Jenkins: The Definitive Guide

Jenkins: The Definitive Guide

John Ferguson Smart

O'REILLY®

Beijing · Cambridge · Farnham · Köln · Sebastopol · Tokyo

Jenkins: The Definitive Guide
by John Ferguson Smart

Published by O'Reilly Media, Inc., 1005 Gravenstein Highway North, Sebastopol, CA 95472.

O'Reilly books may be purchased for educational, business, or sales promotional use. Online editions are also available for most titles (*http://my.safaribooksonline.com*). For more information, contact our corporate/institutional sales department: (800) 998-9938 or *corporate@oreilly.com*.

Editors: Mike Loukides and Meghan Blanchette
Production Editor: Adam Zaremba
Proofreader: Jennifer Knight

Indexer: Angela Howard
Cover Designer: Karen Montgomery
Interior Designer: David Futato
Illustrator: Robert Romano

Printing History:

July 2011:	First Edition.

ISBN: 978-1-449-30535-2

[LSI]

1309968863

Table of Contents

Foreword

Seven years ago, I wrote the first line of code that started this whole project that is now known as Jenkins, and was originally called Hudson. I used to be the guy who broke the build, so I needed a program to catch my mistakes before my colleagues did. It was just a simple tool that did a simple thing. But it rapidly evolved, and now I'd like to think that it's the most dominant CI server on the market bar none, encompassing a broad plugin ecosystem, commercial distributions, hosted Jenkins-as-a-Service, user groups, meet-ups, trainings, and so on.

As with most of my other projects, this project was open-sourced since its inception. Over its life it critically relied on the help and love of other people, without which the project wouldn't be in the current state. During this time I've also learned a thing or two about running open source projects. From that experience, I think people often overlook that there are many ways to help an open source project, of which writing code is just one of many. There's spreading words, helping other users, organizing meet-ups, and yes, there's writing documentation.

In this sense, John is an important part of the Jenkins community, even though he hasn't contributed code—instead, he makes Jenkins more approachable to new users. For example, he has a popular blog that's followed by many, where he regularly talks about continuous integration practices and other software development topics. He is good at explaining things so that people new to Jenkins can still understand them, which is something often hard for people like me who develop Jenkins day in day out. He is also well-known for his training courses, of which Jenkins is a part. This is another means by which he makes Jenkins accessible for more people. He clearly has a passion for evangelizing new ideas and teaching fellow developers to be more productive.

These days I spend my time at CloudBees where I focus my time on Open Source Jenkins, the CloudBees pro version of Jenkins where we build plugins on top of Jenkins, and taking Jenkins to the private and public cloud with CloudBees DEV@cloud service. In this role I now have more interaction with John than before, and my respect for his passion has only grown.

So I was truly delighted that he took on the daunting task of writing a book about Jenkins. It gives a great overview of the typical main ingredients of continuous integration. And for me personally, I always get asked if there's a book about Jenkins, and I can finally answer this question positively! But more importantly, this book reflects his passion, and his long experience in teaching people how to use Jenkins, in combination with other things. But don't take my words for it. You'll just need to read on to see it for yourself.

—Kohsuke Kawaguchi
Creator of the Jenkins project and Architect at CloudBees

Preface

Audience

This book is aimed at relatively technical readers, though no prior experience with Continuous Integration is assumed. You may be new to Continuous Integration, and would like to learn about the benefits it can bring to your development team. Or, you might be using Jenkins or Hudson already, and want to discover how you can take your Continuous Integration infrastructure further.

Much of this book discusses Jenkins in the context of Java or JVM-related projects. Nevertheless, even if you are using another technology stack, this book should give you a good grounding in Continuous Integration with Jenkins. We discuss how to build projects using several non-Java technologies, including as Grails, Ruby on Rails and .NET. In addition, many topics, such as general configuration, notification, distributed builds and security are applicable no matter what language you are using.

Book Layout

Continuous Integration is like a lot of things: the more you put in, the more value you will get out. While even a basic Continuous Integration setup will produce positive improvements in your team process, there are significant advantages to gradually assimilating and implementing some of the more advanced techniques as well. To this end, this book is organized as a progressive trek into the world of Continuous Integration with Jenkins, going from simple to more advanced. In the first chapter, we start off with a sweeping overview of what Jenkins is all about, in the form of a high-level guided tour. From there, we progress into how to install and configure your Jenkins server and how to set up basic build jobs. Once we have mastered the basics, we will delve into more advanced topics, including automated testing practices, security, more advanced notification techniques, and measuring and reporting on code quality metrics. Next, we move on to more advanced build techniques such as matrix builds, distributed builds and cloud-based CI, before discussing how to implement Continuous Deployment with Jenkins. Finally, we cover some tips on maintaining your Jenkins server.

Jenkins or Hudson?

As we discuss in the introduction, Jenkins was originally, and up until recently, known as Hudson. In 2009, Oracle purchased Sun and inherited the code base of Hudson. In early 2011, tensions between Oracle and the open source community reached rupture point and the project forked into two separate entities: Jenkins, run by most of the original Hudson developers, and Hudson, which remained under the control of Oracle.

As the title suggests, this book is primarily focused on Jenkins. However, much of the book was initially written before the fork, and the products remain very similar. So, although the examples and illustrations do usually refer to Jenkins, almost all of what is discussed will also apply to Hudson.

Font Conventions

This book follows certain conventions for font usage. Understanding these conventions up-front makes it easier to use this book.

Italic
> Used for filenames, file extensions, URLs, application names, emphasis, and new terms when they are first introduced.

`Constant width`
> Used for Java class names, methods, variables, properties, data types, database elements, and snippets of code that appear in text.

`Constant width bold`
> Used for commands you enter at the command line and to highlight new code inserted in a running example.

`Constant width italic`
> Used to annotate output.

Command-Line Conventions

From time to time, this book discusses command-line instructions. When we do, output produced by the console (e.g., command prompts or screen output) is displayed in normal characters, and commands (what you type) are written in **bold**. For example:

```
$ ls -al
total 168
drwxr-xr-x   16 johnsmart  staff    544 21 Jan 07:20 .
drwxr-xr-x+  85 johnsmart  staff   2890 21 Jan 07:10 ..
-rw-r--r--    1 johnsmart  staff     30 26 May  2009 .owner
-rw-r--r--@   1 johnsmart  staff   1813 16 Apr  2009 config.xml
drwxr-xr-x  181 johnsmart  staff   6154 26 May  2009 fingerprints
drwxr-xr-x   17 johnsmart  staff    578 16 Apr  2009 jobs
drwxr-xr-x    3 johnsmart  staff    102 15 Apr  2009 log
drwxr-xr-x   63 johnsmart  staff   2142 26 May  2009 plugins
```

```
-rw-r--r--      1 johnsmart  staff      46 26 May  2009 queue.xml
-rw-r--r--@     1 johnsmart  staff      64 13 Nov  2008 secret.key
-rw-r--r--      1 johnsmart  staff   51568 26 May  2009 update-center.json
drwxr-xr-x      3 johnsmart  staff     102 26 May  2009 updates
drwxr-xr-x      3 johnsmart  staff     102 15 Apr  2009 userContent
drwxr-xr-x     12 johnsmart  staff     408 17 Feb  2009 users
drwxr-xr-x     28 johnsmart  staff     952 26 May  2009 war
```

Where necessary, the backslash character at the end of the line is used to indicate a line break: you can type this all on one line (without the backslash) if you prefer. Don't forget to ignore the ">" character at the start of the subsequent lines—it's a Unix prompt character:

```
$ wget -O - http://jenkins-ci.org/debian/jenkins-ci.org.key \
> | sudo apt-key add -
```

For consistency, unless we are discussing a Windows-specific issue, we will use Unix-style command prompts (the dollar sign, "$"), as shown here:

```
$ java -jar jenkins.war
```

or:

```
$ svn list svn://localhost
```

However, unless we say otherwise, Windows users can safely use these commands from the Windows command console:

```
C:\Documents and Settings\Owner> java -jar jenkins.war
```

or:

```
C:\Documents and Settings\Owner> svn list svn://localhost
```

Contributors

This book was not written alone. Rather, it has been a collaborative effort involving many people playing different roles. In particular, the following people generously contributed their time, knowledge and writing skill to make this a better book:

- **Evgeny Goldin** is a Russian-born software engineer living in Israel. He is a lead developer at Thomson Reuters where he's responsible for a number of activities, some of which are directly related to Maven, Groovy, and build tools such as Artifactory and Jenkins. He has a vast experience in a range of technologies, including Perl, Java, JavaScript and Groovy. Build tools and dynamic languages are Evgeny's favorite subjects about which he often writes, presents or blogs. These days he is writing for GroovyMag, Methods & Tools and runs two open source projects of his own: Maven-plugins (*http://evgeny-goldin.com/wiki/Maven-plugins*) and GCommons (*http://evgeny-goldin.com/wiki/GCommons*). He blogs at *http://evgeny-goldin.com/blog* and can be found on Twitter as *@evgeny_goldin*.

  Evgeny contributed a section on generating your Maven build jobs automatically in Chapter 10.

- **Matthew McCullough** is an energetic 15 year veteran of enterprise software development, open source education, and co-founder of Ambient Ideas, LLC, a Denver consultancy. Matthew currently is a trainer for GitHub.com, author of the Git Master Class series for O'Reilly, speaker at over 30 national and international conferences, author of 3 of the top 10 DZone RefCards, and President of the Denver Open Source Users Group. His current topics of research center around project automation: build tools (Maven, Leiningen, Gradle), distributed version control (Git), Continuous Integration (Jenkins) and Quality Metrics (Sonar). Matthew resides in Denver, Colorado with his beautiful wife and two young daughters, who are active in nearly every outdoor activity Colorado has to offer.

  Matthew wrote the section on integrating Git with Jenkins in Chapter 5.

- **Juven Xu** is a software engineer from China who works for Sonatype. An active member of the open source community and recognized Maven expert, Juven was responsible for the Chinese translation of *Maven: The Definitive Guide* as well as an original Chinese reference book on Maven. He is also currently working on the Chinese translation of the present book.

  Juven wrote the section on IRC notifications in Chapter 8.

- **Rene Groeschke** is a software engineer at Cassidian Systems, formerly known as EADS Deutschland GmbH, as well as an open source enthusiast. A certified ScrumMaster with about 7 years experience as a programmer in several enterprise Java projects, he is especially focused on Agile methodologies like Continuous Integration and Test-Driven Development. Besides his daily business, the University of Corporate Education in Friedrichshafen allows him to spread the word about scrum and scrum related topics by giving lectures for the bachelor students of information technology.

  Rene contributed the section on building projects with Gradle in Chapter 5.

The Review Team

The technical review process for this book was a little different to the approach taken for most books. Rather than having one or two technical reviewers read the entire book near the end of the book writing process, a team of volunteers from the Jenkins community, including many key Jenkins developers, were able to read chapters as they were written. This review team was made up of the following people: Alan Harder, Andrew Bayer, Carlo Bonamico, Chris Graham, Eric Smalling, Gregory Boissinot, Harald Soevik, Julien Simpson, Juven Xu, Kohsuke Kawaguchi, Martijn Verberg, Ross Rowe, and Tyler Ballance.

Book Sponsors

This book would not have been possible without the help of several organizations who were willing to assist with and fund the book-writing process.

Wakaleo Consulting

Wakaleo Consulting (*http://www.wakaleo.com*) is a consulting company that helps organizations optimize their software development process. Lead by John Ferguson Smart, author of this book and *Java Power Tools* (*http://oreilly.com/catalog/9780596527938*), Wakaleo Consulting provides consulting, training and mentoring services in Agile Java Development and Testing Practices, Software Development Life Cycle optimization, and Agile Methodologies.

Wakaleo helps companies with training and assistance in areas such as Continuous Integration, Build Automation, Test-Driven Development, Automated Web Testing and Clean Code, using open source tools such as Maven, Jenkins, Selenium 2, and Nexus. Wakaleo Consulting also runs public and on-site training around Continuous Integration and Continuous Deployment, Build Automation, Clean Code practices, Test-Driven Development and Behavior-Driven Development, including Certified Scrum Developer (CSD) courses.

CloudBees

CloudBees (*http://www.cloudbees.com*) is the only cloud company focused on servicing the complete develop-to-deploy life cycle of Java web applications in the cloud. The company is also the world's premier expert on the Jenkins/Hudson continuous integration tool.

Jenkins/Hudson creator Kohsuke Kawaguchi leads a CloudBees team of experts from around the world. They've created Nectar, a supported and enhanced version of Jenkins that is available on-premise by subscription. If you depend on Jenkins for mission-critical software processes, Nectar provides a highly-tested, stable, and fully-supported version of Jenkins. It also includes Nectar-only functionality such as automatic scaling to VMWare virtual machines.

If you're ready to explore the power of continuous integration in the cloud, CloudBees makes Jenkins/Hudson available as part of its DEV@cloud build platform. You can get started with Jenkins instantly and can scale as needed—no big up-front investment in build servers, no more limited capacity for builds, and no maintenance hassles. Once an application is ready to go live, you can deploy on CloudBees's RUN@cloud Platform as a Service in just a few clicks.

With CloudBees's DEV@cloud and RUN@cloud services, you don't have to worry about servers, virtual machines or IT staff. And with Nectar, you enjoy the most powerful, stable, supported Jenkins available.

Odd-e

Odd-e (*http://www.odd-e.com*) is an Asian-based company that builds products in innovative ways and helps others achieve the same. The team consists of experienced coaches and product developers who work according to the values of scrum, agile, lean, and craftsmanship, and the company is structured the same way. For example, Odd-e doesn't have an organizational hierarchy or managers making decisions for others. Instead, individuals self-organize and use all their skills to continuously improve their competence. The company provides training and follow-up coaching to help others collaboratively seek and develop a better way of working.

It is not the job but the values that binds Odd-e together. Its members love building software, value learning and contribution over maximizing profit, and are committed to supporting open source development in Asia.

Using Code Examples

This book is an open source book, published under the Creative Commons License. The book was written in DocBook, using XmlMind. The book's source code can be found on GitHub at *http://www.github.org/wakaleo/jenkins-the-definitive-guide*.

The sample Jenkins projects used in this book are open source and freely available online—see the book's web page at *http://www.wakaleo.com/books/jenkins-the-definitive-guide* for more details.

This book is here to help you get your job done. In general, you may use the code in this book in your programs and documentation. You do not need to contact us for permission unless you're reproducing a significant portion of the code. For example, writing a program that uses several chunks of code from this book does not require permission. Selling or distributing a CD-ROM of examples from O'Reilly books does require permission. Answering a question by citing this book and quoting example code does not require permission. Incorporating a significant amount of example code from this book into your product's documentation does require permission.

We appreciate, but do not require, attribution. An attribution usually includes the title, author, publisher, and ISBN. For example: "*Jenkins: The Definitive Guide* by John Ferguson Smart (O'Reilly). Copyright 2011 John Ferguson Smart, 978-1-449-30535-2."

If you feel your use of code examples falls outside fair use or the permission given above, feel free to contact us at *permissions@oreilly.com*.

Safari® Books Online

Safari Books Online is an on-demand digital library that lets you easily search over 7,500 technology and creative reference books and videos to find the answers you need quickly.

With a subscription, you can read any page and watch any video from our library online. Read books on your cell phone and mobile devices. Access new titles before they are available for print, and get exclusive access to manuscripts in development and post feedback for the authors. Copy and paste code samples, organize your favorites, download chapters, bookmark key sections, create notes, print out pages, and benefit from tons of other time-saving features.

O'Reilly Media has uploaded this book to the Safari Books Online service. To have full digital access to this book and others on similar topics from O'Reilly and other publishers, sign up for free at *http://my.safaribooksonline.com*.

How to Contact Us

Please address comments and questions concerning this book to the publisher:

O'Reilly Media, Inc.
1005 Gravenstein Highway North
Sebastopol, CA 95472
800-998-9938 (in the United States or Canada)
707-829-0515 (international or local)
707-829-0104 (fax)

We have a web page for this book, where we list errata, examples, and any additional information. You can access this page at:

http://www.oreilly.com/catalog/9781449305352

To comment or ask technical questions about this book, send email to:

bookquestions@oreilly.com

For more information about our books, courses, conferences, and news, see our website at *http://www.oreilly.com*.

Find us on Facebook: *http://facebook.com/oreilly*

Follow us on Twitter: *http://twitter.com/oreillymedia*

Watch us on YouTube: *http://www.youtube.com/oreillymedia*

Acknowledgments

First and foremost, my wonderful wife, Chantal, and boys, James and William, without whose love, support, and tolerance this book would not have been possible.

I would like to thank Mike Loukides for working with me once again on this book project, and the whole O'Reilly team for their high standards of work.

Thank you to Kohsuke Kawaguchi for having created Jenkins, and for still being the driving force behind this brilliant product. Thanks also to Francois Dechery, Sacha Labourey, Harpreet Singh, and the rest of the CloudBees team for their help and support.

I am also very grateful to those who took the time and energy to contribute work to the book: Evgeny Goldin, Matthew McCullough, Juven Xu, and Rene Groeschke.

A great thanks goes out to the following reviewers, who provided valuable feedback throughout the whole writing process: Alan Harder, Andrew Bayer, Carlo Bonamico, Chris Graham, Eric Smalling, Gregory Boissinot, Harald Soevik, Julien Simpson, Juven Xu, Kohsuke Kawaguchi, Martijn Verberg, Ross Rowe, and Tyler Ballance.

Thank you to Andrew Bayer, Martijn Verburg, Matthew McCullough, Rob Purcell, Ray King, Andrew Walker, and many others, whose discussions and feedback provided me with inspiration and the ideas that made this book what it is.

And many other people have helped in various ways to make this book much richer and more complete than it would have been otherwise: Geoff and Alex Bullen, Pete Thomas, Gordon Weir, Jay Zimmerman, Tim O'Brien, Russ Miles, Richard Paul, Julien Simpson, John Stevenson, Michael Neale, Arnaud Héritier, and Manfred Moser.

And finally a great thank you to the Hudson/Jenkins developer and user community for the ongoing encouragement and support.

CHAPTER 1

Introducing Jenkins

Introduction

Continuous Integration, also know as CI, is a cornerstone of modern software development. In fact it is a real game changer—when Continuous Integration is introduced into an organization, it radically alters the way teams think about the whole development process. It has the potential to enable and trigger a series of incremental process improvements, going from a simple scheduled automated build right through to continuous delivery into production. A good CI infrastructure can streamline the development process right through to deployment, help detect and fix bugs faster, provide a useful project dashboard for both developers and non-developers, and ultimately, help teams deliver more real business value to the end user. Every professional development team, no matter how small, should be practicing CI.

Continuous Integration Fundamentals

Back in the days of waterfall projects and Gantt charts, before the introduction of CI practices, development team time and energy was regularly drained in the period leading up to a release by what was known as the Integration Phase. During this phase, the code changes made by individual developers or small teams were brought together piecemeal and forged into a working product. This was hard work, sometimes involving the integration of months of conflicting changes. It was very hard to anticipate the types of issues that would crop up, and even harder to fix them, as it could involve reworking code that had been written weeks or months before. This painful process, fraught with risk and danger, often lead to significant delivery delays, unplanned costs and, as a result, unhappy clients. Continuous Integration was born to address these issues.

Continuous Integration, in its simplest form, involves a tool that monitors your version control system for changes. Whenever a change is detected, this tool automatically compiles and tests your application. If something goes wrong, the tool immediately notifies the developers so that they can fix the issue immediately.

But Continuous Integration can do much more than this. Continuous Integration can also help you keep tabs on the health of your code base, automatically monitoring code quality and code coverage metrics, and helping keep technical debt down and maintenance costs low. The publicly-visible code quality metrics can also encourage developers to take pride in the quality of their code and strive to improve it. Combined with automated end-to-end acceptance tests, CI can also act as a communication tool, publishing a clear picture of the current state of development efforts. And it can simplify and accelerate delivery by helping you automate the deployment process, letting you deploy the latest version of your application either automatically or as a one-click process.

In essence, Continuous Integration is about reducing risk by providing faster feedback. First and foremost, it is designed to help identify and fix integration and regression issues faster, resulting in smoother, quicker delivery, and fewer bugs. By providing better visibility for both technical and non-technical team members on the state of the project, Continuous Integration can open and facilitate communication channels between team members and encourage collaborative problem solving and process improvement. And, by automating the deployment process, Continuous Integration helps you get your software into the hands of the testers and the end users faster, more reliably, and with less effort.

This idea of automated deployment is important. Indeed, if you take automating the deployment process to its logical conclusion, you could push every build that passes the necessary automated tests into production. The practice of automatically deploying every successful build directly into production is generally known as *Continuous Deployment*.

However, a pure Continuous Deployment approach is not always appropriate for everyone. For example, many users would not appreciate new versions falling into their laps several times a week, and prefer a more predictable (and transparent) release cycle. Commercial and marketing considerations might also play a role in when a new release should actually be deployed.

The notion of *Continuous Delivery* is a slight variation on the idea of Continuous Deployment that takes into account these considerations. With Continuous Delivery, any and every successful build that has passed all the relevant automated tests and quality gates can *potentially* be deployed into production via a fully automated one-click process, and be in the hands of the end-user within minutes. However, the process is not automatic: it is the business, rather than IT, that decides the best time to deliver the latest changes.

So Continuous Integration techniques, and in particular Continuous Deployment and Continuous Delivery, are very much about providing value to the end user faster. How long does it take your team to get a small code change out to production? How much of this process involves problems that could have been fixed earlier, had you known about the code changes that Joe down the corridor was making? How much is taken up by labor-intensive manual testing by QA teams? How much involves manual deployment steps, the secrets of which are known only to a select few? CI is not a silver bullet by any means, but it can certainly help streamline many of these problems.

But Continuous Integration is a mindset as much as a toolset. To get the most out of CI, a team needs to adopt a CI mentality. For example, your projects must have a reliable, repeatable, and automated build process, involving no human intervention. Fixing broken builds should take an absolute priority, and not be left to stagnate. The deployment process should be automated, with no manual steps involved. And since the trust you place in your CI server depends to a great extent on the quality of your tests, the team needs to place a very strong emphasis on high quality tests and testing practices.

In this book we will be looking at how to implement a robust and comprehensive Continuous Integration solution using Jenkins or Hudson.

Introducing Jenkins (née Hudson)

Jenkins, originally called Hudson, is an open source Continuous Integration tool written in Java. Boasting a dominant market share, Jenkins is used by teams of all sizes, for projects in a wide variety of languages and technologies, including .NET, Ruby, Groovy, Grails, PHP and more, as well as Java. So what has made Jenkins such a success? And why use Jenkins for your CI infrastructure?

Firstly, Jenkins is easy to use. The user interface is simple, intuitive, and visually appealing, and Jenkins as a whole has a very low learning curve. As we will see in the next chapter, you can get started with Jenkins in a matter of minutes.

However Jenkins does not sacrifice power or extensibility: it is also extremely flexible and easy to adapt to your own purposes. Hundreds of open source plugins are available, with more coming out every week. These plugins cover everything from version control systems, build tools, code quality metrics, build notifiers, integration with external systems, UI customization, games, and much more. And installing them is quick and easy.

Last, but certainly not least, much of Jenkins's popularity comes from the size and vibrancy of its community. The Jenkins community is a large, dynamic, reactive and welcoming bunch, with passionate champions, active mailing lists, IRC channels and a very vocal blog and twitter account. The development pace is fast, with releases coming out weekly with the latest new features, bug fixes, and plugin updates.

However Jenkins also caters to users who are not comfortable with upgrading on a weekly basis. For those who prefer a less-hectic release pace, there is also a Long-term Support, or LTS, release line that lags behind the latest release in favor of more stability and a slower rate of change. New LTS releases come out every three months or so, with important bug fixes being backported. This concept is similar to the Ubuntu LTS releases.

From Hudson to Jenkins—A Short History

Jenkins is the result of one visionary developer, Kohsuke Kawaguchi, who started the project as a hobby project under the name of Hudson in late 2004 whilst working at Sun. As Hudson evolved over the years, it was adopted by more and more teams within Sun for their own projects. By early 2008, Sun recognized the quality and value of the tool, and ask Kohsuke to work on Hudson full-time, starting to provide professional services and support around Hudson. By 2010, Hudson had become the leading Continuous Integration solution with a market share of over 70%.

In 2009, Oracle purchased Sun. Towards the end of 2010, tensions arose between the Hudson developer community and Oracle, initially triggered by problems with the Java.net infrastructure, and aggravated by issues related to Oracle's claim to the Hudson trademark. These tensions also reflected strong underlying disagreements about the way the project was being managed by Oracle. Indeed, Oracle wanted to move towards a more strictly controlled development process with a slower release schedule, whereas most of the core Hudson developers, led by Kohsuke, preferred to continue with the open, flexible, and fast-paced community-focused model that had worked so well for Hudson in the past.

In January 2011, the Hudson developer community decisively voted to rename the project to Jenkins. They subsequently migrated the original Hudson code base to a new GitHub project (*https://github.com/jenkinsci*) and continued their work there. The vast majority of core and plugin developers upped camp and followed Kohsuke Kawaguchi and other core contributors to the Jenkins camp, where the bulk of the development activity can be seen today.

After the fork, a majority of users also followed the Jenkins developer community and switched to Jenkins. At the time of writing, polls show that some 75% of Hudson users had switched to Jenkins, while 13% were still using Hudson, and another 12% were using both Hudson and Jenkins or in the process of migrating to Jenkins.

Nevertheless, Oracle and Sonatype (the company behind Maven and Nexus) have continued to work on the Hudson code base (now also hosted on GitHub at *https://github .com/hudson*), but with a very different focus. Indeed, the Sonatype developers have concentrating on major underlying infrastructure changes around, among other areas, Maven integration, the dependency injection framework and the plugin architecture.

Should I Use Jenkins or Hudson?

So should you use Jenkins or Hudson? Since this is a book on Jenkins, here are a few reasons why you might want to opt for Jenkins:

- *Jenkins is the new Hudson.* In fact, Jenkins is simply the old Hudson with a new name, so if you liked Hudson, you'll like Jenkins! Jenkins uses the Hudson code base, and the development team and project philosophy remain the same. In a nutshell, the original developers, who wrote the vast majority of the Hudson core, simply resumed business as usual after the fork working on the Jenkins project.

- *The Jenkins community.* Like many of the more successful Open Source projects, much of Hudson's strength came from its large and dynamic community, and its massive adoption. Bugs are identified (and generally fixed) much more rapidly, and, if you have a problem, chances are someone else will have had it too! If you run into trouble, post a question on the mailing list or IRC channel—there's sure to be someone who can help.

- *The fast development pace.* Jenkins continues the rapid release cycles that typified Hudson, which many developers love. New features, new plugins and bug fixes come out weekly, and the turn-around time for bug fixes can be very short indeed. And, if you prefer more stability, there are always the LTS releases

And, in the interest of balance, here are some reasons you might prefer to stick with Hudson:

- *If it ain't broke, don't fix it.* You already have a Hudson installation that you are happy with, and don't feel the need to upgrade to the latest version.

- *Enterprise integration and Sonatype tools.* Hudson is likely to place a strong emphasis on integration with enterprise tools such as LDAP/Active Directory, and the Sonatype products such as Maven 3, Nexus and M2Eclipse, whereas Jenkins is more open to other competing tools such as Artifactory and Gradle.

- *Plugin architecture.* If you intend to write your own Jenkins/Hudson plugins, you should be aware that Sonatype is working on providing JSR-330 dependency injection for Hudson plugins. New developers may find this approach easier to use, though it does raise issues about future plugin compatibility between Jenkins and Hudson.

The good news is, no matter whether you are using Jenkins or Hudson, the products remain very similar, and the vast majority of techniques and tips discussed in this book will apply equally well to both. Indeed, to illustrate this point, many screenshots in this book refer to Hudson rather than Jenkins.

Introducing Continuous Integration into Your Organization

Continuous Integration is not an all-or-nothing affair. In fact, introducing CI into an organization takes you on a path that progresses through several distinct phases. Each of these phases involves incremental improvements to the technical infrastructure as well as, perhaps more importantly, improvements in the practices and culture of the development team itself. In the following paragraphs, I have tried to paint an approximate picture of each phase.

Phase 1—No Build Server

Initially, the team has no central build server of any kind. Software is built manually on a developer's machine, though it may use an Ant script or similar to do so. Source code may be stored in a central source code repository, but developers do not necessarily commit their changes on a regular basis. Some time before a release is scheduled, a developer manually integrates the changes, a process which is generally associated with pain and suffering.

Phase 2—Nightly Builds

In this phase, the team has a build server, and automated builds are scheduled on a regular (typically nightly) basis. This build simply compiles the code, as there are no reliable or repeatable unit tests. Indeed, automated tests, if they are written, are not a mandatory part of the build process, and may well not run correctly at all. However developers now commit their changes regularly, at least at the end of every day. If a developer commits code changes that conflict with another developer's work, the build server alerts the team via email the following morning. Nevertheless, the team still tends to use the build server for information purposes only—they feel little obligation to fix a broken build immediately, and builds may stay broken on the build server for some time.

Phase 3—Nightly Builds and Basic Automated Tests

The team is now starting to take Continuous Integration and automated testing more seriously. The build server is configured to kick off a build whenever new code is committed to the version control system, and team members are able to easily see what changes in the source code triggered a particular build, and what issues these changes address. In addition, the build script compiles the application and runs a set of automated unit and/or integration tests. In addition to email, the build server also alerts team members of integration issues using more proactive channels such as Instant Messaging. Broken builds are now generally fixed quickly.

Phase 4—Enter the Metrics

Automated code quality and code coverage metrics are now run to help evaluate the quality of the code base and (to some extent, at least) the relevance and effectiveness of the tests. The code quality build also automatically generates API documentation for the application. All this helps teams keep the quality of the code base high, alerting team members if good testing practices are slipping. The team has also set up a "build radiator," a dashboard view of the project status that is displayed on a prominent screen visible to all team members.

Phase 5—Getting More Serious About Testing

The benefits of Continuous Integration are closely related to solid testing practices. Now, practices like Test-Driven Development are more widely practiced, resulting in a growing confidence in the results of the automated builds. The application is no longer simply compiled and tested, but if the tests pass, it is automatically deployed to an application server for more comprehensive end-to-end tests and performance tests.

Phase 6—Automated Acceptance Tests and More Automated Deployment

Acceptance-Test Driven Development is practiced, guiding development efforts and providing high-level reporting on the state of the project. These automated tests use Behavior-Driven Development and Acceptance-Test Driven Development tools to act as communication and documentation tools and documentation as much as testing tools, publishing reports on test results in business terms that non-developers can understand. Since these high-level tests are automated at an early stage in the development process, they also provide a clear idea of what features have been implemented, and which remain to be done. The application is automatically deployed into test environments for testing by the QA team either as changes are committed, or on a nightly basis; a version can be deployed (or "promoted") to UAT and possibly production environments using a manually-triggered build when testers consider it ready. The team is also capable of using the build server to back out a release, rolling back to a previous release, if something goes horribly wrong.

Phase 7—Continuous Deployment

Confidence in the automated unit, integration and acceptance tests is now such that teams can apply the automated deployment techniques developed in the previous phase to push out new changes directly into production.

The progression between levels here is of course somewhat approximate, and may not always match real-world situations. For example, you may well introduce automated web tests before integrating code quality and code coverage reporting. However, it should give a general idea of how implementing a Continuous Integration strategy in a real world organization generally works.

Where to Now?

Throughout the remainder of this book, as we study the various features Jenkins has to offer, as well as the practices required to make the most of these features, we will see how we can progress through each of these levels with Jenkins. And remember, most of the examples used in the book are available online (see *http://www.wakaleo.com/ books/jenkins-the-definitive-guide* for more details), so you can get your hands dirty too!

CHAPTER 2

Your First Steps with Jenkins

Introduction

In this chapter, we are going to take a quick guided tour through some of Jenkins's key features. You'll get to see first-hand just how easy it is to install Jenkins and set up your first Jenkins automated build job. We won't dwell on the details too much—there are more details to come in the following chapters, as well as a detailed chapter on Jenkins Administration at the end of the book (Chapter 13). This chapter is just an introduction. Still, by the end of the chapter, you will also be keeping tabs on test results, generating javadoc and publishing code coverage reports! We've got a lot of ground to cover, so let's get started!

Preparing Your Environment

There are two ways you can tackle this chapter. You can read through it without touching a keyboard, just to get an overview of what Jenkins is about. Or you can get your hands dirty, and follow along on your own machine.

If you do want to follow along at home, you may need to set up some software on your local machine. Remember, the most basic function of any Continuous Integration tool is to monitor source code in a version control system and to fetch and build the latest version of your source code whenever any changes are committed. So you'll need a version control system. In our case, we'll be using Git (*http://git-scm.com*). The central source code repository for our simple project is stored on GitHub (*https://github.com*). Don't worry about messing up this repository with your own changes, though: you'll be creating your own fork of the repository that you can use as you wish. If you haven't used Git and/or don't have an account on GitHub yet, don't worry, we'll walk through the basics, and the whole installation process is well documented on the GitHub website. We'll explain how to set it all up in great detail further on.

In this chapter, we'll be using Jenkins to build a Java application using Maven. Maven is a widely-used build tool in the Java world, with many powerful features such as declarative dependency management, convention over configuration, and a large range of plugins. For our build, we will also be using recent versions of the Java Development Kit (JDK) and Maven, but if you don't have these installed on your machine, don't fret! As we will see, Jenkins will install them for you.

Installing Java

The first thing you will need to install on your machine is Java. Jenkins is a Java web application, so you will need at least the Java Runtime Environment, or JRE to run it. For the examples in this chapter, you will need a recent version of Java 6 (these examples were written with Java 6 update 17, and the latest release at the time of writing was Java 6 update 19). If you are not sure, you can check this from the command line (by opening a DOS console on Windows), and running `java -version`. If Java is installed on your machine should get something like this:

```
$ java -version
java version "1.6.0_17"
Java(TM) SE Runtime Environment (build 1.6.0_17-b04-248-10M3025)
Java HotSpot(TM) 64-Bit Server VM (build 14.3-b01-101, mixed mode)
```

If you don't have a version already installed, or if your version is an older one, download and install the latest JRE installer from the Java website (*http://java.sun.com/javase/downloads/index.jsp*), as shown in Figure 2-1.

Installing Git

Since we will be using Git, you will need to install and configure Git on your machine. If you are new to Git, you might want to run through the basics on the Git Reference website (*http://gitref.org*). And if you get lost, the whole process is well documented on the GitHub help pages (*http://help.github.com*).

First of all, you need to install Git on your machine. This involves downloading the appropriate installer for your operating system from the Git website (*http://git-scm.com*). There are packaged installers for both Windows and Mac OS X. If you are using Linux, you are in Git's home ground: most Linux distributions. On Ubuntu or some other Debian-based distribution, you could run something like:

```
$ sudo apt-get install git-core
```

On Fedora or another RPM-based distribution, you could use yum instead:

```
$ sudo yum install git-core
```

And, being Linux, you also have the option of installing the application from source. There are instructions on how to do this on the Git website.

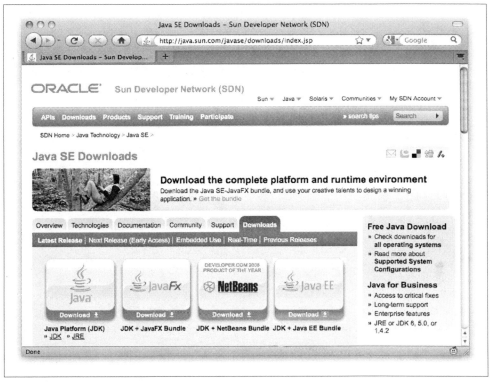

Figure 2-1. Installing Java

Once you are done, check that Git is installed and available by invoking it from the command line:

```
$ git --version
git version 1.7.1
```

Setting Up a GitHub Account

Next, if you don't already have one, you will need to create a GitHub account. This is easy and (for our purposes, at least) free of charge, and all the cool kids have one. Go to the GitHub signup page (*https://github.com/plans*) and choose the "Create a free account" option. You will just need to provide a username, a password, and your email address (see Figure 2-2).

Configuring SSH Keys

GitHub uses SSH keys to establish a secure connection between your computer and the GitHub servers. Setting these up is not hard, but involves a bit of work: fortunately there are clear and detailed instructions for each operating system on the GitHub website (*http://help.github.com/set-up-git-redirect*).

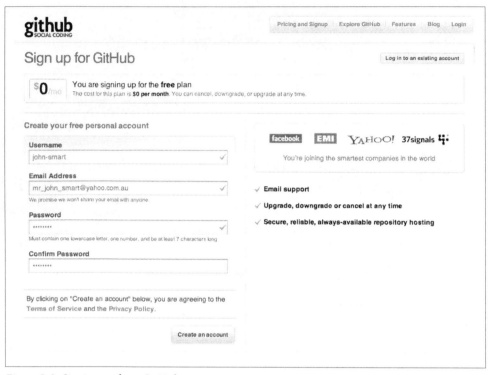

Figure 2-2. Signing up for a GitHub account

Forking the Sample Repository

As we mentioned earlier, all the sample code for this book is stored on GitHub, at the following URL: *https://github.com/wakaleo/game-of-life*. This is a public repository, so you can freely view the source code online and check out your own working copy. However, if you want to make changes, you will need to create your own fork. A fork is a personal copy of a repository that you can use as you wish. To create a fork, login to your GitHub account and navigate to the repository URL. Then click on the Fork button (see Figure 2-3). This will create your own personal copy of the repository.

Once you have forked the repository, you should clone a local copy to make sure everything is set up correctly. Go to the command line and run the following command (replacing *<username>* with your own GitHub username):

```
$ git clone git@github.com:<username>/game-of-life.git
```

This will "clone" (or check out, in Subversion terms) a copy of the project onto your local drive:

```
git clone git@github.com:john-smart/game-of-life.git
Initialized empty Git repository in /Users/johnsmart/.../game-of-life/.git/
remote: Counting objects: 1783, done.
```

```
remote: Compressing objects: 100% (589/589), done.
remote: Total 1783 (delta 1116), reused 1783 (delta 1116)
Receiving objects: 100% (1783/1783), 14.83 MiB | 119 KiB/s, done.
Resolving deltas: 100% (1116/1116), done.
```

You should now have a local copy of the project that you can build and execute. We will be using this project later on to trigger changes in the repository.

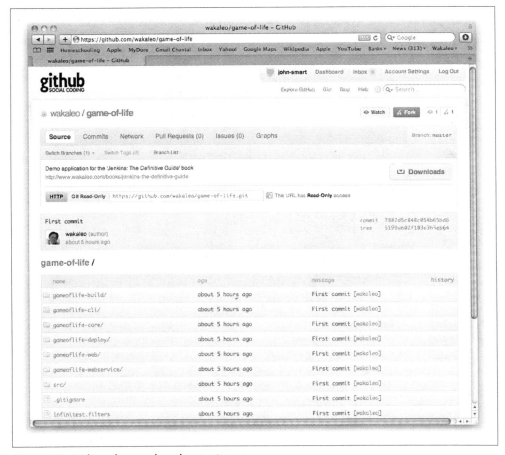

Figure 2-3. Forking the sample code repository

Starting Up Jenkins

There are several ways to run Jenkins on your machine. One of the easiest ways to run Jenkins for the first time is to use Java Web Start. Java Web Start is a technology that lets you start up a Java application on your local machine via a URL on a web page— it comes bundled with the Java JRE. In our case, this will start a Jenkins server running on your machine, and let you experiment with it as if it were installed locally. All you need for this to work is a recent (Java 6 or later) version of the Java Runtime Environment (JRE), which we installed in the previous section.

For convenience, there is a link to the Jenkins Java Web Start instance on the book resources page (*http://www.wakaleo.com/books/jenkins-the-definitive-guide*). Here you will find a large orange Launch button in the Book Resources section (see Figure 2-4). You can also find this link on the Meet Jenkins page on the Jenkins website (*http://wiki .jenkins-ci.org/display/JENKINS/Meet+Jenkins*), where, if you scroll down far enough, you should find a Test Drive section with an identical Launch button.

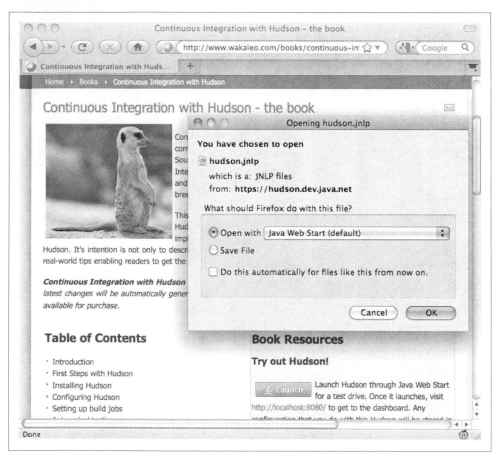

Figure 2-4. Running Jenkins using Java Web Start from the book's website

Java Web Start seems to work best on Firefox. When you click on the Launch button on either of these sites in Firefox, the browser will ask if you want to open a file called *jenkins.jnlp* using Java Web Start. Click on OK—this will download Jenkins and start it up on your machine (see Figure 2-5).

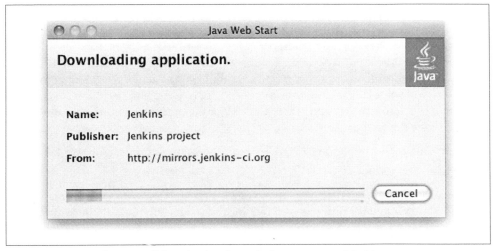

Figure 2-5. Java Web Start will download and run the latest version of Jenkins

In other browsers, clicking on this button may simply download the JNLP file. In Internet Explorer, you may even need to right click on the link and select "Save Target As" to save the JNLP file, and then run it from Windows Explorer. However, in both of these cases, when you open the JNLP file, Java Web Start will download and start Jenkins.

Java Web Start will only need to download a particular version of Jenkins once. From then on, when you click on the "Launch" button again, Java Web Start will use the copy of Jenkins it has already downloaded (that is, until the next version comes out). Ignore any messages your operating system or anti-virus software may bring up—it is perfectly safe to run Jenkins on your local machine.

Once it has finished downloading, it will start up Jenkins on your machine. You will be able to see it running in a small window called "Jenkins Console" (see Figure 2-6). To stop Jenkins at any time, just close this window.

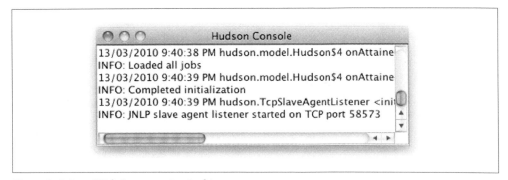

Figure 2-6. Java Web Start running Jenkins

There are also installers available for the principal operating systems available on the Jenkins website (*http://jenkins-ci.org*). Or, if you are an experienced Java user versed in the ways of WAR files, you may prefer to simply download the latest version of Jenkins and run it from the command line. Jenkins comes in the form of an executable WAR file—you can download the most recent version from the Jenkins website home page (*http://http://jenkins-ci.org*). For convenience, there is also a link to the latest version of Jenkins in the Resources section of this book's website (*http://www.wakaleo.com/books/jenkins-the-definitive-guide*).

Once downloaded, you can start Jenkins from the command line as shown here:

```
$ java -jar jenkins.war
```

Whether you have started Jenkins using Java Web Start or from the command line, Jenkins should now be running on your local machine. By default, Jenkins will be running on port 8080, so you can access Jenkins in your web browser on *http://localhost:8080*.

Alternatively, if you are familiar with Java application servers such as Tomcat, you can simply deploy the Jenkins WAR file to your application server—with Tomcat, for example, you could simply place the *jenkins.war* file in Tomcat's *webapps* directory. If you are running Jenkins on an application server, the URL that you use to access Jenkins will be slightly different. On a default Tomcat installation, for example, you can access Jenkins in your web browser on *http://localhost:8080/jenkins*.

When you open Jenkins in your browser, you should see a screen like the one shown in Figure 2-7. You are now ready to take your first steps with Jenkins!

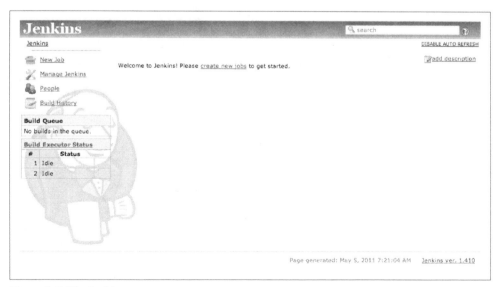

Figure 2-7. The Jenkins start page

Configuring the Tools

Before we get started, we do need to do a little configuration. More precisely, we need to tell Jenkins about the build tools and JDK versions we will be using for our builds.

Click on the Manage Jenkins link on the home page (see Figure 2-7). This will take you to the Manage Jenkins page, the central one-stop-shop for all your Jenkins configuration. From this screen, you can configure your Jenkins server, install and upgrade plugins, keep track of system load, manage distributed build servers, and more! For now, however, we'll keep it simple. Just click on the Configuring System link at the top of the list (see Figure 2-8).

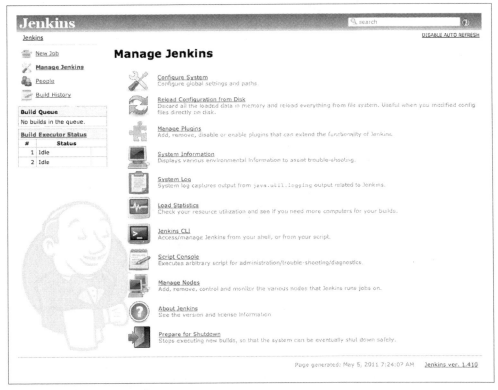

Figure 2-8. The Manage Jenkins screen

This will take you to Jenkins's main configuration screen (see Figure 2-9). From here you can configure everything from security configuration and build tools to email servers, version control systems and integration with third-party software. The screen contains a lot of information, but most of the fields contain sensible default values, so you can safely ignore them for now.

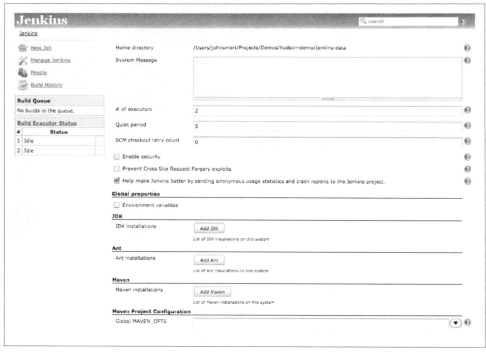

Figure 2-9. The Configure Jenkins screen

For now, you will just need to configure the tools required to build our sample project. The application we will be building is a Java application, built using Maven. So in this case, all we need to do is to set up a recent JDK and Maven installation.

However before we start, take a look at the little blue question mark icons lined to the right of the screen. These are Jenkins's contextual help buttons. If you are curious about a particular field, click on the help icon next to it and Jenkins will display a very detailed description about what it is and how it works.

Configuring Your Maven Setup

Our sample project uses Maven, so we will need to install and configure Maven first. Jenkins provides great out-of-the-box support for Maven. Scroll down until you reach the Maven section in the Configure System screen (see Figure 2-10).

Jenkins provides several options when it comes to configuring Maven. If you already have Maven installed on your machine, you can simply provide the path in the MAVEN_HOME field. Alternatively, you can install a Maven distribution by extracting a zip file located in a shared directory, or execute a home-rolled installation script. Or you can let Jenkins do all the hard work and download Maven for you. To choose this option, just tick the Install automatically checkbox. Jenkins will download and install Maven from the Apache website the first time a build job needs it. Just choose the

Figure 2-10. Configuring a Maven installation

Maven version you want to install and Jenkins will do the rest. You will also need to give a name for your Maven version (imaginatively called "Maven 2.2.1" in the example), so that you can refer to it in your build jobs.

For this to work, you need to have an Internet connection. If you are behind a proxy, you'll need to provide your proxy information—we discuss how to set this up in "Configuring a Proxy" on page 77.

One of the nice things about the Jenkins Maven installation process is how well it works with remote build agents. Later on in the book, we'll see how Jenkins can also run builds on remote build servers. You can define a standard way of installing Maven for all of your build servers (downloading from the Internet, unzipping a distribution bundle on a shared server, etc.)—all of these options will work when you add a new remote build agent or set up a new build server using this Jenkins configuration.

Configuring the JDK

Once you have configured your Maven installation, you will also need to configure a JDK installation (see Figure 2-11). Again, if you have a Java JDK (as opposed to a Java Runtime Environment—the JDK contains extra development tools such as the Java compiler) already installed on your workstation, you can simply provide the path to your JDK in the JAVA_HOME field. Otherwise, you can ask Jenkins to download the JDK from the Oracle website (*http://www.oracle.com/technetwork/java/index.html*) the first time a build job requires it. This is similar to the automatic Maven installation feature—just pick the JDK version you need and Jenkins will take care of all the logistics. However, for licensing reasons, you will also need to tick a checkbox to indicate that you agree with the Java SDK License Agreement.

Now go to the bottom of the screen and click on the Save button.

Figure 2-11. Configuring a JDK installation

Notification

Another important aspect you would typically set up is notification. When a Jenkins build breaks, and when it works again, it can send out email messages to the team to spread the word. Using plugins, you can also get it to send instant messages or SMS messages, post entries on Twitter, or get people notified in a few other ways. It all depends on what works best for your organizational culture. Email notification is easy enough to set up if you know your local SMTP server address—just provide this value in the Email Notification section towards the bottom of the main configuration page. However, to keep things simple, we're not going to worry about notifications just yet.

Setting Up Git

The last thing we need to configure for this demo is to get Jenkins working with Git. Jenkins comes with support for Subversion and CVS out of the box, but you will need to install the Jenkins Git plugin to be able to complete the rest of this tutorial. Don't worry, the process is pretty simple. First of all, click on the Manage Jenkins link to the left of the screen to go back to the main configuration screen (see Figure 2-8). Then click on Manage Plugins. This will open the plugin configuration screen, which is where you manage the extra features you want to install on your Jenkins server. You should see four tabs: Updates, Available, Installed, and Advanced (see Figure 2-12).

For now, just click on the Available tab. Here you will see a very long list of available plugins. Find the Git Plugin entry in this list and tick the corresponding checkbox (see Figure 2-13), and then scroll down to the bottom of the screen and click on Install. This will download and install the Jenkins Git plugin into your local Jenkins instance.

Once it is done, you will need to restart Jenkins for the changes to take effect. To do this, you can simply click on the "Restart Jenkins when no jobs are running" button displayed on the installation screen, or alternatively shut down and restart Jenkins by hand.

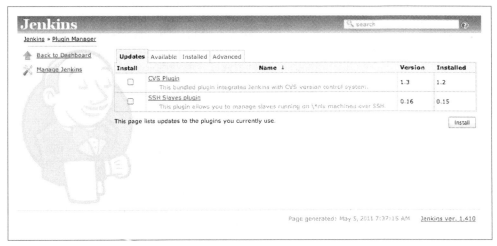

Figure 2-12. Managing plugins in Jenkins

	CMVC Plugin	0.3
	This plugin integrates CMVC to Hudson.	
	Darcs Plugin	0.3.5
	This plugin integrates Darcs version control system to Jenkins. The plugin requires the Darcs binary (darcs) to be installed on the target machine.	
	Dimensions Plugin	0.8.1
	This plugin integrates Hudson with Dimensions, the Serena SCM solution.	
	File System SCM	1.10
	Use File System as SCM.	
☑	Git Plugin	1.1.6
	This plugin allows use of GIT as a build SCM. Git 1.3.3 or newer is required.	
	Harvest Plugin	0.4
	This plugin allows you to use CA Harvest as a SCM.	

Figure 2-13. Installing the Git plugin

That is all we need to configure at this stage. You are now ready to set up your first Jenkins build job!

Your First Jenkins Build Job

Build jobs are at the heart of the Jenkins build process. Simply put, you can think of a Jenkins build job as a particular task or step in your build process. This may involve simply compiling your source code and running your unit tests. Or you might want a build job to do other related tasks, such as running your integration tests, measuring code coverage or code quality metrics, generating technical documentation, or even deploying your application to a web server. A real project usually requires many separate but related build jobs.

Our sample application is a simple Java implementation of John Conway's "Game of Life."* The Game of Life is a mathematical game which takes place on a two dimensional grid of cells, which we will refer to as the Universe. Each cell can be either alive or dead. Cells interact with their direct neighbors to determine whether they will live or die in the next generation of cells. For each new generation of cells, the following rules are applied:

- Any live cell with fewer than two live neighbors dies of underpopulation.
- Any live cell with more than three live neighbors dies of overcrowding.
- Any live cell with two or three live neighbors lives on to the next generation.
- Any dead cell with exactly three live neighbors becomes a live cell.

Our application is a Java module, built using Maven, that implements the core business logic of the Game of Life. We'll worry about the user interfaces later on. For now, let's see how we can automate this build in Jenkins. If you are not familiar with Maven, or prefer Ant or another build framework—don't worry! The examples don't require much knowledge of Maven, and we'll be looking at plenty of examples of using other build tools later on in the book.

For our first build job, we will keep it simple: we are just going to compile and test our sample application. Click on the New Job link. You should get to a screen similar to Figure 2-14. Jenkins supports several different types of build jobs. The two most commonly-used are the freestyle builds and the Maven 2/3 builds. The freestyle projects allow you to configure just about any sort of build job: they are highly flexible and very configurable. The Maven 2/3 builds understand the Maven project structure, and can use this to let you set up Maven build jobs with less effort and a few extra features. There are also plugins that provide support for other types of build jobs. Nevertheless, although our project does use Maven, we are going to use a freestyle build job, just to keep things simple and general to start with. So choose "Build a freestyle software project", as shown in Figure 2-14.

You'll also need to give your build job a sensible name. In this case, call it *gameoflife-default*, as it will be the default CI build for our Game of Life project.

Once you click on OK, Jenkins will display the project configuration screen (see Figure 2-15).

In a nutshell, Jenkins works by checking out the source code of your project and building it in its own workspace. So the next thing you need to do is to tell Jenkins where it can find the source code for your project. You do this in the Source Code Management section (see Figure 2-15). Jenkins provides support for CVS and Subversion out of the box, and many others such as Git, Mercurial, ClearCase, Perforce and many more via plugins.

---

* See *http://en.wikipedia.org/wiki/Conway%27s_Game_of_Life*.

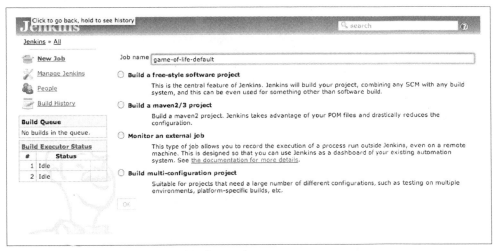

Figure 2-14. Setting up your first build job in Jenkins

For this project, we will be getting the source code from the GitHub repository we set up earlier. On the Jenkins screen, choose "Git" and enter the Repository URL we defined in "Forking the Sample Repository" on page 12 (see Figure 2-15). Make sure this is the URL of your fork, and not of the original repository: it should have the form *git@github.com:<username>/game-of-life.git*, where *<username>* is the username for your own GitHub account. You can leave all of the other options up until here with their default values.

Once we have told Jenkins where to find the source code for our application, we need to tell it how often it should check for updates. We want Jenkins to monitor the repository and start a build whenever any changes have been committed. This is a common way to set up a build job in a Continuous Integration context, as it provides fast feedback if the build fails. Other approaches include building on regular intervals (for example, once a day), requiring a user to kick of the build manually, or even triggering a build remotely using a "post-commit" hook in your SCM.

We configure all of this in the Build Triggers section (see Figure 2-16). Pick the Poll SCM option and enter "* * * * *" (that's five asterisks separated by spaces) in the Schedule box. Jenkins schedules are configured using the `cron` syntax, well-known in the Unix world. The `cron` syntax consists of five fields separated by white space, indicating respectively the minute (0–59), hour (0–23), day of the month (1–31), month (1–12) and the day of the week (0–7, with 0 and 7 being Sunday). The star is a wildcard character which accepts any valid value for that field. So five stars basically means "every minute of every hour of every day." You can also provide ranges of values: "* 9-17 * * *" would mean "every minute of every day, between 9am and 5pm." You can also space out the schedule using intervals: "*/5 * * * *" means "every 5 minutes," for example. Finally, there are some other convenient short-hands, such as "@daily" and "@hourly".

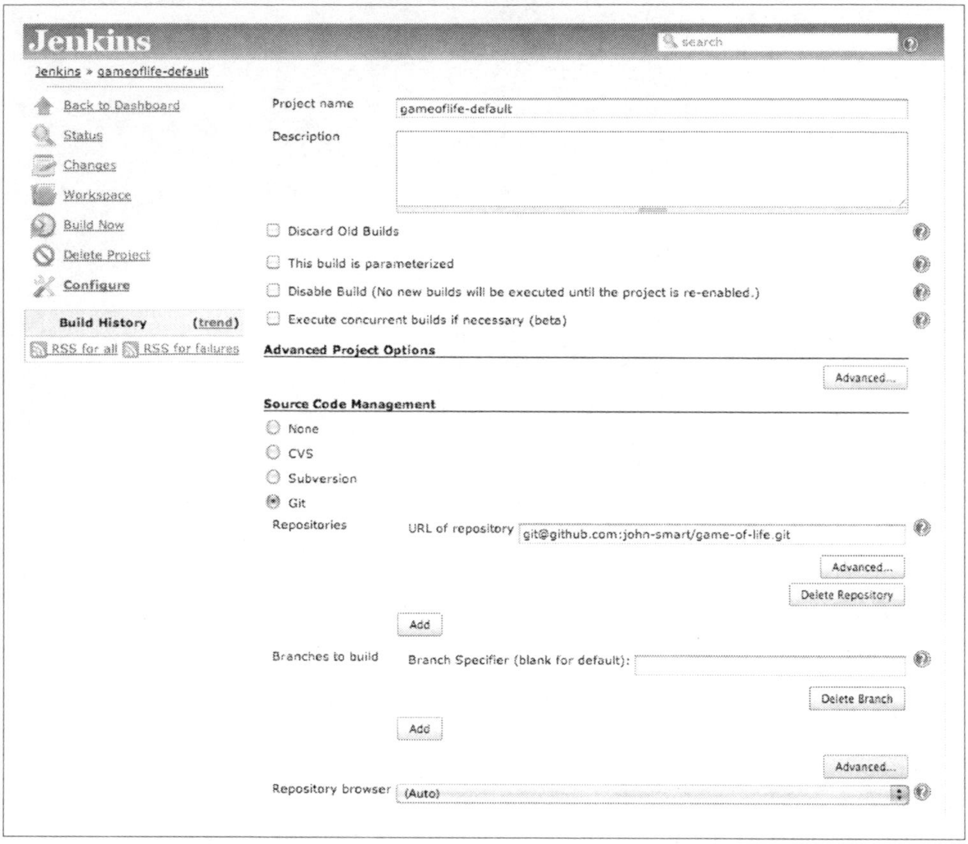

Figure 2-15. Telling Jenkins where to find the source code

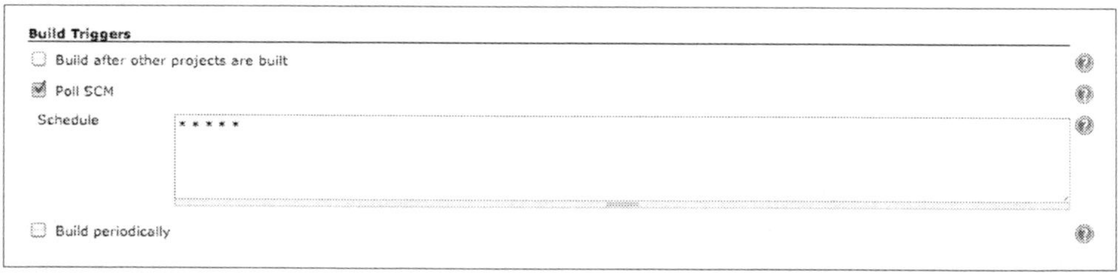

Figure 2-16. Scheduling the build jobs

Don't worry if your Unix skills are a little rusty—if you click on the blue question mark icon on the side of the schedule box, Jenkins will bring up a very complete refresher.

The next step is to configure the actual build itself. In a freestyle build job, you can break down your build job into a number of build steps. This makes it easier to organize builds in clean, separate stages. For example, a build might run a suite of functional tests in one step, and then tag the build in a second step if all of the functional tests succeed. In technical terms, a build step might involve invoking an Ant task or a Maven target, or running a shell script. There are also Jenkins plugins that let you use additional types of build steps: Gant, Grails, Gradle, Rake, Ruby, MSBuild and many other build tools are all supported.

For now, we just want to run a simple Maven build. Scroll down to the Build section and click on the "Add build step" and choose "Invoke top-level Maven targets" (see Figure 2-17). Then enter "clean package" in the Goals field. If you are not familiar with Maven, this will delete any previous build artifacts, compile our code, run our unit tests, and generate a JAR file.

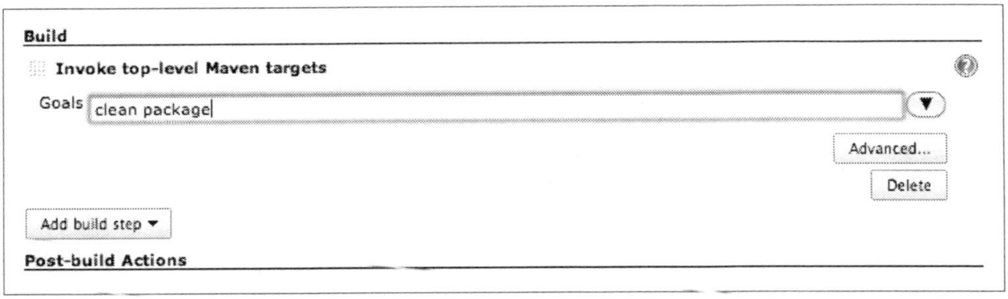

Figure 2-17. Adding a build step

By default, this build job will fail if the code does not compile or if any of the unit tests fail. That's the most fundamental thing that you'd expect of any build server. But Jenkins also does a great job of helping you display your test results and test result trends.

The de facto standard for test reporting in the Java world is an XML format used by JUnit. This format is also used by many other Java testing tools, such as TestNG, Spock and Easyb. Jenkins understands this format, so if your build produces JUnit XML test results, Jenkins can generate nice graphical test reports and statistics on test results over time, and also let you view the details of any test failures. Jenkins also keeps track of how long your tests take to run, both globally, and per test—this can come in handy if you need to track down performance issues.

So the next thing we need to do is to get Jenkins to keep tabs on our unit tests.

Go to the Post-build Actions section (see Figure 2-18) and tick "Publish JUnit test result report" checkbox. When Maven runs unit tests in a project, it automatically generates the XML test reports in a directory called *surefire-reports* in the *target* directory. So enter "**/target/surefire-reports/*.xml" in the "Test report XMLs" field. The two asterisks at the start of the path ("**") are a best practice to make the configuration a bit more robust: they allow Jenkins to find the target directory no matter how we have configured Jenkins to check out the source code.

Figure 2-18. Configuring JUnit test reports and artifact archiving

Another thing you often want to do is to archive your build results. Jenkins can store a copy of the binary artifacts generated by your build, allowing you to download the binaries produced by a build directly from the build results page. It will also post the latest binary artifacts on the project home page, which is a convenient way to distribute the latest and greatest version of your application. You can activate this option by ticking the "Archive the artifacts" checkbox and indicating which binary artifacts you want Jenkins to archive. In Figure 2-18, for example, we have configured Jenkins to store all of the JAR files generated by this build job.

Now we're done—just click on the Save button at the bottom of the screen. Our build job should now be ready to run. So let's see it in action!

Your First Build Job in Action

Once you save your new build job, Jenkins will display the home page for this job (see Figure 2-19). This is where Jenkins displays details about the latest build results and the build history.

If you wait a minute or so, the build should kick off automatically—you can see the stripy progress bar in the Build History section in the bottom left hand corner of Figure 2-19. Or, if you are impatient, you can also trigger the build manually using the Build Now button.

The build will also now figure proudly on your Jenkins server's home page (see Figure 2-20). This page shows a summary of all of your build jobs, including the current build status and general state of heath of each of your builds. It tells you when each build ran successfully for the last time, and when it last failed, and also the result of the last build.

Once of Jenkins's specialities is the way it lets you get an idea of build behavior over time. For example, Jenkins uses a weather metaphor to help give you an idea of the stability of your builds. Essentially, the more your builds fail, the worse the weather gets. This helps you get an idea of whether a particular broken build is an isolated event,

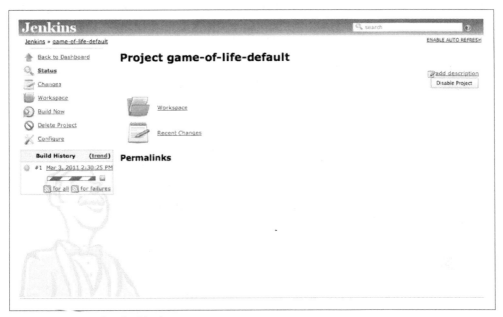

Figure 2-19. Your first build job running

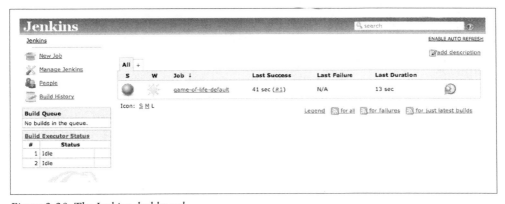

Figure 2-20. The Jenkins dashboard

or if the build is breaking on a regular basis, in which case it might need some special attention.

You can also manually trigger a build job here, using the build schedule button (that's the one that looks a bit like a green play button on top of a clock).

When the build finishes, the ball in the Build History box becomes solid blue. This means the build was a success. Build failures are generally indicated by a red ball. For some types of project, you can also distinguish between a build error (such as a compiler error), indicated by a red ball, and other sorts of build failures, such as unit test failures or insufficient code coverage, which are indicated by a yellow ball. There are also some other details about the latest test results, when the last build was run, and so on. But before we look at the details, let's get back to the core business model of a Continuous Integration server—kicking off builds when someone changes the code!

We are going to commit a code change to GitHub and see what happens, using the source code we checked out in "Forking the Sample Repository" on page 12. We now have Jenkins configured to monitor our GitHub fork, so if we make any changes, Jenkins should be able to pick them up.

So let's make a change. The idea is to introduce a code change that will cause the unit tests to fail. If your Java is a bit rusty, don't worry, you won't need to know any Java to be able to break the build—just follow the instructions!

Now in normal development, you would first modify the unit test that describes this behaviour. Then you would verify that the test fails with the existing code, and implement the code to ensure that the test passes. *Then* you would commit your changes to your version control system, allowing Jenkins to build them. However this would be a poor demonstration of how Jenkins handles unit test failures. So in this example, we will, against all best practices, simply modify the application code directly.

First of all, open the *Cell.java* file, which you will find in the *gameoflife-core/src/main/java/com/wakaleo/gameoflife/domain* directory. Open this file in your favorite text editor. You should see something like this:

```
package com.wakaleo.gameoflife.domain;

public enum Cell {
    LIVE_CELL("*"), DEAD_CELL(".");

    private String symbol;

    private Cell(String symbol) {
        this.symbol = symbol;
    }

    @Override
    public String toString() {
        return symbol;
    }

    static Cell fromSymbol(String symbol) {
        Cell cellRepresentedBySymbol = null;
        for (Cell cell : Cell.values()) {
            if (cell.symbol.equals(symbol)) {
                cellRepresentedBySymbol = cell;
                break;
            }
        }
        return cellRepresentedBySymbol;
    }
```

```
        public String getSymbol() {
            return symbol;
        }
    }
```

The application can print the state of the grid as a text array. Currently, the application prints our live cells as an asterisk (*), and dead cells appear as a minus character (–). So a five-by-five grid containing a single living cell in the center would look like this:

```
-----
--*--
-----
```

Now users have asked for a change to the application—they want pluses (+) instead of stars! So we are going to make a slight change to the Cell class method, and rewrite it as follows (the modifications are in **bold**):

```
package com.wakaleo.gameoflife.domain;

public enum Cell {
    LIVE_CELL("+"), DEAD_CELL(".");

    private String symbol;

    private Cell(String symbol) {
        this.symbol = symbol;
    }

    @Override
    public String toString() {
        return symbol;
    }

    static Cell fromSymbol(String symbol) {
        Cell cellRepresentedBySymbol = null;
        for (Cell cell : Cell.values()) {
            if (cell.symbol.equals(symbol)) {
                cellRepresentedBySymbol = cell;
                break;
            }
        }
        return cellRepresentedBySymbol;
    }

    public String getSymbol() {
        return symbol;
    }
}
```

Save this change, and then commit them to the local Git repository by running `git commit`:

```
$ git commit -a -m "Changes stars to pluses"
[master 61ce946] Changes stars to pluses
 1 files changed, 1 insertions(+), 1 deletions(-)
```

This will commit the changes locally, but since Git is a distributed repository, you now have to push these changes through to your fork on GitHub. You do this by running git push:

```
$ git push
Counting objects: 21, done.
Delta compression using up to 4 threads.
Compressing objects: 100% (7/7), done.
Writing objects: 100% (11/11), 754 bytes, done.
Total 11 (delta 4), reused 0 (delta 0)
To git@github.com:john-smart/game-of-life.git
   7882d5c..61ce946  master -> master
```

Now go back to the Jenkins web page. After a minute or so, a new build should kick off, and fail. In fact, there are several other places which are affected by this change, and the regression tests related to these features are now failing. On the build job home page, you will see a second build in the build history with an ominous red ball (see Figure 2-21)—this tells you that the latest build has failed.

You might also notice some clouds next to the Build History title—this is the same "weather" icon that we saw on the home page, and serves the same purpose—to give you a general idea of how stable your build is over time.

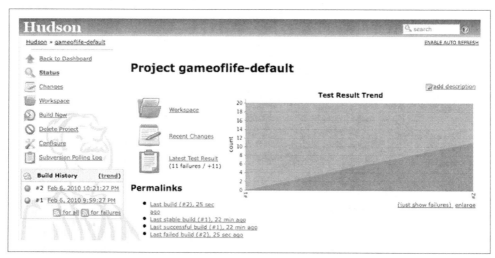

Figure 2-21. A failed build

If you click on the new build history entry, Jenkins will give you some more details about what went wrong (see Figure 2-22). Jenkins tells us that there were 11 new test failures in this build, something which can be seen at a glance in the Test Result Trend graph—red indicates test failures. You can even see which tests are failing, and how long they have been broken.

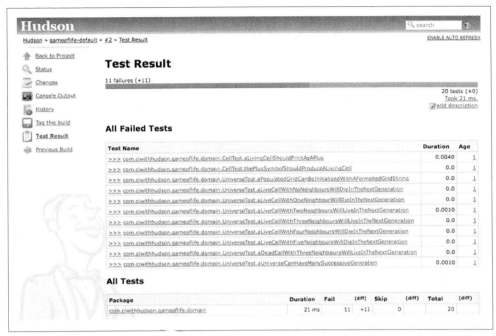

Figure 2-22. The list of all the broken tests

If you want to know exactly what went wrong, that's easy enough to figure out as well. If you click on the failed test classes, Jenkins brings up the actual details of the test failures (see Figure 2-23), which is a great help when it comes to reproducing and fixing the issue.

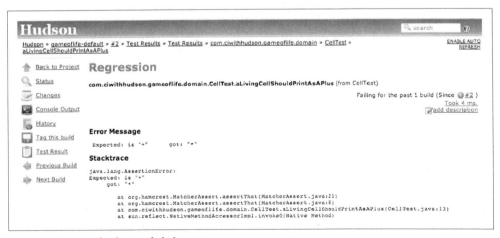

Figure 2-23. Details about a failed test

Jenkins displays a host of information about the failed test in a very readable form, including the error message the test produced, the stack trace, how long the test has been broken, and how long it took to run. Often, this in itself is enough to put a developer on the right track towards fixing the issue.

Now let's fix the build. To make things simple, we'll just back out our changes and recommit the code in its original state (the end users just changed their mind about the asterisks, anyway). So just undo the changes you made to the Cell class (again, the changes are highlighted in **bold**):

```
package com.wakaleo.gameoflife.domain;

public enum Cell {
    LIVE_CELL("*"), DEAD_CELL(".");

    private String symbol;

    private Cell(String symbol) {
        this.symbol = symbol;
    }

    @Override
    public String toString() {
        return symbol;
    }

    static Cell fromSymbol(String symbol) {
        Cell cellRepresentedBySymbol = null;
        for (Cell cell : Cell.values()) {
            if (cell.symbol.equals(symbol)) {
                cellRepresentedBySymbol = cell;
                break;
            }
        }
        return cellRepresentedBySymbol;
    }

    public String getSymbol() {
        return symbol;
    }
}
```

When you've done this, commit your changes again:

```
$ git commit -a -m "Restored the star"
[master bc924be] Restored the star
 1 files changed, 1 insertions(+), 1 deletions(-)
$ git push
Counting objects: 21, done.
Delta compression using up to 4 threads.
Compressing objects: 100% (7/7), done.
Writing objects: 100% (11/11), 752 bytes, done.
Total 11 (delta 4), reused 6 (delta 0)
To git@github.com:john-smart/game-of-life.git
   61ce946..bc924be  master -> master
```

Once you've committed these changes, Jenkins should pick them up and kick off a build. Once this is done, you will be able to see the fruit of your work on the build job home page (see Figure 2-24)—the build status is blue again and all is well. Also notice the way we are building up a trend graph showing the number of succeeding unit tests over time—this sort of report really is one of Jenkins's strong points.

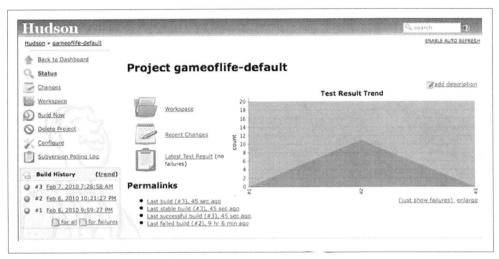

Figure 2-24. Now the build is back to normal

More Reporting—Displaying Javadocs

For many Java projects, Javadoc comments are an important source of low-level technical documentation. There are even tools, such as UmlGraph, that let you produce Javadoc with embedded UML diagrams to give you a better picture of how the classes fit together in the application. This sort of technical documentation has the advantage of being cheap to produce, accurate and always up-to-date.

Jenkins can integrate Javadoc API documentation directly into the Jenkins website. This way, everyone can find the latest Javadoc easily, in a well known place. Often, this sort of task is performed in a separate build job, but for simplicity we are going to add another build step to the *gameoflife-default* build job to generate and display Javadoc documention for the Game of Life API.

Start off by going into the "gameoflife-default" configuration screen again. Click on "Add build step", and add a new build step to "Invoke top level Maven targets" (see Figure 2-25). In the Goals field, place javadoc:javadoc—this will tell Maven to generate the Javadoc documentation.

Now go to the "Post-build Action" and tick the "Publish Javadoc" checkbox. This project is a multimodule project, so a separate subdirectory is generated for each module (core, services, web and so forth). For this example, we are interested in

Figure 2-25. Adding a new build step and report to generate Javadoc

displaying the documentation for the core module. In the Javadoc directory field, enter **gameoflife-core/target/site/apidocs**—this is where Maven will place the Javadocs it generates for the core module. Jenkins may display an error message saying that this directory doesn't exist at first. Jenkins is correct—this directory won't exist until we run the javadoc:javadoc goal, but since we haven't run this command yet we can safely ignore the message at this stage.

If you tick "Retain Javadoc for each successful build", Jenkins will also keep track of the Javadocs for previous builds—not always useful, but it can come in handy at times.

Now trigger a build manually. You can do this either from the build job's home page (using the Build Now link), or directly from the server home page. Once the build is finished, open the build job summary page. You should now see a Javadoc link featuring prominently on the screen—this link will open the latest version of the Javadoc documentation (see Figure 2-26). You will also see this link on the build details page, where it will point to the Javadoc for that particular build, if you have asked Jenkins to store Javadoc for each build.

Adding Code Coverage and Other Metrics

As we mentioned earlier, reporting is one of Jenkins's strong points. We have seen how easy it is to display test results and to publish Javadocs, but you can also publish a large number of other very useful reports using Jenkins's plugins.

Plugins are another one of Jenkins's selling points—there are plugins for doing just about anything, from integrating new build tools or version control systems to

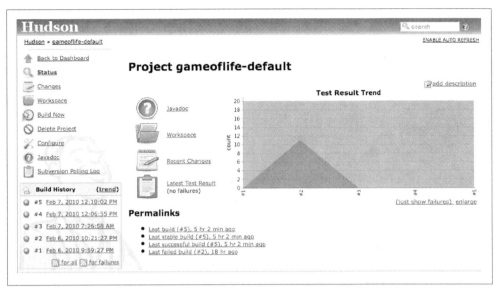

Figure 2-26. Jenkins will add a Javadoc link to your build results

notification mechanisms and reporting. In addition, Jenkins plugins are very easy to install and integrate smoothly into the existing Jenkins architecture.

To see how the plugins work, we are going to integrate code coverage metrics using the Cobertura plugin. Code coverage is an indication of how much of your application code is actually executed during your tests—it can be a useful tool in particular for finding areas of code that have not been tested by your test suites. It can also give some indication as to how well a team is applying good testing practices such as Test-Driven Development or Behavior-Driven Development.

Cobertura (*http://cobertura.sourceforge.net*) is an open source code coverage tool that works well with both Maven and Jenkins. Our Maven demonstration project is already configured to record code coverage metrics, so all we need to do is to install the Jenkins Cobertura plugin and generate the code coverage metrics for Jenkins to record and display.

To install a new plugin, go to the Manage Jenkins page and click on the Manage Plugins entry. This will display a list of the available plugins as well as the plugins already installed on your server (see Figure 2-27). If your build server doesn't have an Internet connection, you can also manually install a plugin by downloading the plugin file elsewhere and uploading it to your Jenkins installation (just open the Advanced tab in Figure 2-27), or by copying the plugin to the *$JENKINS_HOME/plugins* directory.

In our case, we are interested in the Cobertura plugin, so go to the Available tab and scroll down until you find the Cobertura Plugin entry in the Build Reports section. Click on the checkbox and then click on the Install button at the bottom of the screen.

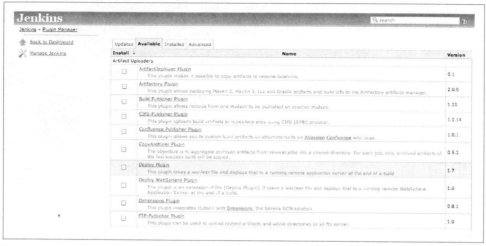

Figure 2-27. Jenkins has a large range of plugins available

This will download and install the plugin for you. Once it is done, you will need to restart your Jenkins instance to see the fruits of your labor. When you have restarted Jenkins, go back to the Manage Plugins screen and click on the Installed tab—there should now be a Cobertura Plugin entry in the list of installed plugins on this page.

Once you have made sure the plugin was successfully installed, go to the configuration page for the *gameoflife-default* build job.

To set up code coverage metrics in our project, we need to do two things. First we need to generate the Cobertura coverage data in an XML form that Jenkins can use; then we need to configure Jenkins to display the coverage reports.

Our Game of Life project already has been configured to generate XML code coverage reports if we ask it. All you need to do is to run `mvn cobertura:cobertura` to generate the reports in XML form. Cobertura can also generate HTML reports, but in our case we will be letting Jenkins take care of the reporting, so we can save on build time by not generating the For this example, for simplicity, we will just add the `cobertura:cober tura` goal to the second build step (see Figure 2-28). You could also add a new build step just for the code coverage metrics. In a real-world project, code quality metrics like this are typically placed in a distinct build job, which is run less frequently than the default build.

Next, we need to tell Jenkins to keep track of our code coverage metrics. Scroll down to the "Post-build Actions" section. You should see a new checkbox labeled Publish Cobertura Reports. Jenkins will often add UI elements like this when you install a new plugin. When you tick this box, Jenkins will display the configuration options for the Cobertura plugin that we installed earlier (see Figure 2-29).

gameoflife-default Config [Hudson]
http://localhost:8080/job/gameoflife-default/c
Google
gameoflife-default Config [Hudson]
Build
Invoke top-level Maven targets
Goals
clean test
Advanced...
Delete
Invoke top-level Maven targets
Goals
javadoc:javadoc cobertura:cobertura
Advanced...
Delete
Add build step
Transferring data from hudson.dev.java.net...

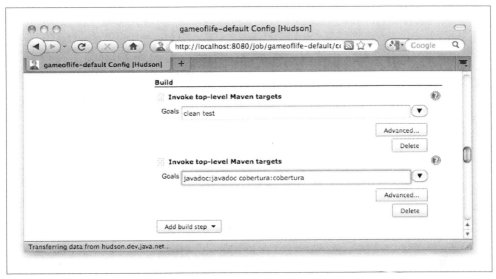

Figure 2-28. Adding another Maven goal to generating test coverage metrics

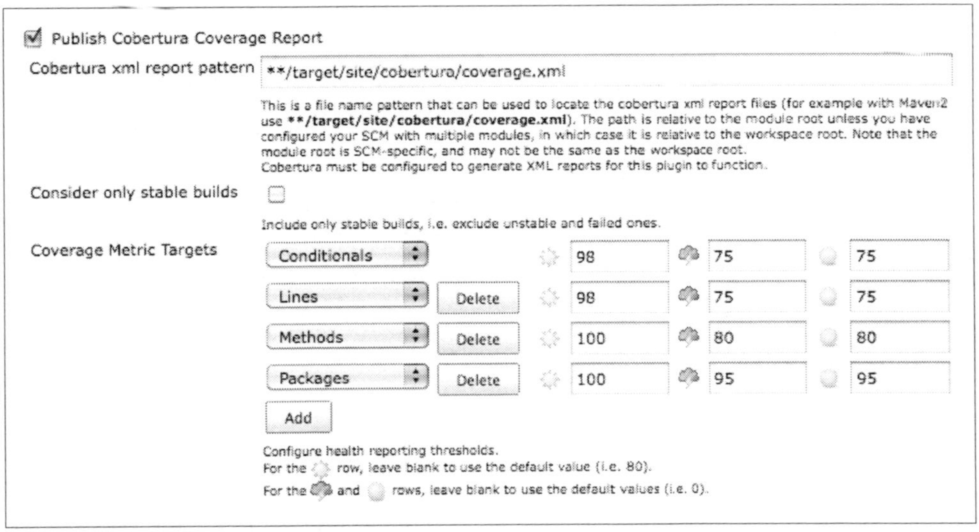

Publish Cobertura Coverage Report
Cobertura xml report pattern
**/target/site/cobertura/coverage.xml
This is a file name pattern that can be used to locate the cobertura xml report files (for example with Maven2 use **/target/site/cobertura/coverage.xml). The path is relative to the module root unless you have configured your SCM with multiple modules, in which case it is relative to the workspace root. Note that the module root is SCM-specific, and may not be the same as the workspace root.
Cobertura must be configured to generate XML reports for this plugin to function.
Consider only stable builds
Include only stable builds, i.e. exclude unstable and failed ones.
Coverage Metric Targets
Conditionals
98
75
75
Lines
Delete
98
75
75
Methods
Delete
100
80
80
Packages
Delete
100
95
95
Add
Configure health reporting thresholds.
For the row, leave blank to use the default value (i.e. 80).
For the and rows, leave blank to use the default values (i.e. 0).

Figure 2-29. Configuring the test coverage metrics in Jenkins

Like most of the code-quality related plugins in Jenkins, the Cobertura plugin lets you fine-tune not only the way Jenkins displays the report data, but also how it interprets the data. In the Coverage Metrics Targets section, you can define what you consider to be the minimum acceptable levels of code coverage. In Figure 2-29, we have configured Jenkins to list any builds with less than 50% test coverage as "unstable" (indicated by a yellow ball), and notify the team accordingly.

This fine-tuning often comes in handy in real-world builds. For example, you may want to impose a special code coverage constraint in release builds, to ensure high code coverage in release versions. Another strategy that can be useful for legacy projects is to gradually increase the minimum tolerated code coverage level over time. This way you can avoid having to retro-fit unit tests on legacy code just to raise the code coverage, but you do encourage all new code and bug fixes to be well tested.

Now trigger a build manually. The first time you run the build job with Cobertura reporting activated, you will see coverage statistics for your build displayed on the build home page, along with a Coverage Report link when you can go for more details (see Figure 2-30). The Cobertura report shows different types of code coverage for the build we just ran. Since we have only run the test coverage metrics once, the coverage will be displayed as red and green bars.

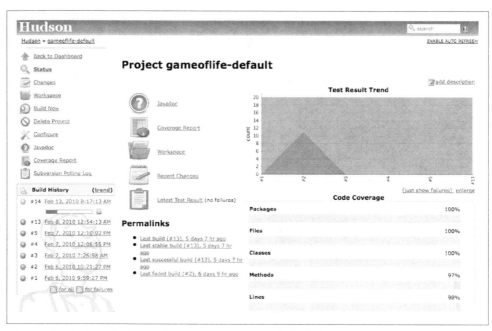

Figure 2-30. Jenkins displays code coverage metrics on the build home page

If you click on the Coverage Report icon, you will see code coverage for each package in your application, and even drill down to see the code coverage (or lack thereof) for an individual class (see Figure 2-31). When you get to this level, Jenkins displays both the overall coverage statistics for the class, and also highlights the lines that were executed in green, and those that weren't in red.

This reporting gets better with time. Jenkins not only reports metrics data for the latest build, but also keeps track of metrics over time, so that you can see how they evolve throughout the life of the project.

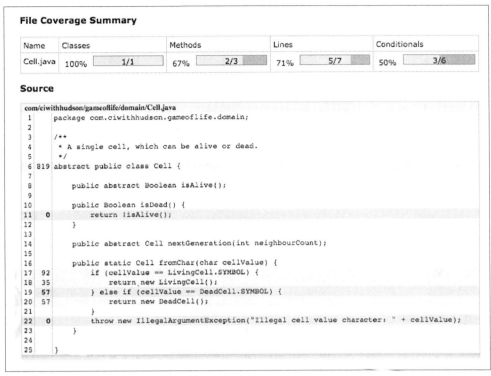

File Coverage Summary

Name	Classes		Methods		Lines		Conditionals	
Cell.java	100%	1/1	67%	2/3	71%	5/7	50%	3/6

Source

```
com/ciwithhudson/gameoflife/domain/Cell.java
 1      package com.ciwithhudson.gameoflife.domain;
 2
 3      /**
 4       * A single cell, which can be alive or dead.
 5       */
 6 819  abstract public class Cell {
 7
 8          public abstract Boolean isAlive();
 9
10          public Boolean isDead() {
11  0           return !isAlive();
12          }
13
14          public abstract Cell nextGeneration(int neighbourCount);
15
16          public static Cell fromChar(char cellValue) {
17  92          if (cellValue == LivingCell.SYMBOL) {
18  35              return new LivingCell();
19  57          } else if (cellValue == DeadCell.SYMBOL) {
20  57              return new DeadCell();
21          }
22  0           throw new IllegalArgumentException("Illegal cell value character: " + cellValue);
23          }
24
25      }
```

Figure 2-31. Jenkins lets you display code coverage metrics for packages and classes

For example, if you drill down into the coverage reports, you will notice that certain parts of this code are not tested (for example the Cell.java class in Figure 2-31).

Code coverage metrics are a great way to isolate code that has not been tested, in order to add extra tests for corner cases that were not properly tested during the initial development, for example. The Jenkins code coverage graphs are also a great way of keeping track of your code coverage metrics as the project grows. Indeed, as you add new tests, you will notice that Jenkins will display a graph of code coverage over time, not just the latest results (see Figure 2-32).

Note that our objective here is not to improve the code coverage just for the sake of improving code coverage—we are adding an extra test to verify some code that was not previously tested, and as a result the code coverage goes up. There is a subtle but important difference here—code coverage, as with any other metric, is very much a means to an end (high code quality and low maintenance costs), and not an end in itself.

Nevertheless, metrics like this can give you a great insight into the health of your project, and Jenkins presents them in a particularly accessible way.

This is just one of the code quality metrics plugins that have been written for Jenkins. There are many more (over fifty reporting plugins alone at the time of writing). We'll look at some more of them in Chapter 9.

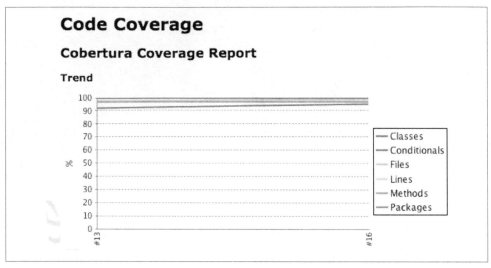

Figure 2-32. Jenkins also displays a graph of code coverage over time

Conclusion

In this chapter, we have gone through what you need to know to get started with Jenkins. You should be able to set up a new build job, and setting up reporting on JUnit test results and javadocs. And you have seen how to add a reporting plugin and keep tabs on code coverage. Well done! But there's still a lot more to learn about Jenkins—in the following chapters, we will be looking at how Jenkins can help you improve your build automation process in many other areas as well.

CHAPTER 3

Installing Jenkins

Introduction

One of the first things you will probably notice about Jenkins is how easy it is to install. Indeed, in less than five minutes, you can have a Jenkins server up and running. However, as always, in the real world, things aren't always that simple, and there are a few details you should take into account when installing your Jenkins server for production use. In this chapter, we look at how to install Jenkins onto both your local machine and onto a fully fledged build server. We will also look at how to take care of your Jenkins installation once it's up and running, and how to perform basic maintenance tasks such as backups and upgrades.

Downloading and Installing Jenkins

Jenkins is easy to install, and can run just about anywhere. You can run it either as a stand-alone application, or deployed on a conventional Java application server such as Tomcat or JBoss. This first option makes it easy to install and try out on your local machine, and you can be up and running with a bare-bones installation in a matter of minutes.

Since Jenkins is a Java application, you will need a recent version of Java on your machine. More precisely, you will need at least Java 5. In fact, on your build server, you will almost certainly need the full features of the Java Development Kit (JDK) 5.0 or better to execute your builds. If you're not sure, you can check the version of Java on your machine by executing the `java -version` command:

```
$ java -version
java version "1.6.0_17"
Java(TM) SE Runtime Environment (build 1.6.0_17-b04-248-10M3025)
Java HotSpot(TM) 64-Bit Server VM (build 14.3-b01-101, mixed mode)
```

Jenkins is distributed in the form of a bundled Java web application (a WAR file). You can download the latest version from the Jenkins website (*http://jenkins-ci.org*—see Figure 3-1) or from the book website. Jenkins is a dynamic project, and new releases come out at a regular rate.

For Windows users, there is a graphical Windows installation package for Jenkins. The installer comes in the form of a ZIP file containing an MSI package for Jenkins, as well as a *setup.exe* file that can be used to install the .NET libraries if they have not already been installed on your machine. In most cases, all you need to do is to unzip the zip file and run the *jenkins-x.x.msi* file inside (see Figure 3-2). The MSI installer comes bundled with a bundled JRE, so no separate Java installation is required.

Figure 3-1. You can download the Jenkins binaries from the Jenkins website

Once you have run the installer, Jenkins will automatically start on port 8080 (see Figure 3-3). The installer will have created a new Jenkins service for you, that you can start and stop just like any other Windows service.

There are also excellent native packages for Mac OS X and most of the major Linux distributions, including Ubuntu, RedHat (including CentOS and Fedora) and Open-Solaris. We discuss how to install Jenkins on Ubuntu and Redhat below.

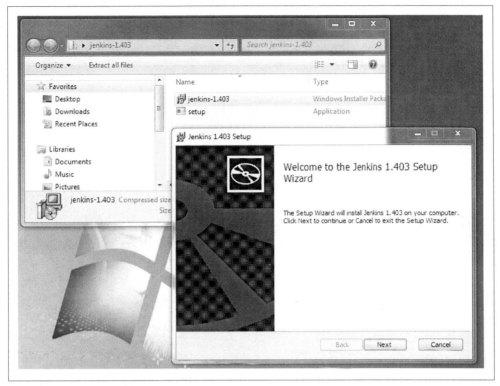

Figure 3-2. Jenkins setup wizard in Windows

If you are not installing Jenkins using one of the native packages, you can simply download the latest binary distribution from the Jenkins website. Once you have downloaded the latest and greatest Jenkins release, place it in an appropriate directory on your build server. On a Windows environment, you might put it in a directory called *C:\Tools\Jenkins* (it's a good idea *not* to place Jenkins in a directory containing spaces in the path, such as *C:\Program Files*, as this can cause problems for Jenkins in some circumstances). On a Linux or Unix box, it might go in */usr/local/jenkins*, */opt/jenkins*, or in some other directory, depending on your local conventions and on the whim of your system administrator.

Before we go any further, let's just start up Jenkins and take a look. If you didn't try this out in the previous chapter, now is the time to get your hands dirty. Open a console in the directory containing the *jenkins.war* file and run the following command:

```
$ java -jar jenkins.war
[Winstone 2008/07/01 20:54:53] - Beginning extraction from war file
...
INFO: Took 35 ms to load
...
[Winstone 2008/07/01 20:55:08] - HTTP Listener started: port=8080
[Winstone 2008/07/01 20:55:08] - Winstone Servlet Engine v0.9.10 running:
```

```
                controlPort=disabled
    [Winstone 2008/07/01 20:55:08] - AJP13 Listener started: port=8009
```

Jenkins should now be running on port 8080. Open your browser at *http://localhost: 8080* and take a look. (see Figure 3-3).

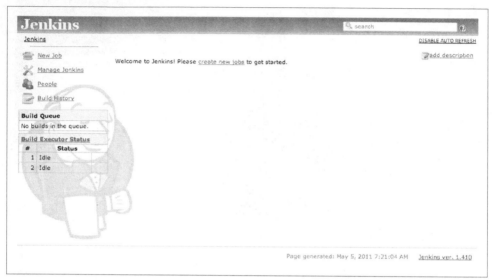

Figure 3-3. The Jenkins start page

Preparing a Build Server for Jenkins

Installing Jenkins on your local development machine is one thing, but installing Jenkins on a proper build server deserves a little more forethought and planning.

Before you start your installation, the first thing you will need is a build server. To work well, Jenkins needs both processor power and memory. Jenkins itself is a relatively modest Java web application. However, in most configurations, at least some of the builds will be run on the principal build server. Builds tend to be both memory and processor-intensive operations, and Jenkins can be configured to run several builds in parallel. Depending on the number of build jobs you are managing, Jenkins will also need memory of its own for its own internal use. The amount of memory required will depend largely on the nature of your builds, but memory is cheap these days (at least in non-hosted environments), and it's best not to be stingy.

A build server also needs CPU horsepower. As a rule of thumb, you will need one processor per parallel build, though, in practice, you can capitalize on I/O delays to do a little better than this. It is also in your best interest to dedicate your build server as much as possible to the task of running continuous builds. In particular, you should avoid memory or CPU-intensive applications such as test servers, heavily-used enterprise applications, enterprise databases such as Oracle, enterprise mail servers, and so on.

One very practical option available in many organizations today is to use a virtual machine. This way, you can choose the amount of memory and number of processors you think appropriate for your initial installation, and easily add more memory and processors later on as required. However, if you are using a virtual machine, make sure that it has enough memory to support the maximum number of parallel builds you expect to be running. The memory usage of a Continuous Integration server is best described as spiky—Jenkins will be creating additional JVMs as required for its build jobs, and these need memory.

Another useful approach is to set up multiple build machines. Jenkins makes it quite easy to set up "slaves" on other machines that can be used to run additional build jobs. The slaves remain inactive until a new build job is requested—then the main Jenkins installation dispatches the build job to the slave and reports on the results. This is a great way to absorb sudden spikes of build activity, for example just before a major release of your principal product. It is also a useful strategy if certain heavy-weight builds tend to "hog" the main build server—just put them on their own dedicated build agent! We will look at how to do this in detail later on in the book.

If you are installing Jenkins on a Linux or Unix build server, it is a good idea to create a special user (and user group) for Jenkins. This makes it easier to monitor at a glance the system resources being used by the Jenkins builds, and to troubleshoot problematic builds in real conditions. The native binary installation packages discussed below do this for you. If you did not use one of these, you can create a dedicated Jenkins user from the command line as shown here:

```
$ sudo groupadd build
$ sudo useradd --create-home --shell /bin/bash --groups build jenkins
```

The exact details may vary depending on your environment. For example, you may prefer to use a graphical administration console instead of the command line, or, on a Debian-based Linux server (such as Ubuntu), you might use the more user-friendly adduser and addgroup commands.

In most environments, you will need to configure Java correctly for this user. For example, you can do this by defining the JAVA_HOME and PATH variables in the *.bashrc* file, as shown here:

```
export JAVA_HOME=/usr/local/java/jdk1.6.0
export PATH=$JAVA_HOME/bin:$PATH
```

You will now be able to use this user to run Jenkins in an isolated environment.

The Jenkins Home Directory

Before we install Jenkins, however, there are some things you need to know about how Jenkins stores its data. Indeed, no matter where you store the Jenkins WAR file, Jenkins keeps all its important data in a special separate directory called the Jenkins home directory. Here, Jenkins stores information about your build server configuration, your build jobs, build artifacts, user accounts, and other useful information, as well as any plugins you may have installed. The Jenkins home directory format is backward compatible across versions, so you can freely update or reinstall your Jenkins executable without affecting your Jenkins home directory.

Needless to say, this directory will need a lot of disk space.

By default, the Jenkins home directory will be called *.jenkins,* and will be placed in your home directory. For example, if you are running a machine under Windows 7, if your username is "john", you would find the Jenkins home directory under *C:\Users\john \.jenkins*. Under Windows XP, it would be *C:\Documents and Settings\John\.jenkins*. On a Linux machine, it would most likely be under */home/john/.jenkins*. And so on.

You can force Jenkins to use a different directory as its home directory by defining the `JENKINS_HOME` environment variable. You may need to do this on a build server to conform to local directory conventions or to make your system administrator happy. For example, if your Jenkins WAR file is installed in */usr/local/jenkins*, and the Jenkins home directory needs to be in the */data/jenkins* directory, you might write a startup script along the following lines:

```
export JENKINS_BASE=/usr/local/jenkins
export JENKINS_HOME=/var/jenkins-data
java -jar ${JENKINS_BASE}/jenkins.war
```

If you are running Jenkins in a Java EE container such as Tomcat or JBoss, you can configure the webapp to expose its own environments variables. For example, if you are using Tomcat, you could create a file called *jenkins.xml* in the *$CATALINA_BASE/ conf/localhost* directory:

```
<Context docBase="../jenkins.war">
  <Environment name="JENKINS_HOME" type="java.lang.String"
               value="/data/jenkins" override="true"/>
</Context>
```

In a previous life, Jenkins was known as Hudson. Jenkins remains compatible with previous Hudson installations, and upgrading from Hudson to Jenkins can be as simple as replacing the old *hudson.war* file with *jenkins.war*. Jenkins will look for its home directory in the following places (by order of precedence):

1. A JNDI environment entry called JENKINS_HOME
2. A JNDI environment entry called HUDSON_HOME
3. A system property named JENKINS_HOME
4. A system property named HUDSON_HOME

5. An environment variable named JENKINS_HOME

6. An environment variable named HUDSON_HOME

7. The *.hudson* directory in the user's home directory, if it already exists

8. The *.jenkins* directory in the user's home directory

Installing Jenkins on Debian or Ubuntu

If you are installing Jenkins on Debian and Ubuntu, it is convenient to install the native binary package for these platforms. This is easy enough to do, though these binaries are not provided in the standard repositories because of the high frequency of updates. First, you need to add the key to your system as shown here:

```
$ wget -q -O - http://pkg.jenkins-ci.org/debian/jenkins-ci.org.key \
  | sudo apt-key add -
$ sudo echo "deb http://pkg.jenkins-ci.org/debian binary/" > \
  /etc/apt/sources.list.d/jenkins.list
```

Now, update the Debian package repository:

```
$ sudo aptitude update
```

Once this is done, you can install Jenkins using the *aptitude* tool:

```
$ sudo aptitude install -y jenkins
```

This will install Jenkins as a service, with a correctly configured startup script in */etc/init.d/jenkins* and a corresponding system user called "jenkins". If you didn't already have Java installed on your server, it will also install the OpenJDK version of Java. By default, you will find the Jenkins WAR file in the */usr/share/jenkins* directory, and the Jenkins home directory in */var/lib/jenkins*.

The installation process should have started Jenkins. In general, to start Jenkins, simply invoke this script:

```
$ sudo /etc/init.d/jenkins start
```

Jenkins will now be running on the default port of 8080 (*http://localhost:8080/*).

You can stop Jenkins as follows:

```
$ sudo /etc/inid.d/jenkins stop
```

Jenkins will write log files to */var/log/jenkins/jenkins.log*. You can also fine-tune the configuration parameters in the */etc/default/jenkins* file. This is useful if you need to modify the Java startup arguments (JAVA_ARGS). You can also use this file to configure arguments that will be passed to Jenkins in this file, such as the HTTP port or web application context (see "Running Jenkins as a Stand-Alone Application" on page 49).

Installing Jenkins on Redhat, Fedora, or CentOS

There are also native binary packages available for Redhat, Fedora, and CentOS. First you need to set up the repository as follows:

```
$ sudo wget -O /etc/yum.repos.d/jenkins.repo \
  http://jenkins-ci.org/redhat/jenkins.repo
$ sudo rpm --import http://pkg.jenkins-ci.org/redhat/jenkins-ci.org.key
```

On a fresh installation, you may need to install the JDK:

```
$ sudo yum install java-1.6.0-openjdk
```

Next, you can install the package as shown here:

```
$ sudo yum install jenkins
```

This will install the latest version of Jenkins into the */usr/lib/jenkins* directory. The default Jenkins home directory will be in */var/lib/jenkins*.

Now you can start Jenkins using the `service` command:

```
$ sudo service jenkins start
```

Jenkins will now be running on the default port of 8080 (*http://localhost:8080/*).

Jenkins's configuration parameters are placed in the */etc/sysconfig/jenkins* file. However at the time of writing the configuration options are more limited than those provided by the Ubuntu package: you can define the HTTP port using the JENKINS_PORT parameter, for example, but to specify an application context you need to modify the startup script by hand. The principal configuration options are listed here:

JENKINS_JAVA_CMD
> The version of Java you want to use to run Jenkins

JENKINS_JAVA_OPTIONS
> Command-line options to pass to Java, such as memory options

JENKINS_PORT
> The port that Jenkins will to run on

Installing Jenkins on SUSE or OpenSUSE

Binary packages are also available for SUSE and OpenSUSE, so the installation process on these platforms is straightforward. First, you need to add the Jenkins repository to the SUSE repository list:

```
$ sudo zypper addrepo http://pkg.jenkins-ci.org/opensuse/ jenkins
```

Finally, you simply install Jenkins using the zypper command:

```
$ sudo zypper install jenkins
```

As you can gather from the console output, this will install both Jenkins and the latest JDK from Sun, if the latter is not already installed. OpenSuse installations typically have the OpenJDK version of Java, but Jenkins prefers the Sun variety. When it downloads the Sun JDK, it will prompt you to validate the Sun Java license before continuing with the installation.

This installation process will also create a *jenkins* user and install Jenkins as a service, so that it will start up automatically whenever the machine boots. To start Jenkins manually, you can invoke the jenkins startup script in the */etc/init.d* directory:

```
$ sudo /etc/init.d/jenkins jenkins start
```

Jenkins will now be running on the default port of 8080 (*http://localhost:8080/*).

The configuration options are similar to the Redhat installation (see "Installing Jenkins on Redhat, Fedora, or CentOS" on page 48). You can define a limited number of configuration variables in the */etc/sysconfig/jenkins* file, but for any advanced configuration options, you need to modify the startup script in */etc/init.d/jenkins*.

The zypper tool also makes it easy to update your Jenkins instance:

```
$ sudo zypper update jenkins
```

This will download and install the latest version of Jenkins from the Jenkins website.

Running Jenkins as a Stand-Alone Application

You can run the Jenkins server in one of two ways: either as a stand-alone application, or deployed as a standard web application onto a Java Servlet container or application server such as Tomcat, JBoss, or GlassFish. Both approaches have their pros and cons, so we will look at both here.

Jenkins comes bundled as a WAR file that you can run directly using an embedded servlet container. Jenkins uses the lightweight Winstone servlet engine to allow you to run the server out of the box, without having to configure a web server yourself. This is probably the easiest way to get started, allowing you to be up and running with Jenkins in a matter of minutes. It is also a very flexible option, and provides some extra features unavailable if you deploy Jenkins to a conventional application server. In particular, if you are running Jenkins as a stand-alone server, you will be able to install plugins and upgrades on the fly, and restart Jenkins directly from the administration screens.

To run Jenkins using the embedded servlet container, just go to the command line and type the following:

```
C:\Program Files\Jenkins>
        java -jar jenkins.war
[Winstone 2011/07/01 20:54:53] - Beginning extraction from war file
[Winstone 2011/07/01 20:55:07] - No webapp classes folder found - C:\Users\john\
    .jenkins\war\WEB-INF\classes
```

```
jenkins home directory: C:\Users\john\.jenkins
...
INFO: Took 35 ms to load
...
[Winstone 2011/07/01 20:55:08] - HTTP Listener started: port=8080
[Winstone 2011/07/01 20:55:08] - Winstone Servlet Engine v0.9.10 running:
    controlPort=disabled
[Winstone 2011/07/01 20:55:08] - AJP13 Listener started: port=8009
```

In a Linux environment, the procedure is similar. Note how we start the Jenkins server from with the "jenkins" user account we created earlier:

```
john@lambton:~$ sudo su - jenkins
jenkins@lambton:~$ java -jar /usr/local/jeknins/jenkins.war
[Winstone 2011/07/16 02:11:24] - Beginning extraction from war file
[Winstone 2011/07/16 02:11:27] - No webapp classes folder found - /home/jenkins/
    .jenkins/war/WEB-INF/classes
jenkins home directory: /home/jenkins/.jenkins
...
[Winstone 2011/07/16 02:11:31] - HTTP Listener started: port=8080
[Winstone 2011/07/16 02:11:31] - AJP13 Listener started: port=8009
[Winstone 2011/07/16 02:11:31] - Winstone Servlet Engine v0.9.10 running:
    controlPort=disabled
```

This will start the embedded servlet engine in the console window. The Jenkins web application will now be available on port 8080. When you run Jenkins using the embedded server, there is no web application context, so you access Jenkins directly using the server URL (e.g., *http://localhost:8080*).

To stop Jenkins, just press Ctrl-C.

By default, Jenkins will run on the 8080 port. If this doesn't suit your environment, you can specify the port manually, using the --httpPort option:

```
$ java -jar jenkins.war --httpPort=8081
```

In a real-world architecture, Jenkins may not be the only web application running on your build server. Depending on the capacity of your server, Jenkins may have to cohabit with other web applications or Maven repository managers, for example. If you are running Jenkins along side another application server, such as Tomcat, Jetty, or GlassFish, you will also need to override the ajp13 port, using the --ajp13Port option:

```
$ java -jar jenkins.war --httpPort=8081 --ajp13Port=8010
```

Some other useful options are:

--prefix

> This option lets you define a context path for your Jenkins server. By default Jenkins will run on the port 8080 with no context path (*http://localhost:8080*). However, if you use this option, you can force Jenkins to use whatever context path suits you, for example:

```
$ java -jar jenkins.war --prefix=jenkins
```

> In this case, Jenkins will be accessible on *http://localhost:8080/hudson*.

This option is often used when integrating a stand-alone instance of Jenkins with Apache.

`--daemon`

If you are running Jenkins on a Unix machine, you can use this option to start Jenkins as a background task, running as a unix daemon.

`--logfile`

By default, Jenkins writes its logfile into the current directory. However, on a server, you often need to write your log files into a predetermined directory. You can use this option to redirect your messages to some other file:

```
$ java -jar jenkins.war --logfile=/var/log/jenkins.log
```

Stopping Jenkins using Ctrl-C is a little brutal, of course—in practice, you would set up a script to start and stop your server automatically.

If you are running Jenkins using the embedded Winstone application server, you can also restart and shutdown Jenkins elegantly by calling the Winstone server directly. To do this, you need to specify the `controlPort` option when you start Jenkins, as shown here:

```
$ java -jar jenkins.war --controlPort=8001
```

A slightly more complete example in a Unix environment might look like this:

```
$ nohup java -jar jenkins.war --controlPort=8001 > /var/log/jenkins.log 2>&1 &
```

The key here is the `controlPort` option. This option gives you the means of stopping or restarting Jenkins directly via the Winstone tools. The only problem is that you need a matching version of the Winstone JAR file. Fortunately, one comes bundled with your Jenkins installation, so you don't have to look far.

To restart the server, you can run the following command:

```
$ java -cp $JENKINS_HOME/war/winstone.jar winstone.tools.WinstoneControl reload: \
  --host=localhost --port=8001
```

And to shut it down completely, you can use the following:

```
$ java -cp $JENKINS_HOME/war/winstone.jar winstone.tools.WinstoneControl shutdown \
  --host=localhost --port=8001
```

Another way to shut down Jenkins cleanly is to invoke the special "/exit" URL, as shown here:

```
$ wget http://localhost:8080/exit
```

On a real server, you would typically have set up security, so that only a system administrator could access this URL. In this case, you will need to provide a username and a password:

```
$ wget --user=admin --password=secret http://localhost:8080/exit
```

Note that you can actually do this from a different server, not just the local machine:

```
$ wget --user=admin --password=secret http://buildserver.acme.com:8080/exit
```

Note that while both these methods will shut down Jenkins relatively cleanly (more so than killing the process directly, for example), they will interrupt any builds in progress. So it is recommended practice to prepare the shutdown cleanly by using the Prepare for Shutdown button on the Manage Jenkins screen (see "The Configuration Dashboard—The Manage Jenkins Screen" on page 65).

Running Jenkins as a stand-alone application may not be to everyone's taste. For a production server, you might want to take advantage of the more sophisticated monitoring and administration features of a full blown Java application server such as JBoss, GlassFish, or WebSphere Application Server. And system administrators may be wary of the relatively little-known Winstone server, or may simply prefer Jenkins to fit into a known pattern of Java web application development. If this is the case, you may prefer to, or be obliged to, deploy Jenkins as a standard Java web application. We look at this option in the following section.

Running Jenkins Behind an Apache Server

If you are running Jenkins in a Unix environment, you may want to hide it behind an Apache HTTP server in order to harmonize the server URLs and simplify maintenance and access. This way, users can access the Jenkins server using a URL like *http://myserver.myorg.com/jenkins* rather than *http://myserver.myorg.com:8081*.

One way to do this is to use the Apache mod_proxy and mod_proxy_ajp modules. These modules let you use implement proxying on your Apache server using the AJP13 (Apache JServer Protocol version 1.3). Using this module, Apache will transfer requests to particular URL patterns on your Apache server (running on port 80) directly to the Jenkins server running on a different port. So when a user opens a URL like *http://www.myorg.com/jenkins*, Apache will transparently forward traffic to your Jenkins server running on *http://buildserver.myorg.com:8081/jenkins*. Technically, this is known as "Reverse Proxying," as the client has no knowledge that the server is doing any proxying, or where the proxied server is located. So you can safely tuck your Jenkins server away behind a firewall, while still providing broader access to your Jenkins instance via the public-facing URL.

The exact configuration of this module will vary depending on the details of your Apache version and installation details, but one possible approach is shown here.

First of all, if you are running Jenkins as a stand-alone application, make sure you start up Jenkins using the --prefix option. The prefix you choose must match the suffix in the public-facing URL you want to use. So if you want to access Jenkins via the URL *http://myserver.myorg.com/jenkins*, you will need to provide jenkins as a prefix:

```
$ java -jar jenkins.war --httpPort=8081 --ajp13Port=8010 --prefix=jenkins
```

If you are running Jenkins on an application server such as Tomcat, it will already be running under a particular web context (/jenkins by default).

Next, make sure the mod_proxy and mod_proxy_ajp modules are activated. In your *httpd.conf* file (often in the */etc/httpf/conf* directory), you should have the following line:

```
LoadModule proxy_module modules/mod_proxy.so
```

The proxy is actually configured in the *proxy_ajp.conf* file (often in the */etc/httpd/conf.d* directory). Note that the name of the proxy path (/jenkins in this example) must match the prefix or web context that Jenkins is using. An example of such a configuration file is given here:

```
LoadModule proxy_ajp_module modules/mod_proxy_ajp.so

ProxyPass        /jenkins  http://localhost:8081/jenkins
ProxyPassReverse /jenkins  http://localhost:8081/jenkins
ProxyRequests    Off
```

Once this is done, you just need to restart your Apache server:

```
$ sudo /etc/init.d/httpd restart
Stopping httpd:                                    [  OK  ]
Starting httpd:                                    [  OK  ]
```

Now you should be able to access your Jenkins server using a URL like *http://my-server.myorg.com/jenkins*.

Running Jenkins on an Application Server

Since Jenkins is distributed as an ordinary WAR file, it is easy to deploy it on any standard Java application server such as Tomcat, Jetty, or GlassFish. Running Jenkins on an application server is arguably more complicated to setup and to maintain. You also loose certain nice administration features such as the ability to upgrade Jenkins or restart the server directly from within Jenkins. On the other hand, your system administrators might be more familiar with maintaining an application running on Tomcat or GlassFish than on the more obscure Winstone server.

Let's look at how you would typically deploy Jenkins onto a Tomcat server. The easiest approach is undoubtedly to simply unzip the Tomcat binary distribution onto your disk (if it is not already installed) and copy the *jenkins.war* file into the Tomcat *webapps* directory. You can download the Tomcat binaries from the Tomcat website (*http://tomcat.apache.org*).

You start Tomcat by running the *startup.bat* or *startup.sh* script in the Tomcat bin directory. Jenkins will be available when you start Tomcat. You should note that, in this case, Jenkins will be executed in its own web application context (typically "jenkins"), so you will need to include this in the URL you use to access your Jenkins server (e.g., *http://localhost:8080/jenkins*).

However, this approach is not necessarily the most flexible or robust option. If your build server is a Windows box, for example, you probably should install Tomcat as a Windows service, so that you can ensure that it starts automatically whenever the server reboots. Similarly, if you are installing Tomcat in a Unix environment, it should be set up as a service.

Memory Considerations

Continuous Integration servers use a lot of memory. This is the nature of the beast—builds will consume memory, and multiple builds being run in parallel will consume still more memory. So you should ensure that your build server has enough RAM to cope with however many builds you intend to run simultaneously.

Jenkins naturally needs RAM to run, but if you need to support a large number of build processes, it is not enough just to give Jenkins a lot of memory. In fact Jenkins spans a new Java process each time it kicks off a build, so during a large build, the build process needs the memory, not Jenkins.

You can define build-specific memory options for your Jenkins build jobs—we will see how to do this later on in the book. However if you have a lot of builds to maintain, you might want to define the JAVA_OPTS, MAVEN_OPTS and ANT_OPTS environment variables to be used as default values for your builds. The JAVA_OPTS options will apply for the main Jenkins process, whereas the other two options will be used when Jenkins kicks off new JVM processes for Maven and Ant build jobs respectively.

Here is an example of how these variables might be configured on a Unix machine in the *.profile* file:

```
export JAVA_OPTS=-Djava.awt.headless=true -Xmx512m -DJENKINS_HOME=/data/jenkins
export MAVEN_OPTS="-Xmx512m -XX:MaxPermSize=256m"
export ANT_OPTS="-Xmx512m -XX:MaxPermSize=256m"
```

Installing Jenkins as a Windows Service

If you are running a production installation of Jenkins on a Windows box, it is essential to have it running as a Windows service. This way, Jenkins will automatically start whenever the server reboots, and can be managed using the standard Windows administration tools.

One of the advantages of running Jenkins on an application server such as Tomcat is that it is generally fairly easy to configure these servers to run as a Windows service. However, it is also fairly easy to install Jenkins as a service, without having to install Tomcat.

Jenkins has a very convenient feature designed to make it easy to install Jenkins as a Windows servers. There is currently no graphical installer that does this for you, but you get the next best thing—a web-based graphical installer.

First, you need to start the Jenkins server on your target machine. The simplest approach is to run Jenkins using Java Web Start (see Figure 3-4). Alternatively, you can do this by downloading Jenkins and running it from the command line, as we discussed earlier:

```
C:\jenkins> java -jar jenkins.war
```

This second option is useful if the default Jenkins port (8080) is already being used by another application. It doesn't actually matter which port you use—you can change this later.

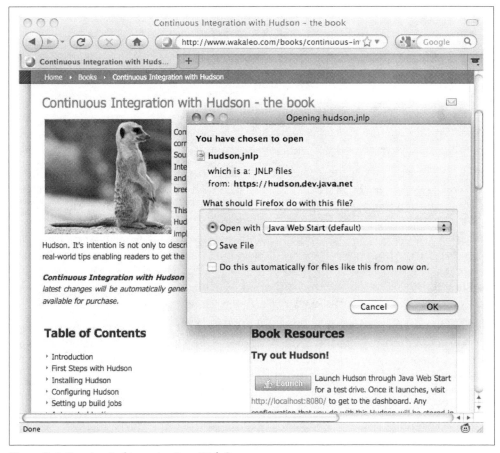

Figure 3-4. Starting Jenkins using Java Web Start

Once you have Jenkins running, connect to this server and go to the Manage Jenkins screen. Here you will find an Install as Windows Service button. This will create a Jenkins service on the server that will automatically start and stop Jenkins in an orderly manner (see Figure 3-5).

Figure 3-5. Installing Jenkins as a Windows service

Jenkins will prompt you for an installation directory. This will be the Jenkins home directory (JENKINS_HOME). The default value is the default JENKINS_HOME value: a directory called *.jenkins* in the current user's home directory. This is often not a good choice for a Windows installation. When running Jenkins on Windows XP, you should avoid installing your Jenkins home directory anywhere near your *C:\\Documents And Settings* directory—not only is it a ridiculously long name, the spaces can wreak havoc with your Ant and Maven builds and any tests using classpath-based resources. It is much better to use a short and sensible name such as *C:\Jenkins*. The Vista and Windows 7 home directory paths like *C:\Users\john* will also work fine.

A short home directory path is sometimes required for other reasons, too. On many versions of Windows (Windows XP, Windows Server 2003, etc.), file path lengths are limited to around 260 characters. If you combine a nested Jenkins work directory and a deep class path, you can often overrun this, which will result in very obscure build errors. To minimize the risks of over-running the Windows file path limits, you need to redefine the JENKINS_HOME environment variable to point to a shorter path, as we discussed above.

This approach won't always work with Windows Vista or Windows 7. An alternative strategy is to use the *jenkins.exe* program that the Web Start installation process will have installed in the directory you specified above. Open the command line prompt as an administrator (right-click, "Run as administrator") and run the *jenkins.exe* executable with the install option:

```
C:\Jenkins> jenkins.exe install
```

This basic installation will work fine in a simple context, but you will often need to fine-tune your service. For example, by default, the Jenkins service will be running under the local System account. However, if you are using Maven, Jenkins will need an *.m2* directory and a *settings.xml* file in the home directory. Similarly, if you are using Groovy, you might need a *.groovy/lib* directory. And so on. To allow this, and to make testing your Jenkins install easier, make sure you run this service under a real user account with the correct development environment set up (see Figure 3-6). Alternatively, run the application as the system user, but use the System Information page in Jenkins to check the *${user.dir}* directory, and place any files that must be placed in the user home directory here.

Figure 3-6. Configuring the Jenkins Windows Service

You configure the finer details of the Jenkins service in a file called *jenkins.xml*, in the same directory as your *jenkins.war* file. Here you can configure (or reconfigure) ports, JVM options, an the Jenkins work directory. In the following example, we give Jenkins a bit more memory and get it to run on port 8081:

```
<service>
  <id>jenkins</id>
  <name>Jenkins</name>
  <description>This service runs the Jenkins continuous integration system
    </description>
  <env name="JENKINS_HOME" value="D:\jenkins" />
  <executable>java</executable>
  <arguments>-Xrs -Xmx512m
  -Dhudson.lifecycle=hudson.lifecycle.WindowsServiceLifecycle
  -jar "%BASE%\jenkins.war" --httpPort=8081 --ajp13Port=8010</arguments>
</service>
```

Finally, if you need to uninstall the Jenkins service, you can do one of two things. The simplest is to run the Jenkins executable with the `uninstall` option:

```
C:\jenkins> jenkins.exe uninstall
```

The other option is to use the Windows service tool `sc`:

```
C:> sc delete jenkins
```

What's in the Jenkins Home Directory

The Jenkins home directory contains all the details of your Jenkins server configuration, details that you configure in the Manage Jenkins screen. These configuration details are stored in the form of a set of XML files. Much of the core configuration, for example, is stored in the *config.xml* file. Other tools-specific configuration is stored in other appropriately-named XML files: the details of your Maven installations, for example, are stored in a file called *hudson.tasks.Maven.xml*. You rarely need to modify these files by hand, though occasionally it can come in handy.

The Jenkins home directory also contains a number of subdirectories (see Figure 3-7). Not all of the files and directories will be present after a fresh installation, as some are created when required by Jenkins. And if you look at an existing Jenkins installation, you will see additional XML files relating to Jenkins configuration and plugins.

The main directories are described in more detail in Table 3-1.

Table 3-1. The Jenkins home directory structure

Directory	Description
.jenkins	The default Jenkins home directory (may be *.hudson* in older installations).
fingerprints	This directory is used by Jenkins to keep track of artifact fingerprints. We look at how to track artifacts later on in the book.
jobs	This directory contains configuration details about the build jobs that Jenkins manages, as well as the artifacts and data resulting from these builds. We look at this directory in detail below.
plugins	This directory contains any plugins that you have installed. Plugins allow you to extend Jenkins by adding extra feature. Note that, with the exception of the Jenkins core plugins (subversion, cvs, ssh-slaves, maven, and scid-ad), plugins are not stored with the `jenkins` executable, or in the expanded web application directory. This means that you can update your Jenkins executable and not have to reinstall all your plugins.
updates	This is an internal directory used by Jenkins to store information about available plugin updates.
userContent	You can use this directory to place your own custom content onto your Jenkins server. You can access files in this directory at *http://myserver/hudson/userContent* (if you are running Jenkins on an application server) or *http://myserver/userContent* (if you are running in stand-alone mode).
users	If you are using the native Jenkins user database, user accounts will be stored in this directory.

Directory	Description
war	This directory contains the expanded web application. When you start Jenkins as a stand-alone application, it will extract the web application into this directory.

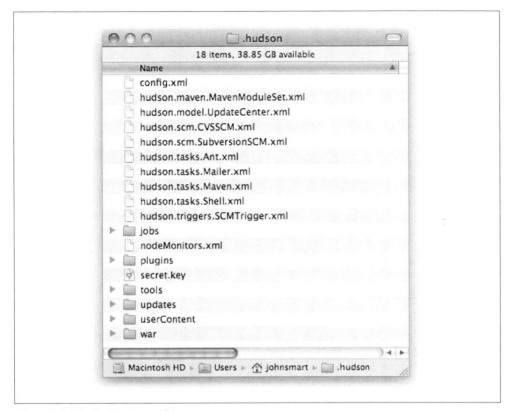

Figure 3-7. The Jenkins home directory

The *jobs* directory is a crucial part of the Jenkins directory structure, and deserves a bit more attention. You can see an example of a real Jenkins jobs directory in Figure 3-8.

This directory contains a subdirectory for each Jenkins build job being managed by this instance of Jenkins. Each job directory in turn contains two subdirectories: *builds* and *workspace*, along with some other files. In particular, it contains the build job *config.xml* file, which contains, as you might expect, the configuration details for this build job. There are also some other files used internally by Jenkins, that you usually wouldn't touch, such as the *nextBuildNumber* file (which contains the number that will be assigned to the next build in this build job), as well as symbolic links to the most recent successful build and the last stable one. A successful build is one that does not have any compilation errors. A stable build is a successful build that has passed whatever quality criteria you may have configured, such as unit tests, code coverage and so forth.

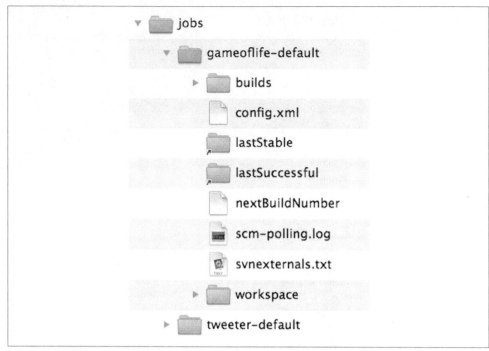

Figure 3-8. The Jenkins jobs directory

Both the *build* and the *workspace* directories are important. The *workspace* directory is where Jenkins builds your project: it contains the source code Jenkins checks out, plus any files generated by the build itself. This workspace is reused for each successive build—there is only ever one *workspace* directory per project, and the disk space it requires tends to be relatively stable.

The *builds* directory contains a history of the builds executed for this job. You rarely need to intervene directly in these directories, but it can be useful to know what they contain. You can see a real example of the builds directory in Figure 3-9, where three builds have been performed. Jenkins stores build history and artifacts for each build it performs in a directory labeled with a timestamp ("2010-03-12_20-42-05" and so forth in Figure 3-9). It also contains symbolic links with the actual build numbers that point to the build history directories.

Each build directory contains information such as the build result log file, the Subversion revision number used for this build (if you are using Subversion), the changes that triggered this build, and any other data or metrics that you have asked Jenkins to keep track of. For example, if your build job keeps track of unit test results or test coverage metrics, this data will be stored here for each build. The build directory also contains any artifacts you are storing—binary artifacts, but also other generated files such as javadoc or code coverage metrics. Some types of build jobs, such as the Jenkins Maven build jobs, will also archive binary artifacts by default.

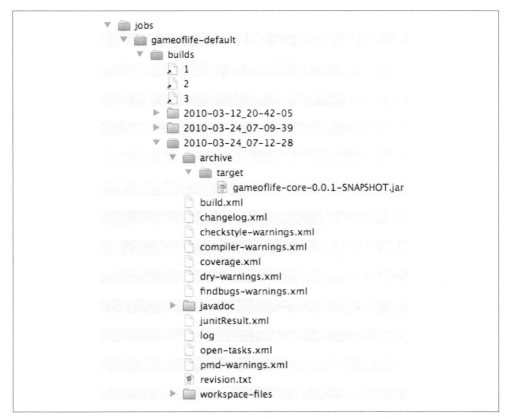

Figure 3-9. The builds directory

The size of the *build* directory will naturally grow over time, as the build history cumulates. You will probably want to take this into account when designing your build server directory structure, especially if your build server is running in a Unix-style environment with multiple disk partitions. A lot of this data takes the form of text or XML files, which does not consume a large amount of extra space for each build. However, if your build archives some of your build artifacts, such as JAR or WAR files, they too will be stored here. The size of these artifacts should be factored into your disk space requirements. We will see later on how to limit the number of builds stored for a particular build job if space is an issue. Limiting the number of build jobs that Jenkins stores is always a trade-off between disk space and keeping useful build statistics, as Jenkins does rely on this build history for its powerful reporting features.

Jenkins uses the files in this directory extensively to display build history and metrics data, so you should be particularly careful not to delete any of the build history directories without knowing exactly what you are doing.

Backing Up Your Jenkins Data

It is important to ensure that your Jenkins data is regularly backed up. This applies in particular to the Jenkins home directory, which contains your server configuration details as well as your build artifacts and build histories. This directory should be backed up frequently and automatically. The Jenkins executable itself is less critical, as it can easily be reinstalled without affecting your build environment.

Upgrading Your Jenkins Installation

Upgrading Jenkins is easy—you simply replace your local copy of the *jenkins.war* file and restart Jenkins. However you should make sure there are no builds running when you restart your server. Since your build environment configuration details, plugins, and build history are stored in the Jenkins home directory, upgrading your Jenkins executable will have no impact on your installation. You can always check what version of Jenkins you are currently running by referring to the version number in the bottom right corner of every screen.

If you have installed Jenkins using one of the Linux packages, Jenkins can be upgraded using the same process as the other system packages on the server.

If you are running Jenkins as a stand-alone instance, you can also upgrade your Jenkins installation directly from the web interface, in the Manage Jenkins section. Jenkins will indicate if a more recent version is available, and give you the option to either download it manually or upgrade automatically (see Figure 3-10).

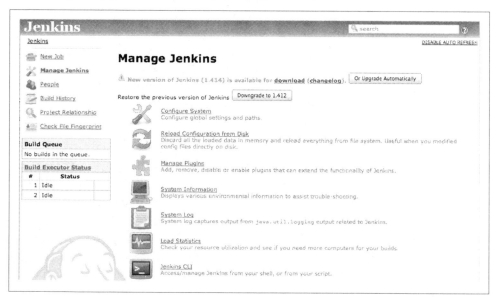

Figure 3-10. Upgrading Jenkins from the web interface

Once Jenkins has downloaded the upgrade, you can also tell it to restart when no jobs are running. This is probably the most convenient way to upgrade Jenkins, although it will not work in all environments. In particular, you need to be running Jenkins as a stand-alone application, and the user running Jenkins needs to have read-write access to the *jenkins.war* file.

If you are running Jenkins on an application server such as Tomcat or JBoss, you might need to do a bit more tidying up when you upgrade your Jenkins instance. Tomcat, for example, places compiled JSP pages in the *CATALINA_BASE/work* directory. When you upgrade your Jenkins version, these files need to be removed to prevent the possibility of any stale pages being served.

Any plugins you have installed will be unaffected by your Jenkins upgrades. However, plugins can also be upgraded, independently of the main Jenkins executable. You upgrade your plugins directly in the Jenkins web application, using the Jenkins Plugin Manager. We discuss plugins in more detail further on in this book.

Conclusion

In this chapter, we have seen how to install and run Jenkins in different environments, and learned a few basic tips on how to maintain your Jenkins installation once running. Jenkins is easy to install, both as a stand-alone application and as a WAR file deployed to an existing application server. The main things you need to consider when choosing a build server to host Jenkins are CPU, memory, and disk space.

CHAPTER 4

Configuring Your Jenkins Server

Introduction

Before you can start creating your build jobs in Jenkins, you need to do a little configuration, to ensure that your Jenkins server works smoothly in your particular environment. Jenkins is highly configurable, and, although most options are provided with sensible default values, or are able to find the right build tools in the system path and environment variables, it is always a good idea to know exactly what your build server is doing.

Jenkins is globally very easy to configure. The administration screens are intuitive, and the contextual online help (the blue question mark icons next to each field) is detailed and precise. In this chapter, we will look at how to configure your basic server setup in detail, including how to configure Jenkins to use different versions of Java, build tools such as Ant and Maven, and SCM tools such as CVS and Subversion. We will look at more advanced server configuration, such as using other version control systems or notification tools, further on in the book.

The Configuration Dashboard—The Manage Jenkins Screen

In Jenkins, you manage virtually all aspects of system configuration in the Manage Jenkins screen (see Figure 4-1). You can also get to this screen directly from anywhere in the application by typing "manage" in the Jenkins search box. This screen changes depending on what plugins you install, so don't be surprised if you see more than what we show here.

This screen lets you configure different aspects of your Jenkins server. Each link on this page takes you to a dedicated configuration screen, where you can manage different parts of the Jenkins server. Some of the more interesting options are discussed here:

Configure System
> This is where you manage paths to the various tools you use in your builds, such as JDKs, and versions of Ant and Maven, as well as security options, email servers,

Figure 4-1. You configure your Jenkins installation in the Manage Jenkins screen

and other system-wide configuration details. Many of the plugins that you install will also need to be configured here—Jenkins will add the fields dynamically when you install the plugins.

Reload Configuration from Disk

As we saw in the previous chapter, Jenkins stores all its system and build job configuration details as XML files stored in the Jenkins home directory (see "The Jenkins Home Directory" on page 46). It also stores all of the build history in the same directory. If you are migrating build jobs from one Jenkins instance to another, or archiving old build jobs, you will need to add or remove the corresponding build job directories to Jenkins's *builds* directory. You don't need to take Jenkins offline to do this—you can simply use the "Reload Configuration from Disk" option to reload the Jenkins system and build job configurations directly. This process can be a little slow if there is a lot of build history, as Jenkins loads not only the build configurations but also all of the historical data as well.

Manage Plugins

One of the best features of Jenkins is its extensible architecture. There is a large ecosystem of third-party open source plugins available, enabling you to add extra features to your build server, from support for different SCM tools such as Git,

Mercurial or ClearCase, to code quality and code coverage metrics reporting. We will be looking at many of the more popular and useful plugins throughout this book. Plugins can be installed, updated and removed through the Manage Plugins screen. Note that removing plugins needs to be done with some care, as it can sometimes affect the stability of your Jenkins instance—we will look at this in more detail in "Migrating Build Jobs" on page 354.

System Information

This screen displays a list of all the current Java system properties and system environment variables. Here, you can check exactly what version of Java Jenkins is running in, what user it is running under, and so forth. You can also check that Jenkins is using the correct environment variable settings. Its main use is for troubleshooting, so that you can make sure that your server is running with the system properties and variables you think it is.

System Log

The System Log screen is a convenient way to view the Jenkins log files in real time. Again, the main use of this screen is for troubleshooting.

You can also subscribe to RSS feeds for various levels of log messages. For example, as a Jenkins administrator, you might want to subscribe to all the ERROR and WARNING log messages.

Load Statistics

Jenkins keeps track of how busy your server is in terms of the number of concurrent builds and the length of the build queue (which gives an idea of how long your builds need to wait before being executed). These statistics can give you an idea of whether you need to add extra capacity or extra build nodes to your infrastructure.

Script Console

This screen lets you run Groovy scripts on the server. It is useful for advanced troubleshooting: since it requires a strong knowledge of the internal Jenkins architecture, it is mainly useful for plugin developers and the like.

Manage Nodes

Jenkins handles parallel and distributed builds well. In this screen, you can configure how many builds you want. Jenkins runs simultaneously, and, if you are using distributed builds, set up build nodes. A build node is another machine that Jenkins can use to execute its builds. We will look at how to configure distributed builds in detail in Chapter 11.

Prepare for Shutdown

If you need to shut down Jenkins, or the server Jenkins is running on, it is best not to do so when a build is being executed. To shut down Jenkins cleanly, you can use the Prepare for Shutdown link, which prevents any new builds from being started. Eventually, when all of the current builds have finished, you will be able to shut down Jenkins cleanly.

We will come back to some of these features in more detail later on in the book. In the following sections, we will focus on how to configure the most important Jenkins system parameters.

Configuring the System Environment

The most important Jenkins administration page is the Configure System screen (Figure 4-2). Here, you set up most of the fundamental tools that Jenkins needs to do its daily work. The default screen contains a number of sections, each relating to a different configuration area or external tool. In addition, when you install plugins, their system-wide configuration is also often done in this screen.

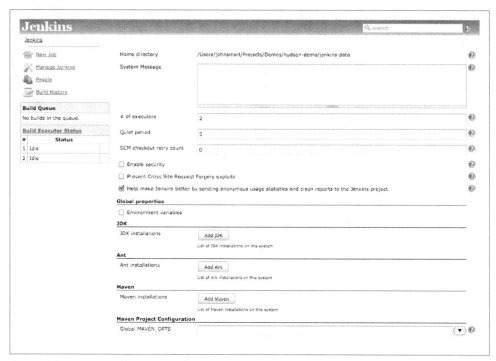

Figure 4-2. System configuration in Jenkins

The Configure System screen lets you define global parameters for your Jenkins installation, as well as external tools required for your build process. The first part of this screen lets you define some general system-wide parameters.

The Jenkins home directory is displayed, for reference. This way, you can check at a glance that you are working with the home directory that you expect. Remember, you can change this directory by setting the JENKINS_HOME environment variable in your environment (see "The Jenkins Home Directory" on page 46).

The System Message field is useful for several purposes. This text is displayed at the top of your Jenkins home page. You can use HTML tags, so it is a simple way to customize your build server by including the name of your server and a short blurb describing its purpose. You can also use it to display messages for all users, such as to announce system outages and so on.

The Quiet Period is useful for SCM tools like CVS that commit file changes one by one, rather than grouped together in a single atomic transaction. Normally, Jenkins will trigger a build as soon as it detects a change in the source repository. However, this doesn't suit all environments. If you are using an SCM tool like CVS, you don't want Jenkins kicking off a build as soon as the first change comes in, as the repository will be in an inconsistent state until all of the changes have been committed. You can use the Quiet Period field to avoid issues like this. If you set a value here, Jenkins will wait until no changes have been detected for the specified number of seconds before triggering the build. This helps to ensure that all of the changes have been committed and the repository is in a stable state before starting the build.

For most modern version control systems, such as Subversion, Git or Mercurial, commits are atomic. This means that changes in multiple files are submitted to the repository as a single unit, and the source code on the repository is guaranteed to be in a stable state at all times. However, some teams still use an approach where one logical change set is delivered in several commit operations. In this case, you can use the Quiet Period field to ensure that the build always uses a stable source code version.

The Quiet Period value specified here is in fact the default system-wide value—if required, you can redefine this value individually for each project.

You also manage user accounts and user rights here. By default, Jenkins lets any user do anything. If you want a more restrictive approach, you will need to activate Jenkins security here using the Enable Security field. There are many ways to do this, and we look at this aspect of Jenkins later on (see Chapter 7).

Configuring Global Properties

The Global Properties (see Figure 4-3) section lets you define variables that can be managed centrally but used in all of your build jobs. You can add as many properties as you want here, and use them in your build jobs. Jenkins will make them available within your build job environment, so you can freely use them within your Ant and Maven build scripts. Note that you shouldn't put periods (".") in the property names, as they won't be processed correctly. So `ldapserver` or `ldap_server` is fine, but not `ldap.server`.

There are two ways you typically use these variables. Firstly, you can use them directly in your build script, using the `${key}` or `$key` notation (so `${ldapserver}` or `$ldap server` in the example give above. This is the simplest approach, but means that there is a tight coupling between your build job configuration and your build scripts.

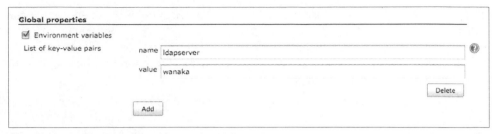

Figure 4-3. Configuring environment variables in Jenkins

If your script uses a different property name (one containing dots, for example), you can also pass the value to your build script in the build job configuration. In Figure 4-4 we pass the `ldapserver` property value defined in Figure 4-3 to a Maven build job. Using the `-D` option means that this value will be accessible from within the build script. This is a flexible approach, as we can assign the global properties defined within Jenkins to script-specific variables in our build scripts. In Figure 4-4, for example, the `ldapserver` property will be available from within the Maven build via the internal `${ldap.server}` property.

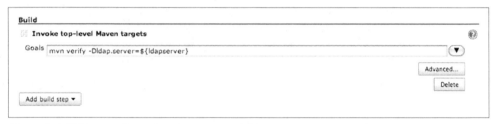

Figure 4-4. Using a configured environment variable

Configuring Your JDKs

Historically, one of the most common uses of Jenkins has been to build Java applications. So Jenkins naturally provides excellent built-in support for Java.

By default, Jenkins will build Java applications using whatever version of Java it finds on the system path, which is usually the version that Jenkins itself is running under. However, for a production build server, you will probably want more control than this. For example, you may be running your Jenkins server under Java 6, for performance reasons. However, your production server might be running under Java 5 or even Java 1.4. Large organizations are often cautious when it comes to upgrading Java versions in their production environments, and some of the more heavyweight application servers on the market are notoriously slow to be certified with the latest JDKs.

In any case, it is always a wise practice to build your application using a version of Java that is close to the one running on your production server. While an application compiled with Java 1.4 will usually run fine under Java 6, the inverse is not always true.

Or you may have different applications that need to be built using different versions of Java.

Jenkins provides good support for working with multiple JVMs. Indeed, Jenkins makes it very easy to configure and use as many versions of Java as you want. Like most system-level configuration, we do this in the Configure System screen (see Figure 4-2). Here, you will find a section called JDK which allows you to manage the JDK installations you need Jenkins to work with.

The simplest way to declare a JDK installation is simply to supply an appropriate name (which will be used to identify this Java installation later on when you configure your builds), along with the path to the Java installation directory (the same path you would use for the JAVA_HOME variable), as shown in Figure 4-5. Although you need to type the path manually, Jenkins will check in real time both that the directory exists and that it looks like a valid JDK directory.

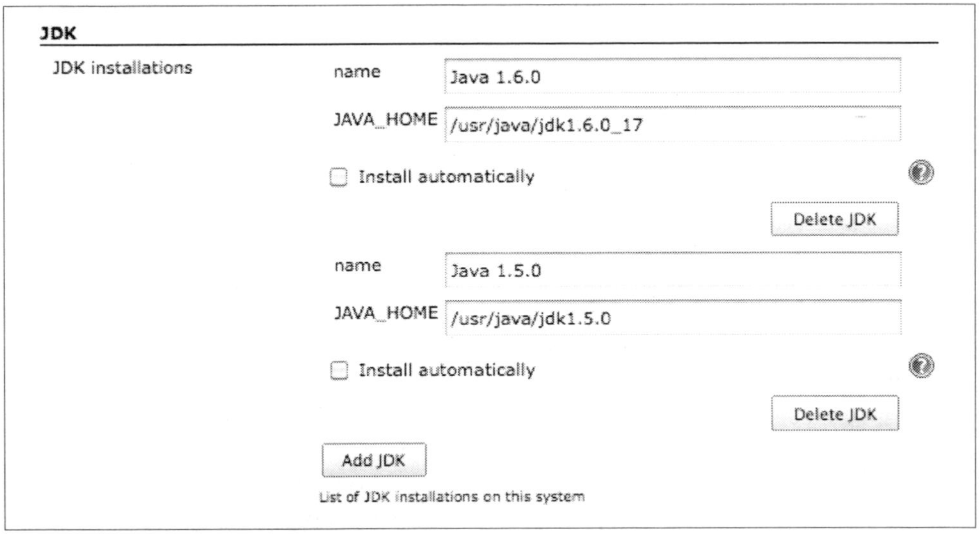

Figure 4-5. JDK configuration in Jenkins

You can also ask Jenkins to install Java for you. In this case, Jenkins will download the JDK installation and install a copy on your machine (see Figure 4-6). The first time a build needs to use this JDK, Jenkins will download and install the specified version of Java into the *tools* directory in the Jenkins home directory. If the build is running on a new build agent that doesn't have this JDK installed, it will download and install it onto the build agent machine as well.

This is also a great way to configure build agents. As we'll see later on in the book, Jenkins can delegate build jobs to other machines, or build agents. A build agent (or "slave") is simply another computer that Jenkins can use to run some of its builds. If you use Jenkins's Install automatically option, you don't need to manually install all

Figure 4-6. Installing a JDK automatically

the JDK versions you need on the build agent machines—Jenkins will do it for you the first time it needs to.

By default, Jenkins proposes to download the JDK from the Oracle website. If your Jenkins installation is behind a proxy server, you may need to configure your proxy settings to ensure that Jenkins can access the external download sites (see "Configuring a Proxy" on page 77). Another option is to provide a URL pointing to your own internal copy of the JDK binaries (either in the form of a ZIP or a GZip-compressed TAR file), stored on a local server within your organization. This lets you provide standard installations on a local server and makes for faster automatic installations. When you use this option, Jenkins also lets you specify a label, which will restrict the use of this installation to the build notes with this label. This is a useful technique if you need to install a specific version of a tool on certain build machines. The same approach can also be used for other build tools (such as Maven and Ant).

The automatic installer will not work in all environments (if it can't find or identify your operating system to its satisfaction, for example, the installation will fail), but it is nevertheless a useful and convenient way to set up new build servers or distributed build agents in a consistent manner.

Configuring Your Build Tools

Build tools are the bread-and-butter of any build server, and Jenkins is no exception. Out of the box, Jenkins supports three principal build tools: Ant, Maven, and the basic shell-script (or Batch script in Windows). Using Jenkins plugins, you can also add support for other build tools and other languages, such as Gant, Grails, MSBuild, and many more.

Maven

Maven is a high-level build scripting framework for Java that uses notions such as a standard directory structure and standard life cycles, Convention over Configuration, and Declarative Dependency Management to simplify a lot of the low-level scripting that you find in a typical Ant build script. In Maven, your project uses a standard, well-defined build life cycle—compile, test, package, deploy, and so forth. Each life cycle phase is associated with a Maven plugin. The various Maven plugins use the standard directory structure to carry out these tasks with a minimum of intervention on your part. You can also extend Maven by overriding the default plugin configurations or by invoking additional plugins.

Jenkins provides excellent support for Maven, and has a good understanding of Maven project structures and dependencies. You can either get Jenkins to install a specific version of Maven automatically (as we are doing with Maven 3 in the example), or provide a path to a local Maven installation (see Figure 4-7). You can configure as many versions of Maven for your build projects as you want, and use different versions of Maven for different projects.

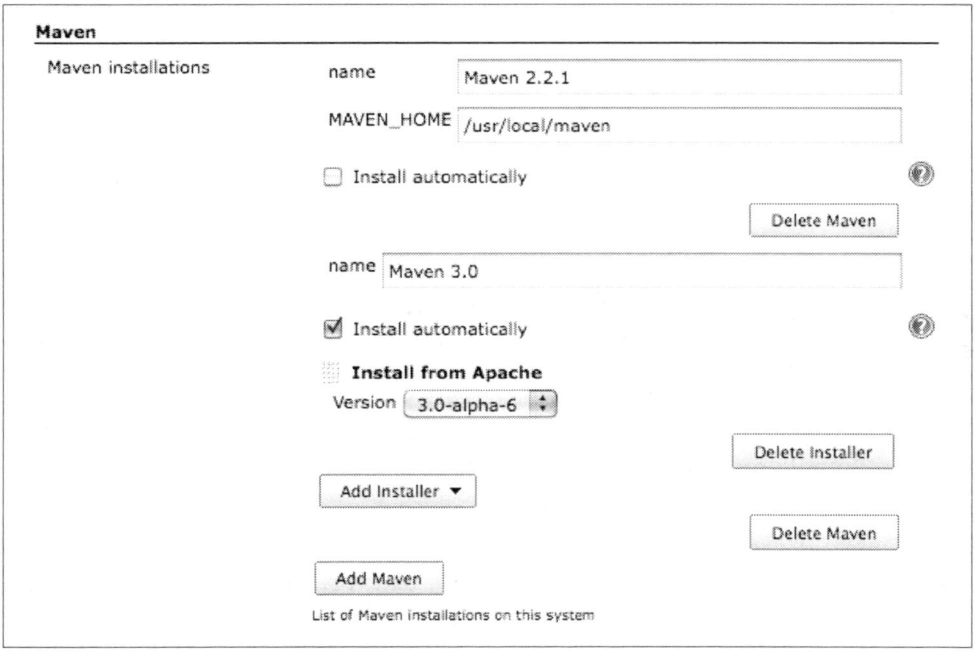

Figure 4-7. Configuring Maven in Jenkins

If you tick the Install automatically checkbox, Jenkins will download and install the requested version of Maven for you. You can either ask Jenkins to download Maven directly from the Apache site, or from a (presumably local) URL of your choice. This is an excellent choice when you are using distributed builds, and, since Maven is cross-platform, it will work on any machine. You don't need to install Maven explicitly on each build machine—the first time a build machine needs to use Maven, it will download a copy and install it to the *tools* directory in the Jenkins home directory.

Sometimes you need to pass Java system options to your Maven build process. For instance it is often useful to give Maven a bit of extra memory for heavyweight tasks such as code coverage or site generation. Maven lets you do this by setting the MAVEN_OPTS variable. In Jenkins, you can set a system-wide default value, to be used across all projects (see Figure 4-8). This comes in handy if you want to use certain standard memory options (for example) across all projects, without having to set it up in each project by hand.

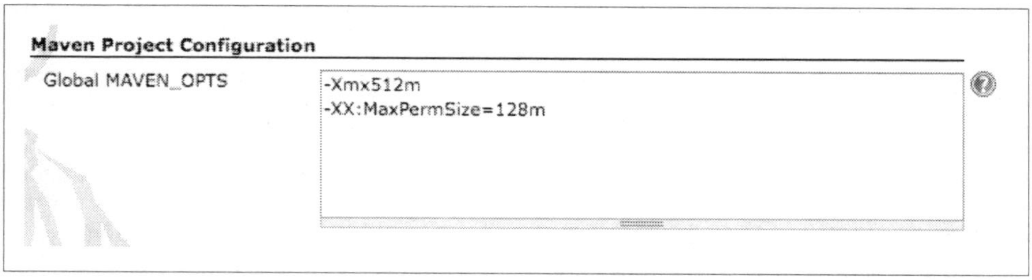

Maven Project Configuration

Global MAVEN_OPTS

```
-Xmx512m
-XX:MaxPermSize=128m
```

Figure 4-8. Configuring system-wide MVN_OPTS

Ant

Ant is a widely-used and very well-known build scripting language for Java. It is a flexible, extensible, relatively low-level scripting language, used in a large number of open source projects. An Ant build script (typically called *build.xml*) is made up of a number of *targets*. Each target performs a particular job in the build process, such as compiling your code or running your unit tests. It does so by executing *tasks*, which carry out a specific part of the build job, such as invoking *javac* to compile your code, or creating a new directory. Targets also have *dependencies*, indicating the order in which your build tasks need to be executed. For example, you need to compile your code before you can run your unit tests.

Jenkins provides excellent build-in support for Ant—you can invoke Ant targets from your build job, providing properties to customize the process as required. We look at how to do this in detail later on in this book.

If Ant is available on the system path, Jenkins will find it. However, if you want to know precisely what version of Ant you are using, or if you need to be able to use several different versions of Ant on different build jobs, you can configure as many installations of Ant as required (see Figure 4-9). Just provide a name and installation directory for each version of Ant in the Ant section of the Configure System screen. You will then be able to choose what version of Ant you want to use for each project.

Figure 4-9. Configuring Ant in Jenkins

If you tick the Install automatically checkbox, Jenkins will download and install Ant into the *tools* directory of your Jenkins home directory, just like it does for Maven. It will download an Ant installation the first time a build job needs to use Ant, either from the Apache website or from a local URL. Again, this is a great way to standardize build servers and make it easier to add new distributed build servers to an existing infrastructure.

Shell-Scripting Language

If you are running your build server on Unix or Linux, Jenkins lets you insert shell scripts into your build jobs. This is handy for performing low-level, OS-related tasks that you don't want to do in Ant or Maven. In the Shell section, you define the default shell that will be used when executing these shell scripts. By default, this is */bin/sh*, but there are times you may want to modify this to another command interpreter such as *bash* or *Perl*.

In Windows, the Shell section does not apply—you use Windows batch scripting instead. So, on a Windows build server, you should leave this field blank.

Configuring Your Version Control Tools

Jenkins comes preinstalled with plugins for CVS and Subversion. Other version control systems are supported by plugins that you can download from the Manage Plugins screen.

Configuring Subversion

Subversion needs no special configuration, since Jenkins uses native Java libraries to interact with Subversion repositories. If you need to authenticate to connect to a repository, Jenkins will prompt you when you enter the Subversion URL in the build job configuration.

Configuring CVS

CVS needs little or no configuration. By default, Jenkins will look for tools like CVS on the system path, though you can provide the path explicitly if it isn't on the system path. CVS keeps login and password details in a file called *.cvspass*, which is usually in your home directory. If this is not the case, you can provide a path where Jenkins can find this file.

Configuring the Mail Server

The last of the basic configuration options you need to set up is the email server configuration. Email is Jenkins's more fundamental notification technique—when a build fails, it will send an email message to the developer who committed the changes, and optionally to other team members as well. So Jenkins needs to know about your email server (see Figure 4-10).

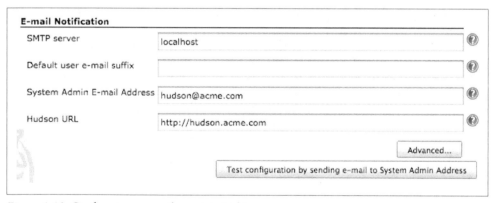

Figure 4-10. Configuring an email server in Jenkins

The System Admin email address is the address from which the notification messages are sent. You can also use this field to check the email setup—if you click on the Test configuration button, Jenkins will send a test email to this address.

In many organizations, you can derive a user's email address from their login by adding the organization domain name. For example, at ACME, user John Smith will have a login of "jsmith" and an email address of "jsmith@acme.com". If this extends to your version control system, Jenkins can save you a lot of configuration effort in this area. In the previous example, you could simply specify the default user email suffix of acme.com and Jenkins will figure out the rest.

You also need to provide a proper base URL for your Jenkins server (one that does not use localhost). Jenkins uses this URL in the email notifications so that users can go directly from the email to the build failure screen on Jenkins.

Jenkins also provides for more sophisticated email configuration, using more advanced features such as SMTP authentication and SSL. If this is your case, click on the Advanced button to configure these options.

For example, many organizations use Google Apps for their email services. You can configure Jenkins to work with the Gmail service as shown in Figure 4-11. All you need to do in this case is to use the Gmail SMTP server, and provide your Gmail username and password in the SMTP Authentication (you also need to use SSL and the non-standard port of 465).

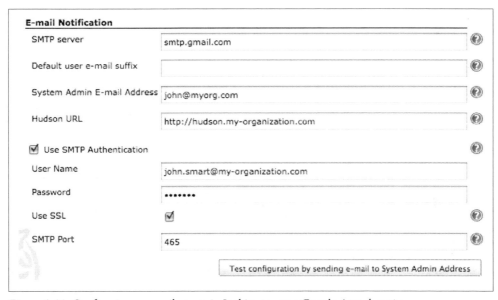

Figure 4-11. Configuring an email server in Jenkins to use a Google Apps domain

Configuring a Proxy

In most enterprise environments, your Jenkins server will be situated behind a firewall, and will not have direct access to the Internet. Jenkins needs Internet access to download plugins and updates, and also to install tools such as the JDK, Ant and Maven from remote sites. If you need to go through an HTTP proxy server to get to the Internet, you can configure the connection details (the server and port, and if required the username and password) in the Advanced tab on the Plugin Manager screen (see Figure 4-12).

If your proxy is using Microsoft's NTLM authentication scheme, then you will need to provide a domain name as well as a username. You can place both in the User name field: just enter the domain name, followed by a back-slash (\), followed by the user-name, such as "MyDomain\Joe Bloggs".

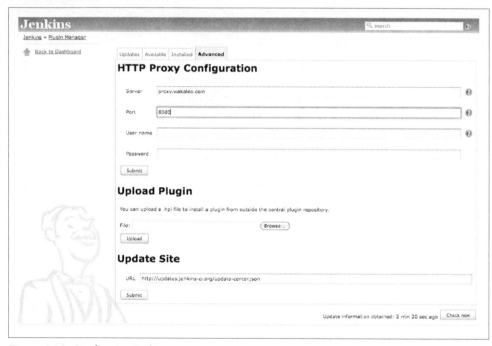

Figure 4-12. Configuring Jenkins to use a proxy

Finally, if you are setting up Proxy access on your Jenkins build server, remember that all of the other tools running on this server will need to know about the proxy as well. In particular, this may include tools such as Subversion (if you are accessing an external repository) and Maven (if you are not using an Enterprise Repository Manager).

Conclusion

You don't need a great deal of configuration to get started with Jenkins. The configu-ration that is required is fairly straightforward, and is centralised in the Configure Sys-tem screen. Once this is done, you are ready to create your first Jenkins build job!

CHAPTER 5

Setting Up Your Build Jobs

Introduction

Build jobs are the basic currency of a Continuous Integration server.

A build job is a particular way of compiling, testing, packaging, deploying or otherwise doing something with your project. Build jobs come in a variety of forms; you may want to compile and unit test your application, report on code quality metrics related to the source code, generate documentation, bundle up an application for a release, deploy it to production, run an automated smoke test, or do any number of other similar tasks.

A software project will usually have several related build jobs. For example, you might choose to start off with a dedicated build job that runs all of your unit tests. If these pass, you might proceed to a build job that executes longer-running integration tests, runs code quality metrics, or generates technical documentation, before finally bundling up your web application and deploying it to a test server.

In Jenkins, build jobs are easy to set up. In this chapter, we will look at the main types of build jobs and how to configure them. In later chapters, we will take things further, looking at how to organize multiple build jobs, how to set up build promotion pipelines, and how to automate the deployment process. But, for now, let's start off with how to set up your basic build jobs in Jenkins.

Jenkins Build Jobs

Creating a new build job in Jenkins is simple: just click on the "New Job" menu item on the Jenkins dashboard. Jenkins supports several different types of build jobs, which are presented to you when you choose to create a new job (see Figure 5-1).

Freestyle software project
> Freestyle build jobs are general-purpose build jobs, which provides a maximum of flexibility.

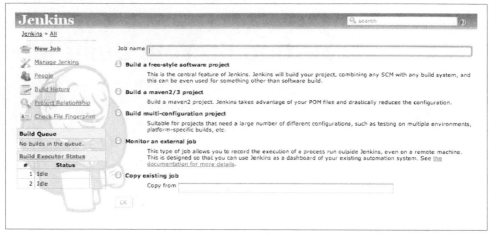

Figure 5-1. Jenkins supports four main types of build jobs

Maven project
> The "maven2/3 project" is a build job specially adapted to Maven projects. Jenkins understands Maven *pom* files and project structures, and can use the information gleaned from the *pom* file to reduce the work you need to do to set up your project.

Monitor an external job
> The "Monitor an external job" build job lets you keep an eye on non-interactive processes, such as cron jobs.

Multiconfiguration job
> The "multiconfiguration project" (also referred to as a "matrix project") lets you run the same build job in many different configurations. This powerful feature can be useful for testing an application in many different environments, with different databases, or even on different build machines. We will be looking at how to configure multiconfiguration build jobs later on in the book.

You can also copy an existing job, which is a great way to create a new job that is very similar to an existing build job, except for a few configuration details.

In this chapter, we will focus on the first two types of build jobs, which are the most commonly used. We will discuss the others later on. Let's start with the most flexible option: the freestyle build job.

Creating a Freestyle Build Job

The freestyle build job is the most flexible and configurable option, and can be used for any type of project. It is relatively straightforward to set up, and many of the options we configure here also appear in other build jobs.

General Options

The first section you see when you create a new freestyle job contains general information about the project, such as a unique name and description, and other information about how and where the build job should be executed (see Figure 5-2).

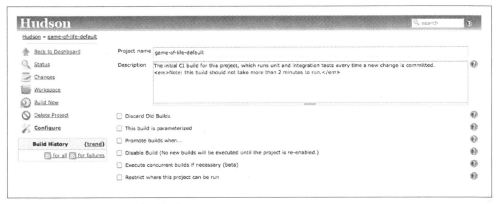

Figure 5-2. Creating a new build job

The project name can be anything you like, but it is worth noting that it will be used for the project directory and the build job URL, so I generally avoid names with spaces. The project description will go on the project home page—use this to provide an overview of the build job's goals and context. HTML tags will work fine in this field.

The other options are more technical, and we will be looking at some of them in detail later on in the book.

One important aspect that you should think about upfront is how you want to handle build history. Build jobs can consume a lot of disk space, especially if you store the build artifacts (the binary files, such as JARs, WARs, TARs, etc., generated by your build job). Even without artifacts, keeping a record of every build job consumes additional disk space and memory, which may or may not be justified, depending on the nature of your build job. For example, for a code quality metrics build that reports on static analysis and code coverage metrics over time, you might want to keep a record of the builds for the duration of the project, whereas, for a build job that automatically deploys an application to a test server, keeping the build history and artifacts for posterity might be less important.

The Discard Old Builds option lets you limit the number of builds you record in the build history. You can either tell Jenkins to only keep recent builds (Jenkins will delete builds after a certain number of days), or to keep no more than a specified number of builds. If a certain build has particular sentimental value, you can always tell Jenkins to keep it forever by using the Keep forever button on the build details page (see Figure 5-3). Note that this button will only appear if you have asked Jenkins to discard old builds.

Figure 5-3. Keeping a build job forever

In addition, Jenkins will never delete the last stable and successful builds, no matter how old they are. For example, if you limit Jenkins to only keep the last twenty builds, and your last successful build was thirty builds ago, Jenkins will still keep the successful build job as well as the last twenty failing builds.

You also have the option to disable the build. A disabled build will not be executed until you enable it again. Using this option when you create a new build job is quite rare. On the other hand, this option often comes in handy to temporarily suspend a build during maintenance work or major refactoring, when notification of the build failures will not be useful for the team.

Advanced Project Options

The Advanced Project options contains, as the name suggests, configuration options that are less frequently required. You need to click on the Advanced button for them to appear (see Figure 5-4).

Figure 5-4. To display the Advanced Options, you need to click on the Advanced button

The Quiet Period option in the build job configuration simply lets you override the system-wide quiet period defined in the Jenkins System Configuration screen (see "Configuring the System Environment" on page 68). This option is mainly used for version control systems that don't support atomic commits, such as CVS, but it is also sometimes used in teams where developers have the habit of committing their work in several small commits.

The "Block build when upstream project is building" option is useful when several related projects are affected by a single commit, but they must be built in a specific order. If you activate this option, Jenkins will wait until any upstream build jobs (see "Build Triggers" on page 97) have finished before starting this build.

For instance, when you release a new version of a multimodule Maven project, version number updates will happen in many, if not all, of the project modules. Suppose, for example, that we have added a web application to the Game of Life project we used in Chapter 2, setting it up as a separate Maven project. When we release a new version of this project, both the core and the web application version numbers will be updated (see Figure 5-5). Before we can build the web application, we need to build a new version of the original Game of Life core module. However if you had a separate freestyle build job for each module, then the build jobs for both the core and the web application would start simultaneously. The web application build job will fail if the core build job hasn't produced a new version of the core module for it, even if there are no test failures.

To avoid this issue, you could set up the web application build job to *only* start once the core build has successfully terminated. However this would mean that the web application would never be built if changes were made that only affected it, and not the core module. A better approach is to use the "Block build when upstream project" option. In this case, when the version numbers are updated in version control, Jenkins will schedule both builds to be executed. However it will wait until the core build has finished before starting the web application build.

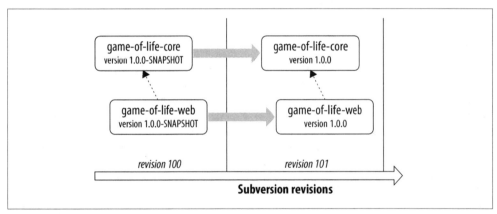

Figure 5-5. The "Block build when upstream project is building" option is useful when a single commit can affect several related projects

You can also override the default workspace used by Jenkins to check out the source code and build your project. Normally, Jenkins will create a special workspace directory for your project, which can be found in the project's build job directory (see "What's in the Jenkins Home Directory" on page 58). This works fine in almost all cases. However, there are times when you need to override this option, and force Jenkins to use a special directory. One common example of this is if you want several build jobs to all work successively in the same directory. You can override the default directory by ticking the "Use custom workspace" option, and providing the path yourself. The path can be either absolute, or relative to Jenkins's home directory.

We will look at some of the other more advanced options that appear in this section later on in the book.

Configuring Source Code Management

In its most basic role, a Continuous Integration server monitors your version control system, and checks out the latest changes as they occur. The server then compiles and tests the most recent version of the code. Alternatively, it may simply check out and build the latest version of your source code on a regular basis. In either case, tight integration with your version control system is essential.

Because of its fundamental role, SCM configuration options in Jenkins are identical across all sorts of build jobs. Jenkins supports CVS and Subversion out of the box, with built-in support for Git, and also integrates with a large number of other version control systems via plugins. At the time of writing, SCM plugin support includes Accurev, Bazaar, BitKeeper, ClearCase, CMVC, Dimensions, Git, CA Harvest, Mercurial, Perforce, PVCS, StarTeam, CM/Synergy, Microsoft Team Foundation Server, and even Visual SourceSafe. In the rest of this section, we will look at how to configure some of the more common SCM tools.

Working with Subversion

Subversion is one of the most widely used version control systems, and Jenkins comes bundled with full Subversion support (see Figure 5-6). To use source code from a Subversion repository, you simply provide the corresponding Subversion URL—it will work fine with any of the three Subversion protocols of (http, svn, or file). Jenkins will check that the URL is valid as soon as you enter it. If the repository requires authentication, Jenkins will prompt you for the corresponding credentials automatically, and store them for any other build jobs that access this repository.

By default, Jenkins will check out the repository contents into a subdirectory of your workspace, whose name will match the last element in the Subversion URL. So if your Subversion URL is *svn://localhost/gameoflife/trunk*, Jenkins will check out the repository contents to a directory called *trunk* in the build job workspace. If you would prefer another directory name, just enter the directory name you want in the *Local module directory* field. Place a period (".") here if you want Jenkins to check the source code directly into the workspace.

Occasionally you may need to get source code from more than one Subversion URL. In this case, just use the "Add more locations..." button to add as many additional repository sources as you need.

A well-designed build process should not modify the source code, or leave any extra files that might confuse your version control system or the build process. Both generated artifacts and temporary files (such as log files, reports, test data or file-based databases)

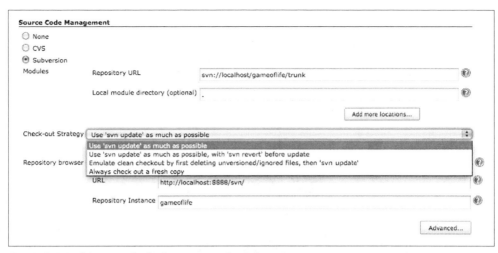

Figure 5-6. Jenkins provides built-in support for Subversion

should go in a directory set aside for this purpose (such as the *target* directory in Maven builds), and/or be configured to be ignored by your version control repository. They should also be deleted as part of the build process, once the build has finished with them. This is also an important part of ensuring a clean and reproducible build process—for a given version of your source code, your build should behave in exactly the same way, no matter where or when it is run. Locally changed source code files, and the presence of temporary files, both have the potential of compromising this.

You can fine-tune the way Jenkins obtains the latest source code from your Subversion repository by selecting an appropriate value in the Check-out Strategy drop-down list. If your project is well-behaved, however, you may be able to speed things up substantially by selecting "Use 'svn update' as much as possible". This is the fastest option, but may leave artifacts and files from previous builds in your workspace. To be on the safe side, you may want to use the second option ("Use 'svn update' as much as possible, with 'svn revert' before update"), which will systematically run svn revert before running svn update. This will ensure that no local files have been modified, though it will not remove any new files that have been created during the build process. Alternatively, you can ask Jenkins to delete any unversioned or ignored files before performing an svn update, or play it safe by checking out a full clean copy for each build.

Another very useful feature is Jenkins's integration with source code browsers. A good source code browser is an important part of your Continuous Integration setup. It lets you see at a glance what changes triggered a given build, which is very useful when it comes to troubleshooting broken builds (see Figure 5-7). Jenkins integrates with most of the major source code browsers, including open source tools such as WebSVN and Sventon, and commercial ones like Atlassian's FishEye.

Jenkins also lets you refine the changes that will trigger a build. In the Advanced section, you can use the Excluded Regions field to tell Jenkins not to trigger a build if only

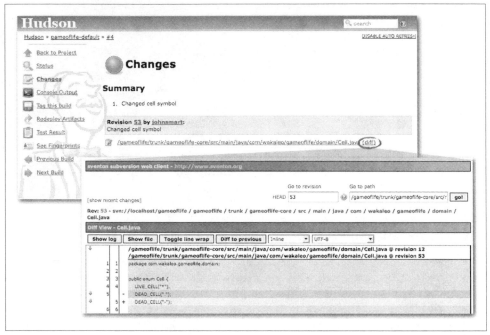

Figure 5-7. Source code browser showing what code changes caused a build

certain files were changed. This field takes a list of regular expressions, which identify files that should *not* trigger a build. For example, suppose you don't want Jenkins to start a new build if only images have been changed. To do this, you could use a set of regular expressions like the following:

```
/trunk/gameoflife/gameoflife-web/src/main/webapp/.*\.jpg
/trunk/gameoflife/gameoflife-web/src/main/webapp/.*\.gif
/trunk/gameoflife/gameoflife-web/src/main/webapp/.*\.png
```

Alternatively, you can specify the Included Regions, if you are only interested in changes in part of the source code directory structure. You can even combine the Excluded Regions and Included Regions fields—in this case a modified file will only trigger a build if it is in the Included Regions but not in the Excluded Regions.

You can also ignore changes coming from certain users (Excluded Users), or with certain commit messages (Excluded Commit Messages). For example, if your project uses Maven, you may want to use the Maven Release Plugin to promote your application from snapshot versions to official releases. This plugin will automatically bump up the version number of your application from a snapshot version used during development (such as 1.0.1-SNAPSHOT) to a release (1.0.1), bundles up and deploys a release of your application with this version number, and then moves the version on to the next snapshot number (e.g., 1.0.2-SNAPSHOT) for ongoing development. During this process Maven takes care of many SCM bookkeeping tasks, such as committing the source code with the release version number and creating a tag for the released version of your application, and then committing the source code with the new snapshot version number.

Now suppose you have a special build job for generating a new release using this process. The many commits generated by the Maven Release Plugin would normally trigger off build jobs in Jenkins. However, since the release build job is already compiling and testing this version of your application, you don't need Jenkins to do it again in a separate build job. To ensure that Jenkins does not trigger a build for this case, you can use the Excluded Commit Messages field with the following value:

```
[maven-release-plugin] prepare release.*
```

This will ensure that Jenkins skips the changes corresponding to the new release version, but not those corresponding to the next snapshot version.

Working with Git

Contributed by Matthew McCullough

Git (*http://git-scm.com/*) is a popular distributed version control system that is a logical successor to Subversion (*http://subversion.tigris.org/*) and a mind-share competitor to Mercurial (*http://mercurial.selenic.com/*). Git support in Jenkins is both mature and full-featured. There are a number of plugins that can contribute to the overall story of Git in Jenkins. We will begin by looking at the Git plugin, which provides core Git support in Jenkins. We'll discuss the supplemental plugins shortly.

Installing the plugin

The Git plugin is available in the Jenkins Plugin Manager and is documented on its own wiki page (*http://wiki.hudson-ci.org/display/HUDSON/Git+Plugin*). The plugin assumes that Git (version 1.3.3 or later) has already been installed on your build server, so you will need to make sure that this is the case. You can do this by running the following command on your build server:

```
$ git --version
git version 1.7.1
```

Next, go back to Jenkins, check the corresponding check box in the Jenkins Plugin Manager page and click the Install button.

System-wide configuration of the plugin. After installing the Git plugin, a small new set of configuration options will be available on the Manage Jenkins→Configure System page (see Figure 5-8). In particular, you need to provide the path to your Git executable. If Git is already installed on the system path, just put "git" here.

SSH key setup. If the Git repository you are accessing uses SSH passphrase-less authentication—for example, if the access address is similar to `git@github.com:mat` `thewmccullough/some-repo.git`—you'll need to provide the private half of the key as

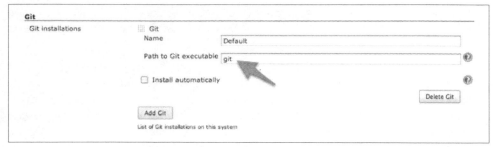

Figure 5-8. System-wide configuration of the Git plugin

file `~/.ssh/id_rsa` where `~` is the home directory of the user account under which Jenkins is running.

The fingerprint of the remote server will additionally need to be placed in `~/.ssh/known_hosts` to prevent Jenkins from invisibly prompting for authorization to access this Git server for the first time.

Alternatively, if logging-in is enabled for the `jenkins` user, SSH into the Jenkins machine as `jenkins` and manually attempt to Git clone a remote repository. This will test your private key setup and establish the `known_hosts` file in the `~/.ssh` directory. This is probably the simplest option for users unfamiliar with the intricacies of SSH configuration.

Using the plugin

On either an existing or a new Jenkins project, a new Source Code Management option for Git will be displayed. From here, you can configure one or more repository addresses (see Figure 5-9). One repository is usually enough for most projects: adding a second repository can be useful in more complicated cases, and lets you specify distinct named locations for `pull` and `push` operations.

Advanced per-project source code management configuration. In most cases, the URL of the Git repository you are using should be enough. However, if you need more options, click on the Advanced button (see Figure 5-10). This provides more precise control of the `pull` behavior.

The *Name of repository* is a shorthand title (a.k.a. `remote` in Git parlance) for a given repository, that you can refer to later on in the merge action configuration.

The *Refspec* is a Git-specific language (*http://progit.org/book/ch9-5.html*) for controlling precisely what is retrieved from remote servers and under what namespace it is stored locally.

Branches to build. The branch specifier (Figure 5-11) is the wildcard pattern or specific branch name that should be built by Jenkins. If left blank, all branches will be built. At the time of this writing, after the first time saving a job with a blank *branches to build* setting, it is populated with `**,` which means "build all branches."

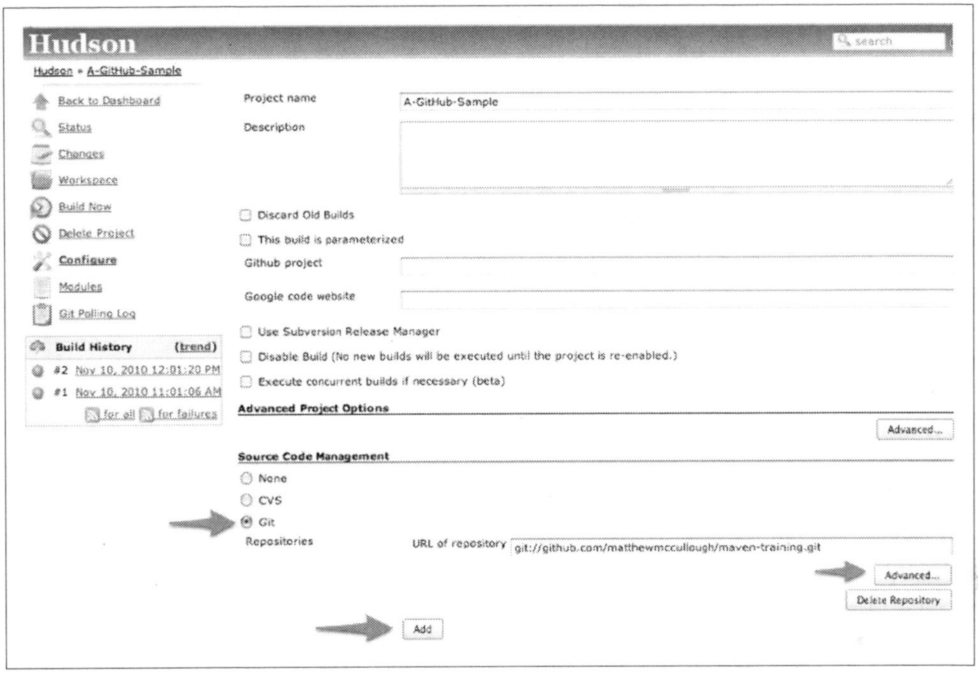

Figure 5-9. Entering a Git repo URL

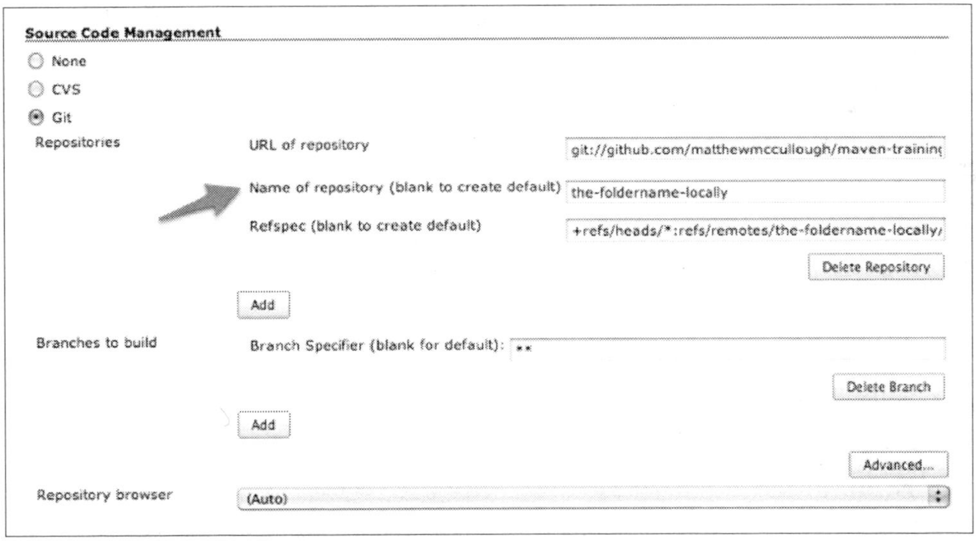

Figure 5-10. Advanced configuration of a Git repo URL

Excluded regions. Regions (seen in Figure 5-12) are named specific or wildcard paths in the codebase that, even when changed, should not trigger a build. Commonly these are

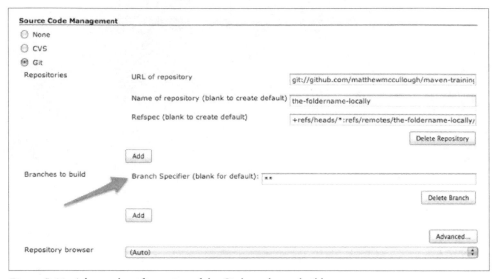

Figure 5-11. Advanced configuration of the Git branches to build

noncompiled files such as localization bundles or images, which, understandably might not have an effect on unit or integration tests.

Excluded users. The Git plugin also lets you ignore certain users, even if they make changes to the codebase that would typically trigger a build.

This is not as spiteful as it sounds: excluded users are typically automated users, not human developers, that happen to have distinct accounts with commit rights in the source control system. These automated users often are performing small numeric changes such as bumping up version numbers in a *pom.xml* file, rather than making actual logic changes. If you want to exclude several users, just place them on separate lines.

Checkout/merge to local branch. There are times when you may want to create a local branch from the tree you've specified, rather than just using a direct *detached HEAD* checkout of the commit's hash. In this case, just specify your local branch in the "Checkout/ merge to a local branch" field.

This is a little easier to illustrate with an example. Without specifying a local branch, the plugin would do something like this:

```
git checkout 73434e4a0af0f51c242f5ae8efc51a88383afc8a
```

On the other hand, if you use a local branch named `mylocalbranch`, Jenkins would do the following:

```
git branch -D mylocalbranch
git checkout -b mylocalbranch 73434e4a0af0f51c242f5ae8efc51a88383afc8a
```

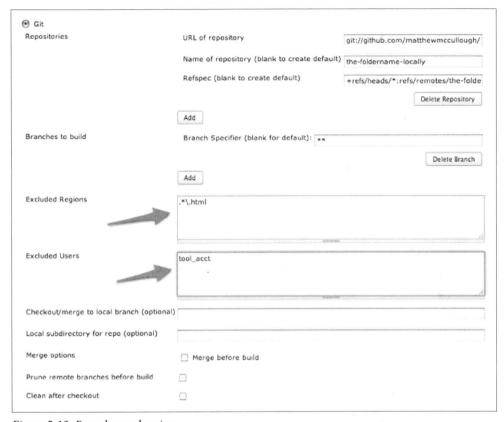

Figure 5-12. Branches and regions

Local subdirectory for repo. By default, Jenkins will clone the Git repository directly into the build job workspace. If you prefer to use a different directory, you can specify it here. Note that the directory you specify is relative to the build job workspace.

Merge before build. The typical recipe for using this option is to fold an integration branch into a branch more similar to master. Keep in mind that only conflict-less merges will happen automatically. More complex merges that require manual intervention will fail the build.

The resultant merged branch will not automatically be pushed to another repository unless the later push post-build action is enabled.

Prune remote branches before build. Pruning removes local copies of remote branches that exist as a remnant of the previous clone, but are no longer present on the remote. In short, this is cleaning the local clone to be in perfect sync with its remote siblings.

Clean after checkout. Activate Git's facilities for purging any untracked files or folders, returning your working copy to a pristine state.

Recursively update submodules. If you are using Git's submodule facilities in the project, this option lets you ensure that every submodule is up-to-date with an explicit call to update, even if submodules are nested within other submodules.

Use commit author in changelog. Jenkins tracks and displays the author of changed code in a summarized view. Git tracks both the committer and author of code distinctly, and this option lets you toggle which of those two usernames is displayed in the changelog.

Wipe out workspace. Typically Jenkins will reuse the workspace, merely freshening the checkout as necessary and, if you activated the "Clean after checkout" option, cleaning up untracked files. However, if you prefer to have a completely clean workspace, you can use the "Wipe out workspace" option to delete and rebuild the workspace from the ground up. Bear in mind that this may significantly lengthen the time it takes to initialize and build the project.

Choosing strategy. Jenkins decides which branches to build based on a *strategy* (see Figure 5-13). Users can influence this branch-search process. The default choice is to search for all branch HEADs. If the Gerrit plugin is installed, additional options for building all Gerrit-notified commits are displayed.

Figure 5-13. Choosing strategy

Git executable. In the global options of Jenkins (see Figure 5-14), different Git executables can be set up and used on a per-build basis. This is infrequently used, and only when the clone or other Git operations are highly sensitive to a particular version of Git. Git tends to be very version-flexible; slightly older repositories can easily be cloned with a newer version of Git and vice-versa.

Repository browser. Like Subversion, Git has several source code browsers that you can use. The most common ones are Gitorious, Git Web, or GitHub. If you provide the URL to the corresponding repository browser, Jenkins will be able to display a link to the source code changes that triggered a build (see Figure 5-15).

Build triggers

The basic Git plugin offers the ability to *Poll SCM* on a timed basis, looking for changes since the last inquiry. If changes are found, a build is started. The polling log (shown in Figure 5-16) is accessible via a link on the left hand side of the page in the navigation bar when viewing a specific job. It offers information on the last time the repository was polled and if it replied with a list of changes (see Figure 5-17).

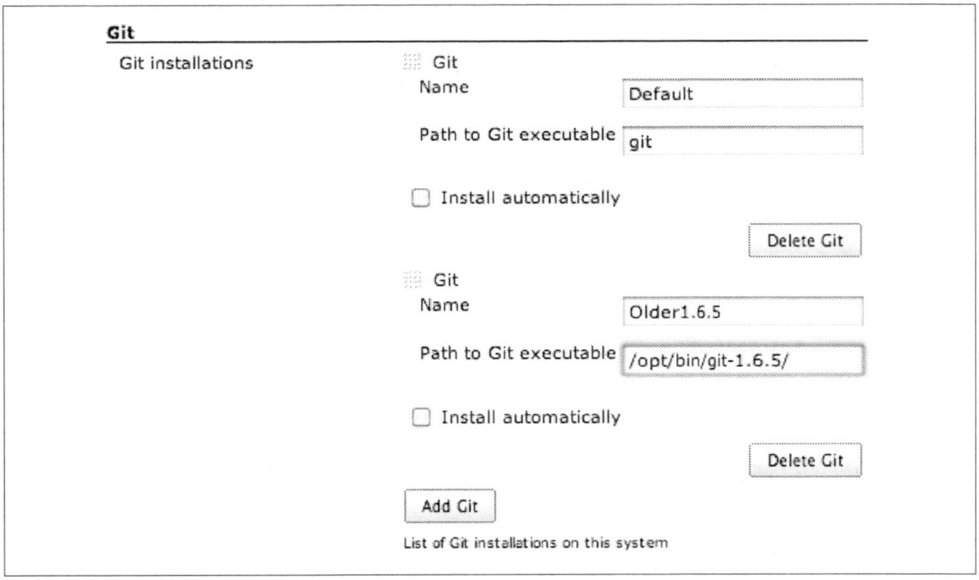

Figure 5-14. Git executable global setup

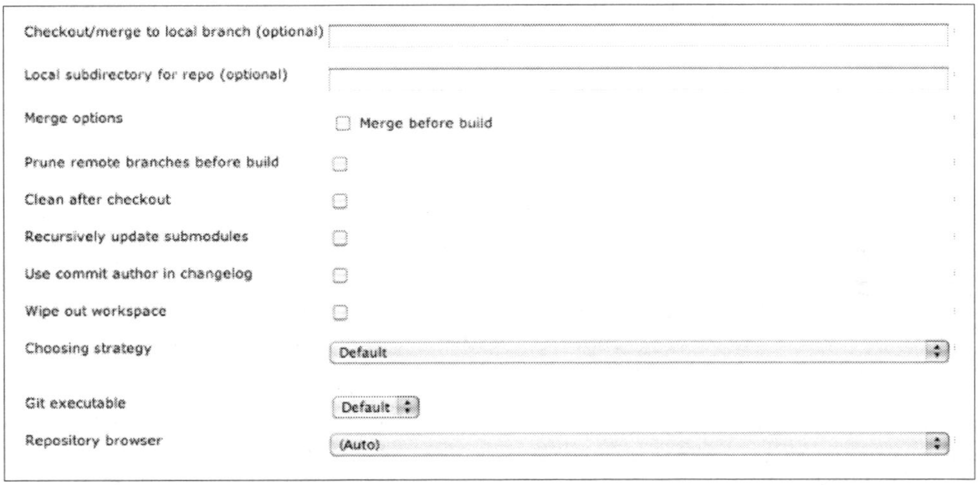

Figure 5-15. Repository browser

The Git polling is distilled into a more developer-useful format that shows commit comments as well as hyperlinking usernames and changed files to more detailed views of each.

Installing the *Gerrit Build Trigger* adds a *Gerrit event* option that can be more efficient and precise than simply polling the repository.

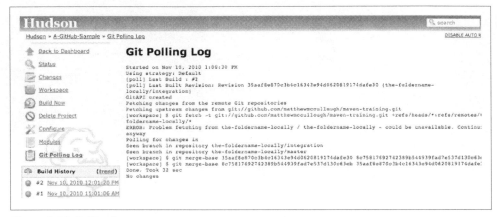

Figure 5-16. Polling log

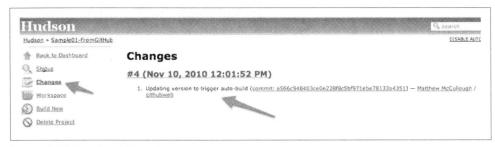

Figure 5-17. Results of Git polling

Gerrit Trigger. Gerrit (*http://code.google.com/p/gerrit/*) is an open source web application that facilitates code reviews (*https://review.source.android.com/#q,status:open,n,z*) for project source hosted on a Git version control system. It reads a traditional Git repository, and provides a side-by-side comparison of changes. As the code is reviewed, Gerrit provides a location to comment and move the patch to an *open*, *merged*, or *abandoned* status.

The Gerrit Trigger (*http://wiki.hudson-ci.org/display/HUDSON/Gerrit+Trigger*) is a Jenkins plugin that can trigger a Jenkins build of the code when any user-specified activity happens in a user-specified project in the Git repository (see Figure 5-18). It is a alternative to the more typically-used *Build periodically* or *Poll SCM*.

The configuration for this plugin is minimal and focused on the *Project Type* and *Pattern* and *Branch Type* and *Pattern*. In each pair, the *type* can be *Plain*, *Path*, or *RegExp*—pattern flavors of what to watch—and then the value (*pattern*) to evaluate using the *type* as the guide.

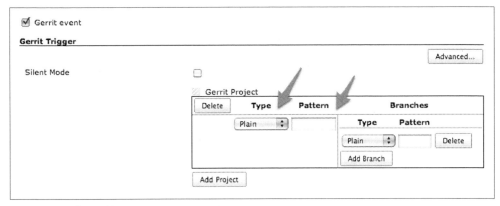

Figure 5-18. Gerrit Trigger

Post-build actions

The Git plugin for Jenkins adds Git-specific capabilities to the post-processing of the build artifacts. Specifically, the Git Publisher (shown in Figure 5-19) offers merging and pushing actions. Check the Git Publisher checkbox to display four options.

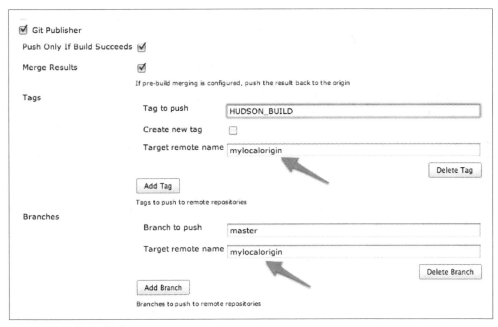

Figure 5-19. Git Publisher

Push only if build succeeds. If a merge or other commit-creating action has been taken during the Jenkins build, it can be enabled to push to a remote.

Merge results. If prebuild merging is configured, push the merge-resultant branch to its origin (see Figure 5-20).

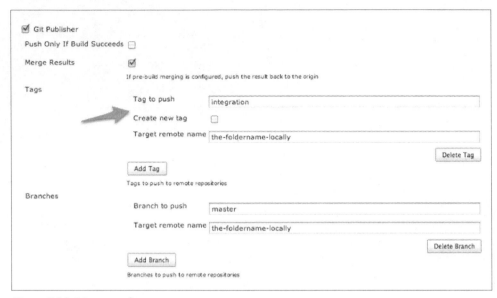

Figure 5-20. Merge results

Tags. When pushing tags, each tag can be named and chosen to be created if it does not exist (which fails if it does already exist). Environment variables can be embedded in the tag name. Examples include the process ID such as `HUDSON_BUILD_$PPID` or even a build number, if that is provided by a Jenkins plugin, such as `$HUDSON_AUTOTAG_$BUILDNUM`. Tags can be targeted to a specific remote such as `origin` or `integrationrepo`.

Branches. The current HEAD used in the Jenkins build of the application can be pushed to other remotes as an after-step of the build. You only need to provide the destination branch name and remote name.

Names of remotes are validated against the earlier configuration of the plugin. If the remote doesn't exist, a warning is displayed.

GitHub plugin

The GitHub plugin offers two integration points. First, it offers an optional link to the project's GitHub home page. Just enter the URL for the project (without the tree/master or tree/branch part). For example, `http://github.com/matthewmccullough/git-work shop`.

Secondly, the GitHub plugin offers per-file-changed links that are wired via the *Repository browser* section of a job's *Source Code Management* configuration (see Figure 5-21).

Figure 5-21. GitHub repository browser

With the `githubweb` repository browser chosen, all changed-detected files will be linked to the appropriate GitHub source-viewing web page (Figure 5-22).

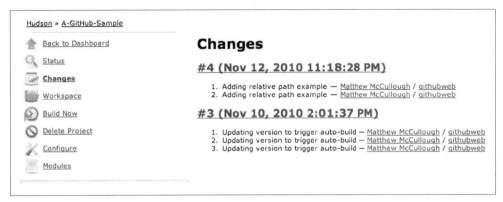

Figure 5-22. GitHub repository browser

Build Triggers

Once you have configured your version control system, you need to tell Jenkins when to kick off a build. You set this up in the Build Triggers section.

In a Freestyle build, there are three basic ways a build job can be triggered (see Figure 5-23):

- Start a build job once another build job has completed
- Kick off builds at periodical intervals
- Poll the SCM for changes

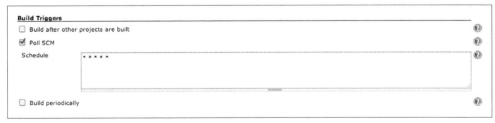

Figure 5-23. There are many ways that you can configure Jenkins to start a build job

Triggering a Build Job Once Another Build Job Has Finished

The first option lets you set up a build that will be run whenever another build has finished. This is an easy way to set up a build pipeline. For example, you might set up an initial build job to run unit and integration tests, followed by another separate build job to run more CPU-intensive code quality metrics. You simply enter the name of the preceding build job in this field. If the build job can be triggered by several other build jobs, just list their names here, separated by commas. In this case, the build job will be triggered once *any* of the build jobs in the list finish.

There is a symmetrical field in the Post-build actions section of the preceding build job called (appropriately enough) "Build other projects". This field will be automatically updated in the corresponding build jobs whenever you modify the "Build after other projects are built" field. However, unlike the "Build after other projects are built" field, this field gives you the option to trigger a build even if the build is unstable (see Figure 5-24). This is useful, for example, if you want to run a code quality metrics build job even if there are unit test failures in the default build job.

Figure 5-24. Triggering another build job even if the current one is unstable

Scheduled Build Jobs

Another strategy is simply to trigger your build job at regular intervals. It is important to note that this is not actually Continuous Integration—it is simply scheduled builds, something you could also do, for example, as a Unix cron job. In the early days of automated builds, and even today in many shops, builds are not run in response to changes committed to version control, but simply on a nightly basis. However, to be effective, a Continuous Integration server should provide feedback much more quickly than once a day.

There are nevertheless a few cases where scheduled builds do make sense. This includes very long running build jobs, where quick feedback is less critical. For example, intensive load and performance tests which may take several hours to run, or Sonar build jobs. Sonar is an excellent way to keep tabs on code quality metrics across your projects and over time, but the Sonar server only stores one set of data per day, so running Sonar builds more frequently than this is not useful.

For all scheduling tasks, Jenkins uses a cron-style syntax, consisting of five fields separated by white space in the following format:

MINUTE HOUR DOM MONTH DOW

with the following values possible for each field:

MINUTE
> Minutes within the hour (0–59)

HOUR
> The hour of the day (0–23) DOM

DOM
> The day of the month (1–31)

MONTH
> The month (1–12)

DOW
> The day of the week (0–7) where 0 and 7 are Sunday.

There are also a few short-cuts:

- "*" represents all possible values for a field. For example, "* * * * *" means "once a minute."
- You can define ranges using the "M–N" notation. For example "1-5" in the DOW field would mean "Monday to Friday."
- You can use the slash notation to defined skips through a range. For example, "*/5" in the MINUTE field would mean "every five minutes."
- A comma-separated list indicates a list of valid values. For example, "15,45" in the MINUTE field would mean "at 15 and 45 minutes past every hour."
- You can also use the shorthand values of "@yearly", "@annually", "@monthly", "@weekly", "@daily", "@midnight", and "@hourly".

Typically, you will only have one line in this field, but for more complicated scheduling setups, you may need multiple lines.

Polling the SCM

As we have seen, scheduled build jobs are usually not the best strategy for most CI build jobs. The value of any feedback is proportional to the speed in which you receive that feedback, and Continuous Integration is no exception. That is why polling the SCM is generally a better option.

Polling involves asking the version control server at regular intervals if any changes have been committed. If any changes have been made to the source code in the project, Jenkins kicks off a build. Polling is usually a relatively cheap operation, so you can poll frequently to ensure that a build kicks off rapidly after changes have been committed. The more frequent the polling is, the faster the build jobs will start, and the more accurate the feedback about what change broke the build will be.

In Jenkins, SCM polling is easy to configure, and uses the same cron syntax we discussed previously.

The natural temptation for SCM polling is to poll as often as possible (for example, using "* * * * *", or once every minute). Since Jenkins simply queries the version control system, and only kicks off a build if the source code has been modified, this approach is often reasonable for small projects. It shows its limits if there are a very large number of build jobs, as this may saturate the SCM server and the network with queries, many of them unnecessary. In this case, a more precise approach is better, where the Jenkins build job is triggered by the SCM when it receives a change. We discuss this option in "Triggering Builds Remotely" on page 100.

If updates are frequently committed to the version control system, across many projects, this may cause many build jobs to be queued, which can in turn slow down feedback times further. You can reduce the build queue to some extent by polling less frequently, but at the cost of less precise feedback.

If you are using CVS, polling may not be a good option. When CVS checks for changes in a project, it checks each file one by one, which is a slow and tedious process. The best solution here is to migrate to a modern version control system such as Git or Subversion. The second-best solution is to use polling at very sparse intervals (for example, every 30 minutes).

Triggering Builds Remotely

Polling can be an effective strategy for smaller projects, but it does not scale particularly well—with large numbers of build jobs, it is wasteful of network resources, and there is always a small delay between the code change being committed and the build job starting. A more precise strategy is to get the SCM system to trigger the Jenkins build whenever a change is committed.

It is easy to start a Jenkins build job remotely. You simply invoke a URL of the following form:

> *http://SERVER/jenkins/job/PROJECTNAME/build*

For example, if my Jenkins server was running on *http://myserver:8080/jenkins*, I could start the *gameoflife* build job by invoking the following URL using a tool like `wget` or `curl`:

```
$ wget http://myserver:8080/jenkins/job/gameoflife/build
```

The trick, then, is to get your version control server to do this whenever a change is committed. The details of how to do this are different for each version control system. In Subversion, for example, you would need to write a post-commit hook script, which would trigger a build. You could, for example, write a Subversion hook script that parses the repository URL to extract the project name, and performs a `wget` operation on the URL of the corresponding build job:

```
JENKINS_SERVER=http://myserver:8080/jenkins
REPOS="$1"
```

```
PROJECT=<Regular Expression Processing Goes Here>❶
/usr/bin/wget $JENKINS_SERVER/job/${PROJECT}/build
```

❶ Use regular expression processing here to extract your project name from the Sub-version repository URL.

However, this approach will only trigger one particular build, and relies on a convention that the default build job is based on the repository name in Subversion. A more flexible approach with Subversion is to use the Jenkins Subversion API directly, as shown here:

```
JENKINS_SERVER=http://myserver:8080/jenkins
REPOS="$1"
REV="$2"
UUID=`svnlook uuid $REPOS`
/usr/bin/wget \
  --header "Content-Type:text/plain;charset=UTF-8" \
  --post-data "`svnlook changed --revision $REV $REPOS`" \
  --output-document "-" \
  --timeout=2 \
  $JENKINS_SERVER/subversion/${UUID}/notifyCommit?rev=$REV
```

This would automatically start any Jenkins build jobs monitoring this Subversion repository.

If you have activated Jenkins security, things become a little more complicated. In the simplest case (where any user can do anything), you need to activate the "Trigger builds remotely" option (see Figure 5-25), and provide a special string that can be used in the URL:

http://SERVER/jenkins/job/PROJECTNAME/build?token=DOIT

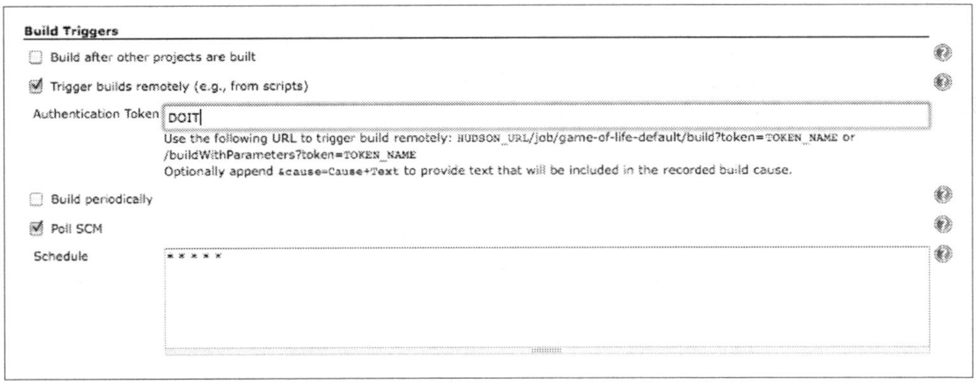

Figure 5-25. Triggering a build via a URL using a token

This won't work if users need to be logged on to trigger a build (for example, if you are using matrix or project-based security). In this case, you will need to provide a user name and password, as shown in the following example:

```
$ wget http://scott:tiger@myserver:8080/jenkins/job/gameoflife/build
```

or:

```
$ curl -u scott:tiger http://scott:tiger@myserver:8080/jenkins/job/gameoflife/build
```

Manual Build Jobs

A build does not have to be triggered automatically. Some build jobs should only be started manually, by human intervention. For example, you may want to set up an automated deployment to a UAT environment, that should only be started on the request of the QA folks. In this case, you can simply leave the Build Triggers section empty.

Build Steps

Now Jenkins should know where and how often to obtain the project source code. The next thing you need to explain to Jenkins is what it what to do with the source code. In a freestyle build, you do this by defining build steps. Build steps are the basic building blocks for the Jenkins freestyle build process. They are what let you tell Jenkins exactly *how* you want your project built.

A build job may have one step, or more. It may even occasionally have none. In a freestyle build, you can add as many build steps as you want to the Build section of your project configuration (see Figure 5-26). In a basic Jenkins installation, you will be able to add steps to invoke Maven and Ant, as well as running OS-specific shell or Windows batch commands. And by installing additional plugins, you can also integrate other build tools, such as Groovy, Gradle, Grails, Jython, MSBuild, Phing, Python, Rake, and Ruby, just to name some of the more well-known tools.

In the remainder of this section, we will delve into some of the more common types of build steps.

Maven Build Steps

Jenkins has excellent Maven support, and Maven build steps are easy to configure and very flexible. Just pick "Invoke top-level Maven targets" from the build step lists, pick a version of Maven to run (if you have multiple versions installed), and enter the Maven goals you want to run. Jenkins freestyle build jobs work fine with both Maven 2 and Maven 3.

Just like on the command line, you can specify as many individual goals as you want. You can also provide command-line options. A few useful Maven options in a CI context are:

`-B, --batch-mode`

> This option tells Maven not to prompt for any input from the user, just using the default values if any are required. If Maven does prompt for any input during the Jenkins build, the build will get stuck indefinitely.

`-U, --update-snapshots`

> Forces Maven to check for updated releases and snapshot dependencies on the remote repository. This makes sure you are building with the latest and greatest snapshot dependencies, and not just using older local copies which may not by in sync with the latest version of the source code.

`-Dsurefire.useFile=false`

> This option forces Maven to write JUnit output to the console, rather than to text files in the target directory as it normally would. This way, any test failure details are directly visible in the build job console output. The XML files that Jenkins needs for its test reporting will still be generated.

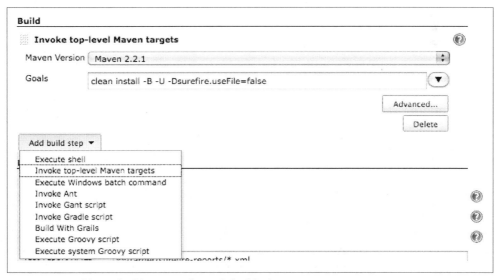

Figure 5-26. Adding a build step to a freestyle build job

The advanced options are also worth investigating (click on the Advanced button).

The optional *POM* field lets you override the default location of the Maven *pom.xml* file. This is the equivalent of running Maven from the command line with the `-f` or `--file` option. This is useful for some multimodule Maven projects where the aggregate *pom.xml* file (the one containing the `<modules>` section) is located in a subdirectory rather than at the top level.

The Properties field lets you set property values that will be passed into the Maven build process, using the standard property file format illustrated here:

```
# Selenium test configuration
selenium.host=testserver.acme.com
selenium.port=8080
selenium.broswer=firefox
```

These properties are passed to Maven as command-line options, as shown here:

```
$ mvn verify -Dselenium.host=testserver.acme.com ...
```

The JVM Options field lets you set any of the standard Java Virtual Machine options for your build job. So if your build process is particularly memory intensive, you might add some extra heap space with the -Xmx option (for example, -Xmx512m would set the maximum heap size to 512 MB).

The final option lets you configure a private Maven repository for this build job. Normally, Maven will just use the default Maven repository (usually in the *.m2/repository* folder in the user's home directory). Occasionally, this can lead to build jobs interfering with each other, or use inconsistent snapshot versions from one build to another. To be sure that your build is run in clean laboratory conditions, you can activate this option. Your build job will get its own private repository, reserved for its own exclusive use. On the downside, the first time the build job runs a build, this may take some time to download all of the Maven artifacts, and private repositories can take up a lot of space. However, it is the best way of guaranteeing that your build is run in a truly isolated environment.

Ant Build Steps

Freestyle build jobs work equally well with Ant. Apache Ant (*http://ant.apache.org/*) is a widely-used and very well-known Java build scripting tool. Indeed, a very large number of Java projects out there rely on Ant build scripts.

Ant is not only used as a primary build scripting tool—even if your project uses Maven, you may resort to calling Ant scripts to do more specific tasks. There are Ant libraries available for many development tools and low-level tasks, such as using SSH, or working with proprietary application servers.

In its most basic form, configuring an Ant build step very is simple indeed—you just provide the version of Ant you want to use and the name of the target you want to invoke. In Figure 5-27, for example, we are invoking an Ant script to run a JMeter test script.

As with the Maven build step, the "Advanced..." button provides you with more detailed options, such as specifying a different build script, or a build script in a different directory (the default will be *build.xml* in the root directory). You can also specify properties and JVM options, just as you can for Maven.

Figure 5-27. Configuring an Ant build step

Executing a Shell or Windows Batch Command

Occasionally you may need to execute a command directly at the Operating System level. Some legacy build processes rely on OS-specific scripts, for example. In other cases, you may need to perform a low-level operation that is most easily done with an OS-level command.

You can do this in Jenkins with the Execute Shell (for Unix) or Execute Windows Batch command (for Windows). As an example, in Figure 5-28 we have added a step to execute the Unix ls command.

Figure 5-28. Configuring an Execute Shell step

The output from this build step is shown here:

```
[workspace] $ /bin/sh -xe /var/folders/.../jenkins2542160238803334344.s
+ ls -al
total 64
drwxr-xr-x  14 johnsmart  staff   476 30 Oct 15:21 .
drwxr-xr-x   9 johnsmart  staff   306 30 Oct 15:21 ..
-rw-r--r--@  1 johnsmart  staff   294 22 Sep 01:40 .checkstyle
-rw-r--r--@  1 johnsmart  staff   651 22 Sep 01:40 .classpath
-rw-r--r--@  1 johnsmart  staff   947 22 Sep 01:40 .project
drwxr-xr-x   5 johnsmart  staff   170 22 Sep 01:40 .settings
-rw-r--r--@  1 johnsmart  staff   437 22 Sep 01:40 .springBeans
drwxr-xr-x   9 johnsmart  staff   306 30 Oct 15:21 .svn
-rw-r--r--@  1 johnsmart  staff  1228 22 Sep 01:40 build.xml
-rw-r--r--@  1 johnsmart  staff    50 22 Sep 01:40 infinitest.filters
-rw-r--r--   1 johnsmart  staff  6112 30 Oct 15:21 pom.xml
```

```
drwxr-xr-x   5 johnsmart  staff   170 22 Sep 01:40 src
drwxr-xr-x   3 johnsmart  staff   102 22 Sep 01:40 target
drwxr-xr-x   5 johnsmart  staff   170 22 Sep 01:40 tools
```

You can either execute an OS-specific command (e.g., `ls`), or store a more complicated script as a file in your version control system, and execute this script. If you are executing a script, you just need to refer to the name of your script relative to the work directory.

Shell scripts are executed using the `-ex` option—the commands are printed to the console, as is the resulting output. If any of the executed commands return a nonzero value, the build will fail.

When Jenkins executes a script, it sets a number of environment variables that you can use within the script. We discuss these variable in more detail in the next section.

In fact, there are some very good reasons why you should avoid using OS-level scripts in your build jobs if you can possibly avoid it. In particular, it makes your build job in the best of cases OS-specific, and at worst dependant on the precise machine configuration. One more portable alternative to executing OS scripts include writing an equivalent script in a more portable scripting language, such as Groovy or Gant.

Using Jenkins Environment Variables in Your Builds

One useful trick that can be used in virtually any build step is to obtain information from Jenkins about the current build job. In fact, when Jenkins starts a build step, it makes the following environment variables available to the build script:

BUILD_NUMBER
> The current build number, such as "153".

BUILD_ID
> A timestamp for the current build id, in the format YYYY-MM-DD_hh-mm-ss.

JOB_NAME
> The name of the job, such as *game-of-life*.

BUILD_TAG
> A convenient way to identify the current build job, in the form of `jenkins-$`
> `{JOB_NAME}-${BUILD_NUMBER}` (e.g., `jenkins-game-of-life-2010-10-30_23-59-59`).

EXECUTOR_NUMBER
> A number identifying the executor running this build among the executors of the same machine. This is the number you see in the "build executor status", except that the number starts from 0, not 1.

NODE_NAME
> The name of the slave if the build is running on a slave, or `""` if the build is running on master.

NODE_LABELS
> The list of labels associated with the node that this build is running on.

JAVA_HOME

If your job is configured to use a specific JDK, this variable is set to the JAVA_HOME of the specified JDK. When this variable is set, PATH is also updated to have *$JAVA_HOME/bin.*

WORKSPACE

The absolute path of the workspace.

HUDSON_URL

The full URL of the Jenkins server, for example *http://ci.acme.com:8080/jenkins/.*

JOB_URL

The full URL for this build job, for example *http://ci.acme.com:8080/jenkins/game-of-life.*

BUILD_URL

The full URL for this build, for example *http://ci.acme.com:8080/jenkins/game-of-life/20.*

SVN_REVISION

For Subversion-based projects, this variable contains the current revision number.

CVS_BRANCH

For CVS-based projects, this variable contains the branch of the module. If CVS is configured to check out the trunk, this environment variable will not be set.

These variables are easy to access. In an Ant script, you can access them using the <property> tag as shown here:

```
<target name="printinfo">
  <property environment="env" />
  <echo message="${env.BUILD_TAG}"/>
</target>
```

In Maven, you can access the variables either in the same way (using the "env." prefix), or directly using the Jenkins environment variable. For example, in the following *pom.xml* file, the project URL will point to the Jenkins build job that ran the mvn site build:

```
<project...>
  ...
  <groupId>com.wakaleo.gameoflife</groupId>
  <artifactId>gameoflife-core</artifactId>
  <version>0.0.55-SNAPSHOT</version>
  <name>gameoflife-core</name>
  <url>${JOB_URL}</url>
```

Alternatively, if you are building a web application, you can also use the *maven-war-plugin* to insert the build job number into the web application manifest, e.g.:

```
<project>
  ...
  <build>
    ...
    <plugins>
```

```
<plugin>
  <artifactId>maven-war-plugin</artifactId>
  <configuration>
    <manifest>
      <addDefaultImplementationEntries>true</addDefaultImplementationEntries>
    </manifest>
    <archive>
      <manifestEntries>
        <Specification-Title>${project.name}</Specification-Title>
        <Specification-Version>${project.version}</Specification-Version>
        <Implementation-Version>${BUILD_TAG}</Implementation-Version>
      </manifestEntries>
    </archive>
  </configuration>
</plugin>
...
    </plugins>
  </build>
  ...
</project>
```

This will produce a *MANIFEST.MF* file along the following lines:

```
Manifest-Version: 1.0
Archiver-Version: Plexus Archiver
Created-By: Apache Maven
Built-By: johnsmart
Build-Jdk: 1.6.0_22
Jenkins-Build-Number: 63
Jenkins-Project: game-of-life
Jenkins-Version: 1.382
Implementation-Version: jenkins-game-of-life-63
Specification-Title: gameoflife-web
Specification-Version: 0.0.55-SNAPSHOT
```

And in a Groovy script, they can be obtained via the `System.getenv()` method:

```
def env = System.getenv()
env.each {
    println it
}
```

or:

```
def env = System.getenv()
println env['BUILD_NUMBER']
```

Running Groovy Scripts

Groovy is not only a popular JVM dynamic language, it is also a convenient language for low-level scripting. The Jenkins Groovy Plugin (*http://wiki.jenkins-ci.org//display/ HUDSON/Groovy+Plugin*) lets you run arbitrary Groovy commands, or invoke Groovy scripts, as part of your build process.

Once you have installed the Groovy plugin in the usual way, you need to add a reference to your Groovy installation in the system configuration page (see Figure 5-29).

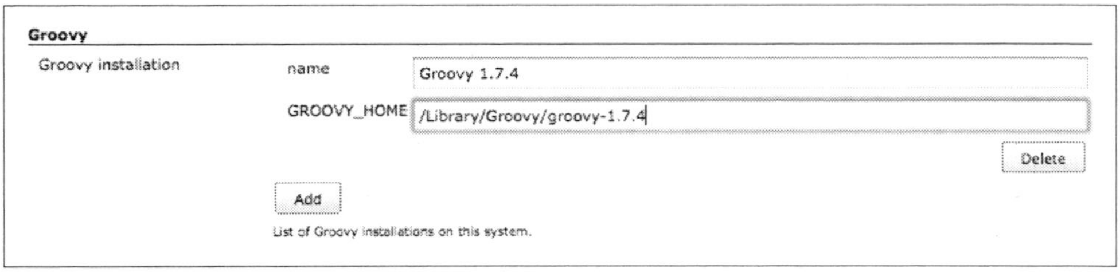

Figure 5-29. Adding a Groovy installation to Jenkins

Now you can add some Groovy scripting to your build job. When you click on "Add build step", you will see two new entries in the drop-down menu: "Execute Groovy script" and "Execute system Groovy script". The first option is generally what you want—this will simply execute a Groovy script in a separate JVM, as if you were invoking Groovy from the command line. The second option runs Groovy commands within Jenkins's own JVM, with full access to Jenkins's internals, and is mainly used to manipulate the Jenkins build jobs or build process itself. This is a more advanced topic that we will discuss later on in the book.

A Groovy build step can take one of two forms. For simple cases, you can just add a small snippet of Groovy, as shown in Figure 5-30. For more involved or complicated cases, you would probably write a Groovy script and place it under version control. Once your script is safely in your SCM, you can run it by selecting the "Groovy script file" option and providing the path to your script (relative to your build job workspace).

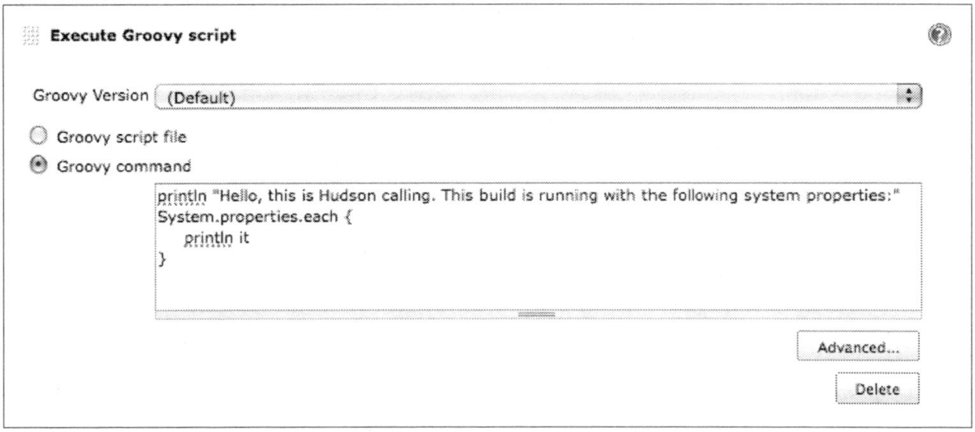

Figure 5-30. Running Groovy commands as part of a build job

In Figure 5-31, you can see a slightly more complicated example. Here we are running a Groovy script called *run-fitness-tests.groovy*, which can be found in the *scripts* directory. This script takes the test suites to be executed as its parameters—we provide these in the Script parameters field. If we want to provide any options for Groovy itself, we can put these in the Groovy Parameters field. Alternatively, we can also provide command-line properties in the Properties field—this is simply a more convenient way of using the -D command-line option to pass property values to the Groovy script.

Figure 5-31. Running Groovy scripts as part of a build job

Building Projects in Other Languages

Jenkins is a flexible tool, and it can be used for much more than just Java and Groovy. For example, Jenkins also works well with Grails, .Net, Ruby, Python and PHP, just to name a few. When using other languages, you generally need to install a plugin to support your favorite language, which will add a new build step type for this language. We will look at some examples in "Using Jenkins with Other Languages" on page 125.

Post-Build Actions

Once the build is completed, there are still a few things you need to look after. You might want to archive some of the generated artifacts, to report on test results, and to notify people about the results. In this section, we look at some of the more common tasks you need to configure after the build is done.

Reporting on Test Results

One of the most obvious requirements of a build job is to report on test results. Not only whether there are any test failures, but also how many tests were executed, how

---

long they took to execute, and so on. In the Java world, JUnit is the most commonly-used testing library around, and the JUnit XML format for test results is widely used and understood by other tools as well.

Jenkins provides great support for test reporting. In a freestyle build job, you need to tick the "Publish JUnit test result report" option, and provide a path to your JUnit report files (see Figure 5-32). You can use a wildcard expression (such as `**/target/surefire-reports/*.xml` in a Maven project) to include JUnit reports from a number of different directories—Jenkins will aggregate the results into a single report.

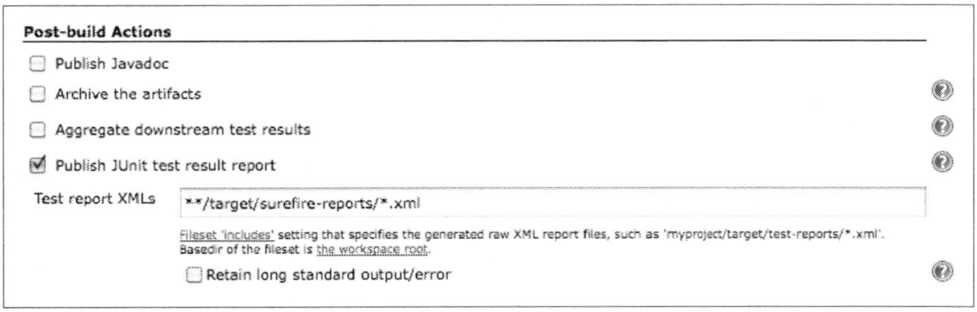

Figure 5-32. Reporting on test results

We look at automated tests in much more detail in Chapter 6.

Archiving Build Results

With a few exceptions, the principal goal of a build job is generally to build something. In Jenkins, we call this something an artifact. An artifact might be a binary executable (a JAR or WAR file for a Java project, for example), or some other related deliverable, such as documentation or source code. A build job can store one or many different artifacts, keeping only the latest copy or every artifact ever built.

Configuring Jenkins to store your artifacts is easy—just tick the "Archive the artifacts" checkbox in the Post-build Actions, and specify which artifacts you want to store (see Figure 5-33).

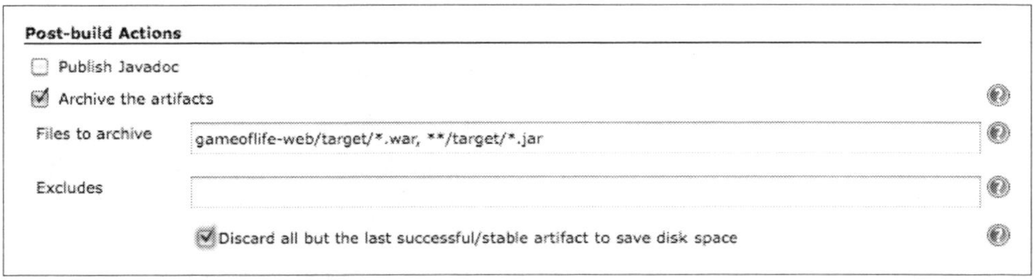

Figure 5-33. Configuring build artifacts

In the "Files to archive" field, you can provide the full paths of the files you want to archive (relative to the job workspace), or, use Ant-like wild cards (e.g., **/*.jar, for all the JAR files, anywhere in the workspace). One advantage of using wild cards is that it makes your build less dependent on your version control set up. For example, if you are using Subversion (see "Configuring Source Code Management" on page 84), Jenkins will check out your project either directly in your workspace, or into a subdirectory, depending on how you set it up. If you use a wild card expression like **/target/*.war, Jenkins will find the file no matter what directory the project is located in.

As usual, the Advanced button give access to a few extra options. If you are using wild cards to find your artifacts, you might need to exclude certain directories from the search. You can do this by filling in the Excludes field. You enter a pattern to match any files that you *don't* want to archive, even if they would normally be included by the "Files to archive" field.

Archived artifacts can take a lot of disk space, especially if builds are frequent. For this reason, you may want to only keep the last successful one. To do this, just tick the "Discard all but the last successful/stable artifact" option. Jenkins will keep artifacts from the last stable build (if there where any). It will also keep the artifacts of the latest unstable build following the stable build (if any), and also from the last failed build that happened.

Archived build artifacts appear on the build results page (see Figure 5-34). The most recent build artifacts are also displayed on the build job home page.

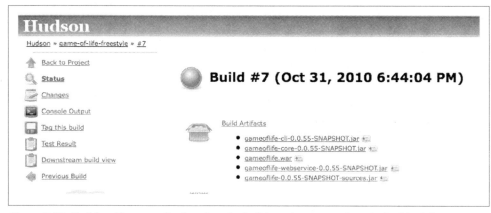

Figure 5-34. Build artifacts are displayed on the build results page and on the build job home page

You can also use permanent URLs to access the most recent build artifacts. This is a great way to reuse the latest artifacts from your builds, either in other Jenkins build jobs or in external scripts, for example. Three URLs are available: last stable build, last successful build and last completed build.

Before we look at the URLs, we should discuss the concept of *stable* and *successful* builds.

A build is *successful* when the compilation reported no errors.

A build is considered *stable* if it was built successfully, and no publisher reports it as unstable. For example, depending on your project configuration, unit test failures, insufficient code coverage, or other code quality metrics issues, could cause a build to be marked as unstable. So a stable build is always successful, but the opposite is not necessarily true—a build can be successful without being stable.

A *completed* build is simply a build that has finished, no matter what its result. Note that the archiving step will take place no matter what the outcome of the build was.

The format of the artifact URLs is intuitive, and takes the following form:

Latest stable build
    `<server-url>`/job/`<build-job>`/lastStableBuild/artifact/`<path-to-artifact>`

Latest successful build
    `<server-url>`/job/`<build-job>`/lastSuccessfulBuild/artifact/`<path-to-artifact>`

Latest completed build
    `<server-url>`/job/`<build-job>`/lastCompletedBuild/artifact/`<path-to-artifact>`

This is best illustrated by some examples. Suppose your Jenkins server is running on *http://myserver:8080*, your build job is called *game-of-life*, and you are storing a file called *gameoflife.war*, which is in the target directory of your workspace. The URLs for this artifact would be the following:

Latest stable build
    http://myserver:8080/job/gameoflife/lastStableBuild/artifact/target/gameoflife.war

Latest successful build
    http://myserver:8080/job/gameoflife/lastSuccessfulBuild/artifact/target/gameoflife.war

Latest completed build
    http://myserver:8080/job/gameoflife/lastCompletedBuild/artifact/target/gameoflife.war

Artifacts don't just have to be executable binaries. Imagine, for example, that your build process involves automatically deploying each build to a test server. For convenience, you want to keep a copy of the exact source code associated with each deployed WAR file. One way to do this would be to generate the source code associated with a build, and archive both this file and the WAR file. We could do this by generating a JAR file containing the application source code (for example, by using the Maven Source Plugin for a Maven project), and then including this in the list of artifacts to store (see Figure 5-35).

Of course, this example is a tad academic: it would probably be simpler just to use the revision number for this build (which is displayed on the build result page) to retrieve the source code from your version control system. But you get the idea.

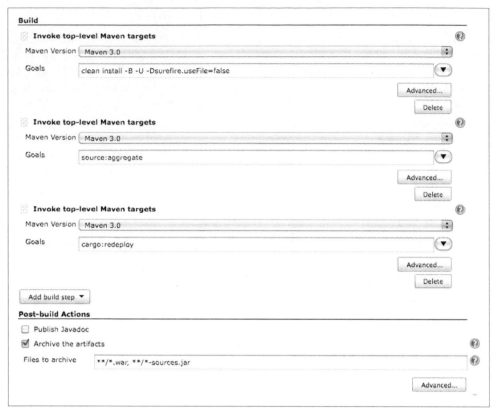

Figure 5-35. Archiving source code and a binary package

Note that if you are using an Enterprise Repository Manager such as Nexus or Artifactory to store your binary artifacts, you may not need to keep them on the Jenkins server. You may prefer simply to automatically deploy your artifacts to your Enterprise Repository Manager as part of the build job, and retrieve them from here when required.

Notifications

The point of a CI server is to let people know when a build breaks. In Jenkins, this comes under the heading of Notification.

Out of the box, Jenkins provides support for email notification. You can activate this by ticking the "E-mail Notification" checkbox in the Post-build Actions (see Figure 5-36). Then enter the email addresses of the team members who will need to know when the build breaks. When the build does break, Jenkins will send a friendly email message to the users in this list containing a link to the broken build.

Figure 5-36. Email notification

You can also opt to send a separate email to the user who's commit (presumably) broke the build. For this to work, you need to have activated Security on your Jenkins server (see Chapter 7).

Normally, Jenkins will send an email notification out whenever a build fails (for example, because of a compilation error). It will also send out a notification when the build becomes unstable for the first time (for example, if there are unit test failures). Unless you configure it to do so, Jenkins will not send emails for every unstable build, but only for the first one.

Finally, Jenkins will send a message when a previously failing or unstable build succeeds, to let everyone know that the problem has been resolved.

Building Other Projects

You can also start other build jobs in the Post-build Actions, using the "Build other projects" option. This is useful if you want to organize your build process in several, smaller steps, rather than one long build job. Just list the projects you want to start after this one. Normally, these projects will only be triggered if the build was stable, but you can optionally trigger another build job even if the current build is unstable. This might be useful, for example, if you wanted to run a code quality metrics reporting build job after a project's main build job, even if there are test failures in the main build.

Running Your New Build Job

Now all you need to do is save your new build job. You can then trigger the first build manually, or just wait for it to kick off by itself. Once the build is finished, you can click on the build number to see the results of your work.

Working with Maven Build Jobs

In this section, we will have a look at the other most commonly used build job: Maven 2/3 build jobs.

Maven build jobs are specifically adapted to Maven 2 and Maven 3 builds. Creating a Maven build job requires considerably less work than configuring the equivalent freestyle build job. Maven build jobs support advanced Maven-related features such as incremental builds on multimodule projects and triggering builds from changes in snapshot dependencies, and make configuration and reporting much simpler.

However, there is a catch: Maven 2/3 build jobs are less flexible than freestyle build jobs, and don't support multiple build steps within the same build job. Some users also report that large Maven projects tend to run more slowly and use more memory when configured as Maven build jobs rather than as Freestyle ones.

In this section, we will investigate how to configure Maven 2/3 builds, when you can use them, as well as their advantages and limitations.

To create a new Maven build job, just choose the ""Build a maven2/3 project" option in the New Job page (see Figure 5-37).

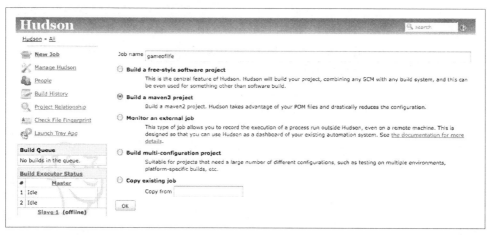

Figure 5-37. Creating a new Maven build job

Building Whenever a SNAPSHOT Dependency Is Built

At first glance, the Maven 2/3 build job configuration screen is very similar to the one we saw for freestyle builds in the previous section. The first difference you may notice is in the Build Triggers section. In this section, an extra option is available: "Build whenever a SNAPSHOT dependency is built". If you select this option, Jenkins will examine your *pom.xml* file (or files) to see if any SNAPSHOT dependencies are being built by other build jobs. If any other build jobs update a SNAPSHOT dependency that your project uses, Jenkins will build your project as well.

Typically in Maven, SNAPSHOT dependencies are used to share the latest bleeding-edge version of a library with other projects within the same team. Since they are by definition unstable, it is not recommended practice to rely on SNAPSHOT dependencies from other teams or from external sources.

For example, imagine that you are working on a new *game-of-life* web application. You are using Maven for this project, so you can use a Maven build job in Jenkins. Your team is also working on a reusable library called *cooltools*. Since these two projects are being developed by the same team, you are using some of the latest *cooltools* features in the *game-of-life* web application. So you have a SNAPSHOT dependency in the `<dependencies>` section of your *game-of-life pom.xml* file:

```
<dependencies>
    <dependency>
        <groupId>com.acme.common</groupId>
        <artifactId>cooltools</artifactId>
        <version>0.0.1-SNAPSHOT</version>
        <scope>test</scope>
    </dependency>
    ...
</dependencies>
```

On your Jenkins server, you have set up Maven build jobs for both the *cooltools* and the *game-of-life* applications. Since your *game-of-life* project needs the latest *cooltools* SNAPSHOT version, you tick the "Build whenever a SNAPSHOT dependency is built" option. This way, whenever the *cooltools* project is rebuilt, the *game-of-life* project will automatically be rebuilt as well.

Configuring the Maven Build

The next area where you will notice a change is in the Build section. In a Maven build job, the build section is entirely devoted to running a single Maven goal (see Figure 5-38). In this section, you specify the version of Maven you want to execute (remember, at the time of Maven, this will only work with Maven), the location of the *pom.xml* file, and the Maven goal (or goals) to invoke. You can also add any command-line options you need here.

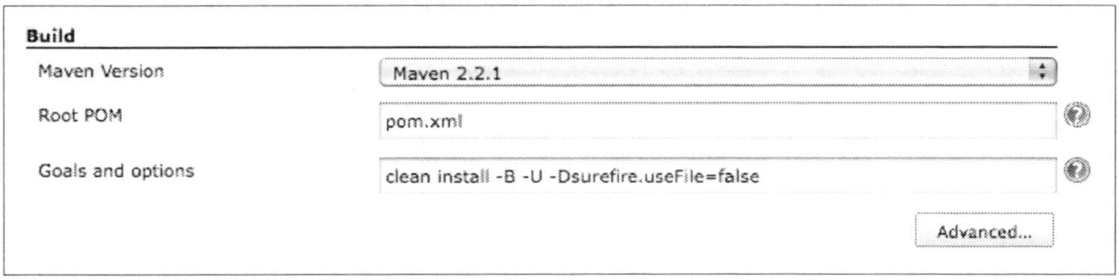

Figure 5-38. Specifying the Maven goals

In many cases, this is all you need to get your Maven build job configured. However, if you click on the "Advanced..." button, you can take your pick of some more advanced features (Figure 5-39).

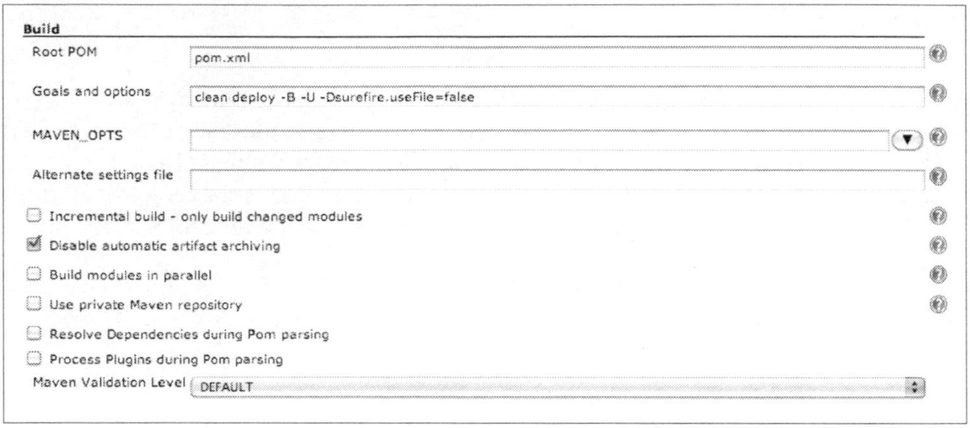

Figure 5-39. Maven build jobs—advanced options

The Incremental Build option comes in very handy for large, multimodule Maven builds. If you tick this option, when a change is made to one of the project modules, Jenkins will only rebuild that module and any modules that use the changed module. It performs this magic by using some new Maven features introduced in Maven 2.1 (so it won't work if you are using Maven 2.0.x). Jenkins detects which modules have been changed, and then uses the -pl (--project-list) option to build only the updated modules, and the -amd (--also-make-dependents) option to build the modules that use the updated modules. If nothing has been changed in the source code, all of the modules are built.

By default, Jenkins will archive all of the artifacts generated by a Maven build job. This can come in handy at times, but it can also be very expensive in disk storage. If you want to turn off this option, just tick the "Disable automatic artifact archiving" option. Alternatively, you can always limit the artifacts stored by using the "Discard Old Builds" option at the top of the configuration page.

The "Build modules in parallel" option tells Jenkins to run each individual module in parallel as a separate build. In theory, this could speed up your builds quite a bit. In practice, it will only really work if your modules are totally independent (that is, you aren't using aggregation), which is rarely the case. If you think building your modules in parallel could really speed up your multimodule project, you may want to try a freestyle build with Maven 3 and its new parallel build feature.

Another useful option is "Use [a] private Maven repository". Normally, when Jenkins runs Maven, it will behave in exactly the same way as Maven on the command line: it will store artifacts in, and retrieve artifacts from the local Maven repository (found in *~/.m2/repository* if you haven't reconfigured it in the *settings.xml* file). This is efficient in terms of disk space, but not always ideal for CI builds. Indeed, if several build jobs are working on and with the same snapshot artifacts, the builds may end up interfering with each other.

When this option is checked, Jenkins will tell Maven to use $WORKSPACE/.repository as the local Maven repository. This means each job will get its own isolated Maven repository just for itself. It fixes the above problems, at the expense of additional disk space consumption.

With this option, Maven will use a dedicated Maven repository for this build job, located in the $WORKSPACE/.repository directory. This takes more disk space, but guarantees a better isolation between build jobs.

Another way of addressing this problem is to override the default repository location by using the maven.repo.local property, as shown here:

```
$ mvn install -Dmaven.repo.local=~/.m2/staging-repository
```

This approach has the advantage of being able to share a repository across several build jobs, which is useful if you need to do a series of related builds. It will also work with freestyle jobs.

Post-Build Actions

The Post-Build actions in a Maven build job are considerably simpler to configure than in a freestyle job. This is simply because, since this is a Maven build, Jenkins knows where to look for a lot of the build output. Artifacts, test reports, Javadoc, and so forth, are all generated in standard directories, which means *you* don't have to tell Jenkins where to find things. So Jenkins will find, and report on, JUnit test results automatically, for example. Later on in the book, we will see how the Maven projects also simplify the configuration of many code quality metrics tools and reports.

Most of the other Post-build Actions are similar to those we saw in the freestyle build job.

Deploying to an Enterprise Repository Manager

One extra option does appear in the Maven build jobs is the ability to deploy your artifacts to a Maven repository (see Figure 5-40). An Enterprise Repository Manager is a server that acts as both a proxy/cache for public Maven artifacts, and as a central storage server for your own internal artifacts. Open Source Enterprise Repository Managers like Nexus (from Sonatype) and Artifactory (from JFrog) provide powerful maintenance and administration features that make configuring and maintaining your Maven repositories a lot simpler. Both these products have commercial versions, with additional features aimed at more sophisticated or high-end build infrastructures.

The advantage of getting Jenkins to deploy your artifacts (as opposed to simply running mvn deploy) is that, if you have a multimodule Maven build, the artifacts will only be deployed once the entire build has finished successfully. For example, suppose you have a multimodule Maven project with five modules. If you run mvn deploy, and the build fails after three modules, the first two modules will have been deployed to your

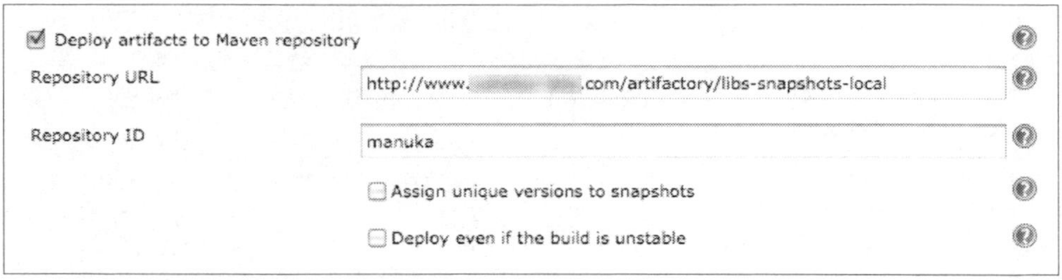

Figure 5-40. Deploying artifacts to a Maven repository

repository, but not the last three, which leaves your repository in an instable state. Getting Jenkins to do the deploy ensures that the artifacts are only deployed as a group once the build has successfully finished.

To do this, just tick the "Deploy artifacts to Maven repository" option in the "Post-Build actions". You will need to specify the URL of the repository you want to deploy to. This needs to be the full URL to the repository (e.g., *http://nexus.acme.com/nexus/ content/repositories/snapshots*, and not just *http://nexus.acme.com/nexus*)

Most repositories need you to authenticate before letting you deploy artifacts to them. The standard Maven way to do this is to place a `<server>` entry in your local *settings.xml* file, as shown here:

```
<settings...>
  <servers>
    <server>
      <id>nexus-snapshots</id>
      <username>scott</username>
      <password>tiger</password>
    </server>
    <server>
      <id>nexus-releases</id>
      <username>scott</username>
      <password>tiger</password>
    </server>
  </servers>
</settings>
```

For the more security-minded, you can also encrypt these passwords if required.

Then, enter the corresponding ID value in the Repository ID field in Jenkins. Jenkins will then be able to look up the right username and password, and deploy your artifacts. Once the build is finished, your artifacts should be available in your Maven Enterprise Repository (see Figure 5-41).

Using this option, you always don't have to deploy straight away—you can always come back and deploy the artifacts from a previous build later. Just click on the "Re-deploy Artifacts" menu on the left and specify the repository URL you want to deploy your artifact to (see Figure 5-42). As in the previous example, the Advanced button lets you provide the ID for the `<server>` entry in your local *settings.xml* file. As we will see

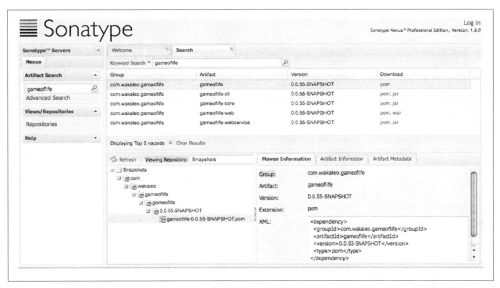

Figure 5-41. After deployment the artifact should be available on your Enterprise Repository Manager

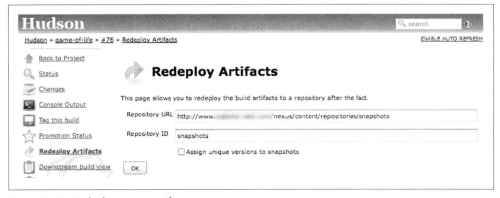

Figure 5-42. Redeploying an artifact

later on in the book, you can also use this deployment as part of a build promotion process, configuring an automatic deployment to a different repository when certain quality metrics have been satisfied, for example.

This approach will work fine for any Enterprise Repository manager. However, if you are using Artifactory, you may prefer to install the Jenkins Artifactory Plugin (*http://wiki.jenkins-ci.org/display/JENKINS/Artifactory+Plugin*), which provides tighter two-way integration with the Artifactory Enterprise Repository Manager. It works by sending additional information to the Artifactory server during the deployment, allowing the server to refer back to the precise build that generated a given artifact. Once you have installed the plugin, you can activate it in your Maven build job by ticking the

"Deploy artifacts to Artifactory" option in the Post-build Actions. Then you choose what repositories your project should deploy to from a list of repositories on the server, along with the username and password required to perform the deployment (see Figure 5-43).

Figure 5-43. Deploying to Artifactory from Jenkins

Your build job will now automatically deploy to Artifactory. In addition, a link to the artifact on the server will now be displayed on the build job home and build results pages (see Figure 5-44).

Figure 5-44. Jenkins displays a link to the corresponding Artifactory repository

This link takes you to a page on the Artifactory server containing the deployed artifact (see Figure 5-45). From this page, there is also a link that takes you back to the build that built the artifact.

Figure 5-45. Viewing the deployed artifact in Artifactory

Deploying to Commercial Enterprise Repository Managers

An Enterprise Repository Manager is an essential part of any Maven-based software development infrastructure. They also play a key role for non-Maven projects using tools like Ivy and Gradle, both of which rely on standard Maven repositories.

Both of the principal Enterprise Repository Managers, Nexus and Artifactory, offer professional versions which come with extra integration features with Jenkins. Later on in the book, we will discuss how you can use advanced features such as Nexus Pro's staging and release management to implement sophisticated build promotion strategies. On the deployment side of things, the commercial edition of Artifactory (Artifactory Pro Power Pack) extends the two-way integration we saw earlier. When you view an artifact in the repository browser, a "Builds" tab displays details about the Jenkins build that created the artifact, and a link to the Jenkins build page (see Figure 5-46). Artifactory also keeps track of the dependencies that were used in the Jenkins build, and will warn you if you try to delete them from the repository.

Managing Modules

When using Maven, it is common to split a project into several modules. Maven build jobs have an intrinsic understand of multimodule projects, and adds a Modules menu item that lets you display the structure of the project at a glance (see Figure 5-47).

Clicking on any of the modules will take you to the build page for that module. From here, you can view the detailed build results for each module, trigger a build of that module in isolation, and if necessary fine tune the configuration of individual module, overriding the configuration of the overall project.

Extra Build Steps in Your Maven Build Jobs

By default, the Maven build job only allows for a single Maven goal. There are times when this is a little limiting, and you would like to add some extra steps before or after the main build. You can do this with the Jenkins M2 Extra Steps Plugin. This plugin

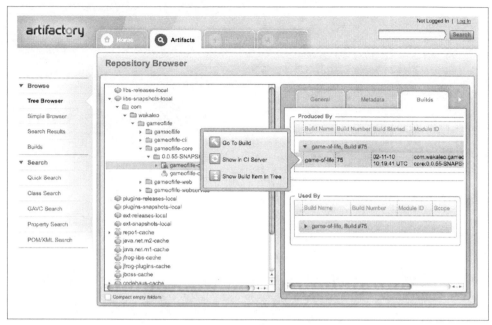

Figure 5-46. Viewing the deployed artifact and the corresponding Jenkins build in Artifactory

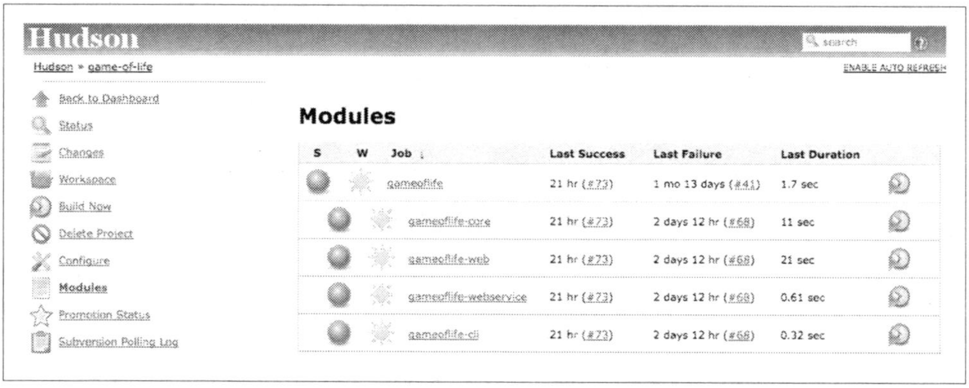

![Hudson modules screenshot]

Figure 5-47. Managing modules in a Maven build job

lets you add normal build steps before and after the main Maven goal, giving you the flexibility of a freestyle build while still having the convenience of the Maven build job configuration.

Install this plugin and go to the Build Environment section of your build job. Tick the "Configure Extra M2 Build Steps" option. You should now be able to add build steps that will be executed before and/or after your main Maven goal is executed (see Figure 5-48).

Figure 5-48. Configuring extra Maven build steps

Using Jenkins with Other Languages

As we mentioned earlier, Jenkins provides excellent support for other languages. In this section, we will look at how to use Jenkins with a few of the more common ones.

Building Projects with Grails

Grails is an open source dynamic web application framework built on Groovy and many well-established open source Java frameworks such as Spring and Hibernate.

Jenkins provides excellent support for Grails builds. First, you need to install the Jenkins Grails plugin (*http://wiki.jenkins-ci.org/display/HUDSON/Grails+Plugin*). Once you have installed this and restarted Jenkins, you will need to provide at least one version of Grails for Jenkins to use in the Grails Builder section of the Configure System screen (see Figure 5-49).

Now you can set up a freestyle build job to build your Grails project. The Grails plugin adds the "Build with Grails" build step, which you can use to build your Grails application (see Figure 5-50). Here, you provide the Grails target, or targets, you want to execute. Unlike the command line, you can execute several targets in the same command. However, if you need to pass any arguments to a particular target, you should

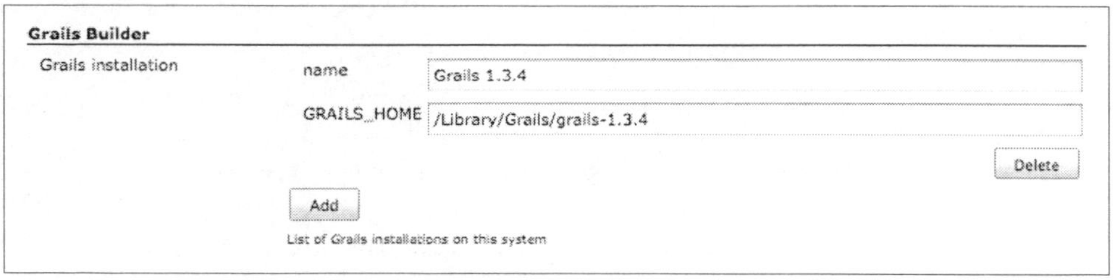

Figure 5-49. Adding a Grails installation to Jenkins

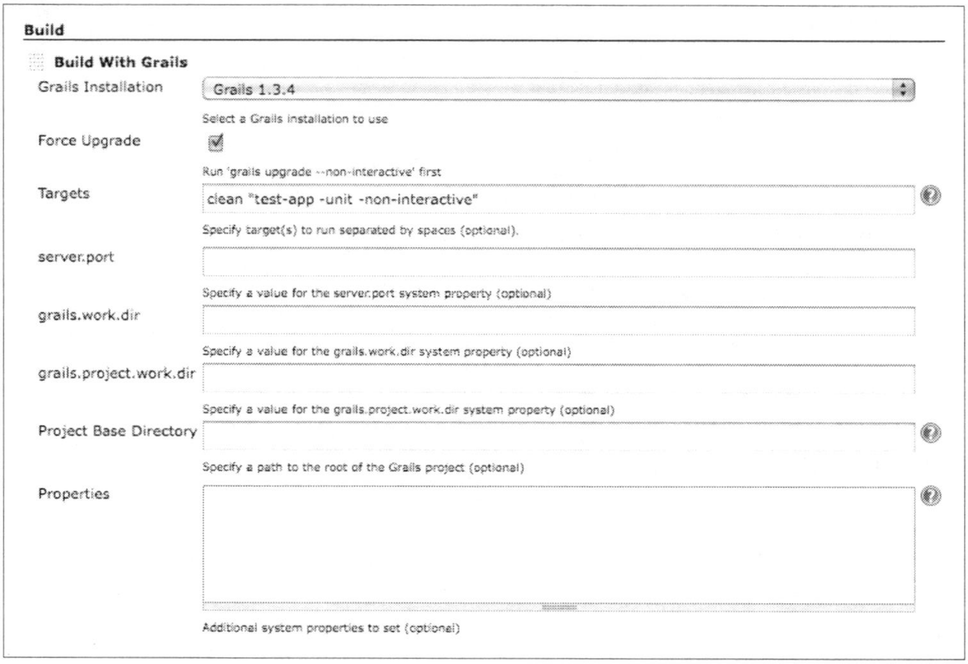

Figure 5-50. Configuring a Grails build step

enclose the target and its arguments in double quotes. In Figure 5-50, for example, we run `grails clean`, followed by `grails test-app -unit -non-interactive`. To get this to work properly, we enclose the options of the second command in quotes, which gives us `grails clean "test-app -unit -non-interactive"`.

The Grails build step takes many optional parameters. For example, Grails is finicky about versions—if your project was created by an older version, Grails will ask you to upgrade it. To be on the safe side, for example, you may want to tick the Force Upgrade checkbox, which makes sure that runs a `grails upgrade --non-interactive` before it runs the main targets.

You can also specify the server port (useful if you are executing web tests), and any other properties you want to pass to the build.

Building Projects with Gradle

Contributed by Rene Groeschke

In comparison to the build tool veterans Ant and Maven, Gradle (*http://gradle.org*) is a relatively new open source build tool for the Java Virtual Machine. Build scripts for Gradle are written in a Domain Specific Language (DSL) based on Groovy. Gradle implements convention over configuration, allows direct access to Ant tasks, and uses Maven-like declarative dependency management. The concise nature of Groovy scripting lets you write very expressive build scripts with very little code, albeit at the cost of loosing the IDE support that exists for established tools like Ant and Maven.

There are two different ways to run your Gradle builds with Jenkins. You can either use the Gradle plugin for Jenkins or the Gradle wrapper functionality.

The Gradle plugin for Jenkins

You can install the Gradle plugin in the usual way—just go to the Manage Plugins screen and select the Jenkins Gradle plugin. Click Install and restart your Jenkins instance.

Once Jenkins has restarted, you will need to configure your new Gradle plugin. You should now find a new Gradle section in your Configure System screen. Here you will need to add the Gradle installation you want to use. The process is similar to that used for the other tool installations. First, click the Add Gradle button to add a new Gradle installation, and enter an appropriate name (see Figure 5-51). If Gradle has already been installed on your build server, you can point to the local Gradle home directory. Alternatively, you can use the "Install automatically" feature to download a Gradle installation, in the form of a ZIP or GZipped TAR file, directly from a URL. You can use a public URL (see *http://gradle.org/downloads.html*), or may prefer to make these installations available on a local server instead.

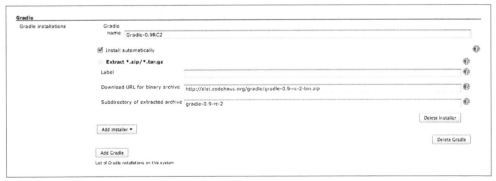

Figure 5-51. Configuring the Gradle plugin

You typically use Freestyle build jobs to configure your Gradle builds. When you add a build step to a Freestyle build job, you will now have a new option called "Invoke Gradle script", which lets you add Gradle specific settings to your build job.

As an example, here is a very simple Gradle build script. It is a simple Java project that uses a Maven directory structure and a Maven repository manager. There is a customizable task, called *uploadArchives*, to deploy the generated archive to the local Enterprise repository manager:

```
apply plugin:'java'
apply plugin:'maven'

version='1.0-SNAPSHOT'
group = "org.acme"

repositories{
  mavenCentral()
    mavenRepo urls: 'http://build.server/nexus/content/repositories/public'
}

dependencies{
  testCompile "junit:junit:4.8.2"
}

uploadArchives {
  repositories.mavenDeployer {
    configuration = configurations.archives
      repository(url: "http://build.server/nexus/content/repositories/snapshots") {
        authentication(userName: "admin", password: "password")
      }
  }
}
```

In Figure 5-52, we use the just configured "Gradle-0.9RC2" instance to run this Gradle build. In this case, we want to run the JUnit tests and upload the build artifacts to our local Maven repository. Furthermore we configure our job to collect the test results from ***/build/test-results*, the default directory for storing test results in Gradle.

Incremental builds

While running a Gradle build job with unchanged sources, Gradle runs its builds incremental. If the output of a Gradle task is still available and the sources haven't changed since the last build, Gradle is able to skip the task execution and marks the according task as up-to-date. This incremental build feature can decrease the duration of a running build job considerably.

If Gradle evaluates the test task as up-to-date even the execution of your unit tests is skipped. This can cause problems when running your Gradle build with Jenkins. In our sample build job above we configured a post build action to publish the JUnit reports of our build. If the test task is skipped by Gradle, the Jenkins job will be marked as failed with the following message:

Test reports were found but none of them are new. Did tests run?

You can easily fix this by invalidating the output and force a re-execution of your tests by adding the following snippet to your Gradle file:

```
test {
    outputs.upToDateWhen { false }
}
```

Figure 5-52. Setting up a Gradle build job

After adding the snippet above to your build file, your job console output should look like the one in Figure 5-53.

```
Console Output

Started by user anonymous
[SampleApp1] $ /Users/Rene/.hudson/tools/Gradle-0.9RC2/gradle-0.9-rc-2/bin/gradle test uploadArchives
:compileJava UP-TO-DATE
:processResources UP-TO-DATE
:classes UP-TO-DATE
:compileTestJava UP-TO-DATE
:processTestResources UP-TO-DATE
:testClasses UP-TO-DATE
:test
:jar UP-TO-DATE
:uploadArchivesUploading: org/acme/SampleApp1/1.0-SNAPSHOT/SampleApp1-1.0-20101123.220032-2.jar to repository remote at
http://localhost:8081/artifactory/gradlerepo
Transferring 1K from remote
Uploaded 1K

BUILD SUCCESSFUL

Total time: 24.325 secs
Recording test results
Finished: SUCCESS
```

Figure 5-53. Incremental Gradle job

As you can see, all of the tasks except *test* and *uploadArchives* have been marked as up-to-date and not executed.

Building Projects with Visual Studio MSBuild

Jenkins is a Java application, but it also provides excellent support for .NET projects.

To build .NET projects in Jenkins, you need to install the MSBuild plugin (*http://wiki .jenkins-ci.org/display/HUDSON/MSBuild+Plugin*).

You may also want to install the MSTest plugin (*http://wiki.jenkins-ci.org//display/ HUDSON/MSTest+Plugin*) and the NUnit plugin (*http://wiki.jenkins-ci.org//display/ HUDSON/NUnit+Plugin*), to display your test results.

Once you have installed the .NET plugins and restarted Jenkins, you need to configure your .NET build tools. Go to the Configure System page and specify the path of the MSBuild executable (see Figure 5-54).

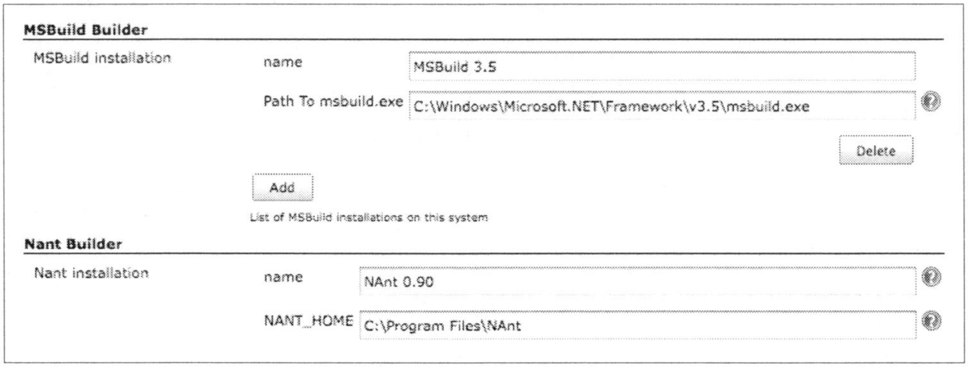

Figure 5-54. Configuring .NET build tools in Jenkins

Once you have this set up, you can return to your freestyle project and add your .NET build step configuration.

Go to the Build section and choose "Build a Visual project or solution using MSBuild" option in the Add Build Step menu. Then enter the path to your MSBuild build script (a *.proj* or *.sln* file), along with any command-line options your build requires (see Figure 5-55).

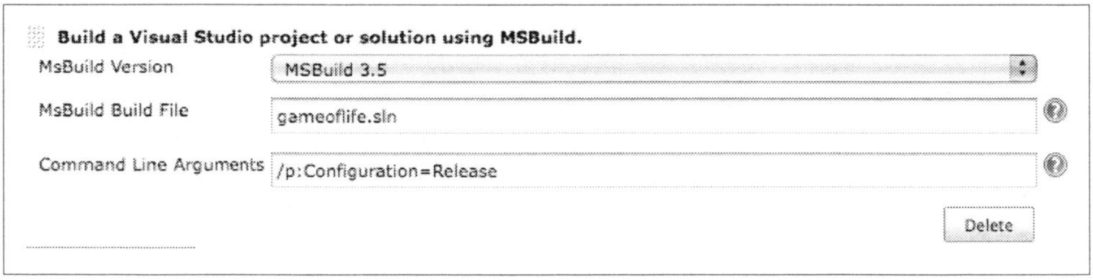

Figure 5-55. A build step using MSBuild

Building Projects with NAnt

Another way to build your .NET projects is to use NAnt. NAnt is a .NET version of the Ant build scripting tool widely used in the Java world. NAnt build scripts are XML files (typically with a *.build* extension), with a very similar format to Ant build scripts.

To build with NAnt in Jenkins, you need to install the Jenkins NAnt plugin (*http://wiki .jenkins-ci.org/display/HUDSON/NAnt+Plugin*). Once you have installed the plugin and restarted Jenkins, go to the Configure System page and specify the NAnt installation directory in the Nant Builders section (see Figure 5-54).

Now go to the Build section of your freestyle project and choose "Execute NAnt build" (see Figure 5-56). Here you specify your build script and the target you want to invoke. If you click on the "Advanced..." option, you can also set property values to be passed into the NAnt script.

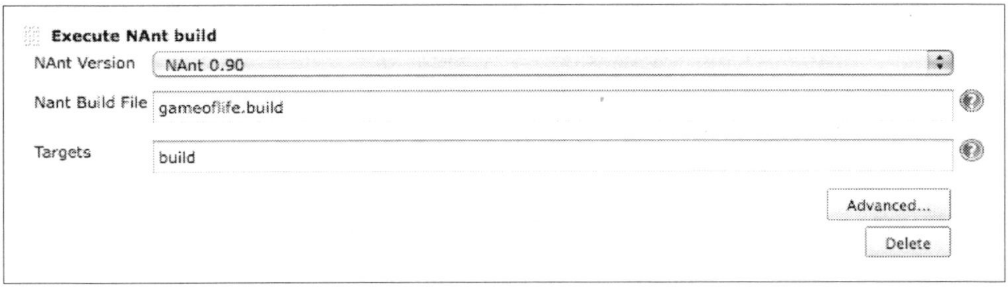

Figure 5-56. A build step using NAnt

Building Projects with Ruby and Ruby on Rails

Jenkins makes an excellent choice when it comes to integrating CI into your Ruby and Ruby on Rails projects. The Rake Plugin lets you add Rake build steps to your build jobs. You can also use the Ruby Plugin lets you run Ruby scripts directly in your build job. Finally, the Ruby Metrics Plugin provides support for Ruby code quality metrics tools such as RCov, Rails stats, and Flog.

Another invaluable tool in this area is `CI:Reporter`. This library is an add-on to `Test::Unit`, `RSpec`, and `Cucumber` that generates JUnit-compatible XML reports for your tests. As we will see, JUnit-compatible test results can be used directly by Jenkins to report on your test results. You would install CI:Reporter using Gem as illustrated here:

```
$ sudo gem install ci_reporter
Successfully installed ci_reporter-1.6.4
1 gem installed
```

Next, you will need to set this up in your Rakefile, by adding the following:

```
require 'rubygems'
gem 'ci_reporter'
require 'ci/reporter/rake/test_unit' # use this if you're using Test::Unit
```

In Chapter 9, we discuss integrating code quality metrics into your Jenkins builds. Jenkins also provides support for code coverage metrics in Ruby. The Ruby Metrics Plugin supports code coverage metrics using *rcov* as well as general code statistics with *Rails stats*. To install the *rcov-plugin*, you will first need to run something along the following lines:

```
$ ./script/plugin install http://svn.codahale.com/rails_rcov
```

Once this is set up, you will be able to display your test results and test result trend in Jenkins.

Finally, you can configure a Rake build simply by using a Rake build step, as illustrated in Figure 5-57.

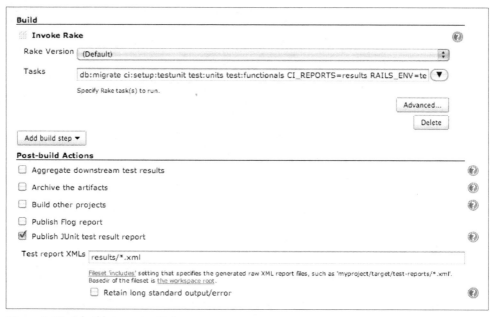

Figure 5-57. A build step using Rake

You also need to configure Jenkins to report on the test and quality metrics results. You can do this by activating the "Publish JUnit test result report", "Publish Rails stats report", and "Public Rcov report" options (see Figure 5-58). The JUnit XML reports will be found in the *results* directory (enter **results/*.xml** in the "Test report XMLs" field), and the Rcov date in the *coverage/units* directory.

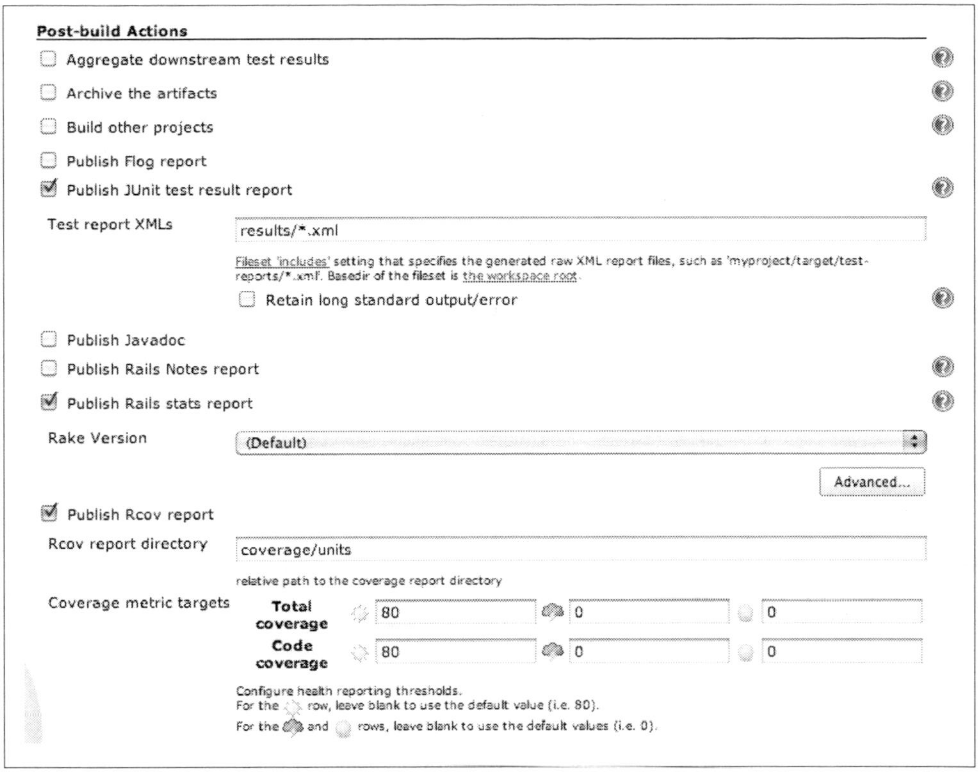

Figure 5-58. Publishing code quality metrics for Ruby and Rails

Conclusion

In this chapter we have covered the basics of creating new build jobs for the most common cases you are likely to encounter. Later on in the book, we will build on these foundations to discuss more advanced options such as parameterized builds, matrix builds, and build promotion strategies.

CHAPTER 6

Automated Testing

Introduction

If you aren't using automated tests with your Continuous Integration setup, you're really missing out on something big. Believe me—CI without automated tests is really just a small improvement on automatically scheduled builds. Now don't get me wrong, if you're coming from nothing, that's already a great step forward—but you can do much better. In short, if you are using Jenkins without any automated tests, you are not getting anywhere near as much value out of your Continuous Integration infrastructure as you should.

One of the basic principles of Continuous Integration is that a build should be verifiable. You have to be able to objectively determine whether a particular build is ready to proceed to the next stage of the build process, and the most convenient way to do this is to use automated tests. Without proper automated testing, you find yourself having to retain many build artifacts and test them by hand, which is hardly in the spirit of Continuous Integration.

There are many ways you can integrate automated tests into your application. One of the most efficient ways to write high quality tests is to write them first, using techniques such as Test-Driven Development (TDD) or Behavior-Driven Development (BDD). In this approach, commonly used in many Agile projects, the aim of your unit tests is to both clarify your understanding of the code's behavior and to write an automated test that the code does indeed implement this behavior. Focusing on testing the expected behavior, rather than the implementation, of your code also makes for more comprehensive and more accurate tests, and thus helps Jenkins to provide more relevant feedback.

Of course, more classical unit testing, done once the code has been implemented, is also another commonly-used approach, and is certainly better than no tests at all.

Jenkins is not limited to unit testing, though. There are many other types of automated testing that you should consider, depending on the nature of your application, including integration testing, web testing, functional testing, performance testing, load testing and so on. All of these have their place in an automated build setup.

Jenkins can also be used, in conjunction with techniques like Behavior-Driven Development and Acceptance Test Driven Development, as a communications tool aimed at both developers and other project stakeholders. BDD frameworks such as easyb, fitnesse, jbehave, rspec, Cucumber, and many others, try to present acceptance tests in terms that testers, product owners, and end users can understand. With the use of such tools, Jenkins can report on project progress in business terms, and so facilitate communication between developers and non-developers within a team.

For existing or legacy applications with little or no automated testing in place, it can be time-consuming and difficult to retro-fit comprehensive unit tests onto the code. In addition, the tests may not be very effective, as they will tend to validate the existing implementation rather than verify the expected business behavior. One useful approach in these situations is to write automated functional tests ("regression") tests that simulate the most common ways that users manipulate the application. For example, automated web testing tools such as Selenium and WebDriver can be effectively used to test web applications at a high level. While this approach is not as comprehensive as a combination of good quality unit, integration and acceptance tests, it is still an effective and relatively cost-efficient way to integrate automated regression testing into an existing application.

In this chapter, we will see how Jenkins helps you keep track of automated test results, and how you can use this information to monitor and dissect your build process.

Automating Your Unit and Integration Tests

The first thing we will look at is how to integrate your unit tests into Jenkins. Whether you are practicing Test-Driven Development, or writing unit tests using a more conventional approach, these are probably the first tests that you will want to automate with Jenkins.

Jenkins does an excellent job of reporting on your test results. However, it is up to you to write the appropriate tests and to configure your build script to run them automatically. Fortunately integrating unit tests into your automated builds is generally relatively easy.

There are many unit testing tools out there, with the xUnit family holding a predominant place. In the Java world, JUnit is the de facto standard, although TestNG is another popular Java unit testing framework with a number of innovative features. For C# applications, the NUnit testing framework proposes similar functionalities to those provided by JUnit, as does Test::Unit for Ruby. For C/C++, there is CppUnit, and PHP developers can use PHPUnit. And this is not an exhaustive list!

These tools can also serve for integration tests, functional tests, web tests and so forth. Many web testing tools, such as Selenium, WebDriver, and Watir, generate xUnit-compatible reports. Behaviour-Driven Development and automated Acceptance-Test tools such as easyb, Fitnesse, Concordion are also xUnit-friendly. In the following sections we make no distinction between these different types of test, as, from a configuration point of view, they are treated by Jenkins in exactly the same manner. However, you will almost certainly need to make the distinction in your build jobs. In order to get the fastest possible feedback loop, your tests should be grouped into well-defined categories, starting with the fast-running unit tests, and then proceeding to the integration tests, before finally running the slower functional and web tests.

A detailed discussion of how to automate your tests is beyond the scope of this book, but we do cover a few useful techniques for Maven and Ant in the Appendix.

Configuring Test Reports in Jenkins

Once your build generates test results, you need to configure your Jenkins build job to display them. As mentioned above, Jenkins will work fine with any xUnit-compatible test reports, no matter what language they are written in.

For Maven build jobs, no special configuration is required—just make sure you invoke a goal that will run your tests, such as mvn test (for your unit tests) or mvn verify (for unit and integration tests). An example of a Maven build job configuration is shown in Figure 6-1.

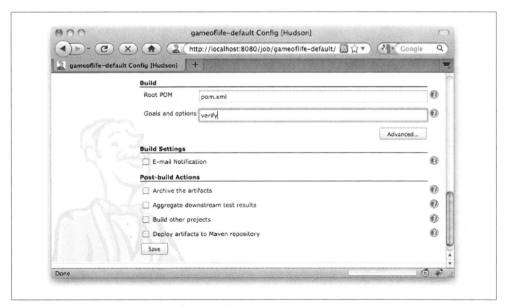

Figure 6-1. You configure your Jenkins installation in the Manage Jenkins screen

For freestyle build jobs, you need to do a little more configuration work. In addition to ensuring that your build actually runs the tests, you need to tell Jenkins to publish the JUnit test report. You configure this in the "Post-build Actions" section (see Figure 6-2). Here, you provide a path to the JUnit or TestNG XML reports. Their exact location will depend on a project—for a Maven project, a path like **/target/surefire-reports/*.xml* will find them for most projects. For an Ant-based project, it will depend on how you configured the Ant JUnit task, as we discussed above.

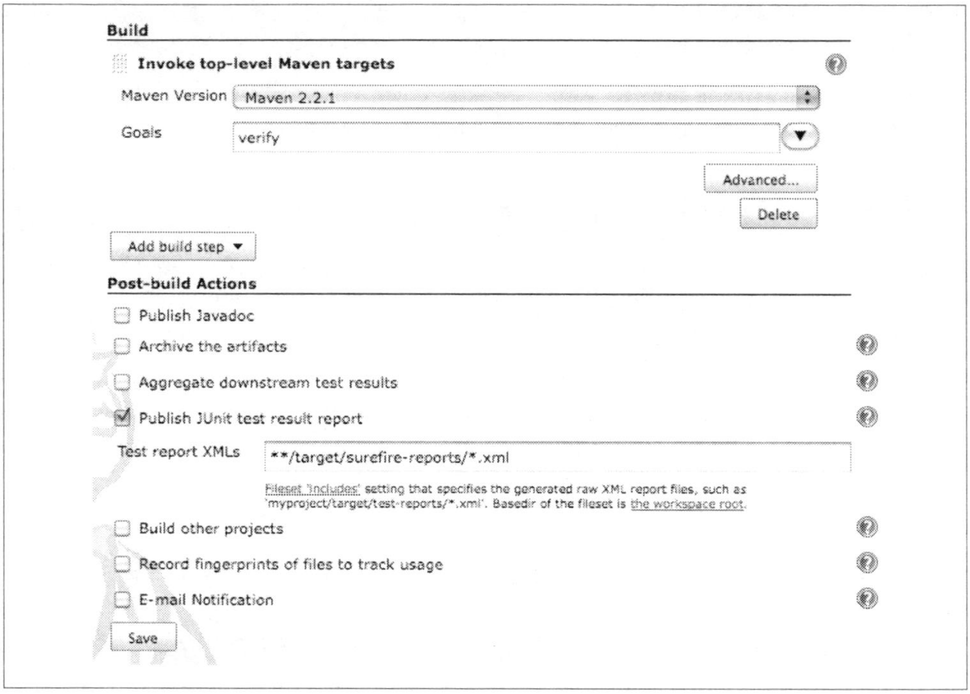

Figure 6-2. Configuring Maven test reports in a freestyle project

For Java projects, whether they are using JUnit or TestNG, Jenkins does an excellent job out of the box. If you are using Jenkins for non-Java projects, you might need the xUnit Plugin. This plugin lets Jenkins process test reports from non-Java tools in a consistent way. It provides support for MSUnit and NUnit (for C# and other .NET languages), UnitTest++ and Boost Test (for C++), PHPUnit (for PHP), as well as a few other xUnit libraries via additional plugins (see Figure 6-3).

Once you have installed the xUnit Plugin, you will need to configure the reporting for your particular xUnit reports in the "Post-build Actions" section. Check the "Publish testing tools result report" checkbox, and enter the path to the XML reports generated by your testing library (see Figure 6-4). When the build job runs, Jenkins will convert these reports to JUnit reports so that they can be displayed in Jenkins.

☐	This plugin provides an eXtreme Feedback Panel that can be used to expose the status of a selected number of Jobs.	1.0.8
☑	**xUnit Plugin** This plugin allows you to publish testing tools test result report.	0.6.1
Build Tools		

Figure 6-3. Installing the xUnit plugin

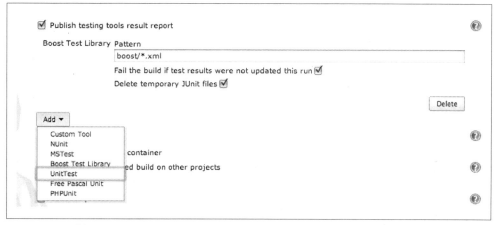

Figure 6-4. Publishing xUnit test results

Displaying Test Results

Once Jenkins knows where to find the test reports, it does a great job of reporting on them. Indeed, one of Jenkins's main jobs is to detect and to report on build failures. And a failing unit test is one of the most obvious symptoms.

As we mentioned earlier, Jenkins makes the distinction between *failed* builds and *unstable* builds. A failed build (indicated by a red ball) indicates test failures, or a build job that is broken in some brutal manner, such as a compilation error. An unstable build, on the other hand, is a build that is not considered of sufficient quality. This is intentionally a little vague: what defines "quality" in this sense is largely up to you, but it is typically related to code quality metrics such as code coverage or coding standards, that we will be discussing later on in the book. For now, let's focus on the *failed* builds.

In Figure 6-5 we can see how Jenkins displays a Maven build job containing test failures. This is the build job home page, which should be your first port of call when a build breaks. When a build results in failing tests, the Latest Test Result link will indicate the current number of test failures in this build job ("5 failures" in the illustration), and also the change in the number of test failures since the last build ("+5" in the illustration—five new test failures). You can also see how the tests have been faring over time—test failures from previous builds will also appear as red in the Test Result Trend graph.

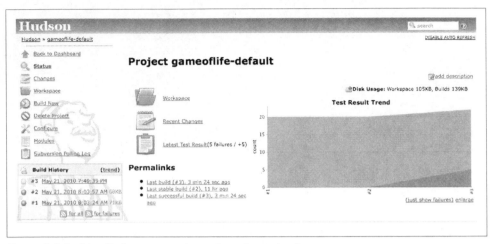

Figure 6-5. Jenkins displays test result trends on the project home page

If you click on the Latest Test Result link, Jenkins will give you a rundown of the current test results (see Figure 6-6). Jenkins understands Maven multimodule project structures, and for a Maven build job, Jenkins will initially display a summary view of test results per module. For more details about the failing tests in a particular module, just click on the module you are interest in.

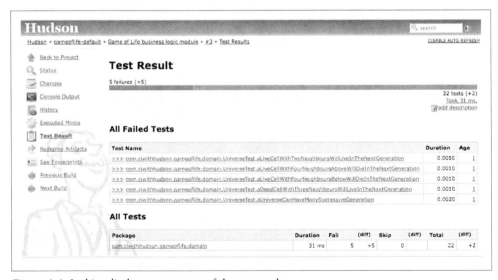

Figure 6-6. Jenkins displays a summary of the test results

For freestyle build jobs, Jenkins will directly give you a summary of your test results, but organized by high-level packages rather than modules.

In both cases, Jenkins starts off by presenting a summary of test results for each package. From here, you can drill down, seeing test results for each test class and then finally the tests within the test classes themselves. And if there are any failed tests, these will be prominently displayed at the top of the page.

This full view gives you both a good overview of the current state of your tests, and an indication of their history. The Age column tells you how for how long a test has been broken, with a hyperlink that takes you back to the first build in which this test failed.

You can also add a description to the test results, using the Edit Description link in the top right-hand corner of the screen. This is a great way to annotate a build failure with some additional details, in order to add extra information about the origin of test failures or some notes about how to fix them.

When a test fails, you generally want to know why. To see the details of a particular test failure, just click on the corresponding link on this screen. This will display all the gruesome details, including the error message and the stack trace, as well as a reminder of how long the test has been failing (see Figure 6-7). You should be wary of tests that have been failing for more than just a couple of builds—this is an indicator of either a tricky technical problem that might need investigating, or a complacent attitude to failed builds (developers might just be ignoring build failures), which is more serious and definitely should be investigated.

Figure 6-7. The details of a test failure

Make sure you also keep an eye on how long your tests take to run, and not just whether they pass or fail. Unit tests should be designed to run fast, and overly long-running tests can be the sign of a performance issue. Slow unit tests also delay feedback, and in CI, fast feedback is the name of the game. For example, running one thousand unit tests in five minutes is good—taking an hour to run them is not. So it is a good idea to regularly check how long your unit tests are taking to run, and if necessary investigate why they are taking so long.

Luckily, Jenkins can easily tell you how long your tests have been taking to run over time. On the build job home page, click on the "trend" link in the Build History box on the left of the screen. This will give you a graph along the lines of the one in Figure 6-8, showing how long each of your builds took to run. Now tests are not the only thing that happens in a build job, but if you have enough tests to worry about, they will probably take a large proportion of the time. So this graph is a great way to see how well your tests are performing as well.

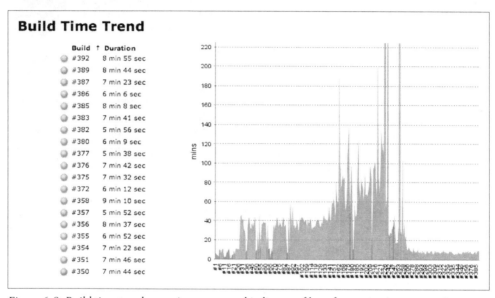

Figure 6-8. Build time trends can give you a good indicator of how fast your tests are running

When you are on the Test Results page (see Figure 6-6), you can also drill down and see how long the tests in a particular module, package or class are taking to run. Just click on the test duration in the test results page ("Took 31 ms" in Figure 6-6) to view the test history for a package, class, or individual test (see Figure 6-9). This makes it easy to isolate a test that is taking more time than it should, or even decide when a general optimization of your unit tests is required.

Ignoring Tests

Jenkins distinguishes between test failures and skipped tests. Skipped tests are ones that have been deactivated, for example by using the @Ignore annotation in JUnit 4:

```
@Ignore("Pending more details from the BA")
@Test
public void cashWithdrawalShouldDeductSumFromBalance() throws Exception {
```

```
        Account account = new Account();
        account.makeDeposit(100);
        account.makeCashWithdraw(60);
        assertThat(account.getBalance(), is(40));
    }
```

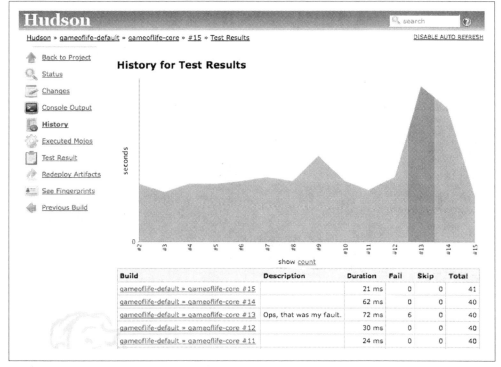

Figure 6-9. Jenkins also lets you see how long your tests take to run

Skipping some tests is perfectly legitimate in some circumstances, such as to place an automated acceptance test, or higher-level technical test, on hold while you implement the lower levels. In such cases, you don't want to be distracted by the failing acceptance test, but you don't want to forget that the test exists either. Using techniques such as the @Ignore annotation are better than simply commenting out the test or renaming it (in JUnit 3), as it lets Jenkins keep tabs on the ignored tests for you.

In TestNG, you can also skip tests, using the enabled property:

```
@Test(enabled=false)
public void cashWithdrawalShouldDeductSumFromBalance() throws Exception {
    Account account = new Account();
    account.makeDeposit(100);
    account.makeCashWithdraw(60);
    assertThat(account.getBalance(), is(40));
}
```

In TestNG, you can also define dependencies between tests, so that certain tests will only run after another test or group of tests has run, as illustrated here:

```
@Test
public void serverStartedOk() {...}

@Test(dependsOnMethods = { "serverStartedOk" })
public void whenAUserLogsOnWithACorrectUsernameAndPasswordTheHomePageIsDisplayed(){..}
```

Here, if the first test (`serverStartedOk()`) fails, the following test will be skipped.

In all of these cases, Jenkins will mark the tests that were not run as yellow, both in the overall test results trend, and in the test details (see Figure 6-10). Skipped tests are not as bad as test failures, but it is important not to get into the habit of neglecting them. Skipped tests are like branches in a version control system: a test should be skipped for a specific reason, with a clear idea as to when they will be reactivated. A skipped test that remains skipped for too long is a bad smell.

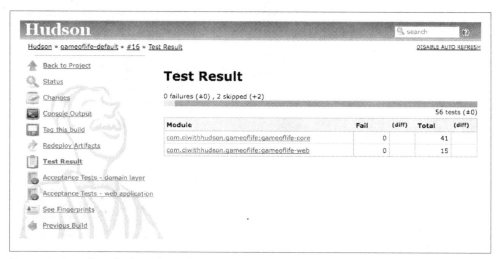

Figure 6-10. Jenkins displays skipped tests as yellow

Code Coverage

Another very useful test-related metric is code coverage. Code coverage gives an indication of what parts of your application were executed during the tests. While this in itself is not a sufficient indication of quality testing (it is easy to execute an entire application without actually testing anything, and code coverage metrics provide no indication of the quality or accuracy of your tests), it is a very good indication of code that has *not* been tested. And, if your team is introducing rigorous testing practices such as Test-Driven-Development, code coverage can be a good indicator of how well these practices are being applied.

Code coverage analysis is a CPU and memory-intensive process, and will slow down your build job significantly. For this reason, you will typically run code coverage metrics in a separate Jenkins build job, to be run after your unit and integration tests are successful.

There are many code coverage tools available, and several are supported in Jenkins, all through dedicated plugins. Java developers can pick between Cobertura and Emma, two popular open source code coverage tools, or Clover, a powerful commercial code coverage tool from Atlassian. For .NET projects, you can use NCover.

The behavior and configuration of all of these tools is similar. In this section, we will look at Cobertura.

Measuring Code Coverage with Cobertura

Cobertura (*http://cobertura.sourceforge.net*) is an open source code coverage tool for Java and Groovy that is easy to use and integrates well with both Maven and Jenkins.

Like almost all of the Jenkins code quality metrics plugins,[*] the Cobertura plugin for Jenkins will not run any test coverage metrics for you. It is left up to you to generate the raw code coverage data as part of your automated build process. Jenkins, on the other hand, does an excellent job of *reporting* on the code coverage metrics, including keeping track of code coverage over time, and providing aggregate coverage across multiple application modules.

Code coverage can be a complicated business, and it helps to understand the basic process that Cobertura follows, especially when you need to set it up in more low-level build scripting tools like Ant. Code coverage analysis works in three steps. First, it modifies (or "instruments") your application classes, to make them keep a tally of the number of times each line of code has been executed.[†] They store all this data in a special data file (Cobertura uses a file called *cobertura.ser*).

When the application code has been instrumented, you run your tests against this instrumented code. At the end of the tests, Cobertura will have generated a data file containing the number of times each line of code was executed during the tests.

Once this data file has been generated, Cobertura can use this data to generate a report in a more usable format, such as XML or HTML.

---

[*] With the notable exception of Sonar, which we will look at later on in the book.

[†] This is actually a slight over-simplification; in fact, Cobertura stores other data as well, such as how many times each possible outcome of a boolean test was executed. However this does not alter the general approach.

Integrating Cobertura with Maven

Producing code coverage metrics with Cobertura in Maven is relatively straightforward. If all you are interested in is producing code coverage data, you just need to add the *cobertura-maven-plugin* to the build section of your *pom.xml* file:

```
<project>
  ...
  <build>
    <plugins>
      <plugin>
        <groupId>org.codehaus.mojo</groupId>
        <artifactId>cobertura-maven-plugin</artifactId>
        <version>2.5.1</version>
        <configuration>
        <formats>
          <format>html</format>
          <format>xml</format>
        </formats>
        </configuration>
      </plugin>
      ...
    </plugins>
  <build>
  ...
</project>
```

This will generate code coverage metrics when you invoke the Cobertura plugin directly:

```
$ mvn cobertura:cobertura
```

The code coverage data will be generated in the *target/site/cobertura* directory, in a file called *coverage.xml*.

This approach, however, will instrument your classes and produce code coverage data for every build, which is inefficient. A better approach is to place this configuration in a special profile, as shown here:

```
<project>
  ...
  <profiles>
   <profile>
     <id>metrics</id>
     <build>
       <plugins>
         <plugin>
           <groupId>org.codehaus.mojo</groupId>
           <artifactId>cobertura-maven-plugin</artifactId>
           <version>2.5.1</version>
           <configuration>
             <formats>
               <format>html</format>
               <format>xml</format>
             </formats>
```

```
            </configuration>
          </plugin>
        </plugins>
      </build>
    </profile>
    ...
  </profiles>
</project>
```

In this case, you would invoke the Cobertura plugin using the metrics profile to generate the code coverage data:

```
$ mvn cobertura:cobertura -Pmetrics
```

Another approach is to include code coverage reporting in your Maven reports. This approach is considerably slower and more memory-hungry than just generating the coverage data, but it can make sense if you are also generating other code quality metrics and reports at the same time. If you want to do this using Maven 2, you need to also include the Maven Cobertura plugin in the reporting section, as shown here:

```
<project>
  ...
  <reporting>
    <plugins>
      <plugin>
        <groupId>org.codehaus.mojo</groupId>
        <artifactId>cobertura-maven-plugin</artifactId>
        <version>2.5.1</version>
        <configuration>
          <formats>
            <format>html</format>
            <format>xml</format>
          </formats>
        </configuration>
      </plugin>
    </plugins>
  </reporting>
</project>
```

Now the coverage data will be generated when you generate the Maven site for this project:

```
$ mvn site
```

If your Maven project contains modules (as is common practice for larger Maven projects), you just need to set up the Cobertura configuration in a parent *pom.xml* file—test coverage metrics and reports will be generated separately for each module. If you use the **aggregate** configuration option, the Maven Cobertura plugin will also generate a high-level report combining coverage data from all of the modules. However, whether you use this option or not, the Jenkins Cobertura plugin will take coverage data from several files and combine them into a single aggregate report.

At the time of writing, there is a limitation with the Maven Cobertura plugin—code coverage will only be recorded for tests executed during the *test* life cycle phase, and not for tests executed during the *integration-test* phase. This can be an issue if you are using this phase to run integration or web tests that require a fully packaged and deployed application—in this case, coverage from tests that are only performed during the integration test phase will not be counted in the Cobertura code coverage metrics.

Integrating Cobertura with Ant

Integrating Cobertura into your Ant build is more complicated than doing so in Maven. However it does give you a finer control over what classes are instrumented, and when coverage is measured.

Cobertura comes bundled with an Ant task that you can use to integrate Cobertura into your Ant builds. You will need to download the latest Cobertura distribution, and unzip it somewhere on your hard disk. To make your build more portable, and therefore easier to deploy into Jenkins, it is a good idea to place the Cobertura distribution you are using within your project directory, and to save it in your version control system. This way it is easier to ensure that the build will use the same version of Cobertura no matter where it is run.

Assuming you have downloaded the latest Cobertura installation and placed it within your project in a directory called *tools*, you could do something like this:

```
<property name="cobertura.dir" value="${basedir}/tools/cobertura" />❶

<path id="cobertura.classpath">❷
    <fileset dir="${cobertura.dir}">
        <include name="cobertura.jar" />❸
        <include name="lib/**/*.jar" />❹
    </fileset>
</path>

<taskdef classpathref="cobertura.classpath" resource="tasks.properties" />
```

❶ Tell Ant where your Cobertura installation is.

❷ We need to set up a classpath that Cobertura can use to run.

❸ The path contains the Cobertura application itself.

❹ And all of its dependencies.

Next, you need to instrument your application classes. You have to be careful to place these instrumented classes in a separated directory, so that they don't get bundled up and deployed to production by accident:

```
<target name="instrument" depends="init,compile">❶
    <delete file="cobertura.ser"/>❷
    <delete dir="${instrumented.dir}" />❸
    <cobertura-instrument todir="${instrumented.dir}">❹
        <fileset dir="${classes.dir}">
            <include name="**/*.class" />
            <exclude name="**/*Test.class" />
        </fileset>
```

```
        </cobertura-instrument>
    </target>
```

❶ We can only instrument the application classes once they have been compiled.

❷ Remove any coverage data generated by previous builds.

❸ Remove any previously instrumented classes.

❹ Instrument the application classes (but not the test classes) and place them in the *${instrumented.dir}* directory.

At this stage, the *${instrumented.dir}* directory contains an instrumented version of our application classes. Now all we need to do to generate some useful code coverage data is to run our unit tests against the classes in this directory:

```
    <target name="test-coverage" depends="instrument">
        <junit fork="yes" dir="${basedir}">❶
            <classpath location="${instrumented.dir}" />
            <classpath location="${classes.dir}" />
            <classpath refid="cobertura.classpath" />❷

            <formatter type="xml" />
            <test name="${testcase}" todir="${reports.xml.dir}" if="testcase" />
            <batchtest todir="${reports.xml.dir}" unless="testcase">
                <fileset dir="${src.dir}">
                    <include name="**/*Test.java" />
                </fileset>
            </batchtest>
        </junit>
    </target>
```

❶ Run the JUnit tests against the instrumented application classes.

❷ The instrumented classes use Cobertura classes, so the Cobertura libraries also need to be on the classpath.

This will produce the raw test coverage data we need to produce the XML test coverage reports that Jenkins can use. To actually produce these reports, we need to invoke another task, as shown here:

```
    <target name="coverage-report" depends="test-coverage">
        <cobertura-report srcdir="${src.dir}" destdir="${coverage.xml.dir}"
                          format="xml" />
    </target>
```

Finally, don't forget to tidy up after your done: the *clean* target should delete not only the generated classes, but also the generated instrumented classes, the Cobertura coverage data, and the Cobertura reports:

```
    <target name="clean"
            description="Remove all files created by the build/test process.">
        <delete dir="${classes.dir}" />
        <delete dir="${instrumented.dir}" />
        <delete dir="${reports.dir}" />
        <delete file="cobertura.log" />
```

```
        <delete file="cobertura.ser" />
    </target>
```

Once this is done, you are ready to integrate your coverage reports into Jenkins.

Installing the Cobertura code coverage plugin

Once code coverage data is being generated as part of your build process, you can configure Jenkins to report on it. This involves installing the Jenkins Cobertura plugin. We went through this process in "Adding Code Coverage and Other Metrics" on page 34, but we'll run through it again to refresh your memory. Go to the Manage Jenkins screen, and click on Manage Plugins. This will take you to the Plugin Manager screen. If Cobertura has not been installed, you will find the Cobertura Plugin in the Available tab, in the Build Reports section (see Figure 6-11). To install it, just tick the checkbox and press enter (or scroll down to the bottom of the screen and click on the "Install" button). Jenkins will download and install the plugin for you. Once the downloading is done, you will need to restart your Jenkins server.

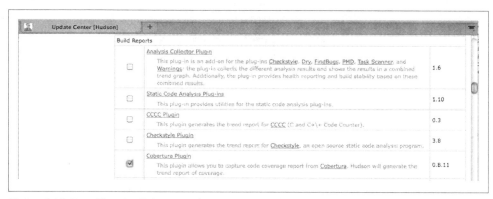

Figure 6-11. Installing the Cobertura plugin

Reporting on code coverage in your build

Once you have installed the plugin, you can set up code coverage reporting in your build jobs. Since code coverage can be slow and memory-hungry, you would typically create a separate build job for this and other code quality metrics, to be run after the normal unit and integration tests. For very large projects, you may even want to set this up as a build that only runs on a nightly basis. Indeed, feedback on code coverage and other such metrics is usually not as time-critical as feedback on test results, and this will leave build executors free for build jobs that can benefit from snappy feedback.

As we mentioned earlier, Jenkins does not do any code coverage analysis itself—you need to configure your build to produce the Cobertura *coverage.xml* file (or files) before you can generate any nice graphs or reports, typically using one of the techniques we discussed previously (see Figure 6-12).

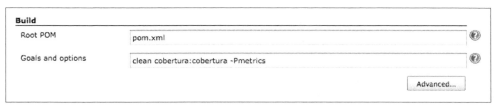

Figure 6-12. Your code coverage metrics build needs to generate the coverage data

Once you have configured your build to produce some code coverage data, you can configure Cobertura in the "Post-build Actions" section of your build job. When you tick the "Publish Cobertura Coverage Report" checkbox, you should see something like Figure 6-13.

![Configuring the test coverage metrics in Jenkins]

☑ Publish Cobertura Coverage Report

Cobertura xml report pattern   **/target/site/cobertura/coverage.xml

This is a file name pattern that can be used to locate the cobertura xml report files (for example with Maven2 use **/target/site/cobertura/coverage.xml). The path is relative to the module root unless you have configured your SCM with multiple modules, in which case it is relative to the workspace root. Note that the module root is SCM-specific, and may not be the same as the workspace root.
Cobertura must be configured to generate XML reports for this plugin to function.

Consider only stable builds   ☐

Include only stable builds, i.e. exclude unstable and failed ones.

Coverage Metric Targets

Conditionals		98	75	75
Lines	Delete	98	75	75
Methods	Delete	100	80	80
Packages	Delete	100	95	95

Add

Configure health reporting thresholds.
For the ☼ row, leave blank to use the default value (i.e. 80).
For the ☁ and ○ rows, leave blank to use the default values (i.e. 0).

Figure 6-13. Configuring the test coverage metrics in Jenkins

The first and most important field here is the path to the Cobertura XML data that we generated. Your project may include a single *coverage.xml* file, or several. If you have a multimodule Maven project, for example, the Maven Cobertura plugin will generate a separate *coverage.xml* file for each module.

The path accepts Ant-style wildcards, so it is easy to include code coverage data from several files. For any Maven project, a path like ***/target/site/cobertura/coverage.xml* will include all of the code coverage metrics for all of the modules in the project.

There are actually several types of code coverage, and it can sometimes be useful to distinguish between them. The most intuitive is Line Coverage, which counts the number of times any given line is executed during the automated tests. "Conditional Coverage" (also referred to as "Branch Coverage") takes into account whether the boolean expressions in `if` statements and the like are tested in a way that checks all the possible outcomes of the conditional expression. For example, consider the following code snippet:

```
if (price > 10000) {
    managerApprovalRequired = true;
}
```

To obtain full Conditional Coverage for this code, you would need to execute it twice: once with a value that is more than 10,000, and one with a value of 10,000 or less.

Other more basic code coverage metrics include methods (how many methods in the application were exercised by the tests), classes and packages.

Jenkins lets you define which of these metrics you want to track. By default, the Cobertura plugin will record Conditional, Line, and Method coverage, which is usually plenty. However it is easy to add other coverage metrics if you think this might be useful for your team.

Jenkins code quality metrics are not simply a passive reporting process—Jenkins lets you define how these metrics affect the build outcome. You can define threshold values for the coverage metrics that affect both the build outcome and the weather reports on the Jenkins dashboard (see Figure 6-14). Each coverage metric that you track takes three threshold values.

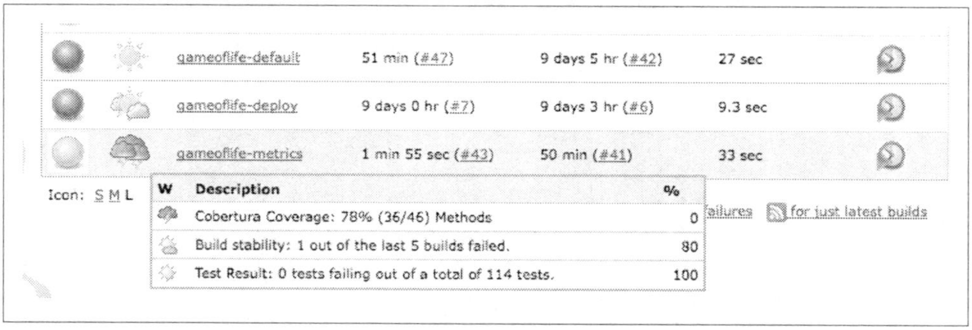

Figure 6-14. Test coverage results contribute to the project status on the dashboard

The first (the one with the sunny icon) is the minimum value necessary for the build to have a sunny weather icon. The second indicates the value below which the build will be attributed a stormy weather icon. Jenkins will extrapolate between these values for the other more nuanced weather icons.

The last threshold value is simply the value below which a build will be marked as "unstable"—the yellow ball. While not quite as bad as the red ball (for a broken build), a yellow ball will still result in a notification message and will look bad on the dashboard.

This feature is far from simply a cosmetic detail—it provides a valuable way of setting objective code quality goals for your projects. Although it cannot be interpreted alone, falling code coverage is generally not a good sign in a project. So if you are serious about code coverage, use these threshold values to provide some hard feedback about when things are not up to scratch.

Interpreting code coverage metrics

Jenkins displays your code coverage reports on the build job home page. The first time it runs, it produces a simple bar chart (see Figure 2-30). From the second build onwards, a graph is shown, indicating the various types of coverage that you are tracking over time (see Figure 6-15). In both cases, the graph will also show the code coverage metrics for the latest build.

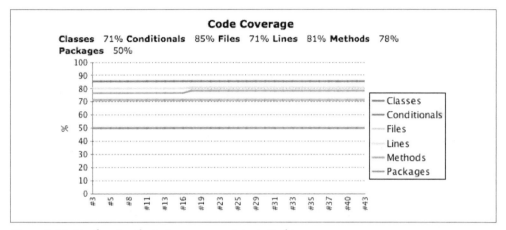

Figure 6-15. Configuring the test coverage metrics in Jenkins

Jenkins also does a great job letting you drill down into the coverage metrics, displaying coverage breakdowns for packages, classes within a package, and lines of code within a class (see Figure 6-16). No matter what level of detail you are viewing, Jenkins will display a graph at the top of the page showing the code coverage trend over time. Further down, you will find the breakdown by package or class.

Once you get to the class details level, Jenkins will also display the source code of the class, with the lines color-coded according to their level of coverage. Lines that have been completely executed during the tests are green, and lines that were never executed are marked in red. A number in the margin indicates the number of times a given line was executed. Finally, yellow shading in the margin is used to indicate insufficient conditional coverage (for example, an `if` statement that was only tested with one outcome).

Measuring Code Coverage with Clover

Clover is an excellent commercial code coverage tool from Atlassian (*http://www.atlas sian.com/software/clover*). Clover works well for projects using Ant, Maven, and even

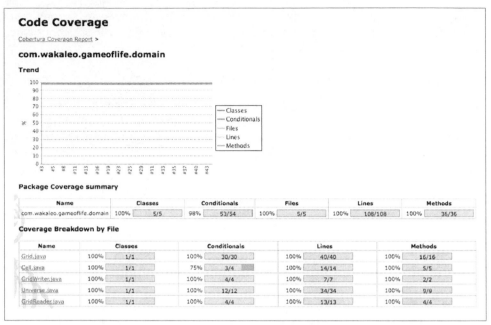

Figure 6-16. Displaying code coverage metrics

Grails. The configuration and use of Clover is well documented on the Atlassian website, so we won't describe these aspects in detail. However, to give some context, here is what a typically Maven 2 configuration of Clover for use with Jenkins would look like:

```
<build>
  ...
  <plugins>
    ...
    <plugin>
      <groupId>com.atlassian.maven.plugins</groupId>
      <artifactId>maven-clover2-plugin</artifactId>
      <version>3.0.4</version>
      <configuration>
        <includesTestSourceRoots>false</includesTestSourceRoots>
        <generateXml>true</generateXml>
      </configuration>
    </plugin>
  </plugins>
</build>
...
```

This will generate both an HTML and XML coverage report, including aggregated data if the Maven project contains multiple modules.

To integrate Clover into Jenkins, you need to install the Jenkins Clover plugin in the usual manner using the Plugin Manager screen. Once you have restarted Jenkins, you will be able to integrate Clover code coverage into your builds.

Running Clover on your project is a multistep project: you instrument your application code, run your tests, aggregate the test data (for multimodule Maven projects) and generate the HTML and XML reports. Since this can be a fairly slow operation, you typically run it as part of a separate build job, and not with your normal tests. You can do this as follows:

```
$ clover2:setup test clover2:aggregate clover2:clover
```

Next, you need to set up the Clover reporting in Jenkins. Tick the Publish Clover Coverage Report checkbox to set this up. The configuration is similar to that of Cobertura—you need to provide the path to the Clover HTML report directory, and to the XML report file, and you can also define threshold values for sunny and stormy weather, and for unstable builds (see Figure 6-17).

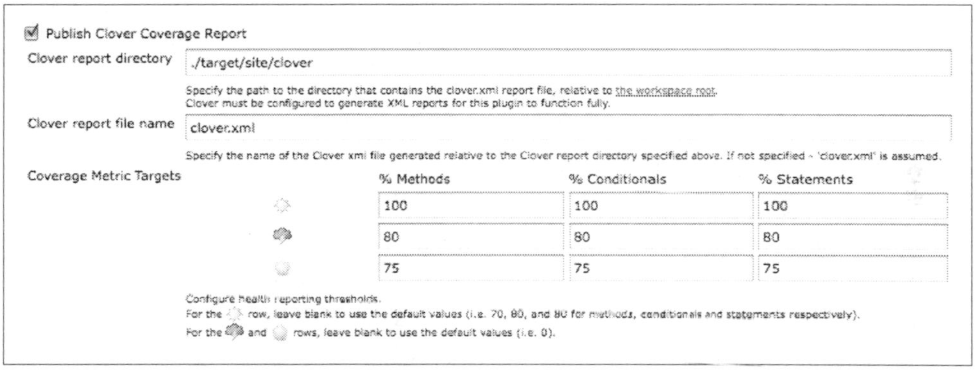

Figure 6-17. Configuring Clover reporting in Jenkins

Once you have done this, Jenkins will display the current level of code coverage, as well as a graph of the code coverage over time, on your project build job home page (see Figure 6-18).

Automated Acceptance Tests

Automated acceptance tests play an important part in many agile projects, both for verification and for communication. As a verification tool, acceptance tests perform a similar role to integration tests, and aim to demonstrate that the application effectively does what is expected of it. But this is almost a secondary aspect of automated Acceptance Tests. The primary focus is actually on communication—demonstrating to nondevelopers (business owners, business analysts, testers, and so forth) precisely where the project is at.

Acceptance tests should not be mixed with developer-focused tests, as both their aim and their audience is very different. Acceptance tests should be working examples of how the system works, with an emphasis on demonstration rather than exhaustive proof. The exhaustive tests should be done at the unit-testing level.

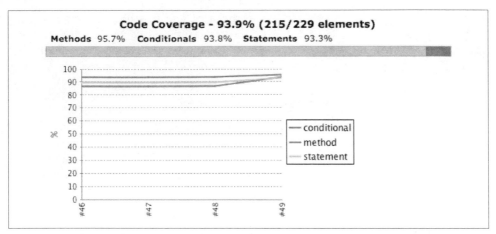

Figure 6-18. Clover code coverage trends

Acceptance Tests can be automated using conventional tools such as JUnit, but there is a growing tendency to use Behavior-Driven Development (BDD) frameworks for this purpose, as they tend to be a better fit for the public-facing nature of Acceptance Tests. Behavior-driven development tools used for automated Acceptance Tests typically generate HTML reports with a specific layout that is well-suited to nondevelopers. They often also produce JUnit-compatible reports that can be understood directly by Jenkins.

Behavior-Driven Development frameworks also have the notion of "Pending tests," tests that are automated, but have not yet been implemented by the development team. This distinction plays an important role in communication with other non-developer stakeholders: if you can automated these tests early on in the process, they can give an excellent indicator of which features have been implemented, which work, and which have not been started yet.

As a rule, your Acceptance Tests should be displayed separately from the other more conventional automated tests. If they use the same testing framework as your normal tests (e.g., JUnit), make sure they are executed in a dedicated build job, so that non-developers can view them and concentrate on the business-focused tests without being distracted by low-level or technical ones. It can also help to adopt business-focused and behavioural naming conventions for your tests and test classes, to make them more accessible to non-developers (see Figure 6-19). The way you name your tests and test classes can make a huge difference when it comes to reading the test reports and understanding the actual business features and behavior that is being tested.

If you are using a tool that generates HTML reports, you can display them in the same build as your conventional tests, as long as they appear in a separate report. Jenkins provides a very convenient plugin for this sort of HTML report, called the HTML Publisher plugin (see Figure 6-20). While it is still your job to ensure that your build produces the right reports, Jenkins can display the reports on your build job page, making them easily accessible to all team members.

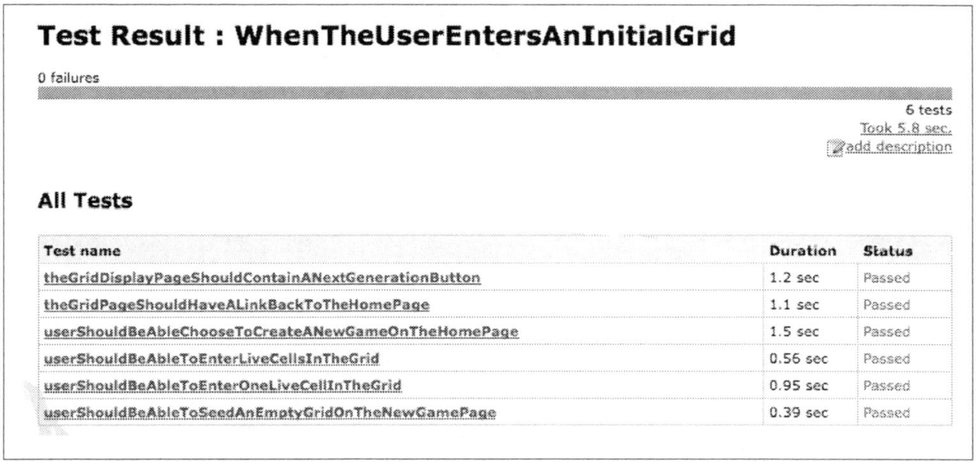

Test Result : WhenTheUserEntersAnInitialGrid

0 failures

6 tests
Took 5.8 sec.
add description

All Tests

Test name	Duration	Status
theGridDisplayPageShouldContainANextGenerationButton	1.2 sec	Passed
theGridPageShouldHaveALinkBackToTheHomePage	1.1 sec	Passed
userShouldBeAbleChooseToCreateANewGameOnTheHomePage	1.5 sec	Passed
userShouldBeAbleToEnterLiveCellsInTheGrid	0.56 sec	Passed
userShouldBeAbleToEnterOneLiveCellInTheGrid	0.95 sec	Passed
userShouldBeAbleToSeedAnEmptyGridOnTheNewGamePage	0.39 sec	Passed

Figure 6-19. Using business-focused, behavior-driven naming conventions for JUnit tests

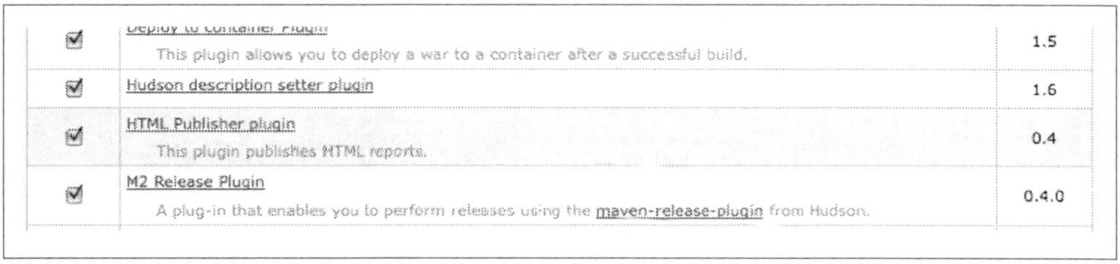

☑	Deploy to Container Plugin This plugin allows you to deploy a war to a container after a successful build.	1.5
☑	Hudson description setter plugin	1.6
☑	HTML Publisher plugin This plugin publishes HTML reports.	0.4
☑	M2 Release Plugin A plug-in that enables you to perform releases using the **maven-release-plugin** from Hudson.	0.4.0

Figure 6-20. Installing the HTML Publisher plugin

This plugin is easy to configure. Just go to the "Post-build Actions" section and tick the "Publish HTML reports" checkbox (see Figure 6-21). Next, give Jenkins the directory your HTML reports were generated to, an index page, and a title for your report. You can also ask Jenkins to store the reports generated for each build, or only keep the latest one.

Figure 6-21. Publishing HTML reports

Once this is done, Jenkins will display a special icon on your build job home page, with a link to your HTML report. In Figure 6-22, you can see the easyb reports we configured previously in action.

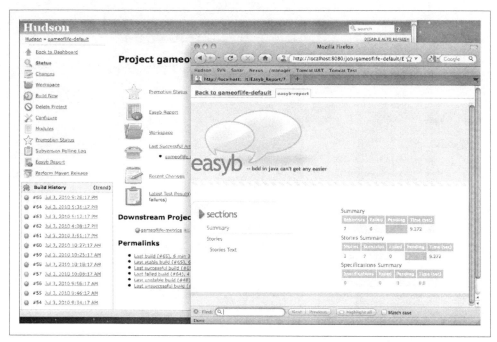

Figure 6-22. Jenkins displays a special link on the build job home page for your report

The HTML Publisher plugin works perfectly for HTML reports. If, on the other hand, you want to (also) publish non-HTML documents, such as text files, PDFs, and so forth, then the DocLinks plugin is for you. This plugin is similar to the HTML Publisher plugin, but lets you archive both HTML reports as well as documents in other formats. For example, in Figure 6-23, we have configured a build job to archive both a PDF document and an HTML report. Both these documents will now be listed on the build home page.

Automated Performance Tests with JMeter

Application performance is another important area of testing. Performance testing can be used to verify many things, such as how quickly an application responds to requests with a given number of simultaneous users, or how well the application copes with an increasing number of users. Many applications have Service Level Agreements, or SLAs, which define contractually how well they should perform.

Performance testing is often a one-off, ad-hoc activity, only undertaken right at the end of the project or when things start to go wrong. Nevertheless, performance issues are like any other sort of bug—the later on in the process they are detected, the more costly they are to fix. It therefore makes good of sense to automate these performance and

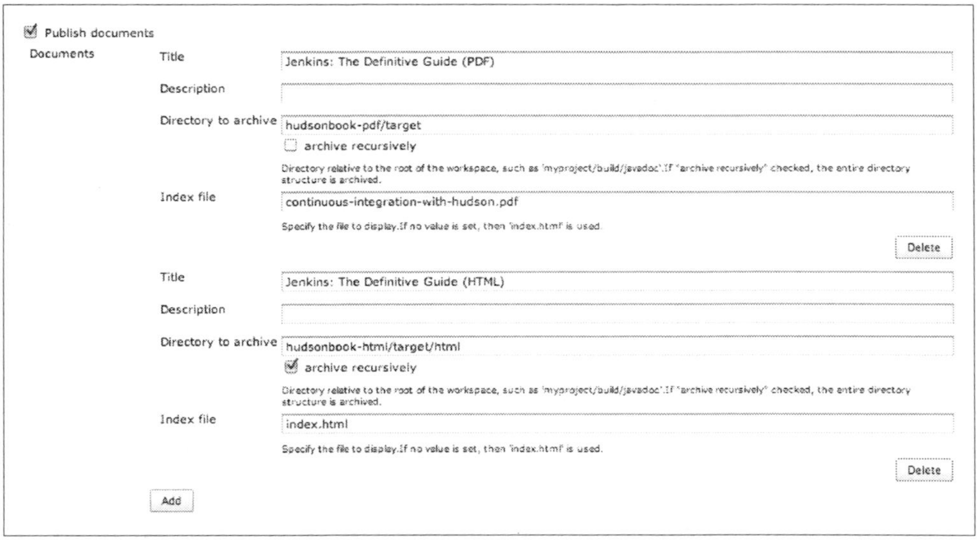

Figure 6-23. The DocLinks plugin lets you archive both HTML and non-HTML artifacts

load tests, so that you can spot any areas of degrading performance before it gets out into the wild.

JMeter (*http://jakarta.apache.org/jmeter/*) is a popular open source performance and load testing tool. It works by simulating load on your application, and measuring the response time as the number of simulated users and requests increase. It effectively simulates the actions of a browser or client application, sending requests of various sorts (HTTP, SOAP, JDBC, JMS and so on) to your server. You configure a set of requests to be sent to your application, as well as random pauses, conditions and loops, and other variations designed to better imitate real user actions.

JMeter runs as a Swing application, in which you can configure your test scripts (see Figure 6-24). You can even run JMeter as a proxy, and then manipulate your application in an ordinary browser to prepare an initial version of your test script.

A full tutorial on using JMeter is beyond the scope of this book. However, it is fairly easy to learn, and you can find ample details about how to use it on the JMeter website. With a little work, you can have a very respectable test script up and running in a matter of hours.

What we are interested in here is the process of automating these performance tests. There are several ways to integrate JMeter tests into your Jenkins build process. Although at the time of writing, there was no official JMeter plugin for Maven available in the Maven repositories, there is an Ant plugin. So the simplest approach is to write an Ant script to run your performance tests, and then either call this Ant script directly, or (if you are using a Maven project, and want to run JMeter through Maven) use the Maven Ant integration to invoke the Ant script from within Maven. A simple Ant script running some JMeter tests is illustrated here:

```
<project default="jmeter">
    <path id="jmeter.lib.path">
        <pathelement location="${basedir}/tools/jmeter/extras/ant-jmeter-1.0.9.jar"/>
    </path>

    <taskdef name="jmeter"
            classname="org.programmerplanet.ant.taskdefs.jmeter.JMeterTask"
            classpathref="jmeter.lib.path" />


    <target name="jmeter">
        <jmeter jmeterhome="${basedir}/tools/jmeter"
                testplan="${basedir}/src/test/jmeter/gameoflife.jmx"
                resultlog="${basedir}/target/jmeter-results.jtl">
            <jvmarg value="-Xmx512m" />
        </jmeter>
    </target>
</project>
```

This assumes that the JMeter installation is available in the *tools* directory of your project. Placing tools such as JMeter within your project structure is a good habit, as it makes your build scripts more portable and easier to run on any machine, which is precisely what we need to run them on Jenkins.

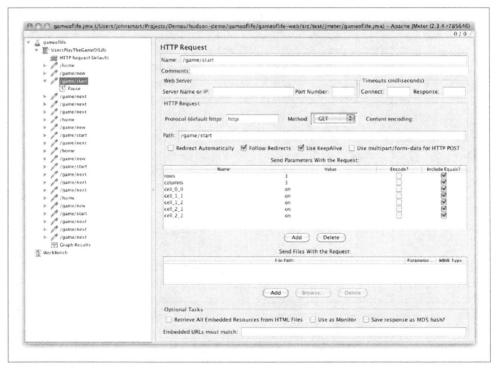

Figure 6-24. Preparing a performance test script in JMeter

Note that we are also using the optional `<jvmarg>` tag to provide JMeter with an ample amount of memory—performance testing is a memory-hungry activity.

The script shown here will execute the JMeter performance tests against a running application. So you need to ensure that the application you want to test is up and running before you start the tests. There are several ways to do this. For more heavy-weight performance tests, you will usually want to deploy your application to a test server before running the tests. For most applications this is not usually too difficult—the Maven Cargo plugin, for example, lets you automate the deployment process to a variety of local and remote servers. We will also see how to do this in Jenkins later on in the book.

Alternatively, if you are using Maven for a web application, you can use the Jetty or Cargo plugin to ensure that the application is deployed before the integration tests start, and then call the JMeter Ant script from within Maven during the integration test phase. Using Jetty, for example, you could so something like this:

```
<project...>
  <build>
    <plugins>
      <plugin>
        <groupId>org.mortbay.jetty</groupId>
        <artifactId>jetty-maven-plugin</artifactId>
        <version>7.1.0.v20100505</version>
        <configuration>
          <scanIntervalSeconds>10</scanIntervalSeconds>
          <connectors>
            <connector
              implementation="org.eclipse.jetty.server.nio.SelectChannelConnector">
              <port>${jetty.port}</port>
              <maxIdleTime>60000</maxIdleTime>
            </connector>
          </connectors>
          <stopKey>foo</stopKey>
          <stopPort>9999</stopPort>
        </configuration>
        <executions>
          <execution>
            <id>start-jetty</id>
            <phase>pre-integration-test</phase>
            <goals>
              <goal>run</goal>
            </goals>
            <configuration>
              <scanIntervalSeconds>0</scanIntervalSeconds>
              <daemon>true</daemon>
            </configuration>
          </execution>
          <execution>
            <id>stop-jetty</id>
            <phase>post-integration-test</phase>
            <goals>
              <goal>stop</goal>
```

```
            </goals>
          </execution>
        </executions>
      </plugin>
      ...
    </plugins>
  </build>
</project>
```

This will start up an instance of Jetty and deploy your web application to it just before the integration tests, and shut it down afterwards.

Finally, you need to run the JMeter performance tests during this phase. You can do this by using the *maven-antrun-plugin* to invoke the Ant script we wrote earlier on during the integration test phase:

```
<project...>
  ...
  <profiles>
    <profile>
      <id>performance</id>
      <build>
        <plugins>
          <plugin>
            <artifactId>maven-antrun-plugin</artifactId>
            <version>1.4</version>
            <executions>
              <execution>
                <id>run-jmeter</id>
                <phase>integration-test</phase>
                <goals>
                  <goal>run</goal>
                </goals>
                <configuration>
                  <tasks>
                    <ant antfile="build.xml" target="jmeter" >
                  </tasks>
                </configuration>
              </execution>
            </executions>
          </plugin>
        </plugins>
      </build>
    </profile>
  </profiles>
  ...
</project>
```

Now, all you need to do is to run the integration tests with the performance profile to get Maven to run the JMeter test suite. You can do this by invoking the *integration-test* or *verify* Maven life cycle phase:

```
$ mvn verify -Pperformance
```

Once you have configured your build script to handle JMeter, you can set up a performance test build in Jenkins. For this, we will use the Performance Test Jenkins plugin, which understands JMeter logs and can generate nice statistics and graphs using this data. So go to the Plugin Manager screen on your Jenkins server and install this plugin (see Figure 6-25). When you have installed the plugin, you will need to restart Jenkins.

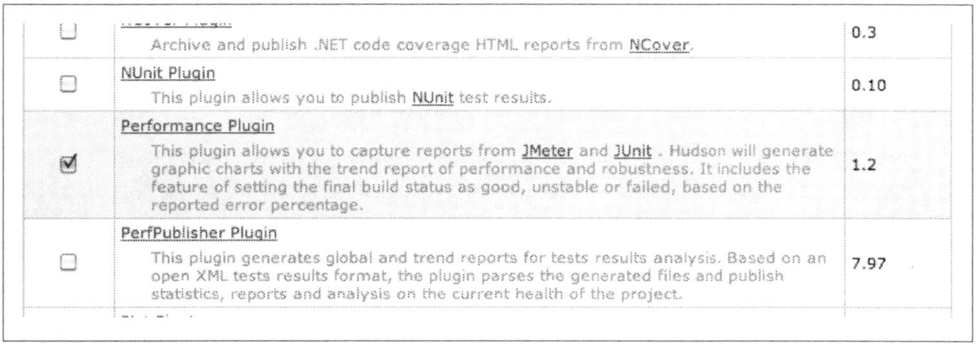

Archive and publish .NET code coverage HTML reports from NCover.
0.3
NUnit Plugin
This plugin allows you to publish NUnit test results.
0.10
Performance Plugin
This plugin allows you to capture reports from JMeter and JUnit . Hudson will generate graphic charts with the trend report of performance and robustness. It includes the feature of setting the final build status as good, unstable or failed, based on the reported error percentage.
1.2
PerfPublisher Plugin
This plugin generates global and trend reports for tests results analysis. Based on an open XML tests results format, the plugin parses the generated files and publish statistics, reports and analysis on the current health of the project.
7.97

Figure 6-25. Preparing a performance test script in JMeter

Once you have the plugin installed, you can set up a performance build job in Jenkins. This build job will typically be fairly separate from your other builds. In Figure 6-26, we have set up the performance build to run on a nightly basis, which is probably enough for a long-running load or performance test.

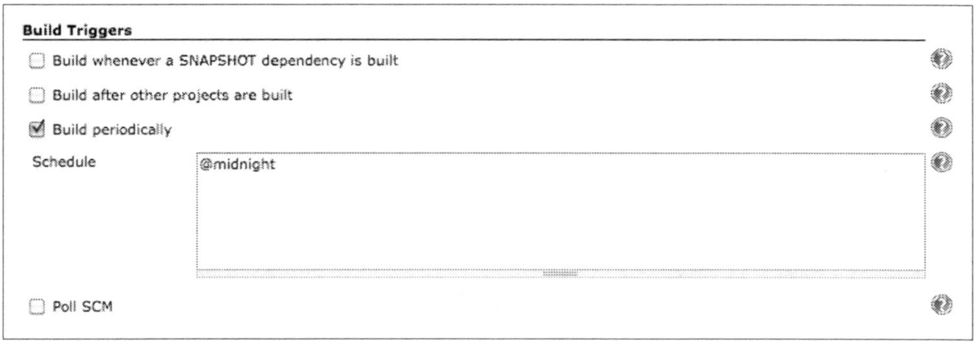

Build Triggers
Build whenever a SNAPSHOT dependency is built
Build after other projects are built
Build periodically
Schedule
@midnight
Poll SCM

Figure 6-26. Setting up the performance build to run every night at midnight

All that remains is to configure the build job to run your performance tests. In Figure 6-27, we are running the Maven build we configured earlier on. Note that we are using the MAVEN_OPTS field (accessible by clicking on the Advanced button) to provide plenty of memory for the build job.

To set up performance reporting, just tick the "Publish Performance test result report" option in the Post-build Actions section (see Figure 6-28). You will need to tell Jenkins

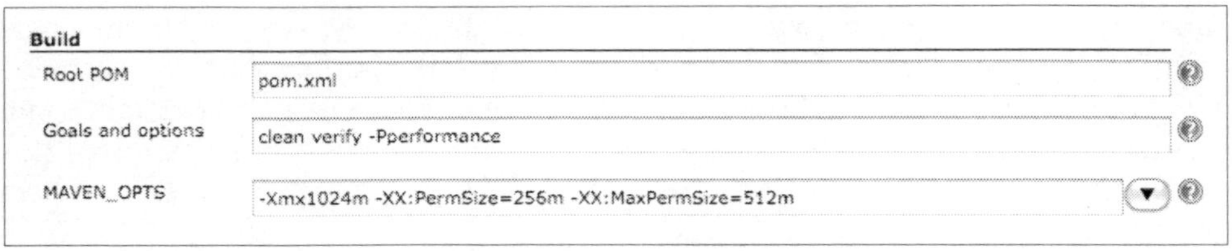

Figure 6-27. Performance tests can require large amounts of memory

where to find your JMeter test results (the output files, not the test scripts). The Performance plugin is happy to process multiple JMeter results, so you can put wildcards in the path to make sure all of your JMeter reports are displayed.

If you take your performance metrics seriously, then the build should fail if the required SLA is not met. In a Continuous Integration environment, any sort of metrics build that does not fail if minimum quality criteria are not met will tend to be ignored.

You can configure the Performance plugin to mark a build as unstable or failing if a certain percentage of requests result in errors. By default, these values will only be raised in the event of real application errors (i.e., bugs) or server crashes. However you really should configure your JMeter test scripts to place a ceiling on the maximum acceptable response time for your requests. This is particularly important if your application has contractual obligations in this regard. One way to do this in JMeter is by adding a Duration Assertion element to your script. This will cause an error if any request takes longer than a certain fixed time to execute.

Figure 6-28. Configuring the Performance plugin in your build job

Now, when the build job runs, the Performance plugin will produce graphs keeping track of overall response times and of the number of errors (see Figure 6-29). There will be a separate graph for each JMeter report you have generated. If there is only one graph, it will appear on the build home page; otherwise you can view them on a dedicated page that you can access via the Performance Trend menu item.

This graph gives you an overview of performance over time. You would typically use this graph to ensure that your average response times are within the expected limits, and also spot any unusually high variations in the average or maximum response times.

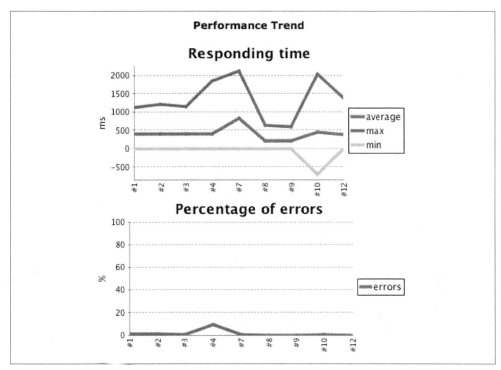

Figure 6-29. The Jenkins Performance plugin keeps track of response time and errors

However if you need to track down and isolate performance issues, the Performance Breakdown screen can be more useful. From within the Performance Trend report, click on the Last Report link at the top of the screen. This will display a breakdown of response times and errors per request (see Figure 6-30). You can do the same thing for previous builds, by clicking on the Performance Report link in the build details page.

With some minor variations, a JMeter test script basically works by simulating a given number of simultaneous users. Typically, however, you will want to see how your application performs for different numbers of users. The Jenkins Performance plugin handles this quite well, and can process graphs for multiple JMeter reports. Just make sure you use a wildcard expression when you tell Jenkins where to find the reports.

Of course, it would be nice to be able to reuse the same JMeter test script for each test run. JMeter supports parameters, so you can easily reuse the same JMeter script with different numbers of simulated users. You just use a property expression in your JMeter script, and then pass the property to JMeter when you run the script. If your property is called `request.threads`, then the property expression in your JMeter script would be `${__property(request.threads)}`. Then, you can use the `<property>` element in the `<jmeter>` Ant task to pass the property when you run the script. The following Ant target, for example, runs JMeter three times, for 200, 500 and 1000 simultaneous users:

```
<target name="jmeter">
  <jmeter jmeterhome="${basedir}/tools/jmeter"
          testplan="${basedir}/src/test/jmeter/gameoflife.jmx"
          resultlog="${basedir}/target/jmeter-results-200-users.jtl">
    <jvmarg value="-Xmx512m" />
    <property name="request.threads" value="200"/>
    <property name="request.loop" value="20"/>
  </jmeter>
  <jmeter jmeterhome="${basedir}/tools/jmeter"
          testplan="${basedir}/src/test/jmeter/gameoflife.jmx"
          resultlog="${basedir}/target/jmeter-results-500-users.jtl">
    <jvmarg value="-Xmx512m" />
    <property name="request.threads" value="500"/>
    <property name="request.loop" value="20"/>
  </jmeter>
  <jmeter jmeterhome="${basedir}/tools/jmeter"
          testplan="${basedir}/src/test/jmeter/gameoflife.jmx"
          resultlog="${basedir}/target/jmeter-results-1000-users.jtl">
    <jvmarg value="-Xmx512m" />
    <property name="request.threads" value="1000"/>
    <property name="request.loop" value="20"/>
  </jmeter>
</target>
```

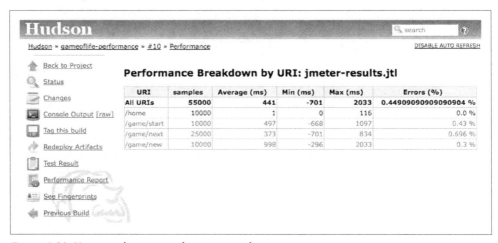

Figure 6-30. *You can also view performance results per request*

Help! My Tests Are Too Slow!

One of the underlying principles of designing your CI builds is that the value of information about a build failure diminishes rapidly with time. In other words, the longer the news of a build failure takes to get to you, the less it is worth, and the harder it is to fix.

Indeed, if your functional or integration tests are taking several hours to run, chances are they won't be run for every change. They are more likely to be scheduled as a nightly build. The problem with this is that a lot can happen in twenty-four hours, and, if the nightly build fails, it will be difficult to figure out which of the many changes committed to version control during the day was responsible. This is a serious issue, and penalizes your CI server's ability to provide the fast feedback that makes it useful.

Of course some builds *are* slow, by their very nature. Performance or load tests fall into this category, as do some more heavyweight code quality metrics builds for large projects. However, integration and functional tests most definitely do *not* fall into this category. You should do all you can to make these tests as fast as possible. Under ten minutes is probably acceptable for a full integration/functional test suite. Two hours is not.

So, if you find yourself needing to speed up your tests, here are a few strategies that might help, in approximate order of difficulty.

Add More Hardware

Sometimes the easiest way to speed up your builds is to throw more hardware into the mix. This could be as simple as upgrading your build server. Compared to the time and effort saved in identifying and fixing integration-related bugs, the cost of buying a shiny new build server is relatively modest.

Another option is to consider using virtual or cloud-based approach. Later on in the book, we will see how you can use VMWare virtual machines or cloud-based infrastructure such as Amazon Web Services (EC2) or CloudBees to increase your build capacity on an "as-needed" basis, without having to invest in permanent new machines.

This approach can also involve distributing your builds across several servers. While this will not in itself speed up your tests, it may result in faster feedback if your build server is under heavy demand, and if build jobs are constantly being queued.

Run Fewer Integration/Functional Tests

In many applications, integration or functional tests are used by default as the standard way to test almost all aspects of the system. However integration and functional tests are not the best way to detect and identify bugs. Because of the large number of components involved in a typical end-to-end test, it can be very hard to know where something has gone wrong. In addition, with so many moving parts, it is extremely difficult, if not completely unfeasible, to cover all of the possible paths through the application.

For this reason, wherever possible, you should prefer quick-running unit tests to the much slower integration and functional tests. When you are confident that the individual components work well, you can complete the picture by a few end-to-end tests that step through common use cases for the system, or use cases that have caused problems in the past. This will help ensure that the components do fit together correctly, which is, after all, what integration tests are supposed to do. But leave the more comprehensive tests where possible to unit tests. This strategy is probably the most sustainable approach to keeping your feedback loop short, but it does require some discipline and effort.

Run Your Tests in Parallel

If your functional tests take two hours to run, it is unlikely that they all need to be run back-to-back. It is also unlikely that they will be consuming all of the available CPU on your build machine. So breaking your integration tests into smaller batches and running them in parallel makes a lot of sense.

There are several strategies you can try, and your mileage will probably vary depending on the nature of your application. One approach, for example, is to set up several build jobs to run different subsets of your functional tests, and to run these jobs in parallel. Jenkins lets you aggregate test results. This is a good way to take advantage of a distributed build architecture to speed up your builds even further. Essential to this strategy is the ability to run subsets of your tests in isolation, which may require some refactoring.

At a lower level, you can also run your tests in parallel at the build scripting level. As we saw earlier, both TestNG and the more recent versions of JUnit support running tests in parallel. Nevertheless, you will need to ensure that your tests can be run concurrently, which may take some refactoring. For example, common files or shared instance variables within test cases will cause problems here.

In general, you need to be careful of interactions between your tests. If your web tests start up an embedded web server such as Jetty, for example, you need to make sure the port used is different for each set of concurrent tests.

Nevertheless, if you can get it to work for your application, running your tests in parallel is one of the more effective way to speed up your tests.

Conclusion

Automated testing is a critical part of any Continuous Integration environment, and should be taken very seriously. As in other areas on CI, and perhaps even more so, feedback is king, so it is important to ensure that your tests run fast, even the integration and functional ones.

CHAPTER 7

Securing Jenkins

Introduction

Jenkins supports several security models, and can integrate with several user repositories. In smaller organizations, where developers work in close proximity, security on your Jenkins machine may not be a large concern—you may simply want to prevent unidentified users tampering with your build job configurations. For larger organizations, with multiple teams, a stricter approach might be required, where only team members and system administrators are allowed to modify their build job configurations. And in situations where the Jenkins server may be exposed to a broader audience, such as on an internal corporate website, or even on the Internet, certain build jobs may be visible to all users whereas others will need to be hidden to unauthorized users.

In this chapter, we will look at how to configure different security configurations in Jenkins, for different environments and circumstances.

Activating Security in Jenkins

Setting up basic security in Jenkins is easy enough. Go to the main configuration page and check the Enable security checkbox (see Figure 7-1). This will display a number of options, that we will investigate in detail in this chapter. The first section, Security Realms, determines where Jenkins will look for users during authentication, and includes options such as using users stored in an LDAP server, using the underlying Unix user accounts (assuming, of course, that Jenkins is running on a Unix machine), or using a simple built-in user database managed by Jenkins.

The second section, Authorization, determines what users can do once they are logged in. This ranges from simple options like "Anyone can do anything" or "Logged-in users can do anything," to more sophisticated role and project-based authorization policies.

In the remainder of this chapter, we will look at how to configure Jenkins security for a number of common scenarios.

Figure 7-1. Enabling security in Jenkins

Simple Security in Jenkins

The most simple usable security model in Jenkins involves allowing authenticated users to do anything, whereas non-authenticated users will just have a read-only view of the build jobs. This is great for small teams—developers can manage the build jobs, whereas other users (testers, BAs, project managers and so on) can view the build jobs as required to view the status of the project. Indeed, certain build jobs may be set up just for this purpose, displaying the results of automated acceptance tests or code quality metrics, for example.

You can set up this sort of configuration to choose "Logged-in users can do anything" in the Authorization section. There are several ways that Jenkins can authenticate users (see "Security Realms—Identifying Jenkins Users" on page 171), but for this example, we will be using the simplest option, which is to use Jenkins's own built in database (see "Using Jenkins's Built-in User Database" on page 171). This is the configuration illustrated in Figure 7-1.

Make sure you tick the "Allow users to sign up" option. This option will display a Sign up link at the top of the screen to let users create their own user account as required (see Figure 7-2). It is a good idea for developers to use their SCM username here: in this case, Jenkins will be able to work out what users contributed to the SCM changes that triggered a particular build.

This approach is obviously a little too simple for many situations—it is useful for small teams working in close proximity, where the aim is to know who's changes caused (or broke) a particular build, rather than to manage access in any more restrictive way. In

Figure 7-2. The Jenkins Sign up page

the following sections, we will discuss the two orthogonal aspects of Jenkins security: identifying your users (Security Realms) and determining what they are allowed to (Authorization).

Security Realms—Identifying Jenkins Users

Jenkins lets you identify and manage users in a number of ways, ranging from a simple, built-in user database suitable for small teams to integration with enterprise directories, with many other options in between.

Using Jenkins's Built-in User Database

The easiest way to manage user accounts in Jenkins is to use Jenkins's internal user database. This is a good option if you want to keep things simple, as very little setup or configuration is required. Users who need to log on to the Jenkins server can sign up and create an account for themselves, and, depending on the security model chosen, an administrator can then decide what these users are allowed to do.

Jenkins automatically adds all SCM users to this database whenever a change is committed to source code monitored by Jenkins. These user names are used mainly to record who is responsible for each build job. You can view the list of currently known users by clicking on the People menu entry (see Figure 7-3). Here, you can visualize the users that Jenkins currently knows about, and also see the last project they committed changes to. Note that this list contains all of the users who have ever committed changes to the projects that Jenkins monitors—they may not be (and usually aren't) all active Jenkins users who are able to log on to the Jenkins server.

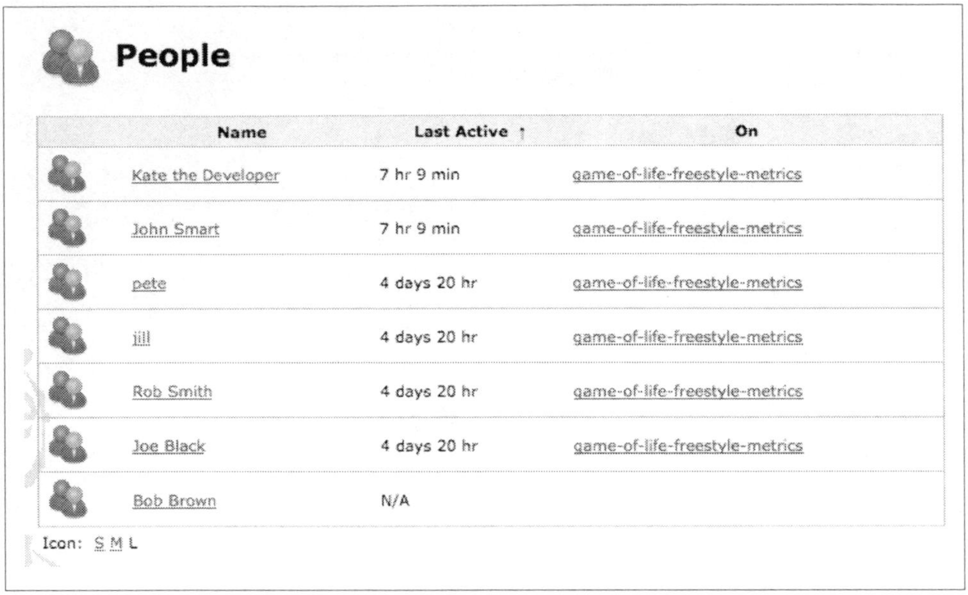

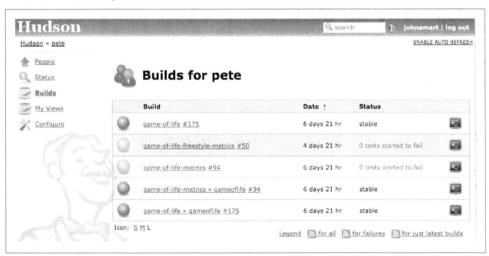

Figure 7-3. The list of users known to Jenkins

If you click on a user in this list, Jenkins takes you to a page displaying various details about this user, including the user's full name and the build jobs they have contributed to (see Figure 7-4). From here, you can also modify or complete the details about this user, such as their password or email address.

Figure 7-4. Displaying the builds that a user participates in

A user appearing in this list cannot necessarily log on to Jenkins. To be able to log on to Jenkins, the user account needs to be set up with a password. There are essentially two ways to do this. If you have activated the "Allow users to sign up" option, users can simply sign up with their SCM user name and provide their email address and a password (see "Simple Security in Jenkins" on page 170). Alternatively, you can activate a user by clicking on the Configure menu option in the user details screen, and provide an email address and password yourself (see Figure 7-5).

Figure 7-5. Creating a new user account by signing up

It is worth noting that, if your email addresses are synchronized with your version control user names (for example, if you work at acme.com, and user "joe" in your version control system has an email address of *joe@acme.com*), you can get Jenkins to derive the email address from a user name by adding a suffix that you configure in the Email Notification section (see Figure 7-6). If you have set up this sort of configuration, you don't need to specify the email address for new users unless it does not respect this convention.

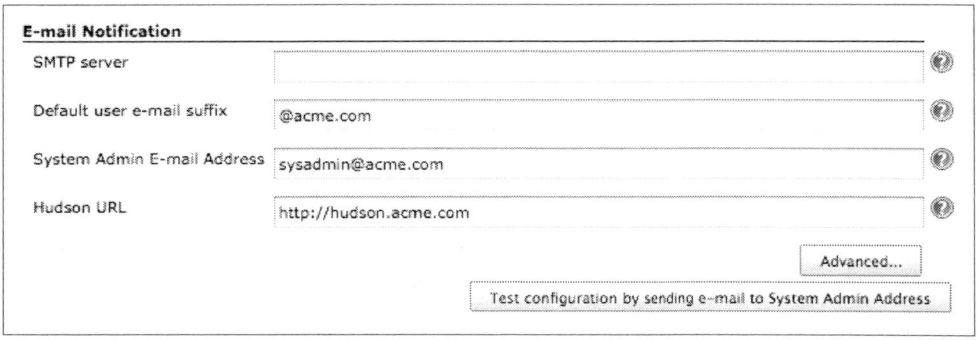

Figure 7-6. Synchronizing email addresses

Another way to manage the current active users (those who can actually log on to Jenkins) is by clicking on the Manage Users link in the main Jenkins configuration page (see Figure 7-7).

Figure 7-7. You can also manage Jenkins users from the Jenkins configuration page

From here, you can view and edit the users who can log in to Jenkins (see Figure 7-8). This includes both users that have signed up manually (if this option has been activated) and SCM users that you have activated by configuring them with a password. You can also edit a user's details (for example modifying their email address or resetting their password), or even remove them from the list of active users. Doing this will not remove them from the overall user list (their name will still appear in the build history, for example), but they will no longer be able to log on to the Jenkins server.

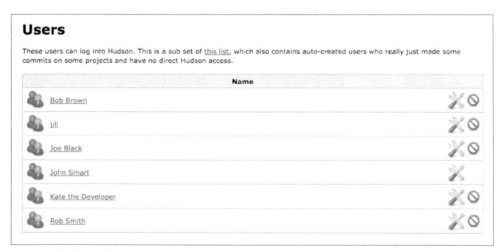

Figure 7-8. The Jenkins user database

The internal Jenkins database is sufficient for many teams and organizations. However, for larger organizations, it may become tedious and repetitive to manage large numbers of user accounts by hand, especially if this information already exists elsewhere. In the following sections, we will look at how to hook Jenkins up to other user management systems, such as LDAP repositories and Unix users and groups.

Using an LDAP Repository

Many organizations use LDAP directories to store user accounts and passwords across applications. Jenkins integrates well with LDAP, with no special plugins required. It can authenticate users using the LDAP repository, check group membership, and retrieve the email address of authenticated users.

To integrate Jenkins with your LDAP repository, Just select "LDAP" in the Security Realm section, and fill in the appropriate details about your LDAP server (see Figure 7-9). The most important field is the repository server. If you are using a non-standard port, you will need to provide this as well (for example, *ldap.acme.org: 1389*). Or, if you are using LDAPS, you will need to specify this as well (for example, *ldaps://ldap.acme.org*)

If your server supports anonymous binding, this will probably be enough to get you started. If not, you can use the Advanced options to fine-tune your configuration.

Most of the Advanced fields can safely be left blank unless you have a good reason to change them. If your repository is extremely large, you may want to specify a root DN value (e.g., dc=acme, dc=com) and/or a User and Group search base (e.g., ou=people) to narrow down the scope of user queries. This is not usually required unless you notice performance issues. Or, if your server does not support anonymous binding, you will need to provide a Manager DN and a Manager DN password, so that Jenkins can connect to the server to perform its queries.

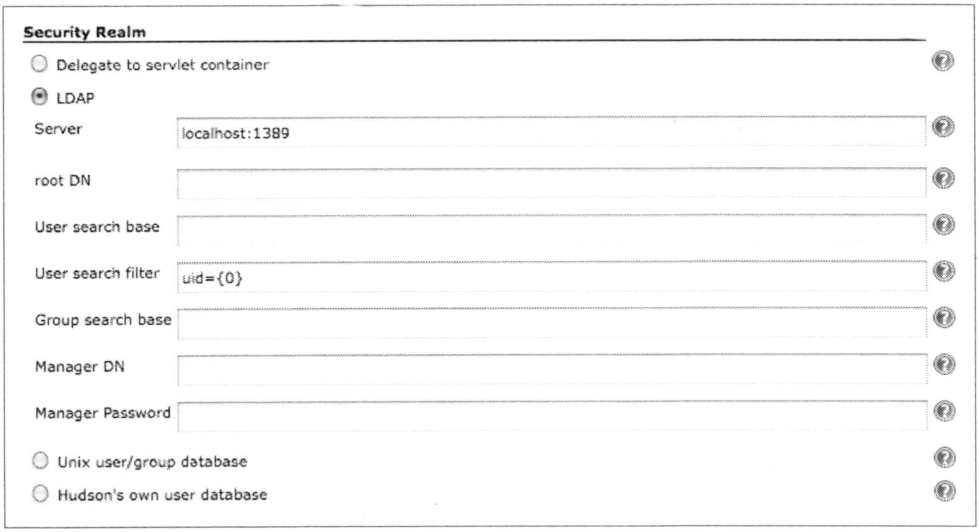

Figure 7-9. Configuring LDAP in Jenkins

Once you have set up LDAP as your Security Realm, you can configure your favorite security model as described previously. When users log on to Jenkins, they will be authenticated against the LDAP repository.

You can also use LDAP groups, though the configuration is not immediately obvious. Suppose you have defined a group called JenkinsAdmin in your LDAP repository, with a DN of `cn=JenkinsAdmin, ou-Groups, dc=acme, dc=com`. To refer to this group in Jenkins, you need to take the common name (cn) in uppercase, and prefix it with `ROLE_`. So `cn=JenkinsAdmin` becomes `ROLE_JENKINSADMIN`. You can see an example of LDAP groups used in this way in Figure 7-10.

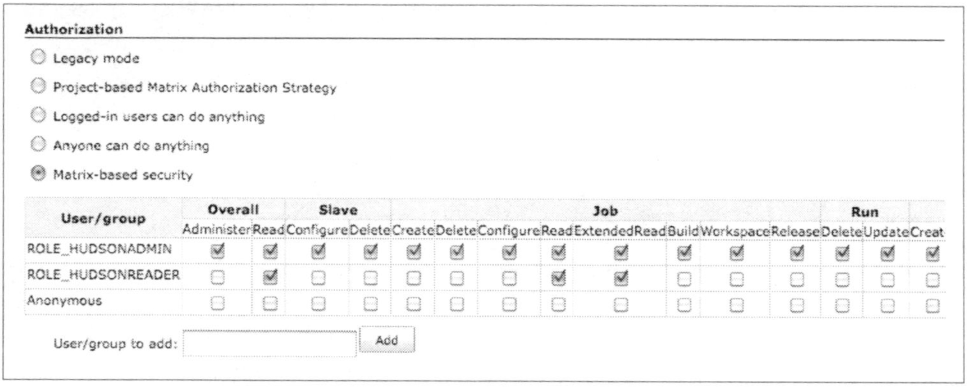

Authorization

- ○ Legacy mode
- ○ Project-based Matrix Authorization Strategy
- ○ Logged-in users can do anything
- ○ Anyone can do anything
- ◉ Matrix-based security

User/group	Overall		Slave			Job							Run		
	Administer	Read	Configure	Delete	Create	Delete	Configure	Read	ExtendedRead	Build	Workspace	Release	Delete	Update	Creat
ROLE_HUDSONADMIN	☑	☑	☑	☑	☑	☑	☑	☑	☑	☑	☑	☑	☑	☑	☑
ROLE_HUDSONREADER	☐	☑	☐	☐	☐	☐	☐	☑	☑	☐	☐	☐	☐	☐	☐
Anonymous	☐	☐	☐	☐	☐	☐	☐	☐	☐	☐	☐	☐	☐	☐	☐

User/group to add: [_____] [Add]

Figure 7-10. Using LDAP Groups in Jenkins

Using Microsoft Active Directory

Microsoft Active Directory is a directory service product widely used in Microsoft architectures. Although Active Directory does provide an LDAP service, it can be a little tricky to set up, and it is simpler to get Jenkins to talk directly to the Active Directory server. Fortunately, there's a plugin for that.

The Jenkins Active Directory plugin lets you configure Jenkins to authenticate against a Microsoft Active Directory server. You can both authenticate users, and retrieve their groups for Matrix and Project-based authorization. Note that, unlike the conventional LDAP integration (see "Using an LDAP Repository" on page 175), there is no need to prefix group names with `ROLE_` —you can use Active Directory groups (such as "Domain Admins") directory.

To configure the plugin, you need to provide the full domain name of your Active Directory server. If you have more than one domain, you can provide a comma-separated list. If you provide the forest name (say "acme.com" instead of "europe.acme.com"), then the search will be done against the global catalog. Note that if you do this without specifying the bind DN (see below), the user would have to login as "europe\joe" or "joe@europe".

The advanced options let you specify a site name (to improve performance by restricting the domain controllers that Jenkins queries), and a Binding DN and password, which come in handy if you are connecting to a multidomain forest. You need to provide a valid Binding DN and password values, that Jenkins can use to connect to your server so that it can establish the full identity of the user being authenticated. This way, the user can simply type in "jack" or "jill", and have the system automatically figure out that they are *jack@europe.acme.com* or *jack@asia.acme.com*. You need to provide the full user principal name with domain name, like *admin@europe.acme.com*, or a LDAP-style distinguished name, such as CN=Administrator,OU=europe,DC=acme,DC=com.

Another nice thing about this plugin is that it works both in a Windows environment and in a Unix environment. So if Jenkins is running on a Unix server, it can still authenticate against a Microsoft Active Directory service running on another machine.

More precisely, if Jenkins is running on a Windows machine and you do not specify a domain, that machine must be a member of the domain you wish to authenticate against. Jenkins will use ADSI to figure out all the details, so no additional configuration is required.

On a non-Windows machine (or you specify one or more domains), you need to tell Jenkins the name of Active Directory domain(s) to authenticate with. Jenkins then uses DNS SRV records and LDAP service of Active Directory to authenticate users.

Jenkins can determine which groups in Active Directory that the user belongs to, so you can use these as part of your authorisation strategy. For example, you can use these groups in matrix-based security, or allow "Domain Admins" to administer Jenkins.

Using Unix Users and Groups

If you are running Jenkins on a Unix machine, you can also ask Jenkins to use the user and group accounts defined on this machine. In this case, users will log into Jenkins using their Unix account logins and passwords. This uses Pluggable Authentication Modules (PAM), and also works fine with NIS.

In its most basic form, this is somewhat cumbersome, as it requires new user accounts to be set up and configured for each new Jenkins user. It is only really useful if these accounts need to be set up for other purposes.

Delegating to the Servlet Container

Another way to identify Jenkins users is to let your Servlet container do it for you. This approach is useful if you are running Jenkins on a Servlet container such as Tomcat or GlassFish, and you already have an established way to integrate the Servlet container with your local enterprise user directory. Tomcat, for example, allows you to authenticate users against a relational database (using direct JDBC or a DataSource), JNDI, JAAS, or an XML configuration file. You can also use the roles defined in the Servlet container's user directory for use with Matrix and Project-based authorization strategies.

In Jenkins, this is easy to configure—just select this option in the Security Realm section (see Figure 7-11). Once you have done this, Jenkins will let the server take care of everything.

Figure 7-11. Selecting the security realm

Using Atlassian Crowd

If your organization is using Atlassian products such as JIRA and Confluence, you may also be using Crowd. Crowd is a commercial Identity Management and Single-Sign On (SSO) application from Atlassian that lets you manage single user accounts across multiple products. It lets you manage both an internal database of users, groups and roles, and integrate with external directories such as LDAP directories or custom user stores.

Using the Jenkins Crowd plugin, you can use Atlassian Crowd as the source of your Jenkins users and groups. Before you start, you need to set up a new application in Crowd (see Figure 7-12). Just set up a new Generic Application called "hudson" (or something similar), and step through the tabs. In the Connections tab, you need to provide the IP address of your Jenkins server. Then map the Crowd directories that you will be using to retrieve Jenkins user accounts and group information. Finally, you will need to tell Crowd which users from these directories can connect to Jenkins. One option is to allow all users to authenticate, and let Jenkins sort out the details. Alternatively, you can list the Crown user groups who are allowed to connect to Jenkins.

Once you have set this up, you need to install the Jenkins Crowd plugin, which you do as usual via the Jenkins Plugin Manager. Once you have installed the plugin and restarted Jenkins, you can define Crowd as your Security Realm in the main Jenkins configuration screen (see Figure 7-13).

With this plugin installed and configured, you can use users and groups from Crowd for any of the Jenkins Authorization strategies we discussed earlier on in the chapter. For example, in Figure 7-14, we are using user groups defined in Crowd to set up Matrix-based security in the main configuration screen.

Integrating with Other Systems

In addition to the authentication strategies discussed here, there are a number of other plugins that allow Jenkins to authenticate against other systems. At the time of writing,

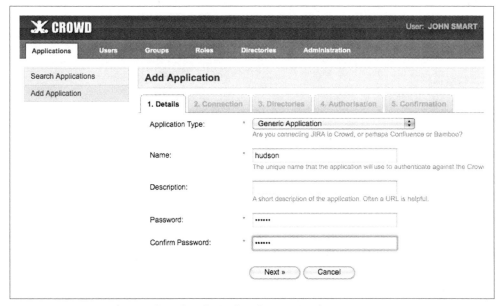

Figure 7-12. *Using Atlassian Crowd as the Jenkins Security Realm*

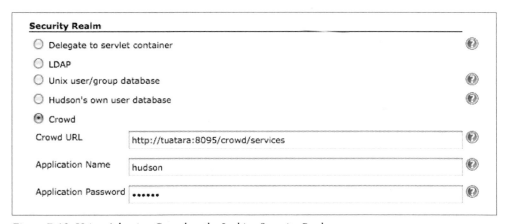

Figure 7-13. *Using Atlassian Crowd as the Jenkins Security Realm*

these include Central Authentication Service (CAS)—an open source single sign-on tool—and the Collabnet Source Forge Enterprise Edition (SFEE) server.

If no plugin is available, you can also write your own custom authentication script. To do this, you need to install the Script Security Realm plugin. Once you have installed the script and restarted Jenkins, you can write two scripts in your favorite scripting language. One script authenticates users, whereas the other determines the groups of a given user (see Figure 7-15).

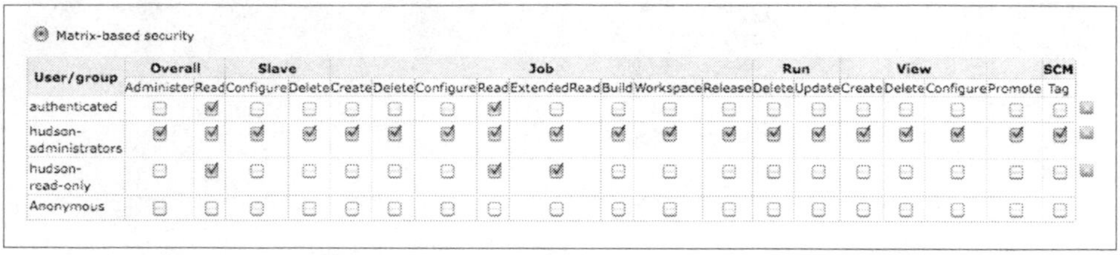

User/group	Overall				Slave			Job							Run		View				SCM
	Administer	Read	Configure	Delete	Create	Delete	Configure	Read	ExtendedRead	Build	Workspace	Release	Delete	Update	Create	Delete	Configure	Promote	Tag		
authenticated	☐	☑	☐	☐	☐	☐	☐	☑	☐	☐	☐	☐	☐	☐	☐	☐	☐	☐	☐		
hudson-administrators	☑	☑	☑	☑	☑	☑	☑	☑	☑	☑	☑	☑	☑	☑	☑	☑	☑	☑	☑		
hudson-read-only	☐	☑	☐	☐	☐	☐	☐	☑	☑	☐	☐	☐	☐	☐	☐	☐	☐	☐	☐		
Anonymous	☐	☐	☐	☐	☐	☐	☐	☐	☐	☐	☐	☐	☐	☐	☐	☐	☐	☐	☐		

Figure 7-14. Using Atlassian Crowd groups in Jenkins

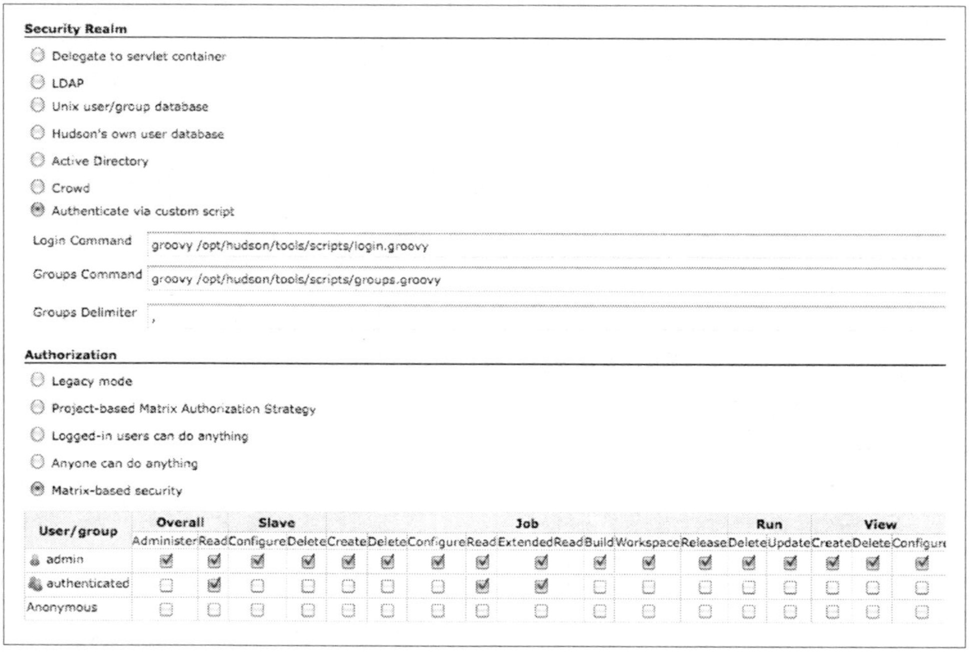

Security Realm

- ○ Delegate to servlet container
- ○ LDAP
- ○ Unix user/group database
- ○ Hudson's own user database
- ○ Active Directory
- ○ Crowd
- ◉ Authenticate via custom script

Login Command   `groovy /opt/hudson/tools/scripts/login.groovy`

Groups Command   `groovy /opt/hudson/tools/scripts/groups.groovy`

Groups Delimiter   `,`

Authorization

- ○ Legacy mode
- ○ Project-based Matrix Authorization Strategy
- ○ Logged-in users can do anything
- ○ Anyone can do anything
- ◉ Matrix-based security

User/group	Overall				Slave			Job							Run		View		
	Administer	Read	Configure	Delete	Create	Delete	Configure	Read	ExtendedRead	Build	Workspace	Release	Delete	Update	Create	Delete	Configure
admin	☑	☑	☑	☑	☑	☑	☑	☑	☑	☑	☑	☑	☑	☑	☑	☑	☑
authenticated	☐	☑	☐	☐	☐	☐	☐	☑	☑	☐	☐	☐	☐	☐	☐	☐	☐
Anonymous	☐	☐	☐	☐	☐	☐	☐	☐	☐	☐	☐	☐	☐	☐	☐	☐	☐

Figure 7-15. Using custom scripts to handle authentication

Before invoking the authentication script, Jenkins sets two environment variables: U, containing the username, and P, containing the password. This script uses these environment variables to authenticate using the specified username and password, returning 0 if the authentication is successful, and some other value otherwise. If authentication fails, the output from the process will be reported in the error message displayed to the user. Here is a simple Groovy authentication script:

```
def env = System.getenv()
def username = env['U']
def password = env['P']

println "Authenticating user $username"

if (authenticate(username, password)) {
```

```
      System.exit 0
} else {
      System.exit 1
}

def authenticate(def username, def password) {
      def userIsAuthenticated = true
      // Authentication logic goes here
      return userIsAuthenticated
}
```

This script is enough if all you have to deal with is basic authentication without groups. If you want to use groups from your custom authentication source in your Matrix-based or Project-based authorizations (see "Authorization—Who Can Do What" on page 181), you can write a second script, which determines the groups for a given user. This groups uses the U environment variable to determine which user is trying to log on, and prints a comma-separated list of groups for this user to the standard output. If you don't like commas, you can override the separating character in the configuration. A simple Groovy script to do this job is shown here:

```
def env = System.getenv()
def username = env['U']

println findGroupsFor(username)

System.exit 0

def findGroupsFor(def username) {
      return "admin,game-of-life-developer"
}
```

Both these scripts must return 0 when called for a user to be authenticated.

Authorization—Who Can Do What

Once you have defined how to identify your users, you need to decide what they are allowed to do. Jenkins supports a variety of strategies in this area, ranging from a simple approach where a logged-in user can do anything to more involved roles and project-based authentication strategies.

Matrix-based Security

Letting signed-in users do anything is certainly flexible, and may be all you need for a small team. For larger or multiple teams, or cases where Jenkins is being used outside the development environment, a more sophisticated approach is generally required.

Matrix-based security is a more sophisticated approach, where different users are assigned different rights, using a role-based approach.

Setting up matrix-based security

The first step in setting up matrix-based security in Jenkins is to create an administrator. *This is an essential step, and must be done before all others.* Now your administrator can be an existing user, or one created specially for the purpose. If you want to create a dedicated administrator user, simply create one by signing up in the usual way (see Figure 7-2). It doesn't have to be associated with an SCM user.

Once you have your admin user ready, you can activate matrix-based security by selecting "Matrix-based security" in the Authorization section of the main configuration page. Jenkins will display a table containing authorized users, and checkboxes corresponding to the various permissions that you can assign to these users (see Figure 7-16).

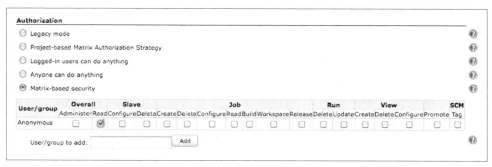

Figure 7-16. Matrix-based security configuration

The special "anonymous" user is always present in the table. This user represents unauthenticated users. Typically, you only grant very limited rights to unauthenticated users, such as read-only access, or no access at all (as shown in Figure 7-16).

The first thing you need to do now is to grant administration rights to your administrator. Add your administration user in the "User/group to add" field and click on Add. Your administrator will now appear in the permissions matrix. Now make sure you grant this user every permission (see Figure 7-17), and save your configuration. You should now be able to log in with your administrator account (if you aren't already logged in with this account) and continue to set up your other users.

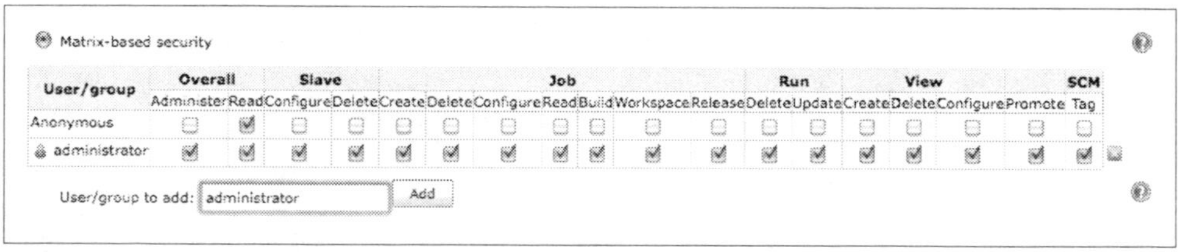

Figure 7-17. Setting up an administrator

Fine-tuning user permissions

Once you have set up your administrator account, you can add any other users that need to access your Jenkins instance. Simply add the user names and tick the permissions you want to grant them (see Figure 7-18). If you are using an LDAP server or Unix users and groups as the underlying authentication schema (see "Using an LDAP Repository" on page 175), you can also configure permissions for groups of users.

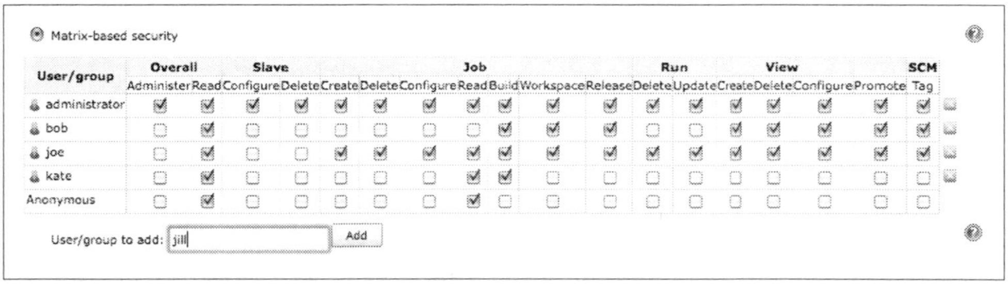

Figure 7-18. Setting up other users

You can grant a range of permissions, which are organized into several groups: Overall, Slave, Job, Run, View and SCM. Most of the permissions are fairly obvious, but some need a little more explanation. The individual permissions are as follows:

Overall
> This group covers basic system-wide permissions:
>
> *Administer*
>> Lets a user make system-wide configuration changes and other sensitive operations, for example in the main Jenkins configuration pages. This should be reserved for the Jenkins administrator.
>
> *Read*
>> This permission provides read-only access to virtually all of the pages in Jenkins. If you want anonymous users to be able to view build jobs freely, but not to be able to modify or start them, grant the Read role to the special "anonymous" user. If not, simply revoke this permission for the Anonymous user. And if you want all authenticated users to be able to see build jobs, then add a special user called "authenticated", and grant this user Overall/Read permission.

Slave
> This group covers permissions about remote build nodes, or slaves:
>
> *Configure*
>> Create and configure new build nodes.
>
> *Delete*
>> Delete build nodes.

Job

This group covers job-related permissions:

Create

Create a new build job.

Delete

Delete an existing build job.

Configure

Update the configuration of an existing build jobs.

Read

View build jobs.

Build

Start a build job.

Workspace

View and download the workspace contents for a build job. Remember, the workspace contains source code and artifacts, so if you want to protect these from general access, you should revoke this permission.

Release

Start a Maven release for a project configured with the M2Release plugin.

Run

This group covers rights related to particular builds in the build history:

Delete

Delete a build from the build history.

Update

Update the description and other properties of a build in the build history. This can be useful if a user wants to leave a note about the cause of a build failure, for example.

View

This group covers managing views:

Create

Create a new view.

Delete

Delete an existing view.

Configure

Configure an existing view.

SCM

Permissions related to your version control system:

Tag

Create a new tag in the source code repository for a given build.

Others

> There can also be other permissions available, depending on the plugins installed. One useful one is:

Promote

> If the Promoted Builds plugin is installed, this permission allows users to manually promote a build.

Help! I've locked myself out!

Now it may happen that, during this process, you may end up locking yourself out of Jenkins. This can happen if, for example, you save the matrix configuration without having correctly set up your administrator. If this happens, do not panic—there is an easy fix, as long as you have access to Jenkins's home directory. Simply open up the *config.xml* file at the root of the Jenkins home directory. This will contain something like this:

```
<hudson>
    <version>1.391</version>
    <numExecutors>2</numExecutors>
    <mode>NORMAL</mode>
    <useSecurity>true</useSecurity>
    ...
```

The thing to look for is the `<useSecurity>` element. To restore your access to Jenkins, change this value to false, and restart your server. You will now be able to access Jenkins again, and set up your security configuration correctly.

Project-based Security

Project-based security lets you build on the matrix-based security model we just discussed, and apply it to individual projects. Not only can you assign system-wide roles for your users, you can also configure more specific rights for certain individual projects.

To activate project-level security, select "Project-based Matrix Authorization Strategy" in the Authorization section of the main configuration screen (see Figure 7-19). Here, you set up the default rights for users and groups, as we saw with Matrix-based security (see "Matrix-based Security" on page 181).

These are the default permissions that apply to all projects that have not been specially configured. However, when you use project-based security, you can also set up special project-specific permissions. You do this by selecting "Enable project-based security" in the project configuration screen (see Figure 7-20). Jenkins will display a table of project-specific permissions. You can configure these permissions for different users and groups just like on the system-wide configuration page. These permissions will be added to the system-wide permissions to produce a project-specific set of permissions applicable for this project.

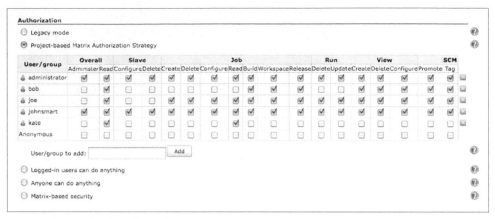

Figure 7-19. Project-based security

Figure 7-20. Configuring project-based security

The way this works is easiest to understand with a few practical examples. In Figure 7-19, for instance, no permissions have been granted to the anonymous user, so by default all build jobs will remain invisible until a user signs on. However, we are using project-based security, so we can override this on a project-by-project basis. In Figure 7-20, for example, we have set up the *game-of-life* project to have read-only access for the special "anonymous" user.

When you save this configuration, unauthenticated users will be able to see the *game-of-life* project in read-only mode (see Figure 7-21). This same principle applies with all of the project-specific permissions.

Note that Jenkins permissions are cumulative—at the time of writing, there is no way to revoke a system-wide permission for a particular project. For example, if the anonymous user has read-access to build jobs at the system level, you can't revoke read-only access for an individual project. So when using project-based security, use the system

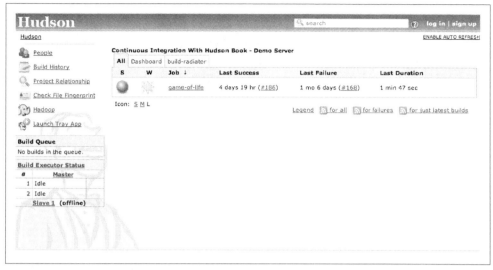

Figure 7-21. Viewing a project

level matrix to define minimum default permissions applicable across all of your projects, and set up projects with additional project-specific authorizations.

There are many approaches to managing project permissions, and they depend as much on organizational culture as on technical considerations. One common strategy approach is to allow team members to have full access to their own projects, and read-only access to other projects. The Extended Read Permission plugin is a useful extension to have for this scenario. This plugin lets you let users from other teams see a read-only view of your project configuration, without being able to modify anything (see Figure 7-22). This is a great way to share build configuration practices and tips with other teams without letting them tamper with your builds.

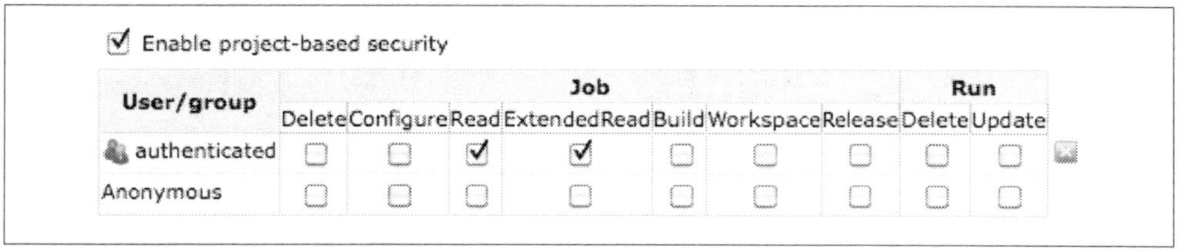

| User/group | Job | | | | | | | Run | |
	Delete	Configure	Read	Extended Read	Build	Workspace	Release	Delete	Update
authenticated	☐	☐	☑	☑	☐	☐	☐	☐	☐
Anonymous	☐	☐	☐	☐	☐	☐	☐	☐	☐

☑ Enable project-based security

Figure 7-22. Setting up Extended Read Permissions

It is worth noting that, whenever large and/or multiple teams are involved, the internal Jenkins database reaches its limits quite quickly, and it is worth considering integrating with a more specialized directory service such as an LDAP server, Active Directory or Atlassian Crowd, or possibly a more sophisticated permission system such as role-based security, discussed in the following section.

Role-based Security

Sometimes managing user permissions individually can be cumbersome, and you may not want to integrate with an LDAP server to set up groups that way. A more recent alternative option is to use the Role Strategy plugin, which allows you to define global and project-level roles, and assign these roles to users.

You install the plugin in the usual way, via the Plugin Manager. Once installed, you can activate this authorization strategy in the main configuration page (see Figure 7-23).

Figure 7-23. Setting up Role-based security

Once you have set this up, you can define roles that regroup sets of related permissions. You set up and configure your roles, and assign these roles to your users, in the Manage Roles screen, which you can access in the Manage Jenkins screen (see Figure 7-24).

Figure 7-24. The Manage Roles configuration menu

In the Manage Roles screen, you can set up global and project-level permissions. Global permissions apply across all projects, and are typically system-wide administration or general access permissions (see Figure 7-25). Setting these roles up is intuitive and similar to setting up user permissions in the other security models we have seen.

Project roles are slightly more complicated. A project role regroups a set of permissions that are applicable to one or more (presumably related) projects. You define the relevant projects using a regular expression, so it helps to have a clear and consistent set of naming conventions in place for your project names (see Figure 7-26). For example,

Figure 7-25. Managing global roles

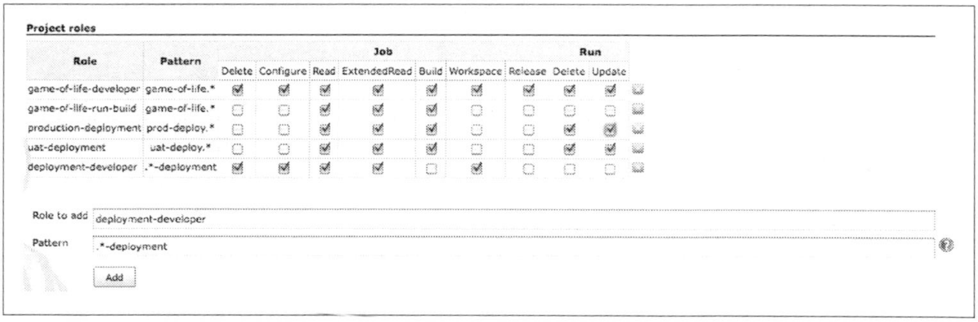

Figure 7-26. Managing project roles

you may wish to create roles distinguishing developers with full configuration rights on their own project from users who can simply trigger a build and view the build results, or create roles where developers can configure certain automated deployment build jobs, but only production teams are allowed to execute these jobs.

Once you have defined these roles, you can go to the Assign Roles screen to set up individual users or groups with these roles (see Figure 7-27).

Role-based strategy is relatively new in Jenkins, but it is an excellent way to simplify the task of managing permissions in large, multiteam and multiproject organizations.

Auditing—Keeping Track of User Actions

In addition to configuring user accounts and access rights, it can also be useful to keep track of the individual user actions: in other words, who did what to your server configuration. This sort of audit trail facility is even required in many organizations.

There are two Jenkins plugins that can help you do this. The Audit Trail plugin keeps a record of user changes in a special log file. And the JobConfigHistory plugin lets you

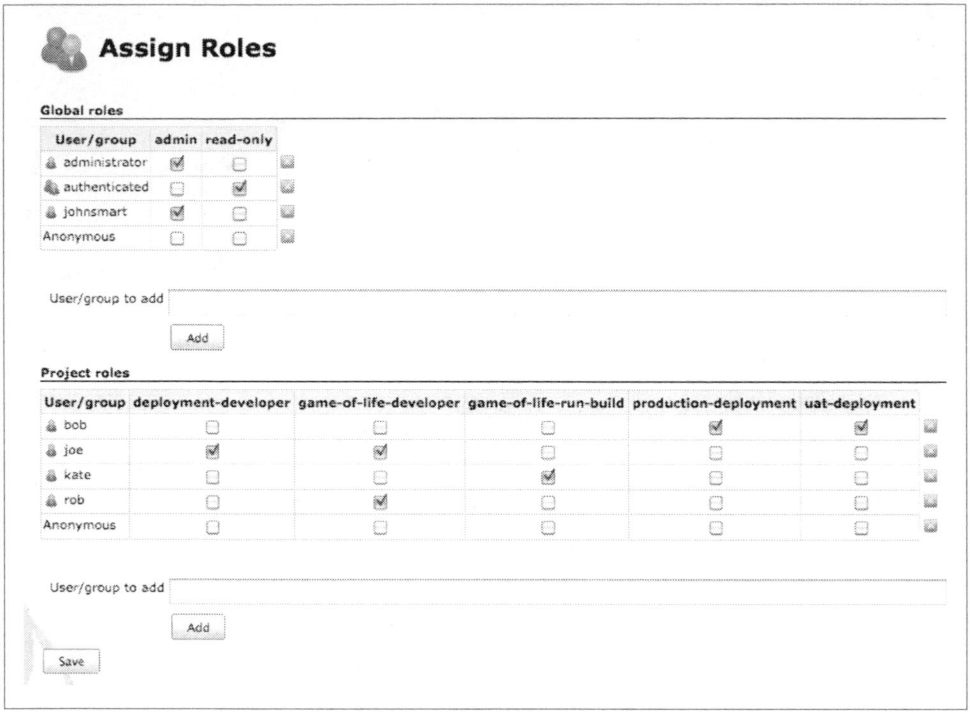

Assign Roles

Global roles

User/group	admin	read-only	
administrator	☑	☐	
authenticated	☐	☑	
johnsmart	☑	☐	
Anonymous	☐	☐	

User/group to add

Add

Project roles

User/group	deployment-developer	game-of-life-developer	game-of-life-run-build	production-deployment	uat-deployment	
bob	☐	☐	☐	☑	☑	
joe	☑	☑	☐	☐	☐	
kate	☐	☐	☑	☐	☐	
rob	☐	☑	☐	☐	☐	
Anonymous	☐	☐	☐	☐	☐	

User/group to add

Add

Save

Figure 7-27. Assigning roles to users

keep a copy of previous versions of the various system and job configuration files that Jenkins uses.

The Audit Trail Plugin keeps track of the main user actions in a set of rolling log files. To set this up, go to the Plugin Manager page and select the Audit Trail plugin in the list of available plugins. Then, as usual, click on Install and restart Jenkins once the plugin has been downloaded.

You can set up the audit trail configuration in the Audit Trail section of the main Jenkins configuration page (see Figure 7-28). The most important field is the Log Location, which is where you indicate the directory in which the log files are to be written. The audit trail is designed to produce system-style log files, which are often placed in a special system directory such as */var/log*. You can also configure the number of log files to be maintained, and the (approximate) maximum size of each file. The simplest option is to provide an absolute path (such as */var/log/hudson.log*), in which case Jenkins will write to log files with names like */var/log/hudson.log.1*, */var/log/hudson.log.2*, and so forth. Of course, you need to ensure that the user running your Jenkins instance is allowed to write to this directory.

You can also use the format defined in the Java logging FileHandler (*http://download .oracle.com/javase/1.5.0/docs/api/java/util/logging/FileHandler.html*) class for more

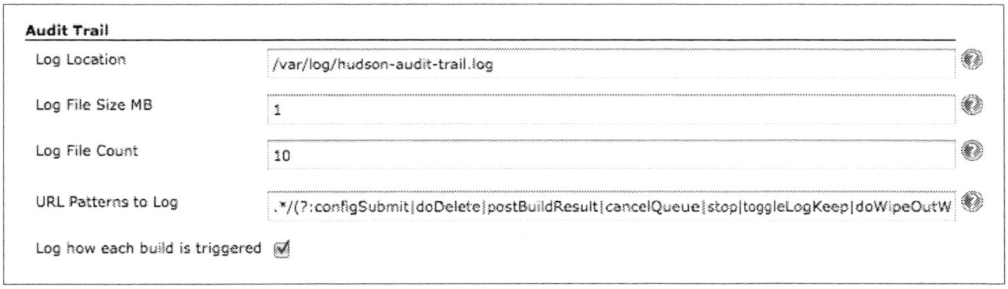

Figure 7-28. Configuring the Audit Trail plugin

control over the generated log files. In this format, you can insert variables such as %h, for the current user's home directory, and %t, for the system temporary directory, to build a more dynamic file path.

By default, the details recorded in the audit logs are fairly sparse—they effectively record key actions performed, such as creating, modifying or deleting job configurations or views, and the user who performed the actions. The log also shows how individual build jobs started. An extract of the default log is shown here:

```
Dec 27, 2010 9:16:08 AM /job/game-of-life/configSubmit by johnsmart
Dec 27, 2010 9:16:42 AM /view/All/createItem by johnsmart
Dec 27, 2010 9:16:57 AM /job/game-of-life-prod-deployment/doDelete by johnsmart
Dec 27, 2010 9:24:38 AM job/game-of-life/ #177 Started by user johnsmart
Dec 27, 2010 9:25:57 AM job/game-of-life-acceptance-tests/ #107 Started by upstream
    project "game-of-life" build number 177
Dec 27, 2010 9:25:58 AM job/game-of-life-functional-tests/ #7 Started by upstream
    project "game-of-life" build number 177
Dec 27, 2010 9:28:15 AM /configSubmit by johnsmart
```

This audit trail is certainly useful, especially from a system administration perspective. However, it doesn't provide any information about the exact changes that were made to the Jenkins configuration. Nevertheless, one of the most important reasons to keep track of user actions in Jenkins is to keep tabs on exactly what changes were made to build job configurations. When something goes wrong, it can be useful to know what changes were done and so be able to undo them. The JobConfigHistory plugin lets you do just this.

The JobConfigHistory plugin is a powerful tool that lets you keep a full history of changes made to both job and system configuration files. You install it from the Plugin Manager in the usual way. Once installed, you can fine-tune the job history configuration in the Manage Jenkins screen (see Figure 7-29).

Here, you can configure a number of useful nonstandard options. In particular, you should specify a directory where Jenkins can store configuration history, in the "Root history folder" field. This is the directory where Jenkins will store a record of both system-related and job-related configuration changes. It can be either an absolute directory (such as */var/hudson/history*), or a relative directory, calculated from the Jenkins

Figure 7-29. Setting up Job Configuration History

home directory (see "The Jenkins Home Directory" on page 46). If you don't do this, job configuration history will be stored with the jobs, and will be lost if you delete a job.

There are a few other useful options in the Advanced section. The "Save system configuration changes" checkbox lets you keep track of system-wide configuration updates, and not just job-specific ones. And the "Do not save duplicate history" checkbox allows you to avoid recording configuration updates if no actual changes have been made. If not, a new version of the configuration will be recorded, even if you have only pressed the Save button without making any changes. Jenkins can also cause this to happen internally—for example, system configuration settings are all saved whenever the main configuration page is saved, even if no changes have been made.

Once you have set up this plugin, you can access the configuration history both for the whole server, including system configuration updates, as well as the changes made to the configuration of each project. In both cases, you can view these changes by clicking on the Job Config History icon to the right of the screen. Clicking on this icon from the Jenkins dashboard will display a view of all of your configuration history, including job changes and system-wide changes (see Figure 7-30).

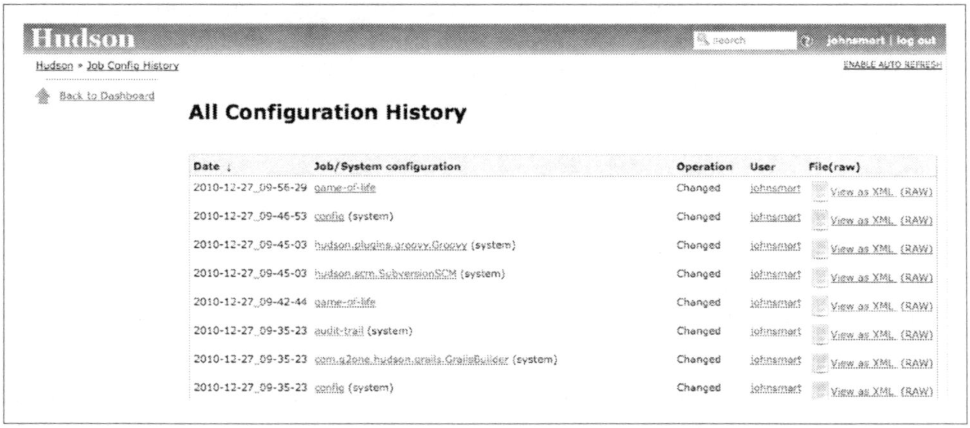

Figure 7-30. Viewing Job Configuration History

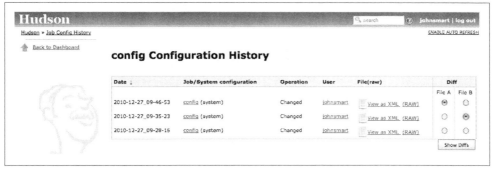

Figure 7-31. Viewing differences in Job Configuration History

If you click on a system-wide change (indicated by the "(system)" suffix in the list), Jenkins takes you to a screen that lists all of the versions of that file, and allows you to view the differences between the different versions (see Figure 7-31). The differences are displayed as *diff* files, which is not particularly readable in itself. However, for small changes, the readable XML format of most of the Jenkins configuration files makes this sufficient to understand what changes were made.

The JobConfigHistory plugin is a powerful tool. However, at the time of writing, it does have its limits. As mentioned, the plugin only displays the differences in raw *diff* format, and you can't restore a previous version of a configuration file (those doing this out of context could be dangerous in some circumstances, particularly for system-wide configuration files). Nevertheless, it gives a very clear picture of the changes that have been made, both to your build jobs and to your system configuration.

Conclusion

In this chapter we have looked at a variety of ways to configure security in Jenkins. The Jenkins security model, with the two orthogonal concepts of Authentication and Authorization, is flexible and extensible. For a Jenkins installation of any size, you should try to integrate your Jenkins security strategy with the organization as a whole. This can go from simply integrating with your local LDAP repository to setting up or using a full-blown SSO solution such as Crown or CAS. In either case, it will make the system considerably easier to administrate in the long run.

CHAPTER 8

Notification

Introduction

While it is important to get your build server building your software, it is even more important to get your build server to let people know when it can't do so. A crucial part of the value proposition of any Continuous Integration environment is to improve the flow of information about the health of your project, be it failing unit tests or regressions in the integration test suite, or other quality related issues such as a drop in code coverage or code quality metrics. In all cases, a CI server must let the right people know about any new issues, and it must be able to do so fast. This is what we call Notification.

There are two main classes of notification strategies, which I call *passive* and *active* (or *pull/push*). Passive notification (pull) requires the developers to consciously consult the latest build status, and includes RSS feeds, build radiators, and (to a certain extent) emails. Active notification (push) will pro-actively alert the developers when a build fails, and includes methods such as desktop notifiers, chat, and SMS. Both approaches have their good and bad points. Passive notification strategies such as build radiators can raise general awareness about failed builds, and help install a team culture where fixing broken builds takes a high priority. More direct forms of notification can actively encourage developers to take matters into their own hands and fix broken builds more quickly.

Email Notification

Email notification is the most obvious and most common form of CI notification. Email is well-known, ubiquitous, easy to use and easy to configure (see "Configuring the Mail Server" on page 76). So, when teams set up their first Continuous Integration environment, it is usually the most common initial notification strategy they try.

You activate email notification in Jenkins by ticking the E-mail Notification checkbox and providing the list of email addresses of the people who need to be notified (see Figure 8-1). By default, Jenkins will send an email for every failed or unstable build.

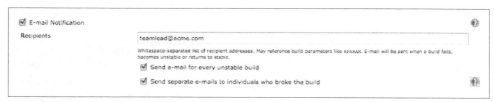

Figure 8-1. Configuring email notification

Remember, it will also send a new email for the first successful build after a series of failed or unstable builds, to indicate that the issue has been fixed.

Normally a build should not take too many tries to get working again—developers should diagnose and reproduce the issue locally, fix it locally, and only then commit their fix to version control. Repeated build failures usually indicate either a chronic configuration issue or poor developer practices (for example, developers committing changes without checking that it works locally first).

You can also opt to send a separate email to any developers who have committed changes to the broken build. This is generally a good idea, as developers who have committed changes since the last build are naturally the people who should be the most interested in the build results. Jenkins will get the email address of the user from the currently-configured security realm (see "Security Realms—Identifying Jenkins Users" on page 171), or by deriving the email address from the SCM username if you have set this up (see "Configuring the Mail Server" on page 76).

If you use this option, it may be less useful to include the entire team in the main distribution list. You may want to simply include people who will be interested in monitoring the result of every build (such as technical leads), and let Jenkins inform contributing developers directly.

This assumes of course that the changes caused the build failure, which is generally (but not always) the case. However, if the builds are infrequent (for example, nightly builds, or if a build is queued for several hours before finally kicking off), many changes may have been committed, and it is hard to know which one was actually responsible for the build failure.

Not all builds are alike when it comes to email notification. Developers committing changes are particularly interested in the results of the unit and integration test builds (especially those triggered by their own changes), whereas BAs and testers might be more interested in keeping tabs on the status of the automated acceptance tests. So the exact email notification setup for each build job will be different. In fact, it is useful to define an email notification strategy. A sample of such an email notification strategy is outlined here:

- Fast builds (unit/integration tests, runs in less than 5 minutes): notification is sent to the team lead and to developers having committed changes.

- Slow builds (acceptance tests builds, run after the fast builds): notification is sent to team lead, testers and developers having committed changes.
- Nightly builds (QA metrics, performance tests and so on; only run if the other builds work): all team members—these provide a snapshot picture of project health before the daily status meeting.

Indeed, you should consider what notification strategy is appropriate for each build job on a case-by-case basis, rather than applying a blanket policy for all build jobs.

More Advanced Email Notification

By default, Jenkins email notification is a rather blunt tool. Notification messages are always sent to basically the same group of people. You cannot send messages to different people depending on what went wrong, or implement any sort of escalation policy. It would be useful, for example, to be able to notify the developers who committed changes the first time a build breaks, and send a different message to the team lead or the entire team if the build breaks a second time

The Email-ext plugin lets you define a more refined email notification strategy. This plugin adds an Editable Email Notification checkbox (see Figure 8-2), which effectively replaces the standard Jenkins email notification. Here, you can define a default recipient list and fine-tune the contents of the email message, and also define a more precise notification strategy with different messages and recipient lists for different events. Note that once you have installed and configured this plugin for your build job, you can deactivate the normal E-mail Notification configuration.

Figure 8-2. Configuring advanced email notification

This plugin has two related but distinct functionalities. Firstly, it lets you customize the email notification message. You can choose from a large number of predefined tokens to create your own customized message title and body. You include a token in your message template using the familiar dollar notation (e.g., `${BUILD_NUMBER}` or `$BUILD_NUMBER`). Some of the tokens accept parameters, which you can specify using a name=value format (e.g., ${BUILD_LOG, maxLines=100} or ${ENV, var="PATH"}). Among the more useful tokens are:

${DEFAULT_SUBJECT}
> The default email subject configured in the Jenkins system configuration page

${DEFAULT_CONTENT}
> The default email content configured in the Jenkins system configuration page

${PROJECT_NAME}
> The project's name

${BUILD_NUMBER}
> Current build number

${BUILD_STATUS}
> Current build status (failing, success, etc.)

${CAUSE}
> The cause of the build

${BUILD_URL}
> A link to the corresponding build job page on Jenkins

${FAILED_TESTS}
> Shows information about failing unit tests, if any have failed

${CHANGES}
> Displays the changes made since the last build

${CHANGES_SINCE_LAST_SUCCESS}
> All the changes made since the last successful build

You can get a full list of the available tokens, and the options for those that accept parameters, by clicking on the Help icon opposite the Context Token Reference label.

The Advanced button lets you define a more sophisticated notification strategy, based on the concept of triggers (see Figure 8-3). Triggers determine when email notification messages should be sent out. The supported triggers include the following:

Failure
> Any time the build fails.

Still Failing
> Any successive build failures.

Unstable
> Any time a build is unstable.

Still Unstable
> Any successive unstable builds.

Success
> Any successful build.

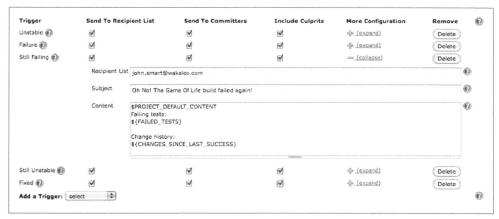

Figure 8-3. Configuring email notification triggers

Fixed

When the build changes from Failure or Unstable to Successful.

Before Build

Sent before every build begins.

You can set up as many (or as few) triggers as you like. The recipients list and message template can be customized for each trigger—for example, by using the Still Failing and Still Unstable triggers, you can set up a notification strategy that only notifies developer having committed changes the first time a build job fails, but proceeds to notify the team leader if it fails a second time. You can choose to send the message only to the developers who have committed to this build ("Send to committers"), or to also include everyone who has committed since the last successful build. This helps ensures that everyone who may be involved in causing the build to break will be notified appropriately.

You can also customize the content of the message by clicking on the More Configuration option (as shown for the Still Failing trigger in Figure 8-3). This way, you can customize different messages to be sent for different occasions.

The triggers interact intelligently. So if you configure both the Failing and the Still Failing triggers, only the Still Failing trigger will be activated on the second build failure.

An example of such a customized message is illustrated in Figure 8-4.

Overall, however, as a notification strategy, email is not without its faults. Some developers shut down their email clients at times to avoid being interrupted. In large organizations, the number of email messages arriving each day can be considerable, and build failure notifications can be hidden among a host of other less important messages. So build failures may not always get the high-priority attention they require in a finely-tuned CI environment. In the following sections, we will look at some other notification strategies that can be used to raise team awareness of failed builds and encourage developers to get them fixed faster.

Figure 8-4. Customized notification message

Claiming Builds

When a build does fail, it can be useful to know that someone has spotted the issue and is working on it. This avoids having more than one developer waste time by trying to fix the same problem separately.

The Claim plugin lets developers indicate that they have taken ownership of the broken build, and are attempting to fix it. You can install this plugin in the usual way. Once installed, developers can claim a failed build as their own, and optionally add a comment to explain the suspected cause of the build and what the developer intends to do about it. The claimed build will then be marked as such in the build history, so that fellow developers can avoid wasting time with unnecessary investigation.

To activate claiming for a build job, you need to tick the "Allow broken build claiming" option in the build job configuration page. From this point on, you will be able to claim a broken build in the build details page (see Figure 8-5). Claimed builds will display an icon in the build history indicating that they have been claimed. You can also make a build claim "sticky," so that all subsequent build failures for this job will also be automatically claimed by this developer, until the issue is resolved.

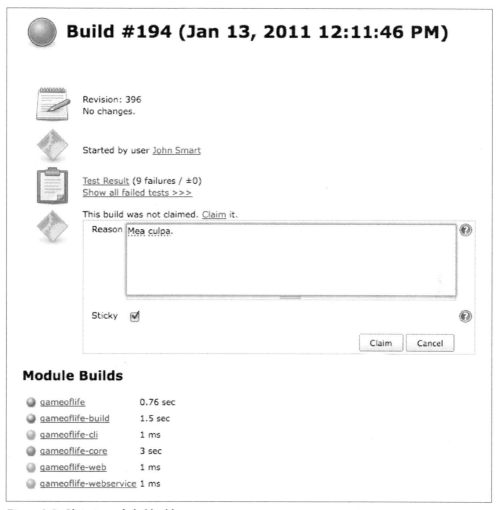

Figure 8-5. Claiming a failed build

RSS Feeds

Jenkins also provides convenient RSS feeds for its build results, both for overall build results across all of your builds (or just the builds on a particular view), or build results for a specific build. RSS Feed icons are available at the bottom of build dashboards (see Figure 8-6) and at the bottom of the build history panel in the individual build jobs, giving you access to either all of the build results, or just the failing builds.

The URLs for RSS feeds are simple, and work for any Jenkins page displaying a set of build results. You just need to append */rssAll* to get an RSS feed of all of the build results on a page, or */rssFailed* to only get the failing builds. And */rssLatest* will provide you

Figure 8-6. RSS Feeds in Jenkins

with a feed containing only the latest build results. But the simplest way to obtain the URL is just to click on the RSS icon in the corresponding Jenkins screen.

There are an abundance of RSS readers out there, both commercial and open source, available for virtually every platform and device, so this can be a great choice to keep tabs on build results. Many common browsers (Firefox in particular) and email clients also support RSS feeds. Some readers have trouble with authentication, however, so if your Jenkins instance is secured, you may need to do a little extra configuration to see your build results.

RSS feeds can be a great information source on overall build results, and let you see the state of your builds at a glance without having to connect to the server. Nevertheless, most RSS Readers are by nature passive devices—you can consult the state of your builds, but the RSS reader will usually not be able to prompt you if a new build failure occurs.

Build Radiators

The concept of information radiators is commonly used in Agile circles. According to Agile guru Alistair Cockburn:

> An Information radiator is a display posted in a place where people can see it as they work or walk by. It shows readers information they care about without having to ask anyone a question. This means more communication with fewer interruptions.

In the context of a CI server, an information radiator is a prominent device or display that allows team members and others to easily see if any builds are currently broken. It typically shows either a summary of all the current build results, or just the failing ones, and is displayed on a large, prominently located wall-mounted flat screen. This sort of specialized information radiator is often known as a *build radiator*.

When used well, build radiators are among the most effective of the passive notification strategies. They are very effective at ensuring that everyone is aware of failing builds. In addition, unlike some of the Extreme Feedback Devices that we discuss later on in

---

this chapter, a build radiator can cater for many build jobs, including many failing build jobs, and so can still be effectively used in a multiteam context.

There are several build radiator solutions for Jenkins. One of the easiest to use is the Jenkins Radiator View plugin. This plugin adds a new type of job that you can create: the (see Figure 8-7).

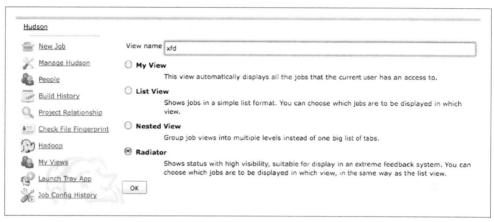

Figure 8-7. Creating a build radiator view

Configuring the build radiator view is similar to configuring the more conventional list views—you just specify the build jobs you want included in the view, either by choosing them individually or by using a regular expression.

Since the build radiator view takes up the entire screen, modifying or deleting a build radiator is a bit tricky. In fact, the only way to open the view configuration screen is to append */configure* to the view URL: so if your build radiator is called "build-radiator," you can edit the view configuration by opening *http://my.hudson.server/view/build-radiator/configure*.

The build radiator view (see Figure 8-8) displays a large red or yellow box for each failing or unstable build, with the build job name in prominent letters, as well as some other details. You can configure the build radiator view to display passing builds as well as failing ones (they will be displayed in small green boxes). However a good build radiator should really only display the failing builds, unless all the builds are passing.

Instant Messaging

Instant Messaging (or IM) is widely used today as a fast, lightweight medium for both professional and personal communication. Instant messaging is, well, instant, which gives it an edge over email when it comes to fast notification. It is also "push" rather than "pull"—when you receive a message, it will pop up on your screen and demand

Figure 8-8. Displaying a build radiator view

your attention. This makes it a little harder to ignore or put off than a simple email message.

Jenkins provides good support for notification via Instant Messaging. The Instant Messaging plugin provides generic support for communicating with Jenkins using IM. Protocol-specific plugins can then be added for the various IM protocols such as Jabber and IRC.

IM Notification with Jabber

Many instant messaging servers today are based on Jabber, an open source, XML-based instant messaging protocol. Jenkins provides good support for Jabber instant messaging, so that developers can receive real-time notification of build failures. In addition, the plugin runs an IM bot that listens to the chat channels and lets developers run commands on the Jenkins server via chat messages.

Setting up IM support in Jenkins is straightforward. First, you need to install both the Jenkins instant-messaging plugin and the Jenkins Jabber notifier plugin using the standard plugin manager page and restart Jenkins (see Figure 8-9).

Once this is done, you need to configure your Instant Messaging server. Any Jabber server will do. You can use a public service like Google Chat, or set up your own internal messaging server locally (the Java-based open source chat server OpenFire (*http://www .igniterealtime.org/projects/openfire/index.jsp*) is a good choice). Using a public service for internal communications may be frowned upon by system administrators, and you may have difficulty getting through corporate fire walls. Setting up your own internal chat service, on the other hand, makes great sense for a development team or organization in general, as it provides another channel of communication that works well for

☑	**Hudson instant-messaging plugin**		1.13
	This plugin provides abstract support for build notification via instant-messaging.		
☑	**Hudson Jabber notifier plugin**		1.13
	Sends build notifications to jabber contacts and/or chatrooms. Also allows control of builds via a jabber 'bot'.		
	Note that the **instant-messaging plugin 1.11** is a requirement for this plugin. *Please make sure that it is installed, too!*		

Figure 8-9. Installing the Jenkins IM plugins

technical questions or comments between developers. The following examples will be using a local OpenFire server, but the general approach will work for any Jabber-compatible server.

The first step involves creating a dedicated account on your Jabber server for Jenkins. This is just an ordinary chat account, but it needs to be distinct from your developer accounts (see Figure 8-10).

User Summary

Total Users: **7** — Sorted by Username — Users per page: [15]

	Online	Username	Name	Created	Last Logout	Edit	Delete
1	🧍	admin ☆	Administrator	Jan 13, 2011		📝	⊗
2	🧍	bill	Bill Smith	Jan 14, 2011		📝	⊗
3	🧍	hudson	hudson	Jan 13, 2011	31 minutes	📝	⊗
4	🧍	joe	Joe Black	Jan 13, 2011		📝	⊗
5	🧍	johnsmart ☆	John Smart	Jan 13, 2011		📝	⊗
6	🧍	kate	Kate Brown	Jan 14, 2011		📝	⊗
7	🧍	pete	Pete Best	Jan 14, 2011		📝	⊗

Figure 8-10. Jenkins needs its own dedicated IM user account

Once you have set up an IM account, you need to configure Jenkins to send IM notifications via this account. Go to the main configuration page and tick the Enable Jabber Notification checkbox (see Figure 8-11). Here, you provide the Jabber ID and password for your IM account. Jenkins can usually figure out the IM server from the Jabber ID (if it is different, you can override this in the Advanced options). If you are using group chat rooms (another useful communication strategy for development teams), you can provide the name of these chat rooms here too. This way, Jenkins will be able to process instructions posted into the chat rooms as well as those received as direct messages.

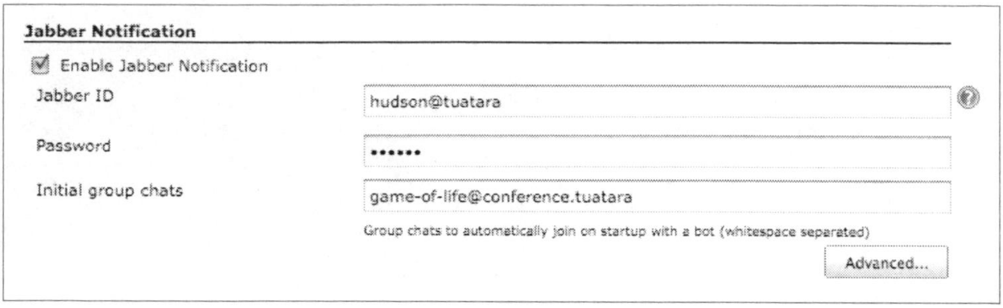

Figure 8-11. Setting up basic Jabber notification in Jenkins

This is all you need for a basic setup. However, you may need to provide some extra details in the Advanced sector for details that are specific to your installation (see Figure 8-12). Here, you can specify the name and port of your Jabber server, if these cannot be derived from the Jenkins Jabber ID. You can also provide a default suffix that can be applied to Jenkins user IDs to generate the corresponding Jabber IDs. Most importantly, if you have secured your Jenkins server, you will need to provide a proper Jenkins username and password so that the IM bot can respond to instructions correctly.

Once this is configured, you need to set up a Jabber notification strategy for each of your build jobs. Open the build job configuration page and click on the Jabber Notification option.

First of all, you define a recipient list for the messages. You can send messages to individuals (just use the corresponding Jabber ID, such as *joe@jabber.acme.com*) or to chat rooms that you have set up. For chat rooms, you normally need to add a "*" to the start of the chat room ID (e.g., "*gameoflife@conference.jabber.acme.org"). However, if the chat room ID contains "@conference.", Jenkins will work out that it is a chat room and append the "*" automatically. The chat room approach is more flexible, though you do have to trust developers to be connected permanently to the chat room for this strategy to be truly effective.

You also need to define a notification strategy. This determines which build results will cause a message to be sent out. Options include:

all
    Send a notification for every build.

failure
    Only send notifications for failed or unstable builds.

failure and fixed
    Send notifications for every failed or unstable builds, and the first successful build following a failed or unstable one.

change
    Send notification whenever the build outcome changes.

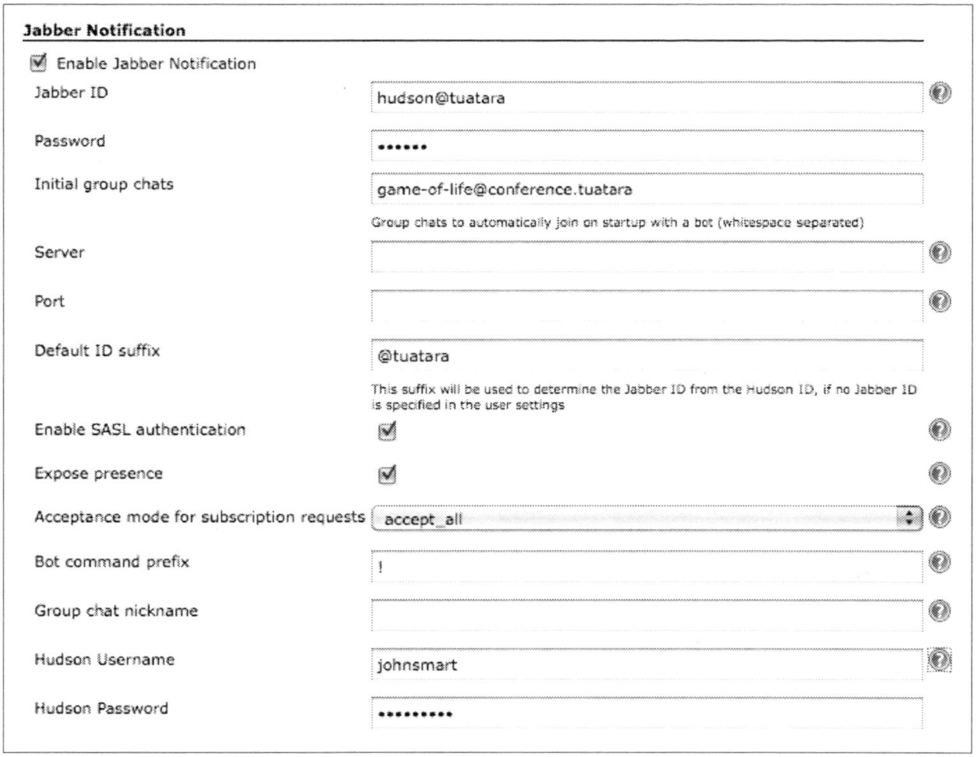

Figure 8-12. Advanced Jabber configuration

If you are using chat rooms, you can also ask Jenkins to send notifications to the chat rooms whenever a build starts (using the "Notify on build starts" option).

For SCM-triggered builds, Jenkins can also notify additional recipients, using the default suffix discussed earlier to build the Jabber ID from the SCM username. You can opt to notify:

SCM committers
> All users having committed changes for the current build, and therefore suspected of breaking the build.

SCM culprits
> SCM committers of all builds since the last successful one.

SCM fixers
> Commiters to the first successful build after a failed or unstable one.

Upstream committers
> Also notifiers committers to upstream builds as well as the current one. This works automatically for Maven build jobs, but needs fingerprinting to be activated for other build types.

At the time of writing, you can only have one notification strategy, so some of the advanced options we saw in "More Advanced Email Notification" on page 197 are not yet possible with IM.

Developers will be notified via their favorite IM client (see Figure 8-13). Developers can also interact with the build server via the chat session, using a set of simple commands. Some examples of a few of the more useful commands are shown here:

- `!build game-of-life`—Start the *game-of-life* build immediately.
- `!build game-of-life 15m`—Start the *game-of-life* build in 15 minutes.
- `!comment game-of-life 207 'oops'`—Add a build description to a given build.
- `!status game-of-life`—display the status of the latest build for this build job.
- `!testresult game-of-life`—display the full test results for the latest build.
- `!health game-of-life`—display a more complete summary of the health status of the latest build.

You can get a full list of commands by sending the `!help` message to the Jenkins user.

Figure 8-13. Jenkins Jabber messages in action

IM Notification using IRC

Another popular form of Internet-based Instant Messaging is Internet Relay Chat, or IRC. IRC is traditionally focused on group discussions (though direct messaging is also supported), and is a very popular form of communication for developers, particularly in the Open Source world.

The Jenkins IRC plugin lets you interact with your Jenkins server via an IRC channel, both to receive notification messages and to issue commands to the server. Like the Jabber plugin, you also need to install the Instant Messaging plugin for this to work.

IRC Notification

Contributed by Juven Xu

Internet Relay Chat (or IRC) is a popular form of instant messaging, primarily designed for group communication in channels. For example, Jenkins has a channel set up on Freenode (*http://jenkins-ci.org/content/chat*) so users and developers can discuss Jenkins related topics. You will see many users ask questions and most of the time more experienced users will be prompt in providing useful answers.

Just like instant messaging through Jabber, you can configure Jenkins to "push" notification through IRC. Some IRC clients such as xchat (*http://xchat.org/*) support alert configuration so that when the message arrives, it can blink the tray icon or make a beep sound. To set up IRC support on Jenkins, first you need to install the IRC plugin (*http://wiki.jenkins-ci.org/display/JENKINS/IRC+Plugin*) and the Instance Messaging plugin (*http://wiki.jenkins-ci.org/display/JENKINS/Instant+Messaging+Plugin*). Simply go to the standard plugin manager, tick their checkbox and then restart Jenkins (see Figure 8-14).

Figure 8-14. Install the Jenkins IRC plugins

Once it's done, you need to enable the IRC plugin and configure it to fit into your own environment. Basically, this involves providing the hostname and port of the IRC server you are using, a dedicated IRC channel, and a nickname for the IRC plugin. It's a good practice to set up a dedicated channel for CI notification, so as people chat in other channels, they won't be disturbed. You may also want to configure extra details in the Advanced sector. All of these are available in the Configure System page (see Figure 8-15).

In addition to the hostname, port, channel, and nickname we mentioned earlier, you can also configure IRC server password or NIckServ password if your environment requires them. Command prefixes need to be configured if you want to interact with the server via IRC messages. This is basically the same as using Jabber (see "Instant Messaging" on page 203). Finally, you may want to let the IRC plugin use

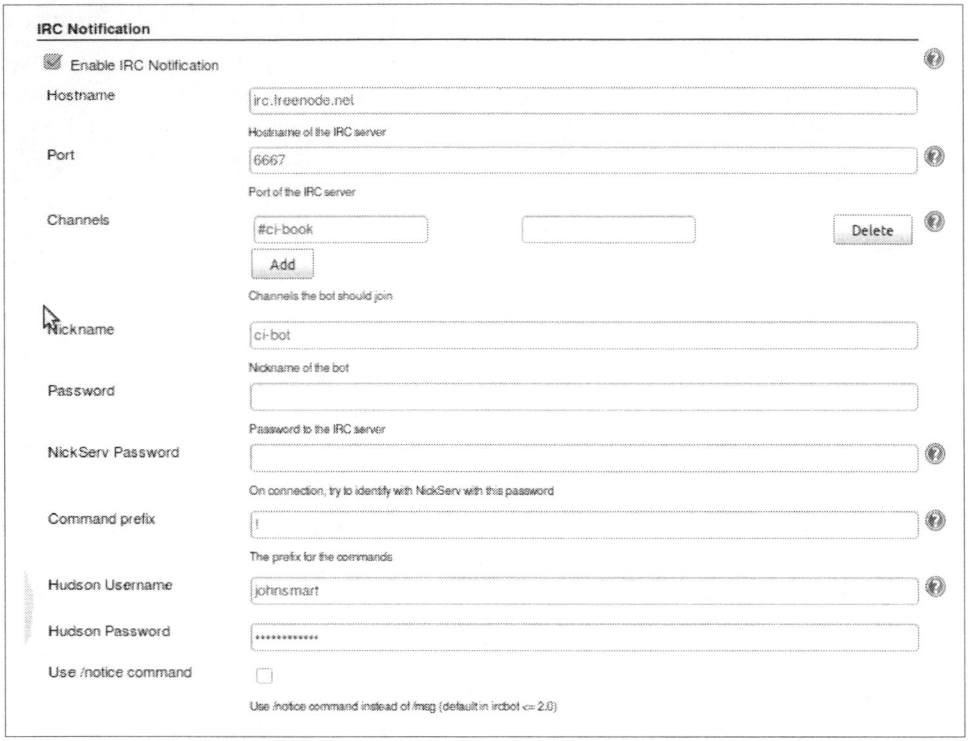

Figure 8-15. Advanced IRC notification configuration

the `/notice` command instead of the default `/msg` command. `/notice` is the same as `/msg` except that the message will be contained in dashes, which will prevent a response from most robots.

Once the global configuration is ready, you can enable IRC notification for each build job and set up a notification strategy. Open the build job configuration page, go to the Post-build Actions section and click on the IRC Notification option. If you want to set up a notification strategy rather than using the default one, click the "Advanced..." button (see Figure 8-16).

Notification strategies (when to send notification messages, and to whom) are discussed in "Instant Messaging" on page 203. Both the Jabber plugin and the IRC plugin depend on the Instant Messaging Plugin, so they share a number of common core features. Some options are specific to IRC plugin, however. Here, for example, you can define a customized channel if you don't like the global default. Finally, for a channel notification message, you can choose what information to send in the notification messages. Your options are build summary, SCM changes, and failed tests.

Once you save the configuration, you should be good to go. Based on what you've configured, this plugin will join the appropriate IRC channels and send notification messages for build jobs.

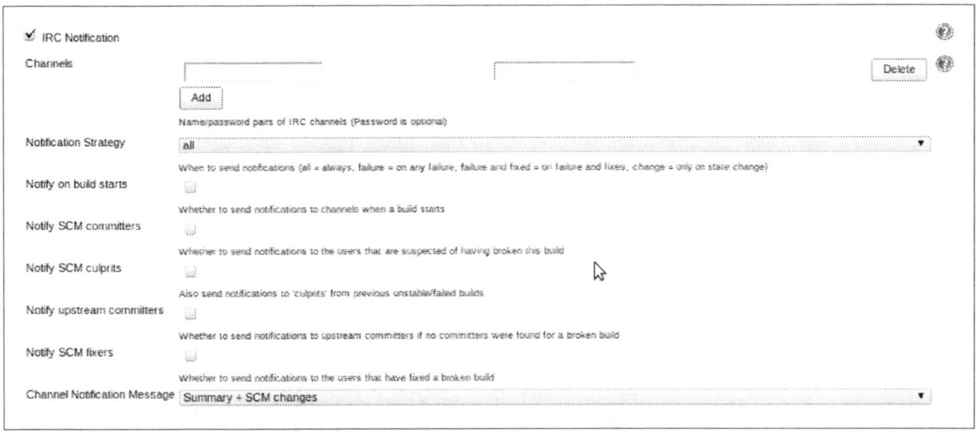

Figure 8-16. Advanced build job IRC notification configuration

In Figure 8-17, for example, the IRC plugin joins the #ci-book channel on freenode. First, user juven committed some change with scm message "feature x added" and IRC plugin let everyone on the channel know that the build was successful. Then juven committed another change for feature y, but this time the build failed. John noticed it and fixed the build error. The IRC plugin now happily said "Yippie, build fixed!" Note that some lines in this screen are highlighted, this is because I logged in as user "juven" and I configured my XChat IRC client to highlight messages containing my nickname.

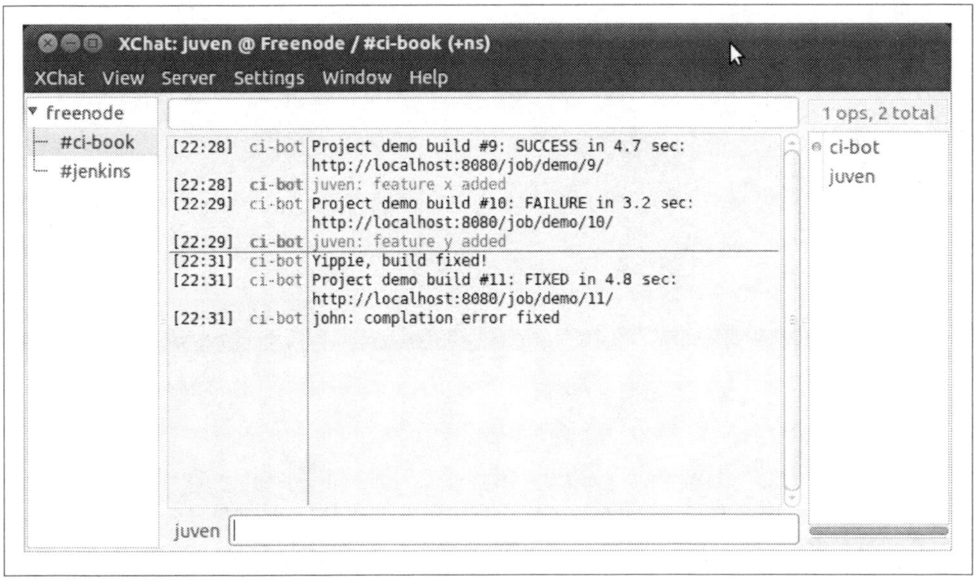

Figure 8-17. IRC notification messages in action

Desktop Notifiers

The best push notification strategies integrate smoothly into the developer's daily work environment. This is why instant messaging can be an effective strategy if developers are already in the habit of using instant messaging for other work-related activities.

Desktop notification tools also fall into this category. Desktop notification tools are tools that run locally on the developer machine, either as an independent application or widget, or as part of the developer's IDE.

If you are using Eclipse, the Jenkins Eclipse plugin (*http://code.google.com/p/hudson -eclipse/*) displays a health icon at the bottom of the Eclipse window. If you click on the icon, you can see a detailed view of the Jenkins projects (see Figure 8-18). In the Eclipse preferences, you provide the URL of your Jenkins server along with any required authentication details. The configuration is fairly simple, however, and you can only connect to a single Jenkins instance for a given Eclipse workspace.

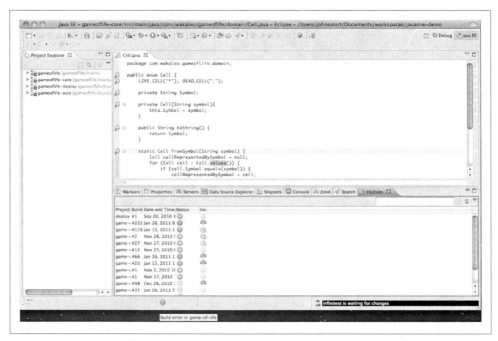

Figure 8-18. Jenkins notifications in Eclipse

The Jenkins Tray Application plugin (see Figure 8-19) lets you start up a small Java client application using Java Web Start from your Jenkins dashboard.

This application sits in your system tray, lets you view the current state of your builds at a glance, and also brings up pop-up windows notifying you of new build failures (see Figure 8-20).

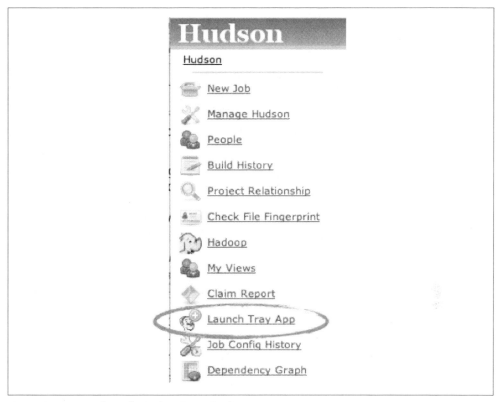

Figure 8-19. Launching the Jenkins Tray Application

This is certainly a useful application, but it suffers from a few limitations. At the time of writing, the Jenkins Tray Application did not support accessing secured Jenkins servers. In addition, the developer needs to remember to restart it each morning. This may seem a minor issue, but in general, when it comes to notification strategies, the less you have to ask of your developers the better.

One of the best options for Jenkins desktop notification is to use a service like Notifo (see "Notification via Notifo" on page 213), which provides both desktop and mobile clients. We will see how this works in detail in the next section.

Notification via Notifo

Notifo (*http://www.notifo.com*) is a fast and economical service to send real-time notifications to your smartphone or desktop. In the context of a Jenkins server, you can use it to set up free or low-cost real-time notification for your Jenkins build results. Individual accounts (which you need to be able to receive notifications) are free. You need to set up a service account to send notification messages from your Jenkins server. This is where Notifo earn their keep, though at the time of writing a service account

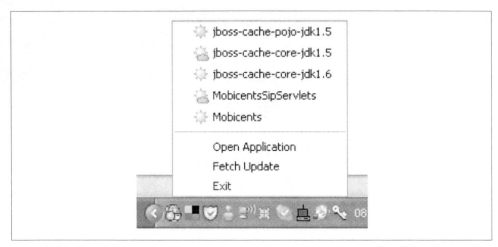

Figure 8-20. Running the Jenkins Tray Application

can send up to 10,000 notifications per month free of charge, which is usually plenty for an average Jenkins instance. One of the strong points of a real-time notification service like Notifo is that notification messages can be sent to the same users on different devices: smartphones and desk top clients, in particular.

Setting up Jenkins notification with Notifo is relatively straightforward. First, go to the Notifio website and sign up to create an account. Each team member who wants to be notified will need their own Notifo account. They will also need to install the Notifo client on each device on which they need to receive notification messages. At the time of writing, Notifo clients were available for Windows and Mac OS X desktops, and iPhones, with support for Linux and other smartphones on the way.

Next, you need to set up a Notifo service account for your Jenkins server. You can do this with one of your developer accounts, or create a new account for the purpose. Log on to the Notifo website, and go to the My Services menu. Here, click on Create Service (see Figure 8-21), and fill in the fields. The most important is the Service Username, which needs to be unique. You can also specify the Site URL and the Default Notification URL to point to your Jenkins instance, so that users can open the Jenkins console by clicking on the notification message.

To receive notification messages from the Jenkins server, developers now need to subscribe to this service. You can then add developers to the list of subscribers in the service Subscribers page, by sending them subscription requests. Once the service has been created and the users are all subscribed, you can configure your project to send out Notifo notifications (see Figure 8-22). You need the provide the API username of the Jenkins service you set up, as well as the API Secret, both of which you can see in the Notifo Service Dashboard.

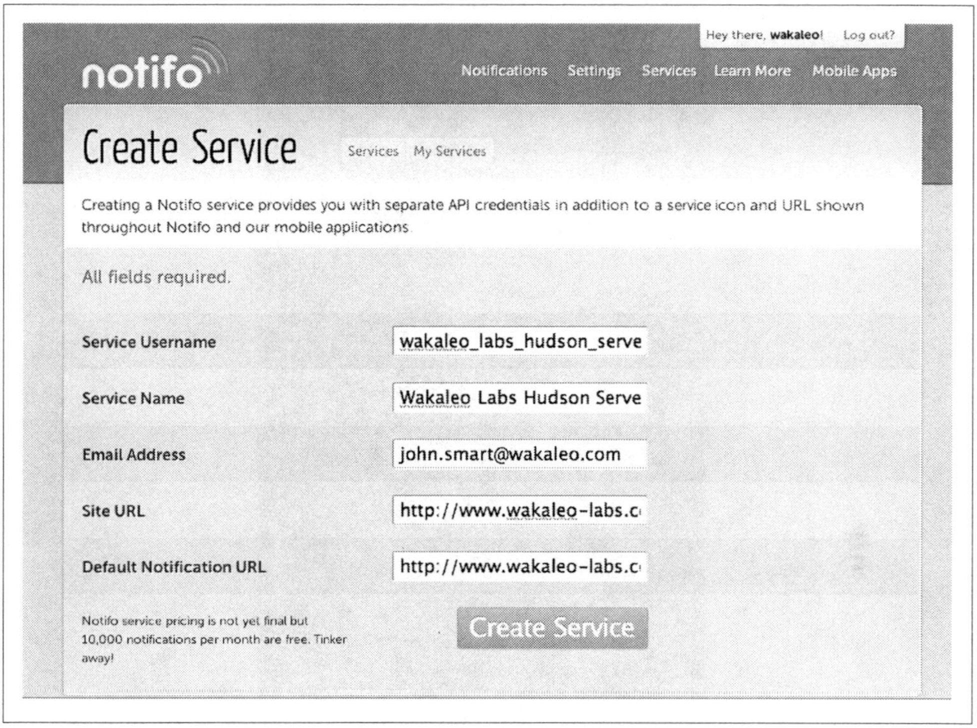

Figure 8-21. Creating a Notifo service for your Jenkins instance

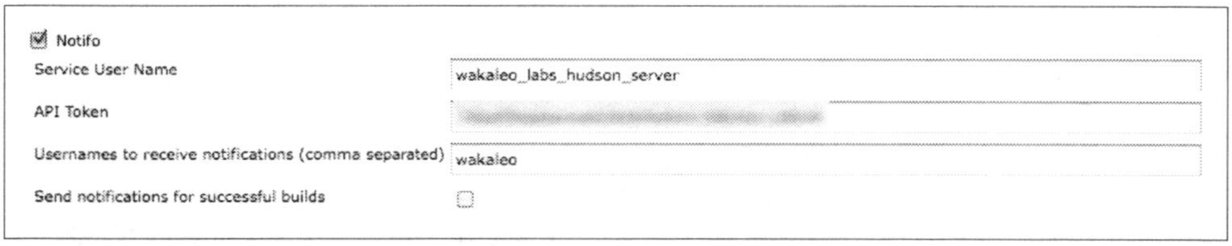

Figure 8-22. Configuring Notifo notifications in your Jenkins build job

Once this is set up, Jenkins will send almost real-time notifications of build failures to any Notifo clients the developer is running, whether it is on a desktop or on a mobile device (see Figure 8-23).

At the time of writing, sophisticated notification strategies are not supported—you just provide a list of Notifo usernames who need to be notified. Nevertheless, this remains a very effective notification tool for frontline developers.

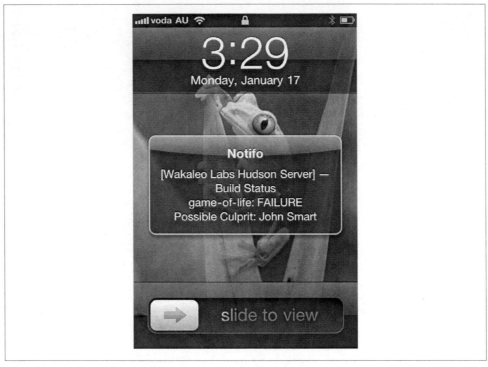

Figure 8-23. Receiving a Notifo notification on an iPhone

Mobile Notification

If your Jenkins server is visible on the Internet (even if you have set up authentication on your Jenkins server), you can also monitor your builds via your iPhone or Android mobile device. The free Hudson Helper application (see Figure 8-24), for example, lets you list your current build jobs (either all of the build jobs on the server, or only the build jobs in a particular view). You can also view the details of a particular build job, including the current status, failing tests and build time, and even start and stop builds.

For Android phones, you can also install the Hudson Mood widget will also provide updates and alerts about build failures.

Note that these mobile applications rely on a data connection, so while they will typically work well locally, you should not rely on them if the developer in question is out of the country.

SMS Notification

These days, SMS is another ubiquitous communication channel which has the added advantage of reaching people even when they are out of the office. For a build engineer,

Figure 8-24. Using the Hudson Helper iPhone app

this can be a great way to monitor critical builds, even when developers or team leads are away from their desks.

SMS gateways (*http://en.wikipedia.org/wiki/SMS_gateway*) are services that let you send SMS notifications via specially-formatted email addresses (for example, *123456789@mysmsgateway.com* might send an SMS message to 123456789). Many mobile vendors provide this service, as do many third-party service providers. There is no built-in support for SMS Gateways in Jenkins, but the basic functionality of these gateways makes integration relatively easy: you simply add the special email addresses to the normal notification list. Alternatively, using the advanced email configuration, you can set up a separate rule containing only the SMS email addresses (see Figure 8-25). Doing this makes it easier to fine-tune the message contents to suit an SMS message format.

Once you have done this, your users will receive prompt notification of build results in the form of SMS messages (see Figure 8-26). The main disadvantage of this approach is arguably that it is not free, and requires the use of a third-party commercial service. That said, it is really the only notification technique capable of reaching developers when they are out of Internet range or who do not have a data-enabled smartphone.

Figure 8-25. Sending SMS notifications via an SMS Gateway Service

Indeed, this technique is popular among system administrators, and can be very useful for certain critical build jobs.

Making Noise

If you have your Jenkins instance running on a machine that is physically located in proximity to the development team, you may also want to add sounds into the mix of notification strategies. This can be an effective strategy for small co-located teams, though it becomes trickier if the build server is set up on a virtual machine or elsewhere in the building.

There are two ways to integrate audio feedback into your build process in Jenkins: the Jenkins Sounds plugin and the Jenkins Speaks plugin. Both can be installed via the Plugin Manager page in the usual manner.

The Jenkins Sounds plugin is the most flexible of the two. It allows you to build a detailed notification strategy based on the latest build result and also (optionally) on the previous build result as well (see Figure 8-27). For example, you can configure Jenkins to play one sound the first time a build fails, a different sound if the build fails a second time, and yet another sound when the build is fixed.

To set this up, you need to tick the Jenkins Sounds checkbox in the Post-build Actions section of your build job configuration page. You can add as many sound configuration rules as you like. Adding a rule is simple enough. First, you need to choose which build result will trigger the sound. You also need to specify the previous build results for

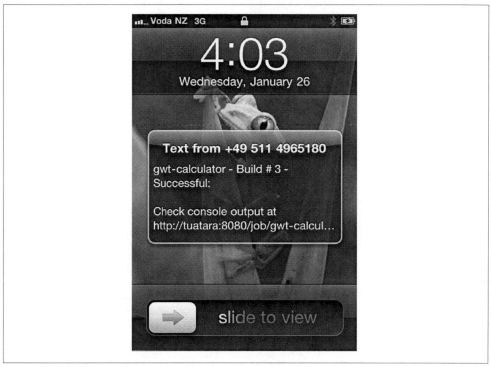

Figure 8-26. Receiving notification via SMS

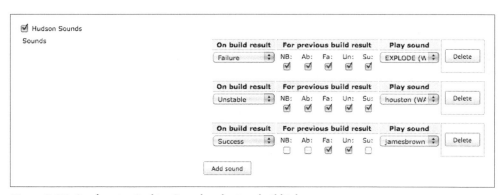

Figure 8-27. Configuring Jenkins Sounds rules in a build job

which this rule is applicable: Not Build (NB), Aborted (Ab), Failed (Fa), Unsuccessful (Un) or Successful (Su).

The Jenkins Sounds plugin proposes a large list of pre-defined sounds, which usually offer plenty of choice for even the most discerning build administrator, but you can add your own to the list if you really want to. Sounds are stored as a ZIP or JAR file containing sound files in a flat directory structure (i.e., no subdirectories). The list of sounds proposed by the plugin is simply the list of filenames, minus the extensions. The plugin supports AIFF, AU, and WAV files.

In the System Configuration page, you can give Jenkins a new sound archive file, using the *http://* notation if your sound archive file is available on a local web server, or the *file://* notation if it is available locally (see Figure 8-28). Once you have saved the configuration, you can test the sounds in your sound archive via the Test Sound button in the Advanced section.

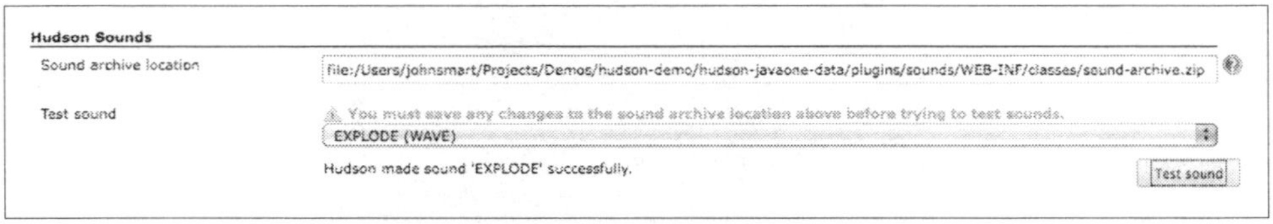

Figure 8-28. Configuring Jenkins Sounds

The Jenkins Sounds plugin is an excellent choice if you want to complement your more conventional notification techniques. Short, recognizable sounds are a great way to grab a developer's attention and let the team know that something needs fixing. They will then be a bit more receptive when the more detailed notifications follow.

Another option is the Jenkins Speaks plugin. With this plugin, you can get Jenkins to broadcast a customized announcement (in a very robotic voice) when your build fails (see Figure 8-29). You can configure the exact message using Jelly. Jelly is an XML-based scripting language used widely in the lower levels of Jenkins.

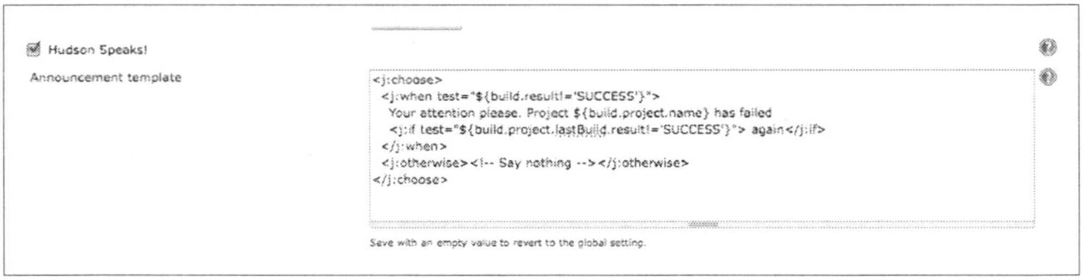

Figure 8-29. Configuring Jenkins Speaks

The advantage of this approach lies in it's precision: since you can use Jenkins variables in the Jelly script, you can get Jenkins to say just about anything you want about the state of the build. Here is a simple example:

```
<j:choose>
  <j:when test="${build.result!='SUCCESS'}">
    Your attention please. Project ${build.project.name} has failed
    <j:if test="${build.project.lastBuild.result!='SUCCESS'}"> again</j:if>
  </j:when>
```

```
        <j:otherwise><!-- Say nothing --></j:otherwise>
    </j:choose>
```

If you leave this field blank, the plugin will use a default template that you can configure in the System Configuration page. In fact, it is usually a good idea to do this, and only to use a project-specific script if you really need to.

The disadvantage is that the robotic voice can make it a little hard to understand. For this reason, it is a good idea to start your announcement with a generic phrase such as "Your attention please," or to combine it with the Jenkins Sounds plugin, so that you have developers' attention before the actual message is broadcast. Using hyphens in your project names (e.g., *game-of-life* rather then *gameoflife*) will also help the plugin know how to pronounce your project names.

Both these approaches are useful for small teams, but can be limited for larger ones, when the server is not physically located in close proximity to the development team. Future versions may support playing sounds on a separate machine, but at the time of writing this feature was not available.

Extreme Feedback Devices

Many more imaginative notification tools and strategies exist, and there is plenty of scope for improvisation if you are willing to improvise with electronics a little. This includes devices such as Ambient Orbs, Lava Lamps, traffic lights, or other more exotic USB-controlled devices. The Build Radiator (see "Build Radiators" on page 202) also falls into this category if you project it onto a big enough screen.

One device that integrates very nicely with Jenkins is the Nabaztag. The Nabaztag (see Figure 8-30) is a popular WiFi-enabled robotic rabbit that can flash colored lights, play music, or even speak. Once advantage of the Nabaztag is that, since it works via WiFi, it is not constrained to be located near the build server, and so will work even if your Jenkins instance is in a server room or on a virtual machine. As far as extreme feedback devices go, these little fellows are hard to beat.

And best of all, there is a Jenkins plugin available for the Nabaztag. Once you have installed the Nabaztag plugin and restarted Jenkins, it is easy to configure. In Jenkins's main Configuration page, go to the Global Nabaztag Settings section and enter the serial number and secret token for your electronic bunny (see Figure 8-31). You can also provide some default information about how your build bunny should react to changes in build status (should it report on starting and successful builds, for example), what voice it should use, and what message it should say when a build fails, succeeds, is fixed, or fails again. Then, to activate Nabaztag notification for a particular build job, you need to tick the Nabaztag Publisher option in your build job configuration. Depending on your environment, for example, you may or may not want all of your builds to send notifications to your Nabaztag.

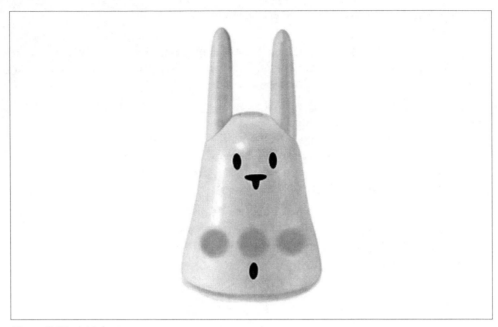

Figure 8-30. A Nabaztag

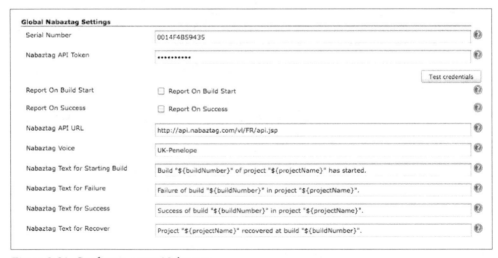

Figure 8-31. Configuring your Nabaztag

With the notable exception of the build radiator, many of these devices have similar limitations to the Jenkins Speaks and Jenkins Sounds plugins (see "Making Noise" on page 218)—they are best suited for small, co-located teams, working on a limited number of projects. Nevertheless, when they work, they can be a useful addition to your general notification strategy.

Conclusion

Notification is a vital part of your overall CI strategy. After all, a failed build is of little use if there is no one listening. Nor is notification a one-size-fits-all affair. You need to think about your organization, and tailor your strategy to suite the local corporate culture and predominant tool set.

Indeed, it is important to define and implement a well thought-out notification strategy that suits your environment. Email, for example, is ubiquitous, so this will form the backbone of many notification strategies, but if you work in a larger team or with a busy technical lead, you may want to consider setting up an escalation strategy based on the advanced email options (see "More Advanced Email Notification" on page 197). But you should complement this with one of the more active strategies, such as instant messaging or a desktop notifier. If your team already uses a chat or IRC channel to communicate, try to integrate this into your notification strategy as well. And SMS notification is a great strategy for really critical build jobs.

You should also ensure that you have both passive and active (or pull and push) notification strategies. A prominent build radiator or an extreme feedback device, for example, sends a strong message to the team that fixing builds is a priority task, and can help install a more agile team culture.

CHAPTER 9

Code Quality

Introduction

Few would deny the importance of writing quality code. High quality code contains less bugs, and is easier to understand and easier to maintain. However, the precise definitions of code quality can be more subjective, varying between organizations, teams, and even individuals within a team.

This is where coding standards come into play. Coding standards are rules, sometimes relatively arbitrary, that define the coding styles and conventions that are considered acceptable within a team or organization. In many cases, agreeing on a set of standards, and applying them, is more important than the standards themselves. Indeed, one of the most important aspects of quality code is that it is easy to read and to understand. If developers within a team all apply the same coding standards and practices, the code will be more readable, at least for members of that team. And if the standards are commonly used within the industry, the code will also be more readable for new developers arriving on the team.

Coding standards include both aesthetic aspects such as code layout and formatting, naming conventions, and so forth, as well as potentially bad practices such as missing curly brackets after a condition in Java. A consistent coding style lowers maintenance costs, makes code clearer and more readable, and makes it easier to work on code written by other team members.

Only an experienced developer can really judge code quality in all its aspects. That is the role of code reviews and, among other things, practices like pair programming. In particular, only a human eye can decide if a piece of code is truly well written, and if it actually does what the requirements ask of it. However, code quality metrics tools can help a great deal. In fact it is unrealistic to try to enforce coding standards without the use of such tools.

These tools analyze your application source code or byte code, and check whether the code respects certain rules. Code quality metrics can encompass many aspects of code quality, from coding standards and best practices right through to code coverage, with everything from compiler warnings to TODO comments in between. Certain metrics concentrate on measurable characteristics of your code base, such as the number of lines of code (NLOC), average code complexity, or the number of lines per class. Others focus on more sophisticated static analysis, or on looking for potential bugs or poor practices in your code.

There are a wide range of code quality reporting plugins available for Jenkins. Many are for Java static analysis tools, such as Checkstyle, PMD, FindBugs, Cobertura, and JDepend. Others, such as fxcop and NCover, are focused on .NET applications.

With all of these tools, you need to configure your build job to generate the code quality metrics data before Jenkins can produce any reports.

The notable exception to this rule is Sonar. Sonar can extract code quality metrics from any Maven project, with no additional configuration required in your Maven project. This is great when you have large numbers of existing Maven projects that you need to integrate into Jenkins, and you want to configure consistent code quality reporting across all of your projects.

In the rest of this chapter, we will see how to set up code quality reporting in your Jenkins builds, and also how you can use it as an effective part of your build process.

Code Quality in Your Build Process

Before we look at how to report on code quality metrics in Jenkins, it can be useful to take a step back and look at the larger picture. Code Quality metrics are of limited value in isolation—they need to be part of a broader process improvement strategy.

The first level of code quality integration should be the IDE. Modern IDEs have great support for many code quality tools—Checkstyle, PMD, and FindBugs all have plugins for Eclipse, NetBeans, and IntelliJ, which provide rapid feedback for developers on code quality issues. This is a much faster and more efficient way to provide feedback for individual developers, and to teach developers about the organizational or project coding standards.

The second level is your build server. In addition to your normal unit and integration test build jobs, set up a dedicated code quality build, which runs after the normal build and test. The aim of this process is to produce project-wide code quality metrics, to keep tabs on how the project is doing as a whole, and to address any issues from a high level. The effectiveness of these reports can be increased by a weekly code quality review, in which code quality issues and trends are discussed within the team.

It is important to run this job separately, because code coverage analysis and many static analysis tools can be quite slow to run. It is also important to keep any code coverage tests well away from builds, as the code coverage process produces instrumented code which should never be deployed to a repository for production use.

Code quality reporting is, by default, a relatively passive process. No one will know the state of the project if they don't seek out the information on the build server. While this is better than nothing, if you are serious about code quality, there is a better way. Rather than simply reporting on code quality, set up a dedicated code quality build, which runs after the normal build and test, and configure the build to fail if code quality metrics are not at an acceptable level. You can do this in Jenkins or in your build script, although one advantage of configuring this outside of your build script is that you can change code quality build failing criteria more easily without changing the project source code.

As a final word, remember that coding standards are guidelines and recommendations, not absolute rules. Use failing code quality builds and code quality reports as indicators of a possible area of improvement, not as measurements of absolute value.

Popular Java and Groovy Code Quality Analysis Tools

There are many open source tools that can help identify poor coding practices.

In the Java world, three static analysis tools have stood the test of time, and are widely used in very complementary ways. Checkstyle excels at checking coding standards and conventions, coding practices, as well as other metrics such code complexity. PMD is a static analysis tool similar to Checkstyle, more focused on coding and design practices. And FindBugs is an innovative tool issued from the ongoing research work of Bill Pugh and his team at the University of Maryland that focuses on identifying potentially dangerous and buggy code. And if you are working with Groovy or Grails, you can use CodeNarc, which checks Groovy coding practices and convention.

All of these tools can be easily integrated into your build process. In the following sections, we will look at how to set up these tools to generate the XML reports that Jenkins can then use for its own reporting.

Checkstyle

Checkstyle (*http://checkstyle.sourceforge.net*) is a static analysis tool for Java. Originally designed to enforce a set of highly-configurable coding standards, Checkstyle now also lets you check for poor coding practices, as well as overly complex and duplicated code. Checkstyle is a versatile and flexible tool that should have its place in any Java-based code quality analysis strategy.

Checkstyle supports a very large number of rules, including ones relating to naming conventions, annotations, javadoc comments, class and method size, code complexity metrics, poor coding practices, and many others.

Duplicated code is another important code quality issue—duplicated or near-duplicated code is harder to maintain and to debug. Checkstyle provides some support for the detection of duplicated code, but more specialized tools such as CPD do a better job in this area.

One of the nice things about Checkstyle is how easy it is to configure. You can start off with the Sun coding conventions and tweak them to suit your needs, or start from scratch. Using the Eclipse plugin (or even directly in XML), you can pick and choose from several hundred different rules, and fine-tune the settings of the rules you do choose (see Figure 9-1). This is important, as different organizations, teams and even projects have different requirements and preferences with regards to coding standards, and it is better to have a precise set of rules that can be adhered to, rather than a broad set of rules that will be ignored. It is especially important where large legacy code bases are involved—in these cases, it is often better to start off with a more limited set of rules than to be overwhelmed with a large number of relatively minor formatting issues.

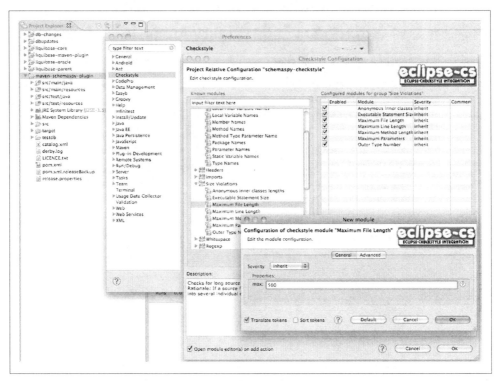

Figure 9-1. It is easy to configure Checkstyle rules in Eclipse

Configuring Checkstyle in your build is usually straightforward. If you are using Ant, you need to download the checkstyle JAR file from the website (*http://checkstyle.sourceforge.net*) and make it available to Ant. You could place it in your Ant *lib* directory, but this would mean customizing the Ant installation on your build server (and any slave nodes), so it is not a very portable solution. A better approach would be to place the Checkstyle JAR file in one of your project directories, or to use Ivy or the Maven

Ant Task library to declare a dependency on Checkstyle. If you opt for keeping the Checkstyle JAR file in the project directories, you could declare the Checkstyle task as shown here:

```
<taskdef resource="checkstyletask.properties"
         classpath="lib/checkstyle-5.3-all.jar"/>
```

Then, to generate Checkstyle reports in an XML format that Jenkins can use, you could do the following:

```
<target name="checkstyle">
  <checkstyle config="src/main/config/company-checks.xml">
    <fileset dir="src/main/java" includes="**/*.java"/>
    <formatter type="plain"/>
    <formatter type="xml"/>
  </checkstyle>
</target>
```

Now, just invoke this task (e.g., `ant checkstyle`) to generate the Checkstyle reports.

In Maven 2, you could add something like the following to the `<reporting>` section:

```
<reporting>
  <plugins>
    <plugin>
      <groupId>org.apache.maven.plugins</groupId>
      <artifactId>maven-checkstyle-plugin</artifactId>
      <version>2.4</version>
      <configuration>
        <configLocation>
          src/main/config/company-checks.xml
        </configLocation>
      </configuration>
    </plugin>
  </plugins>
</reporting>
```

For a Maven 3 project, you need to add the plugin to the `<reportPlugins>` element of the `<configuration>` section of the *maven-site-plugin*:

```
<project>
  <properties>
    <sonar.url>http://buildserver.acme.org:9000</sonar.url>
  </properties>
  <build>
    ...
    <plugins>
      ...
      <plugin>
        <groupId>org.apache.maven.plugins</groupId>
        <artifactId>maven-site-plugin</artifactId>
        <version>3.0-beta-2</version>
        <configuration>
          <reportPlugins>
            <plugin>
              <groupId>org.apache.maven.plugins</groupId>
```

```
    <artifactId>maven-checkstyle-plugin</artifactId>
    <version>2.4</version>
    <configuration>
     <configLocation>
       ${sonar.url}/rules_configuration/export/java/My_Rules/checkstyle.xml
     </configLocation>
    </configuration>
   </plugin>
  </reportPlugins>
 </configuration>
</plugin>
</plugins>
</build>
</project>
```

Now, running `mvn checkstyle:checkstyle` or `mvn site` will analyse your source code and generate XML reports that Jenkins can use.

Note that in the last example, we used a Checkstyle ruleset that we have uploaded to a Sonar server (defined by the `${sonar.url}` property). This strategy makes it easy to use the same set of Checkstyle rules for Eclipse, Maven, Jenkins, and Sonar.

Recent versions of Gradle also offer some integrated Checkstyle support. You can set up Checkstyle for your builds as shown here:

```
apply plugin: 'code-quality'
```

This will use the checkstyle ruleset in *config/checkstyle/checkstyle.xml* by default. You can override this with the `checkstyleConfigFileName` property: at the time of writing, however, you can't get the Gradle code quality plugin to obtain the Checkstyle rules from a URL.

You can generate the Checkstyle reports here by running `gradle checkstyleMain` or `gradle check`.

PMD/CPD

PMD (*http://pmd.sourceforge.net*) is another popular static analysis tool. It focuses on potential coding problems such as unused or suboptimal code, code size and complexity, and good coding practices. Some typical rules include "Empty If Statement," "Broken Null Check," "Avoid Deeply Nested If Statements," "Switch Statements Should Have Default," and "Logger Is Not Static Final." There is a fair amount of overlap with some of the Checkstyle rules, though PMD does have some more technical rules, and more specialized ones such as rules related to JSF and Android.

PMD also comes with CPD, a robust open source detector of duplicated and near-duplicated code.

PMD is a little less flexible than Checkstyle, though you can still pick and choose the rules you want to use in Eclipse, and then export them as an XML file (see Figure 9-2). You can then import this rule set into other Eclipse projects, into Sonar, or use it in your Ant or Maven builds.

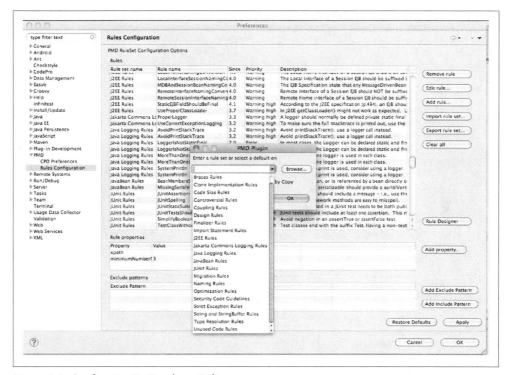

Figure 9-2. Configuring PMD rules in Eclipse

PMD comes with an Ant task that you can use to generate the PMD and CPD reports. First, though, you need to define these tasks, as shown in the following example:

```
<path id="pmd.classpath">
    <pathelement location="${build}"/>
    <fileset dir="lib/pmd">
        <include name="*.jar"/>
    </fileset>
</path>

<taskdef name="pmd" classname="net.sourceforge.pmd.ant.PMDTask"
        classpathref="pmd.classpath"/>

<taskdef name="cpd" classname="net.sourceforge.pmd.cpd.CPDTask"
        classpathref="pmd.classpath"/>
```

Next, you can generate the PMD XML report by invoking the PMD task as illustrated here:

```
<target name="pmd">
 <taskdef name="pmd" classname="net.sourceforge.pmd.ant.PMDTask"
          classpathref="pmd.classpath"/>

 <pmd rulesetfiles="basic" shortFilenames="true">
  <formatter type="xml" toFile="target/pmd.xml" />
  <fileset dir="src/main/java" includes="**/*.java"/>
 </pmd>
</target>
```

And, to generate the CPD XML report, you could do something like this:

```
<target name="cpd">
  <cpd minimumTokenCount="100" format="xml" outputFile="/target/cpd.xml">
    <fileset dir="src/main/java" includes="**/*.java"/>
  </cpd>
</target>
```

You can place this XML ruleset in your project classpath (for example, in src/main/resources for a Maven project), or in a separate module (if you want to share the configuration between projects). An example of how to configure Maven 2 to generate PMD and CPD reports using an exported XML ruleset as shown here:

```
<reporting>
  <plugins>
    <plugin>
      <groupId>org.apache.maven.plugins</groupId>
      <artifactId>maven-pmd-plugin</artifactId>
      <version>2.5</version>
      <configuration>
        <!-- PMD options -->
        <targetJdk>1.6</targetJdk>
        <aggregate>true</aggregate>
        <format>xml</format>
        <rulesets>
          <ruleset>/pmd-rules.xml</ruleset>
        </rulesets>

        <!-- CPD options -->
        <minimumTokens>20</minimumTokens>
        <ignoreIdentifiers>true</ignoreIdentifiers>
      </configuration>
    </plugin>
  </plugins>
</reporting>
```

If you are using Maven 3, you would place the plugin definition in the <maven-site-plugin> configuration section. This example also shows how to use a ruleset in another dependency (in this case the *pmd-rules.jar* file):

```
<project>
  ...
  <build>
```

```
    ...
    <plugins>
      ...
      <plugin>
        <groupId>org.apache.maven.plugins</groupId>
        <artifactId>maven-site-plugin</artifactId>
        <version>3.0-beta-2</version>
        <configuration>
          <reportPlugins>
            <plugin>
              <groupId>org.apache.maven.plugins</groupId>
              <artifactId>maven-pmd-plugin</artifactId>
              <version>2.5</version>
              <configuration>
                <!-- PMD options -->
                <targetJdk>1.6</targetJdk>
                <aggregate>true</aggregate>
                <format>xml</format>
                <rulesets>
                  <ruleset>/pmd-rules.xml</ruleset>
                </rulesets>

                <!-- CPD options -->
                <minimumTokens>50</minimumTokens>
                <ignoreIdentifiers>true</ignoreIdentifiers>
              </configuration>
            </plugin>
          </reportPlugins>
        </configuration>
        <dependencies>
          <dependency>
            <groupId>com.wakaleo.code-quality</groupId>
            <artifactId>pmd-rules</artifactId>
            <version>1.0.1</version>
          </dependency>
        </dependencies>
      </plugin>
    </plugins>
  </build>
</project>
```

Now, you can run either `mvn site` or `mvn pmd:pmd pmd:cpd` to generate the PMD and CPD reports.

Unfortunately there is currently no built-in Gradle support for PMD or CPD, so you have to fall back on invoking the PMD Ant plugin directly, as shown here:

```
configurations {
    pmdConf
}

dependencies {
    pmdConf 'pmd:pmd:4.2.5'
}

task pmd << {
```

```
println 'Running PMD static code analysis'
ant {
    taskdef(name:'pmd', classname:'net.sourceforge.pmd.ant.PMDTask',
            classpath: configurations.pmdConf.asPath)

    taskdef(name:'cpd', classname:'net.sourceforge.pmd.cpd.CPDTask',
                classpath: configurations.pmdConf.asPath)

    pmd(shortFilenames:'true', failonruleviolation:'false',
        rulesetfiles:'conf/pmd-rules.xml') {
        formatter(type:'xml', toFile:'build/pmd.xml')
        fileset(dir: "src/main/java") {
            include(name: '**/*.java')
        }
        fileset(dir: "src/test/java") {
            include(name: '**/*.java')
        }
    }

    cpd(minimumTokenCount:'50', format: 'xml',
        ignoreIdentifiers: 'true',
        outputFile:'build/cpd.xml') {
        fileset(dir: "src/main/java") {
            include(name: '**/*.java')
        }
        fileset(dir: "src/test/java") {
            include(name: '**/*.java')
        }
    }
}
}
```

This configuration will use the PMD rule set in the *src/config* directory, and generate a PMD XML report called *pmd.xml* in the *build* directory. It will also run CPD and generate a CPD XML report called *cpd.xml* in the *build* directory.

FindBugs

FindBugs is a powerful code quality analysis tool that checks your application byte code for potential bugs, performance problems, or poor coding habits. FindBugs is the result of research carried out at the University of Maryland lead by Bill Pugh, that studies byte code patterns coming from bugs in large real-world projects, such as the JDKs, Eclipse, and source code from Google applications. FindBugs can detect some fairly significant issues such as null pointer exceptions, infinite loops, and unintentionally accessing the internal state of an object. Unlike many other static analysis tools, FindBugs tends to find a smaller number of issues, but of those issues, a larger proportion will be important.

FindBugs is less configurable than the other tools we have seen, though in practice you generally don't need to fine-tune the rules as much as the other tools we've discussed.

You can list the individual rules you want to apply, but you can't configure a shared XML file between your Maven builds and your IDE, for example.

FindBugs comes bundled with an Ant task. You can define the FindBugs task in Ant as shown below. FindBugs needs to refer to the FindBugs home directory, which is where the binary distribution of FindBugs has been unzipped. To make the build more portable, we are storing the FindBugs installation in our project directory structure, in the *tools/findbugs* directory:

```
<property name="findbugs.home" value="tools/findbugs" />

<taskdef name="findbugs" classname="edu.umd.cs.findbugs.anttask.FindBugsTask" >
  <classpath>
    <fileset dir="${findbugs.home}/lib" includes="**/*.jar"/>
  </classpath>
</taskdef>
```

Then, to run FindBugs, you could set up a "findbugs" target as shown in the following example. Note that FindBugs runs against your application byte-code, not your source code, so you need to compile your source code first:

```
<target name="findbugs" depends="compile">
  <findbugs home="${findbugs.home}" output="xml" outputFile="target/findbugs.xml">
    <class location="${classes.dir}" />
    <auxClasspath refId="dependency.classpath" />
    <sourcePath path="src/main/java" />
  </findbugs>
</target>
```

If you are using Maven 2, you don't need to keep a local copy of the FindBugs installation. You just need to configure FindBugs in the reporting section as shown here:

```
<reporting>
  <plugins>
    <plugin>
      <groupId>org.codehaus.mojo</groupId>
      <artifactId>findbugs-maven-plugin</artifactId>
      <version>2.3.1</version>
      <configuration>
        <effort>Max</effort>
        <xmlOutput>true</xmlOutput>
      </configuration>
    </plugin>
  </plugins>
</reporting>
```

Or for a Maven 3 project:

```
<project>
  ...
  <build>
    ...
    <plugins>
      ...
      <plugin>
```

```
            <groupId>org.apache.maven.plugins</groupId>
            <artifactId>maven-site-plugin</artifactId>
            <version>3.0-beta-2</version>
            <configuration>
              <reportPlugins>
                  <plugin>
                    <groupId>org.codehaus.mojo</groupId>
                    <artifactId>findbugs-maven-plugin</artifactId>
                    <version>2.3.1</version>
                    <configuration>
                      <effort>Max</effort>
                      <xmlOutput>true</xmlOutput>
                    </configuration>
                  </plugin>
              </reportPlugins>
            </configuration>
        </plugin>
      </plugins>
    </build>
  </project>
```

In both cases, you can generate the XML reports by running `mvn site` or `mvn find
bugs:findbugs`. The XML reports will be placed in the *target* directory.

At the time of writing there is no special support for FindBugs in Gradle, so you need
to invoke the FindBugs Ant plugin.

CodeNarc

CodeNarc is a static analysis tool for Groovy code, similar to PMD for Java. It checks
Groovy source code for potential defects, poor coding practices and styles, overly com-
plex code, and so on. Typical rules include "Constant If Expression," "Empty Else
Block," "GString As Map Key," and "Grails Stateless Service."

For Ant or Maven-based projects, the CodeNarc Ant plugin is the simplest option (a
Maven plugin is under development at the time of writing). A typical Ant configuration
for use with Jenkins would look like this:

```
<taskdef name="codenarc" classname="org.codenarc.ant.CodeNarcTask"/>
<target name="runCodeNarc">
    <codenarc ruleSetFiles="rulesets/basic.xml,rulesets/imports.xml"
              maxPriority1Violations="0">

        <report type="xml">
            <option name="outputFile" value="reports/CodeNarc.xml" />
        </report>

        <fileset dir="src">
            <include name="**/*.groovy"/>
        </fileset>
    </codenarc>
</target>
```

You can integrate CodeNarc into a Grails project simply by installing the CodeNarc plugin:

```
$ grails install-plugin codenarc
```

This will configure CodeNarc to analyse the Groovy files in your Grails application code, as well as in the *src/groovy* and *test* directories.

Gradle 0.8 also provides support for CodeNarc in the code-quality plugin, that you can configure in your builds as shown here:

```
apply plugin: 'code-quality'
```

This will use the CodeNarc configuration file in *config/codenarc/codenarc.xml* by default. You can override this with the `codeNarcConfigFileName` property.

You can generate the CodeNarc reports here by running `gradle codenarcMain` or, more simply, `gradle check`.

Reporting on Code Quality Issues with the Violations Plugin

One of the most useful code quality plugins for Jenkins is the Violations plugin. This plugin will not analyse your project source code (you need to configure your build to do that), but it does a great job on reporting on the code quality metrics generated for individual builds and trends over time. The plugin caters for reports on code quality metrics coming from a large range of static analysis tools, including:

For Java
Checkstyle, CPD, PMD, FindBugs, and jcreport

For Groovy
codenarc

For JavaScript
jslint

For .Net
gendarme and stylecop

Installing the plugin is straightforward. Just go to the Plugin Manager screen and select the Jenkins Violations plugin. Once you have installed the plugin and restarted Jenkins, you will be able to use it for your projects.

The Violations plugin does not generate the code quality metrics data itself—you need to configure your built to do that, as shown in the previous section. An example of doing this for a Maven build job is illustrated in Figure 9-3. Notice that here we are invoking the Maven plugin goals directly. We could also just run `mvn site`, but if we are only interested in the code quality metrics, and not the other elements of the Maven-generated site, calling the plugins directly will result in faster builds.

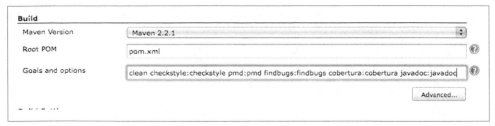

Figure 9-3. Generating code quality reports in a Maven build

Once you have set this up, you can configure the violations plugin to generate reports and, if required, trigger notifications, based on the report results. Just go to the Post-build Actions and check the Report Violations checkbox. The details of the configuration vary depending on the project type. Lets look at Freestyle build jobs first.

Working with Freestyle Build Jobs

Freestyle build jobs allow you the most configuration flexibility, and are your only option for non-Java projects.

When you use the Violations plugin with a Freestyle build job, you need to specify the paths to each of the XML reports generated by the static analysis tools you have used (see Figure 9-4). The plugin can cater for several reports from the same tool, which is useful for Maven multimodule projects—just use a wildcard expression to identify the reports you want (for example, `**/target/checkstyle.xml`).

The Violations plugin will generate a graph tracking the number of each type of issue over time (see Figure 9-5). The graph displays a different-colored line for each type of violations your are tracking, as well as a summary of the latest results.

You can also click on this graph to drill down into a particular build. Here, you can see the number of issues raised for that particular build (see Figure 9-6), with various breakdowns by violation type, severity, and file.

Finally, you can drill down into a particular class, to display the detailed list of issues, along with where they appear in the source code.

But the Violations plugin also allows for a more proactive management of code quality. You can use the results of the code quality analysis reports to influence the weather icon on the Jenkins dashboard. This weather icon is normally related to the number of failing builds in the previous five builds, but Jenkins can also take into account other factors, such as code quality results. Displaying a cloudy or stormy icon for a project on the dashboard is a much better way of raising awareness about code quality issues that simply relying on graphs and reports on the build job page.

To set this up, you need to go back to the Report Violations section in the Post-build Actions. The first three columns in Figure 9-4 show a sunny icon, a stormy icon, and a yellow ball. The one with the sunny icon is the maximum number of violations

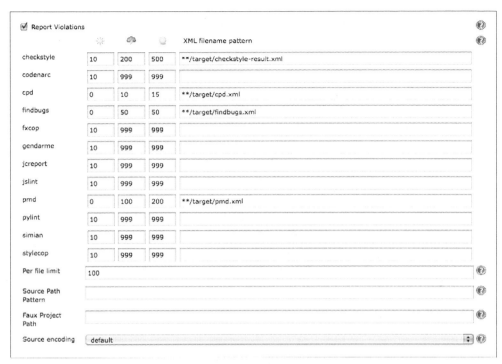

Figure 9-4. Configuring the violations plugin for a Freestyle project

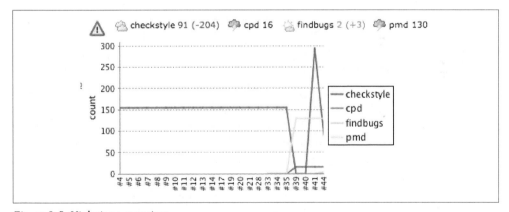

Figure 9-5. Violations over time

tolerated in order to keep the sunny weather icon on the dashboard page. The second column, with the stormy weather icon, is the number of violations that will cause a stormy icon to appear on the dashboard. If you have a number of violations between these two extremes, you will get one of the cloudy icons.

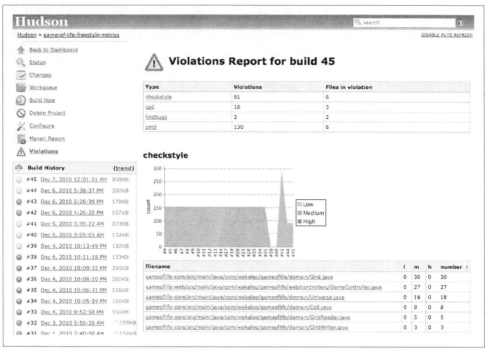

Figure 9-6. Violations for a given build

You can set different values for different tools. The exact thresholds will vary between teams and between projects, and also between tools. For example, Checkstyle will typically raise a lot more issues than FindBugs or CPD, with PMD being somewhere in between. You need to adjust the values you use to reflect how these tools work on your code base, and your expectations.

You can take this even further with the third column (the one with the yellow ball). This column lets you set a number of violations that will cause the build to be declared unstable. Remember, when a build becomes unstable Jenkins will send out notification messages, so this is an even more proactive strategy.

For example, in Figure 9-4, we have configured the minimum number of Checkstyle violations to 10, which means that the sunny weather icon will only appear if there are 10 or fewer Checkstyle violations. If there are more than 10, the weather will degrade progressively, until at the 200 violations mark, it will become stormy. And if there are 500 or more Checkstyle violations, the project will be flagged as unstable.

Now look at the configuration for CPD, the duplicated code detector that comes with PMD. In this project, we have adopted a zero-tolerance policy for duplicated code, so the sunny icon value is set to zero. The stormy icon is set to 10, so if there are 10 or more copy-paste violations, the project weather indicator will appear as stormy. And if the project has 15 or more copy-paste violations, it will be declared unstable.

Now, on the Dashboard page, this project will appear both with a stormy weather icon and as unstable, even though there are no test failures (see Figure 9-7). This particular build is unstable because there are 16 CPD violations. In addition, if you place your mouse over the weather icon, Jenkins will display some more details about how it calculated this particular status.

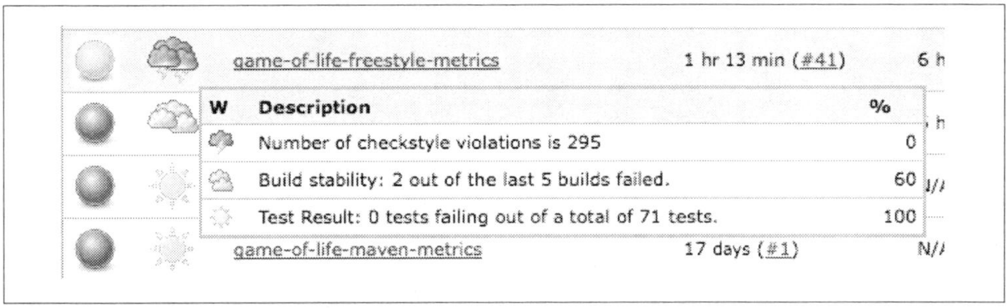

Figure 9-7. Configuring the violations plugin for a Freestyle project

Working with Maven Build Jobs

Maven build jobs in Jenkins use the Maven conventions and information in the project *pom.xml* file to make configuration easier and more lightweight. When you use the Violations plugin with a Maven build job, Jenkins uses these conventions to reduce the amount of work you need to do to configure the plugin. You don't need to tell Jenkins where to find the XML reports for many of the static analysis tools (for example, Checkstyle, PMD, FindBugs, and CPD), as Jenkins can figure this out based from the Maven conventions and plugin configurations (see Figure 9-8). If you do need to override these conventions, you can choose the Pattern option in the "XML filename pattern" drop-down list, and enter a path as you do for freestyle build jobs.

The Violations plugin works well with multimodule Maven projects, but at the time of writing it needs a little tweaking to obtain best results. Maven build jobs understand the structure of multimodule projects (see Figure 9-9); furthermore, you can drill down into any module and get a detailed view of the build results for that build job.

This is a very useful feature, but it means you need to do a little extra work to get all of the benefits out of the Violations plugins for the individual modules. By default, the violations plugin will display an aggregated view of the code quality metrics like the one in Figure 9-5. You can also click on the violations graph, and view the detailed reports for each module.

However, for this to work correctly, you need to activate the violations plugin individually for each module in addition to the main project. To do this, click on the module you want to configure in the Modules screen, and then click on the "Configure" menu. Here, you will see a small subset of the usual configuration options (see Figure 9-10). Here, you just need to activate the Violations option, and configure the thresholds if

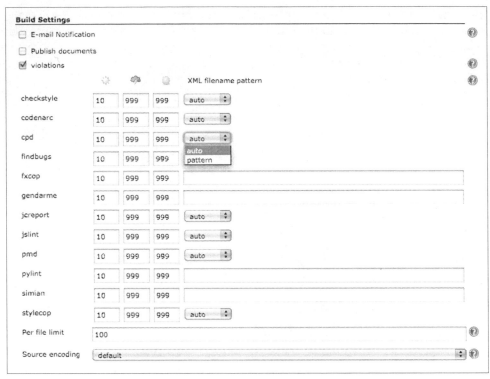

Figure 9-8. Configuring the violations plugin for a Maven project

required. On the positive side, this means that you can define different threshold values for different modules.

Once you have done this, when you click on the violations aggregate graph on the project build job home page, Jenkins will list the individual violations graphs for each module.

Using the Checkstyle, PMD, and FindBugs Reports

You can also report individually on results from Checkstyle, PMD, and FindBugs. In addition to the Violations plugin, there are also Jenkins plugins that produce trend graphs and detailed reports for each of these tools individually. We will look at how to do this for Checkstyle, but the same approach also applies for PMD and FindBugs. You can even use the Analysis Collector Plugin to display the combined results in a graph similar to the one produced by the Violations plugin.

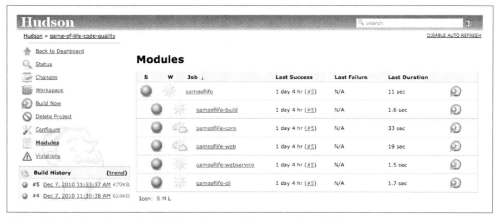

Figure 9-9. Jenkins Maven build jobs understand Maven multimodule structures

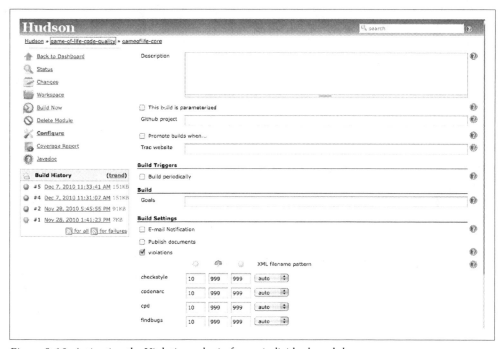

Figure 9-10. Activating the Violations plugin for an individual module

You can install these plugins through the Plugin Manager in the usual way. The plugins in question are called, unsurprisingly, Checkstyle plugin, PMD plugin, and FindBugs plugin. All of these plugins use the Static Analysis Utilities plugin, which you need to install as well (see Figure 9-11).

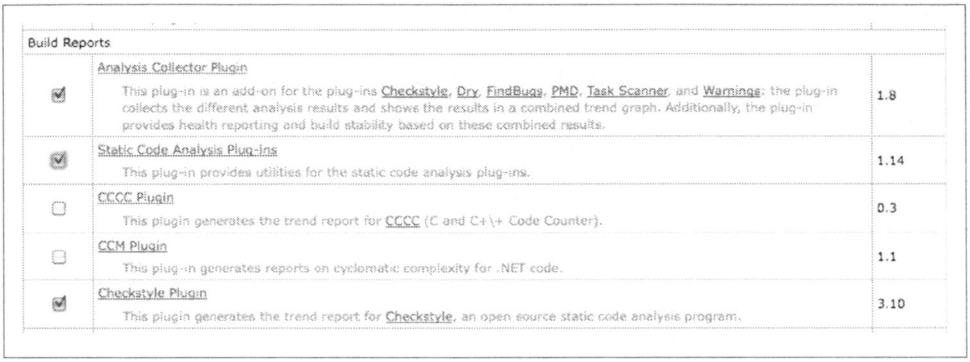

Figure 9-11. Installing the Checkstyle and Static Analysis Utilities plugins

Once you have installed these plugins, you can set up the reporting in your project configuration. Tick the "Publish Checkstyle analysis results" checkbox. In a freestyle build, you will need to specify a path pattern to find the Checkstyle XML reports; in a Maven 2 build, Jenkins will figure out where to look for them by itself.

This will provide basic Checkstyle reporting, but as usual you can fine-tune things further by clicking on the Advanced button. In a Maven 2 build, you can configure the health threshold values (how many violations will cause the build to go from sunny to stormy), and also filter the priority violations you want to include in this calculation. For example, you may only want high priority issues to be taken into account for the weather icon status.

The Freestyle builds have a few more options you can configure: in particular, you can cause the build to become unstable (yellow ball) or even to fail (red ball) if there are more than a given number of violations, or if there are more than a given number of new violations (see Figure 9-12). So, in the configuration in the illustration, if there are more than 50 new checkstyle violations of any priority in a build, the build will be flagged as unstable. This certainly has its uses for Checkstyle, but it can also come in very handy with FindBugs, where high priority issues often represent dangerous and potentially show-stopping bugs.

Now, when the build runs, Jenkins will now generate a trend graph and detailed reports for the Checkstyle violations (see Figure 9-13). From here, you can drill down to see violations per priority, per category, per run type, per package, and so on.

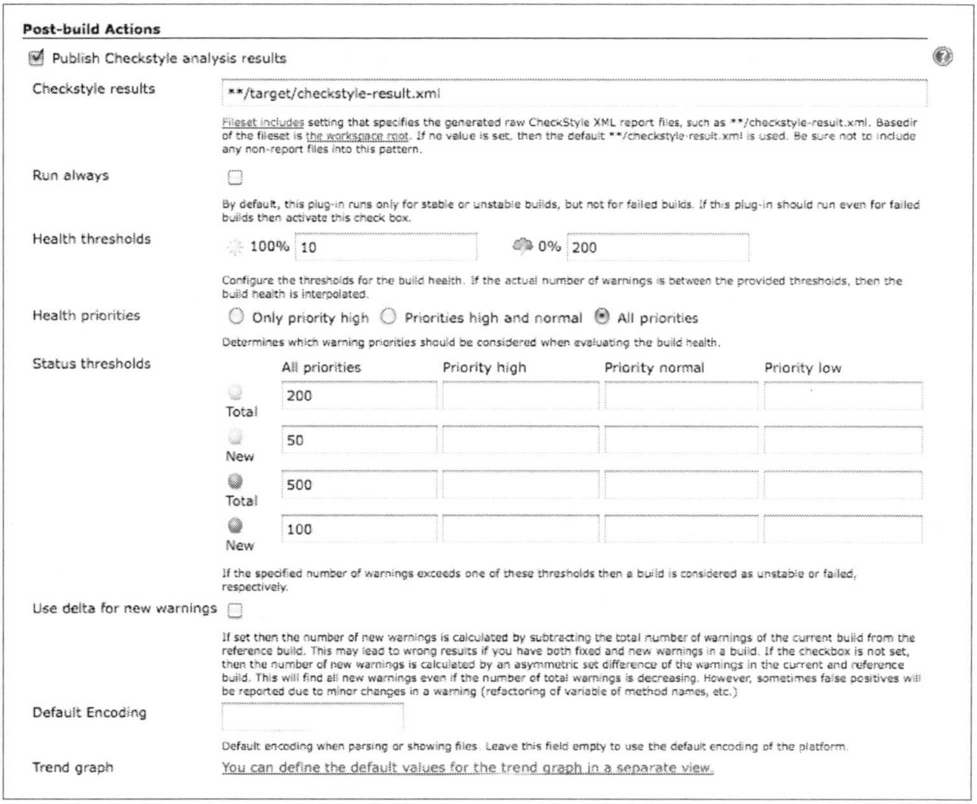

Post-build Actions

☑ Publish Checkstyle analysis results ⊕

Checkstyle results	`**/target/checkstyle-result.xml`

Fileset includes setting that specifies the generated raw CheckStyle XML report files, such as `**/checkstyle-result.xml`. Basedir of the fileset is the workspace root. If no value is set, then the default `**/checkstyle-result.xml` is used. Be sure not to include any non-report files into this pattern.

Run always	☐

By default, this plug-in runs only for stable or unstable builds, but not for failed builds. If this plug-in should run even for failed builds then activate this check box.

Health thresholds	☼ 100% `10` ☁ 0% `200`

Configure the thresholds for the build health. If the actual number of warnings is between the provided thresholds, then the build health is interpolated.

Health priorities   ○ Only priority high   ○ Priorities high and normal   ● All priorities

Determines which warning priorities should be considered when evaluating the build health.

Status thresholds

	All priorities	Priority high	Priority normal	Priority low
○ Total	`200`			
○ New	`50`			
● Total	`500`			
● New	`100`			

If the specified number of warnings exceeds one of these thresholds then a build is considered as unstable or failed, respectively.

Use delta for new warnings ☐

If set then the number of new warnings is calculated by subtracting the total number of warnings of the current build from the reference build. This may lead to wrong results if you have both fixed and new warnings in a build. If the checkbox is not set, then the number of new warnings is calculated by an asymmetric set difference of the warnings in the current and reference build. This will find all new warnings even if the number of total warnings is decreasing. However, sometimes false positives will be reported due to minor changes in a warning (refactoring of variable of method names, etc.)

Default Encoding	

Default encoding when parsing or showing files. Leave this field empty to use the default encoding of the platform.

Trend graph   You can define the default values for the trend graph in a separate view.

Figure 9-12. Configuring the Checkstyle plugin

As we mentioned earlier, the same approach also works with the PMD plugin and the FindBugs plugin. These plugins are a great way to provide more focused reporting on the results of a particular tool, and also give you more control over the impact that these violations will have on the build results.

Reporting on Code Complexity

Code complexity is another important aspect of code quality. Code complexity is measured in a number of ways, but one commonly used (and easy-to-understand) complexity metric is Cyclometric Complexity, which involves measuring the number of different paths through a method. Using this metric, complex code typically has large numbers of nested conditional statements and loops, which make the code harder to understand and to debug.

There is also a code quality theory that correlates code complexity and code coverage, to give a general idea of how reliable a particular piece of code is. This is based on the

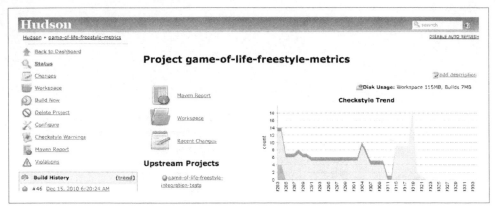

Figure 9-13. Displaying Checkstyle trends

(very understandable) idea that code that is both complex and poorly tested is more likely to contain bugs than simple, well-tested code.

The Coverage Complexity Scatter Plot plugin is designed to let you visualize this information in your Jenkins builds (see Figure 9-14). Dangerously complex and/or untested methods will appear high on the graph, where as the more well-written and well-tested methods will appear lower down.

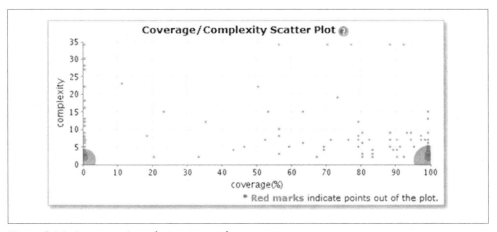

Figure 9-14. A coverage/complexity scatter plot

The scatter graph gives you a good overview of the state of your code in terms of complexity and test coverage, but you can also drill down to investigate further. If you click on any point in the graph, you can see the corresponding methods, with their test coverage and complexity (see Figure 9-15).

Coverage / Complexity Scatter Plot

2 method(s) in the range of coverage (90%~100%) and complexity (5~9)

Method	Complexity	Coverage(%)	Total	Covered
createNextGeneration() : void	7	100	19	19
cellIsOutsideBorders(int,int) : boolean	5	100	3	3

Figure 9-15. You can click on any point in the graph to investigate further

At the time of writing, this plugin requires Clover, so your build needs to have generated a Clover XML coverage report, and you need to have installed and configured the Clover Jenkins plugin (see "Measuring Code Coverage with Clover" on page 153). However support for Cobertura and other tools is planned.

Reporting on Open Tasks

When it comes to code quality, static analysis is not the only tool you can use. Another indicator of the general health of your project can be found in the number of FIXME, TODO, @deprecated, and similar tags scattered through the source code. If there are a lot of these, it can be a sign that your code base has a lot of unfinished work, and is therefore not in a very finalized state.

The Jenkins Task Scanners plugin lets you keep track of these sorts of tags in your source code, and optionally flag a build with a bad weather icon on the dashboard if there are too many open tasks.

To set this up, you need to install both the Static Analysis Utilities plugin and the Task Scanner plugin. Once installed, you can activate the plugin in your project by checking the "Scan workspace for open tasks" checkbox in the Build Settings section of your project job configuration.

Configuring the Task Scanner plugin is pretty straightforward (see Figure 9-16). You simply enter the tags you want to track, with different priorities if you consider certain tags to be more important than others. By default, the plugin will scan all the Java source code in the project, but you can redefine this behavior by entering the Files to scan field. In Figure 9-16, for example, we also check XML and JSP files for tags.

The Advanced button gives you access to a few more sophisticated options. Probably the most useful are the Health thresholds, which let you define the maximum number of issues tolerated before the build can no longer be considered "sunny," and the minimum number of issues required for "stormy weather" status.

The plugin generates a graph that shows tag trends by priority (see Figure 9-17). If you click on the Open Tasks report, you can also see a breakdown of tasks by Maven module, package or file, or even list the open tasks.

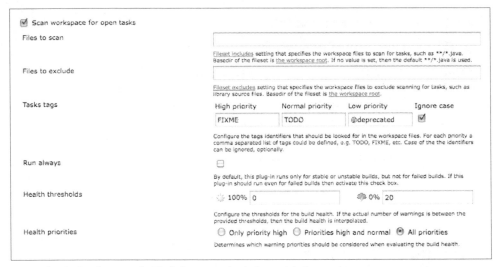

Figure 9-16. Configuring the Task Scanner plugin is straightforward

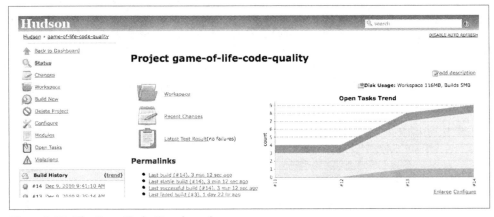

Figure 9-17. The Open Tasks Trend graph

Integrating with Sonar

Sonar (*http://www.sonarsource.org*) is a tool that centralizes a range of code quality metrics into a single website (see Figure 9-18). It uses several Maven plugins (Checkstyle, PMD, FindBugs, Cobertura or Clover, and others) to analyse Maven projects and generate a comprehensive set of code quality metrics reports. Sonar reports on code coverage, rule compliance, and documentation, but also on more high-level metrics such as complexity, maintainability and even technical debt. You can use plugins to extend its features and add support for other languages (such as support for CodeNarc for Groovy source code). The rules used by the various tools are managed and

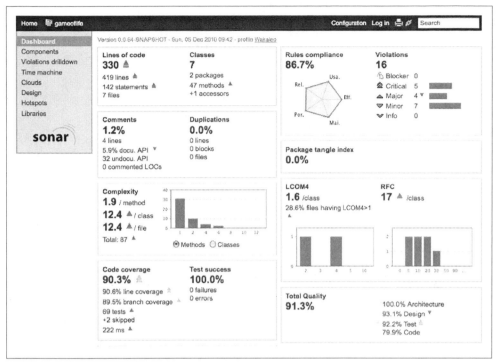

Figure 9-18. Code quality reporting by Sonar

configured centrally on the Sonar website, and the Maven projects being analyzed don't require any particular configuration. This makes Sonar a great fit for working on Maven projects where you have limited control over the pom files.

In one of the most common usages of Sonar, Sonar automatically runs a set of Maven code quality related plugins against your Maven project, and stores the results into a relational database. The Sonar server, which you run separately, then analyzes and displays the results as shown in Figure 9-18.

Jenkins integrates well with Sonar. The Jenkins Sonar Plugin lets you define Sonar instances for all of your projects, and then activate Sonar in particular builds. You can run your Sonar server on a different machine to your Jenkins instance, or on the same. The only constraint is that the Jenkins instance must have JDBC access to the Sonar database, as it injects code quality metrics directly into the database, without going through the Sonar website (see Figure 9-19).

Sonar also has an Ant bootstrap (with a Gradle bootstrap in the making at the time of writing) for non-Maven users.

You install the plugin in the usual way, via the Plugin Manager. Once installed, you configure the Jenkins Sonar plugin in the Configure System screen, in the Sonar section. This involves defining your Sonar instances—you can configure as many instances of

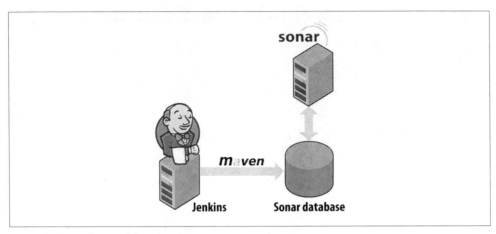

Figure 9-19. Jenkins and Sonar

Sonar as you need. The default configuration assumes that you are running a local instance of Sonar with the default embedded database. This is useful for testing purposes but not very scalable. For a production environment, you will typically run Sonar on a real database such as MySQL or Postgres, and you will need to configure the JDBC connection to the production Sonar database in Jenkins. You do this by clicking on the Advanced button and filling in the appropriate fields (see Figure 9-20).

The other thing you need to configure is when the Sonar build will kick off in a Sonar-enabled build job. You usually configure Sonar to run with one of the long-running Jenkins build jobs, such as the code quality metrics build. It is not very useful to run the Sonar build more than once a day, as Sonar stores metrics in 24-hour slices. The default configuration will kick off a Sonar build in a Sonar-enabled build job whenever the job is triggered by a periodically scheduled build or by a manual build.

To activate Sonar in your build job with the system-wide configuration options, just check the Sonar option in the Post-build Actions (see Figure 9-21). Sonar will run whenever your build is started by one of the trigger mechanisms defined above.

You typically set up Sonar to run on a regular basis, for example every night or once a week. So you can activate Sonar on your normal unit/integration test build job, simply by adding a schedule (see Figure 9-22). This avoids duplicated configuration details between jobs. Or, if you already have a scheduled build job that runs with an appropriate frequency (such as a dedicated code quality metrics build), you can activate Sonar on this build job.

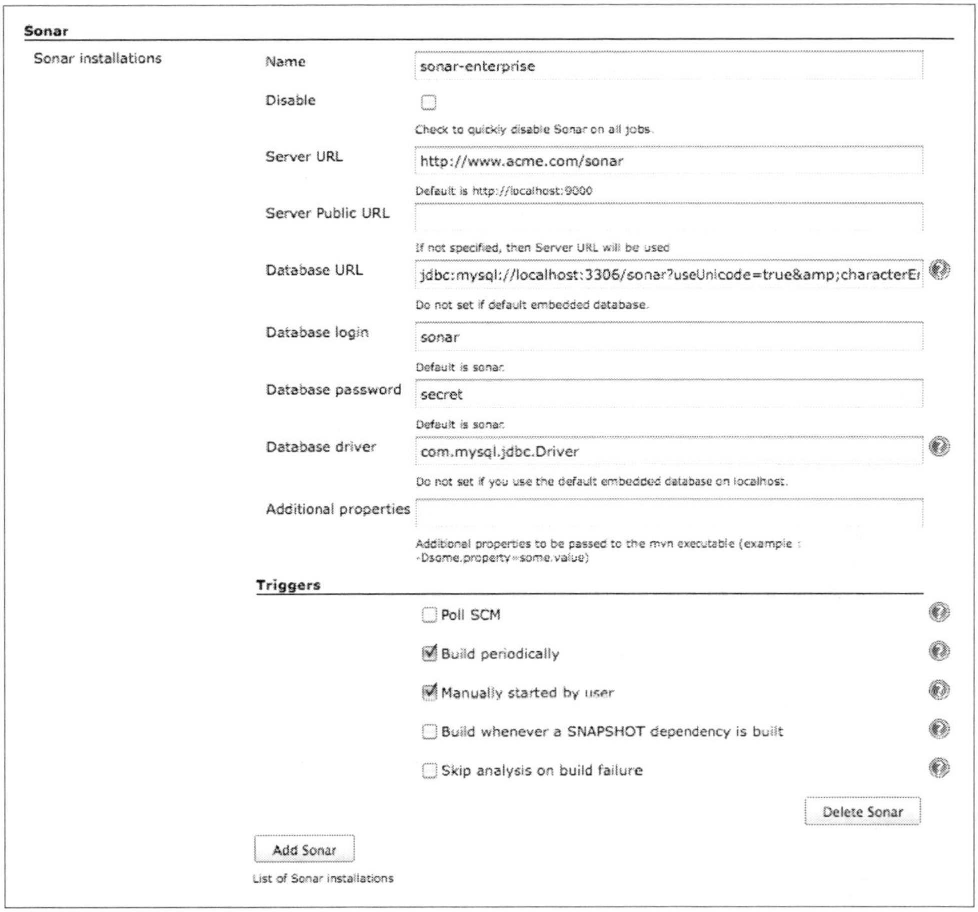

Sonar

Sonar installations

Name	sonar-enterprise	
Disable	☐	
	Check to quickly disable Sonar on all jobs.	
Server URL	http://www.acme.com/sonar	
	Default is http://localhost:9000	
Server Public URL		
	If not specified, then Server URL will be used	
Database URL	jdbc:mysql://localhost:3306/sonar?useUnicode=true&characterEr	
	Do not set if default embedded database.	
Database login	sonar	
	Default is sonar.	
Database password	secret	
	Default is sonar.	
Database driver	com.mysql.jdbc.Driver	
	Do not set if you use the default embedded database on localhost.	
Additional properties		
	Additional properties to be passed to the mvn executable (example : -Dsome.property=some.value)	

Triggers

☐ Poll SCM

☑ Build periodically

☑ Manually started by user

☐ Build whenever a SNAPSHOT dependency is built

☐ Skip analysis on build failure

[Delete Sonar]

[Add Sonar]

List of Sonar installations

Figure 9-20. Configuring Sonar in Jenkins

If you click on the Advanced button, you can specify other more sophisticated options, such as running your Sonar build on a separate branch, passing Maven additional command-line options (such as extra memory), or overriding the default trigger configuration.

By default, Sonar will run even if the normal build fails. This is usually what you want, as Sonar should record build and test failures as well as successful results. However, if required, you can deactivate this option too in the Advanced options.

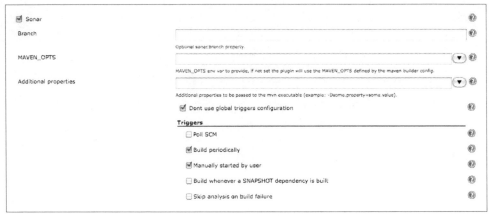

Figure 9-21. Configuring Sonar in a build job

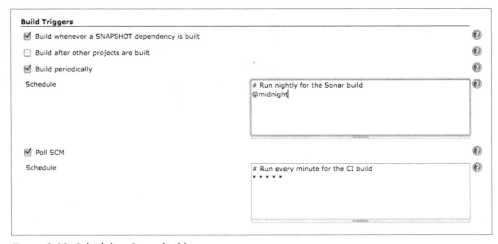

Figure 9-22. Scheduling Sonar builds

Conclusion

Code quality is an important part of the build process, and Jenkins provides excellent support for the wide range of code quality-related tools out there. As a result, Jenkins should be a key part of your code quality strategy.

CHAPTER 10

Advanced Builds

Introduction

In this chapter, we will look at some more advanced build job setups. We will discuss parameterized builds, which allows Jenkins to prompt the user for additional parameters that will be passed into the build job, and multiconfiguration build jobs, which let you run a single build job though a large number of variations. We will look at how to run build jobs in parallel, and wait for the outcome of one or more build jobs before continuing. And we will see how to implement build promotion strategies and build pipelines so that Jenkins can be used not only as a build server, but also as a deployment server.

Parameterized Build Jobs

Parameterized builds are a powerful concept that enable you to add another dimension to your build jobs.

The Parameterized Build plugin lets you configure parameters for your build job, that can be either entered by the user when the build job is triggered, or (as we will see later) from another build job.

For example, you might have a deployment build job, where you want to choose the target environment in a drop-down list when you start the build job. Or you may want to specify the version of the application you want to deploy. Or, when running a build job involving web tests, you might want to specify the browser to run your Selenium or WebDriver tests in. You can even upload a file to be used by the build job.

Note that it is the job of the build script to analyze and process the parameter values correctly—Jenkins simply provides a user interface for users to enter values for the parameters, and passes these parameters to the build script.

Creating a Parameterized Build Job

You install the Parameterized Build plugin as usual, via the Plugin Manager screen. Once you have done this, configuring a parameterized build job is straightforward. Just tick the "This build is parameterized" option and click Add Parameter to add a new build job parameter (see Figure 10-1). You can add parameters to any sort of build, and you can add as many parameters as you want for a given build job.

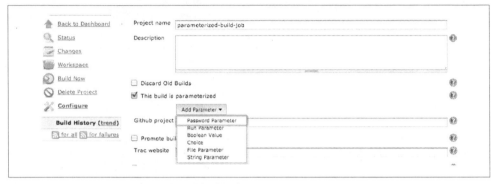

Figure 10-1. Creating a parameterized build job

To add a parameter to your build job, just pick the parameter type in the drop-down list. This will let you configure the details of your parameter (see Figure 10-2). You can choose from several different parameter types, such as Strings, Booleans, and drop-down lists. Depending on the type you choose, you will have to enter slightly different configuration values, but the basic process is identical. All parameter types, with the exception of the File parameter, have a name and a description, and most often a default value.

In Figure 10-3, for example, we are adding a parameter called `version` to a deployment build job. The default value (`RELEASE`) will be initially displayed when Jenkins prompts the user for this parameter, so if the user doesn't change anything, this value will be used.

When the user starts a parameterized build job (parameterized build jobs are very often started manually), Jenkins will propose a page where the user can enter values for each of the build job's parameters (see Figure 10-3).

Adapting Your Builds to Work with Parameterized Build Scripts

Once you have added a parameter, you need to configure your build scripts to use it. Choosing the parameter name well is important here, as this is also the name of the variable that Jenkins will pass through as an environment variable when it runs the build job. To illustrate this, consider the very basic build job configuration in Figure 10-4, where we are simply echoing the build parameter back out to the console.

Figure 10-2. Adding a parameter to the build job

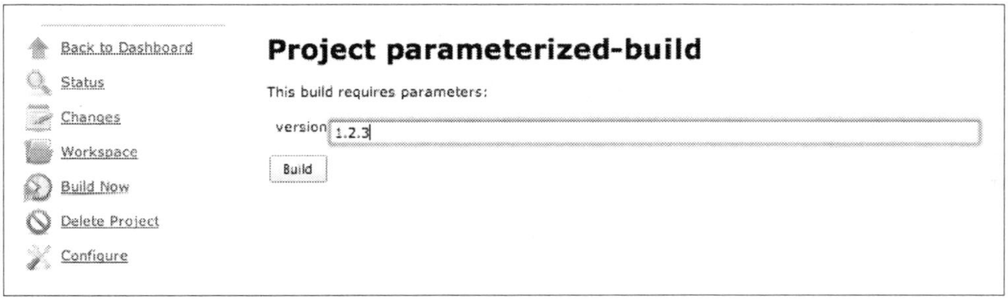

Figure 10-3. Adding a parameter to the build job

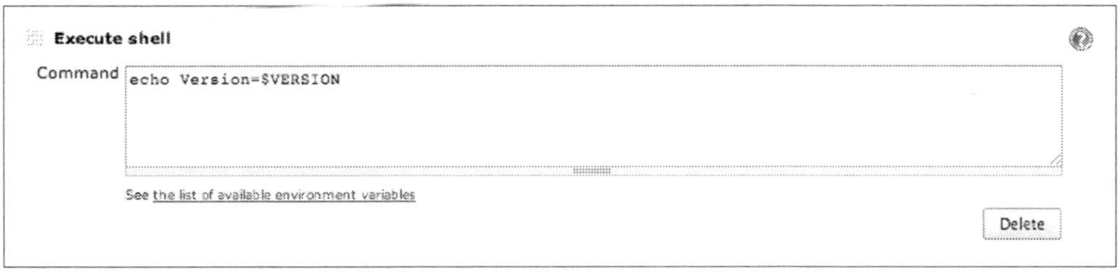

Figure 10-4. Demonstrating a build parameter

Note that, to make the environment variables more portable across operating systems, it is good practice to put them all in upper case.

When we run this, we get a console output along the following lines:

```
Started by user anonymous
Building on master
[workspace] $ /bin/sh -xe /var/folders/y+/y+a+wZ-jG6WKHEm9KwnSvE+++TI/-Tmp-/
jenkins5862957776458050998.sh
+ echo Version=1.2.3
Version=1.2.3
Notifying upstream projects of job completion
Finished: SUCCESS
```

You can also use these environment variables from within your build scripts. For example, in an Ant or Maven build, you can use the special env property to access the current environment variables:

```
<target name="printversion">
  <property environment="env" />
  <echo message="${env.VERSION}"/>
</target>
```

Another option is to pass the parameter into the build script as a property value. The following is a more involved example from a Maven POM file. In this example, Maven is configured to deploy a specific WAR file. We provide the version of the WAR file to be deployed in the target.version property, which is used in the dependency declaration, as shown below:

```
...
<dependencies>
  <dependency>
    <groupId>com.wakaleo.gameoflife</groupId>
    <artifactId>gameoflife-web</artifactId>
    <type>war</type>
    <version>${target.version}</version>
  </dependency>
</dependencies>
<properties>
  <target.version>RELEASE</target.version>
  ...
</properties>
```

When we invoke Maven, we pass in the parameter as one of the build properties (see Figure 10-5). We can then use a tool like Cargo to do the actual deployment—Maven will download the requested version of the WAR file from the local Enterprise Repository Manager, and deploy it to an application server.

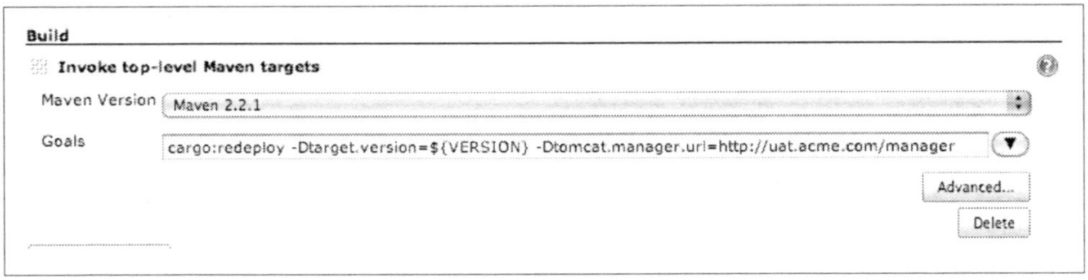

Figure 10-5. Adding a parameter to a Maven build job

That, in a nutshell, is how you can integrate build job parameters into your build. In addition to plain old String parameters, however, there are a few more sophisticated parameter types, that we will look at in the following paragraphs (see Figure 10-6).

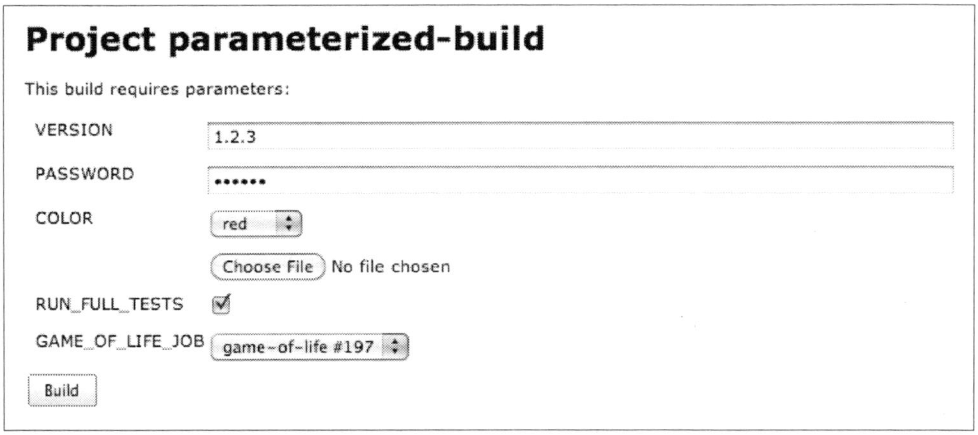

Project parameterized-build

This build requires parameters:

VERSION	`1.2.3`
PASSWORD	`•••••`
COLOR	red ▲▼
	(Choose File) No file chosen
RUN_FULL_TESTS	☑
GAME_OF_LIFE_JOB	game~of~life #197 ▲▼

[Build]

Figure 10-6. Many different types of parameters are available

More Advanced Parameter Types

Password parameters are, as you would expect, very similar to String parameters, except that they are displayed as a password field.

There are many cases where you which to present a limited set of parameter options. In a deployment build, you might want to let the user choose one of a number of target servers. Or you may want to present a list of supported browsers for a suite of acceptance tests. *Choice parameters* let you define a set of values that will be displayed as a drop-down list (see Figure 10-7). You need to provide a list of possible values, one per line, starting with the default value.

Choice	
Name	`COLOR`

Choices	`red`
	`green`
	`blue`

Description	

Figure 10-7. Configuring a Choice parameter

Boolean parameters are, as you would expect, parameters that take a value of true or false. They are presented as checkboxes.

Two more exotic parameter types, which behave a little differently to the others, are *Run parameters* and *File parameters*.

Run parameters let you select a particular run (or build) of a given build job (see Figure 10-8). The user picks from a list of build run numbers. The URL of the corresponding build run is stored in the specified parameter.

Figure 10-8. Configuring a Run parameter

The URL (which will look something like *http://jenkins.myorg.com/job/game-of-life/ 197/*) can be used to obtain information or artifacts from that build run. For example, you could obtain the JAR or WAR file archived in a previous build and run further tests with this particular binary in a separate build job. For example, to access the WAR file of a previous build in a multimodule Maven project, the URL would look something like this:

```
http://buildserver/job/game-of-life/197/artifact/gameoflife-web/target/
    gameoflife.war
```

So, using the parameter configured in Figure 10-8, you could access this WAR file using the following expression:

```
${RELEASE_BUILD}gameoflife-web/target/gameoflife.war
```

File parameters let you upload a file into the build job workspace, so that it can then be used by the build script (see Figure 10-9). Jenkins will store the file into the specified location in the project workspace, where you can access it in your build scripts. You can use the WORKSPACE variable to refer to the current Jenkins workspace directory, so you could manipulate the file uploaded in Figure 10-9 by using the expression ${WORK SPACE}/deploy/app.war.

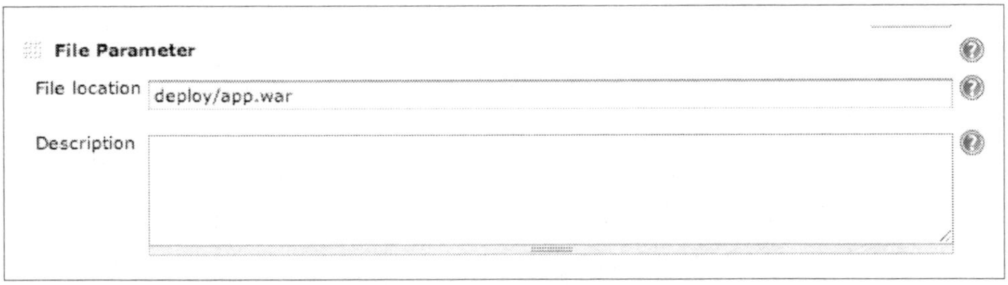

Figure 10-9. Configuring a File parameter

Building from a Subversion Tag

The parameterized trigger has special support for Subversion, allowing you to build against a specific Subversion tag. This is useful if you want to run a release build using a tag generated by a previous build job. For example, an upstream build job may tag a particular revision. Alternatively, you might use the standard Maven release process (see "Managing Maven Releases with the M2Release Plugin" on page 282) to generate a new release. In this case, a tag with the Maven release number will automatically be generated in Subversion.

This approach is useful for projects that need to be partially or entirely rebuilt before they can be deployed to a given platform. For example, you may need to run the Ant or Maven build using different properties or profiles for different platforms, so that platform-specific configuration files can be embedded in the deployed WAR or EAR files.

You can configure a Jenkins build to run against a selected tag by using the "List Subversion Tag" parameter type (see Figure 10-10). You just need to provide the Subversion repository URL pointing to the tags directory of your project.

Figure 10-10. Adding a parameter to build from a Subversion tag

When you run this build, Jenkins will propose a list of tags to choose from (see Figure 10-11).

Figure 10-11. Building from a Subversion tag

Building from a Git Tag

Building from a Git tag is not as simple as doing so from a Subversion tag, though you can still use a parameter to indicate which tag to use. Indeed, because of the very nature of Git, when Jenkins obtains a copy of the source code from Git, it clones the Git repository, including all of the tags. Once you have the latest version of the repository on your Jenkins server, you can then proceed to checkout a tagged version using `git checkout <tagname>`.

To set this up in Jenkins, you first need to add a String parameter to your build job (called `RELEASE` in this example—see Figure 10-12). Unlike the Subversion support, there is no way to list the available Git tags in a drop-down list, so users will need to know the name of the tag they want to release.

Figure 10-12. Configuring a parameter for a Git tag

Once you have added this parameter, you need to checkout the corresponding tag once the repository has been cloned locally. So if you have a freestyle build, the first build step would be a command-line call to Git to check out the tag referenced by the `RELEASE` parameter (see Figure 10-13). Of course a more portable way to do this would be to write a simple Ant or Groovy script to do the same thing in a more OS-neutral way.

Starting a Parameterized Build Job Remotely

You can also start a parameterized build job remotely, by invoking the URL of the build job. The typical form of a parameterized build job URL is illustrated here:

```
http://jenkins.acme.org/job/myjob/buildWithParameters?PARAMETER=Value
```

So, in the example shown above, you could trigger a build like this:

```
http://jenkins.acme.org/job/parameterized-build/buildWithParameters?VERSION=1.2.3
```

When you use a URL to start a build job in this way, remember that the parameter names are case-sensitive, and that the values need to be escaped (just like any other

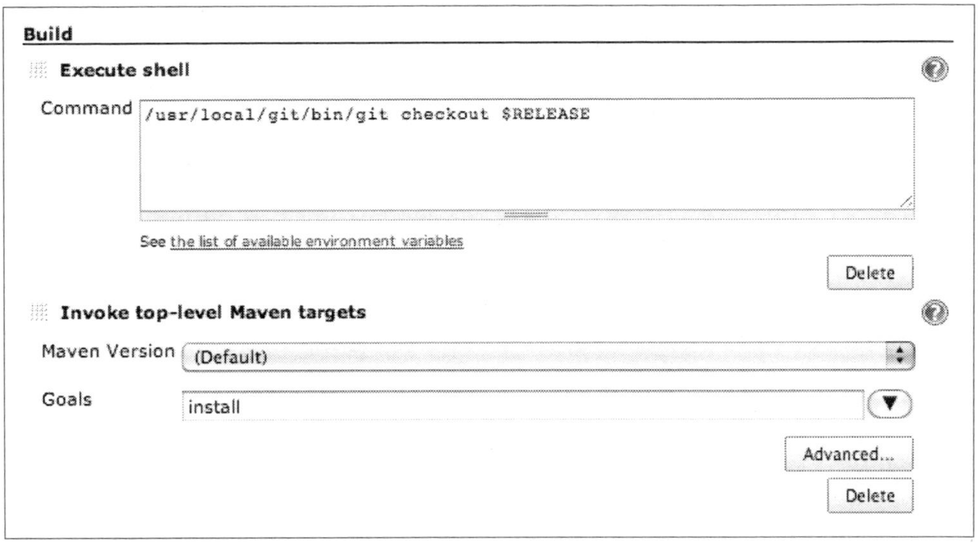

```
Build
    Execute shell                                                          ⓘ

    Command  /usr/local/git/bin/git checkout $RELEASE




            See the list of available environment variables

                                                              Delete

    Invoke top-level Maven targets                                         ⓘ

    Maven Version  (Default)                                          ⇕

    Goals          install                                          ▼

                                                      Advanced...

                                                              Delete
```

Figure 10-13. Building from a Git tag

HTTP parameter). And if you are using a Run parameter, you need to provide the name of the build job *and* the run number (e.g., game-of-life#197) and not just the run number.

Parameterized Build Job History

Finally, it is indispensable to know what parameters were used to run a particular parameterized build. For example, in an automated deployment build job, it is useful to know exactly what version was actually deployed. Fortunately, Jenkins stores these values in the build history (see Figure 10-14), so you can always go back and take a look.

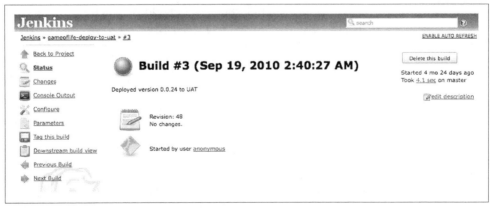

Figure 10-14. Jenkins stores what parameter values where used for each build

Parameterized Triggers

When you trigger another build job from within a parameterized build job, it is often useful to be able to pass the parameters of the current build job to the new one. Suppose, for example, that you have an application that needs to be tested against several different databases. As we have seen, you could do this by setting up a parameterized build job that accepts the target database as a parameter. You may want to kick of a series of builds, all of which will need this parameter.

If you try to do this using the conventional "Build other projects" option in the Post-Build Actions section, it won't work. In fact, you can't trigger a parameterized build in this way.

However, you can do this using the Jenkins Parameterized Trigger plugin. This plugin lets you configure your build jobs to both trigger parameterized builds, and to pass arbitrary parameters to these builds.

Once you install this plugin, you will find the option of "Triggering parameterized builds on other projects" in your build job configuration page (see Figure 10-16). This lets you start another build job in a number of ways. In particular, it lets you kick off a subsequent build job, passing the current parameters to this new build job, which is impossible to do with a normal triggered build. The best way to see how this works is through an example.

In Figure 10-15 we have an initial build job. This build job takes a single parameter, DATABASE, which specifies the database to be used for the tests. As we have seen, the user will be prompted to enter this value whenever the build is started.

Now suppose we want to trigger a second build job to run more comprehensive integration tests once this first build job has finished. However we need it to run the tests against the same database. We can do this by setting up a parameterized trigger to start this second build job (see Figure 10-16).

In this case, we are simple passing through the current build parameters. This second build job will automatically be started after the first one, with the DATABASE parameter value provided by the user. You can also fine-tune the triggering policy, by telling Jenkins when the build should be triggered. Typically, you would only trigger a downstream build after your build has completed successfully, but with the Parameterized Trigger plugin you can also configure builds to be triggered even if the build is unstable, only when the build fails or ask for it to be triggered no matter what the outcome of the first build. You can even set up multiple triggers for the same build job.

Naturally, the build job that you trigger must be a parameterized build job (as illustrated in Figure 10-17), and you must pass through all of the parameters it requires.

This feature actually has much broader applications than simply passing through the current build parameters. You can also trigger a parameterized build job with an arbitrary set of parameters, or use a combination of parameters that were passed to the

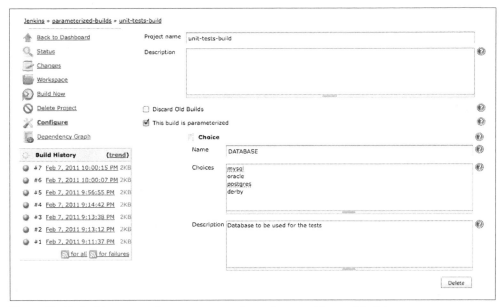

Figure 10-15. Jenkins stores what parameter values where used for each build

Figure 10-16. Adding a parameterized trigger to a build job

current build, and your own additional ones. Or, if you have a lot of parameters, you can load them from a properties file. In Figure 10-18, we are passing both the current build parameters (the DATABASE variable in this case), and an additional parameter called TARGET_PLATFORM.

Multiconfiguration Build Jobs

Multiconfiguration build jobs are an extremely powerful feature of Jenkins. A multi-configuration build job can be thought of as a parameterized build job that can be automatically run with all the possible combinations of parameters that it can accept. They are particularly useful for tests, where you can test your application using a single build job, but under a wide variety of conditions (browsers, databases, and so forth).

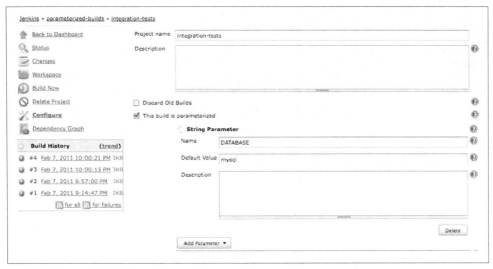

Figure 10-17. The build job you trigger must also be a parameterized build job

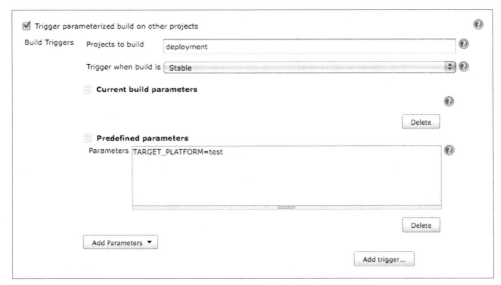

Figure 10-18. Passing a predefined parameter to a parameterized build job

Setting Up a Multiconfiguration Build

To create a new multiconfiguration build job, simply choose this option on the New Job page (see Figure 10-19).

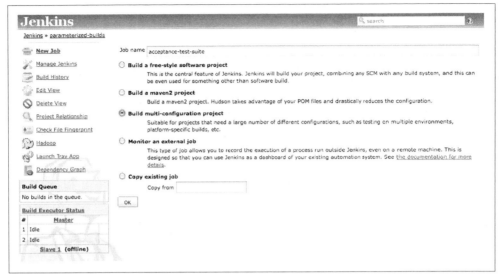

Figure 10-19. Creating a multiconfiguration build job

A multiconfiguration build job is just like any other build job, but with one very important additional element: the *Configuration Matrix* (see Figure 10-20). This is where you define the different configurations that will be used to run your builds.

Figure 10-20. Adding an axis to a multiconfiguration build

You can define different axes of configuration options, including running the build job on different slaves or on different JDKs, or providing your own custom properties to the build. For example, in the build jobs discussed earlier, we might want to test our application for different databases and different operating systems. We could define one axis defining slave machines with different operating systems we wanted our build to run on, and another axis defining all the possible database values. Jenkins will then run the build job for each possible database and each possible operating system.

Let's look at the types of axis you can define.

Configuring a Slave Axis

The first option is to configure your build to run simultaneously on different slave machines (see Chapter 11). Now of course, the idea of having a set of slave machines is usually that you can run your build job on any of them. But there are cases where it makes sense to be a little more choosy. For example, you might want your tests to run on Windows, Mac OS X, and Linux. In this case, you create a new axis for your slave nodes, as shown in Figure 10-21. You can choose the nodes you want to use in two ways: by label or by individual node. Using labels lets you identify categories of build nodes (for example, Windows machines), without tying the build to any one machine. This is a more flexible option, and makes it easier to expand your build capacity as required. Sometimes, however, you may really want to run a build on a specific machine. In this case, you can use the "Individual nodes" option, and choose the machine in this list.

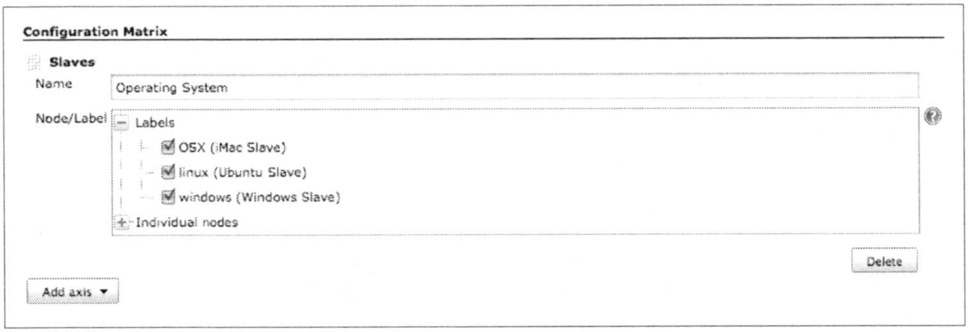

Figure 10-21. Defining an axis of slave nodes

If you need more flexibility, you can also use a Label Expression, which lets you define which slave nodes should be used for builds on a particular axis using boolean expressions and logical operators to combine labels. For example, suppose you have defined labels for slave machines based on operating system ("windows", "linux") and installed databases ("oracle", "mysql", "db2"). To define an axis running tests only on Windows machines installed with MySQL, you could use an expression like `windows && mysql`.

We discuss working with slave nodes and distributed builds in more detail in Chapter 11.

Configuring a JDK Axis

If you are deploying your application to a broad client base where you have limited control over the target environment, you may need to test your application using different versions of Java. In cases like this it is useful to be able to set up a JDK axis in a multiconfiguration build. When you add a JDK axis, Jenkins will automatically propose the list of JDK versions that it knows about (see Figure 10-22). If you need to use additional JDKs, just add them to your Jenkins configuration page.

Figure 10-22. Defining an axis of JDK versions

Custom Axis

The third type of axis lets you define different ways to run your build job, based on arbitrary variables that you define. For example, you might provide a list of databases you need to test against, or a list of browsers to use in your web tests. These are like parameters for a parameterized build job, except that you provide the complete list of possible values, and rather than prompting for you to enter a value, Jenkins will run the build with *all* of the values you provide (Figure 10-23).

Figure 10-23. Defining a user-defined axis

Running a Multiconfiguration Build

Once you have set up the axes, you can run your multiconfiguration build just like any other. However, Jenkins will treat each combination of variables as a separate build job. Jenkins displays the aggregate results in a table, where all of the combinations are shown (see Figure 10-24). If you click on any of the balls, Jenkins will take you to the detailed results for that particular build.

By default, Jenkins will run the build jobs in parallel. However there are some cases where this is not a good idea. For example, many Java web applications use Selenium or WebDriver tests running against a local instance of Jetty that is automatically started by the build job. Build scripts like this need to be specially configured to be able to run in parallel on the same machine, to avoid port conflicts. Concurrent database access during tests can be another source of problems if concurrency is not designed into the tests. If your builds are not designed to run in parallel, you can force Jenkins to run the tests sequentially by ticking the Run each configuration sequentially checkbox at the bottom of the Configuration Matrix section.

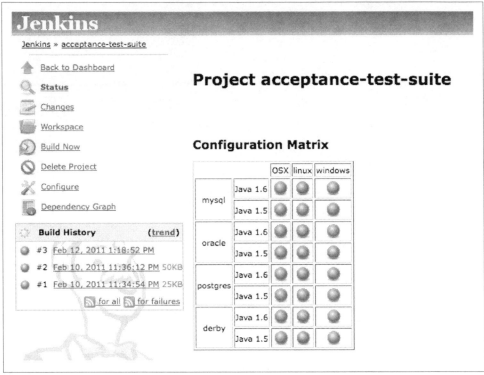

Figure 10-24. Multiconfiguration build results

By default, Jenkins will run all possible combinations of the different axes. So, in the above example, we have three environments, two JDKs, and four databases. This results in a total of 24 builds. However, in some cases, it may not make sense (or be possible) to run certain combinations. For example, suppose you have a build job that runs automated web tests. If one axis contains the web browsers to be tested (Firefox, Internet Explorer, Chrome, etc.) and another the Operating Systems (Linux, Windows, Mac OS), it would make little sense to run Internet Explorer with Linux or Mac OS.

The Combination Filter option lets you set up rules about which combinations of variables are valid. This field is a Groovy boolean expression that uses the names of the variables you defined for each axis. The expression must evaluate to true for the build to execute. For example, suppose you have a build job running web tests in different browsers on different operating systems (see Figure 10-25). The tests need to run Firefox, Internet Explorer and Chrome, on Windows, Mac OS X, and Linux. However Internet Explorer only runs on Windows, and Chrome does not run on Linux.

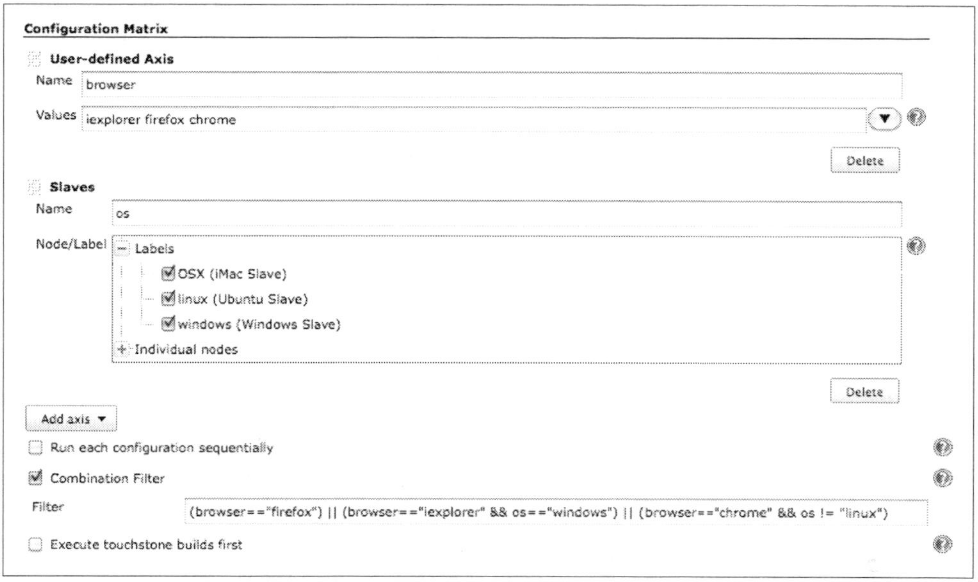

Figure 10-25. Setting up a combination filter

To set this up with a Combination Filter, we could use an expression like the following:

```
(browser=="firefox")
|| (browser=="iexplorer" && os=="windows")
|| (browser=="chrome" && os != "linux")
```

This would result in only the correct browser/operating system combinations being executed (see Figure 10-26). Executed builds are displayed in the usual colors, whereas skipped builds are shown in gray.

Another reason to use a build filter is that there are simply too many valid combinations to run in a reasonable time. In this case, the best solution may be to upscale your build server. The second-best solution, on the other hand, might be to only run a subset of the combinations, possibly running the full set of combinations on a nightly basis. You can do this by using the special index variable. If you include the expression (index%2 == 0), for example, will ensure that only one build job in two is actually executed.

You may also want certain builds to be executed before the others, as a sanity check. For example, you might want to run the default (and, theoretically, the most reliable) configuration for your application first, before continuing on to more exotic combinations. To do this, you can use the "Execute touchstone builds first" option. Here, you enter a filter value (like the one seen above) to define the first build or builds to be executed. You can also specify if the build should proceed only if these builds are successful, or even if they are unsuccessful. Once these builds have completed as expected, Jenkins will proceed with the other combinations.

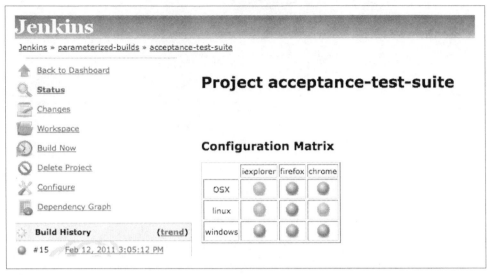

Figure 10-26. Build results using a combination filter

Generating Your Maven Build Jobs Automatically

Contributed by Evgeny Goldin

As mentioned in the previous section, the number of build jobs that your Jenkins server will host can vary. As the number of build jobs grows, it becomes harder not only to view them in Jenkins dashboard, but to configure them as well. Imagine what would it take to configure 20 to 50 Jenkins jobs one-by-one! In addition, many of those jobs may have common configuration elements, such as Maven goals or build memory settings, which results in duplicated configuration and higher maintenance overhead.

For example, if you decide to run `mvn clean install` instead of `mvn clean deploy` for your release jobs and switch to alternative deployment methods, such as those provided by Artifactory plugin (*http://wiki.jenkins-ci.org/display/JENKINS/Artifactory+Plugin*), you'll have no choice but to visit all relevant jobs and update them manually.

Alternatively, you could take an advantage of the fact that Jenkins is a simple and straightforward tool that keeps all of its definitions in plain files on the disk. Indeed you can update the *config.xml* files of your jobs directly in the *.jenkins/jobs* directory where they are kept. While this approach will work, it is still far from ideal as it involves quite a lot of manual picking and fragile replacements in Jenkins XML files.

There is a third way to achieve the nirvana of massive job updates: generate your configuration files automatically using some sort of definition file. The Maven Jenkins Plugin (*http://evgeny-goldin.com/wiki/Maven-jenkins-plugin*) does exactly that, generating *config.xml* files for all jobs using standard Maven definitions kept in a single *pom.xml* file.

Configuring a Job

When configuring a single job with the Maven Jenkins Plugin, you can define all the usual Jenkins configuration elements, such as Maven goals, POM location, repository URLs, e-mail addresses, number of days to keep the logs, and so on. The plugin tries to bring you as close to possible to Jenkins' usual way of configuring a job manually.

Let's take a look on a Google Guice (*http://code.google.com/p/google-guice/*) build job:

```
<job>
    <id>google-guice-trunk</id>
    <description>Building Google Guice trunk.</description>
    <descriptionTable>
        <row>
            <key>Project Page</key>
            <value>
                <a href="http://code.google.com/p/google-guice/">
                    <b><code>code.google.com/p/google-guice</code></b>
                </a>
            </value>
            <escapeHTML>false</escapeHTML>
            <bottom>false</bottom>
        </row>
    </descriptionTable>
    <jdkName>jdk1.6.0</jdkName>
    <mavenName>apache-maven-3</mavenName>
    <mavenOpts>-Xmx256m -XX:MaxPermSize=128m</mavenOpts>
    <daysToKeep>5</daysToKeep>
    <useUpdate>false</useUpdate>
    <mavenGoals>-e clean install</mavenGoals>
    <trigger>
        <type>timer</type>
        <expression>0 0 * * *</expression>
    </trigger>
    <repository>
        <remote>http://google-guice.googlecode.com/svn/trunk/</remote>
    </repository>
    <mail>
        <recipients>jenkins@evgeny-goldin.org</recipients>
    </mail>
</job>
```

This job uses a number of standard configurations such as `<jdkName>`, `<mavenName>`, and `<mavenOpts>`. The code is checked out from a Subversion repository (defined in the `<repository>` element), and a cron `<trigger>` runs the job nightly at 00:00. Email notifications are sent to people specified with the `<mail>` element. This configuration also adds a link back to the project's page in the description table that is generated automatically for each job.

The generated job is displayed in your Jenkins server as illustrated in Figure 10-27.

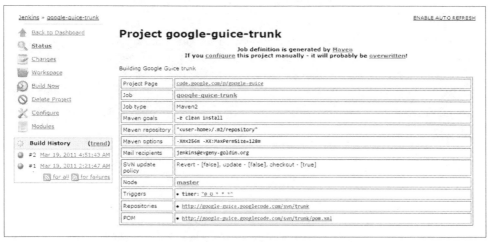

Figure 10-27. A job generated by the Maven Jenkins plugin

Here's another job building the Jenkins master branch at GitHub:

```
<job>
    <id>jenkins-master</id>
    <jdkName>jdk1.6.0</jdkName>
    <numToKeep>5</numToKeep>
    <mavenName>apache-maven-3</mavenName>
    <trigger>
        <type>timer</type>
        <expression>0 1 * * *</expression>
    </trigger>
    <scmType>git</scmType>
    <repository>
        <remote>git://github.com/jenkinsci/jenkins.git</remote>
    </repository>
    <mail>
        <recipients>jenkins@evgeny-goldin.org</recipients>
        <sendForUnstable>false</sendForUnstable>
    </mail>
</job>
```

This would generate the job shown in Figure 10-28.

The plugin's documentation (*http://evgeny-goldin.com/wiki/Maven-jenkins-plugin#.3Cjob.3E*) provides a detailed reference of all settings that can be configured.

Reusing Job Configuration with Inheritance

Being able to generate Jenkins jobs using centralized configuration, such as Maven POM, solves the problem of creating and updating many jobs at once. All you has to do now is to modify the job definitions, re-run the plugin and load definitions updated with Manage Jenkins→"Reload Configuration from Disk". This approach also has the

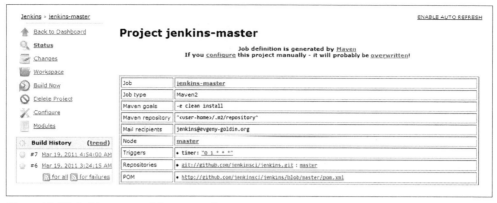

Figure 10-28. jenkins-master job generated

advantage of making it easy to store your job configurations in your version control system, which in turn makes it easier to keep track of changes made to the build configurations.

But we still didn't solve the problem of maintaining jobs that share a number of identical properties, such as Maven goals, email recipients or code repository URL. For that, the Maven Jenkins Plugin provides jobs inheritance, demonstrated in the following example:

```
<jobs>
    <job>
        <id>google-guice-inheritance-base</id>
        <abstract>true</abstract>
        <jdkName>jdk1.6.0</jdkName>
        <mavenName>apache-maven-3</mavenName>
        <daysToKeep>5</daysToKeep>
        <useUpdate>true</useUpdate>
        <mavenGoals>-B -e -U clean install</mavenGoals>
        <mail><recipients>jenkins@evgeny-goldin.org</recipients></mail>
    </job>

    <job>
        <id>google-guice-inheritance-trunk</id>
        <parent>google-guice-inheritance-base</parent>
        <repository>
            <remote>http://google-guice.googlecode.com/svn/trunk/</remote>
        </repository>
    </job>

    <job>
        <id>google-guice-inheritance-3.0-rc3</id>
        <parent>google-guice-inheritance-base</parent>
        <repository>
            <remote>http://google-guice.googlecode.com/svn/tags/3.0-rc3/</remote>
        </repository>
    </job>
```

```
<job>
    <id>google-guice-inheritance-2.0-maven</id>
    <parent>google-guice-inheritance-base</parent>
    <mavenName>apache-maven-2</mavenName>
    <repository>
        <remote>http://google-guice.googlecode.com/svn/branches/2.0-maven/
        </remote>
    </repository>
</job>
</jobs>
```

In this configuration, *google-guice-inheritance-base* is an abstract parent job holding all common properties: JDK name, Maven name, days to keep the logs, SVN update policy, Maven goals, and mail recipients. The three following jobs are very short, merely specifying that they extend a `<parent>` job and add any missing configurations (repository URLs in this case). When generated, they inherit all of the properties from the parent job automatically.

Any inherited property can be overridden, as demonstrated in *google-guice-inheritance-2.0-maven* job where Maven 2 is used instead of Maven 3. If you want to "cancel" an inherited property, you will need to override it with an empty value.

Jobs inheritance is a very powerful concept that allows jobs to form hierarchical groups of any kind and for any purpose. You can group your CI, nightly or release jobs this way, centralizing shared execution triggers, Maven goals or mail recipients in parent jobs. This approach borrowed from an OOP world solves the problem of maintaining jobs sharing a number of identical properties.

Plugin Support

In addition to configuring a job and reusing its definitions, you can apply special support for a number of Jenkins plugins. Right now, a simplified usage of Parameterized Trigger and Artifactory plugins is provided, with support for other popular plugins planned for future versions.

Below is an example of invoking jobs with the Parameterized Trigger plugin. Using this option assumes you have this plugin installed already:

```
<job>
    <id>google-guice-inheritance-trunk</id>
    ...
    <invoke>
        <jobs>
            google-guice-inheritance-3.0-rc3,
            google-guice-inheritance-2.0-maven
        </jobs>
    </invoke>
</job>

<job>
    <id>google-guice-inheritance-3.0-rc3</id>
```

```
    ...
  </job>

  <job>
      <id>google-guice-inheritance-2.0-maven</id>
      ...
  </job>
```

The <invoke> element lets you invoke other jobs each time the current job finishes successfully. You can create a pipeline of jobs this way, making sure each job in a pipeline invokes the following one. Note that if there are more than one Jenkins executors available at the moment of invocation, the specified jobs will start running in parallel. For serial execution you'll need to connect each upstream job to a downstream one with <invoke>.

By default invocation happens only when the current job is stable. This can be modified, as shown in the following examples:

```
<invoke>
    <jobs>jobA, jobB, jobC</jobs>
    <always>true</always>
</invoke>

<invoke>
    <jobs>jobA, jobB, jobC</jobs>
    <unstable>true</unstable>
</invoke>

<invoke>
    <jobs>jobA, jobB, jobC</jobs>
    <stable>false</stable>
    <unstable>false</unstable>
    <failed>true</failed>
</invoke>
```

The first invocation in the example above always invokes the downstream jobs. It can be used for a pipeline of jobs that should always be executed even if some of them or their tests fail.

The second invocation in the example above invokes downstream jobs even if an upstream job is unstable: the invocation happens regardless of test results. It can be used for a pipeline of jobs that are less sensitive to tests and their failures.

The third invocation in the example above invokes downstream jobs only when an upstream job fails but not when it is stable or unstable. You can find this configuration useful when a failing job needs to perform additional actions beyond traditional email notifications.

Artifactory (*http://jfrog.org*) is a general purpose binaries repository that can be used as a Maven repository manager. The Jenkins Artifactory plugin (*http://wiki.jenkins-ci.org/ display/JENKINS/Artifactory+Plugin*), shown in Figure 10-29, provides a number of benefits for Jenkins build jobs. We have already reviewed some of them in "Deploying

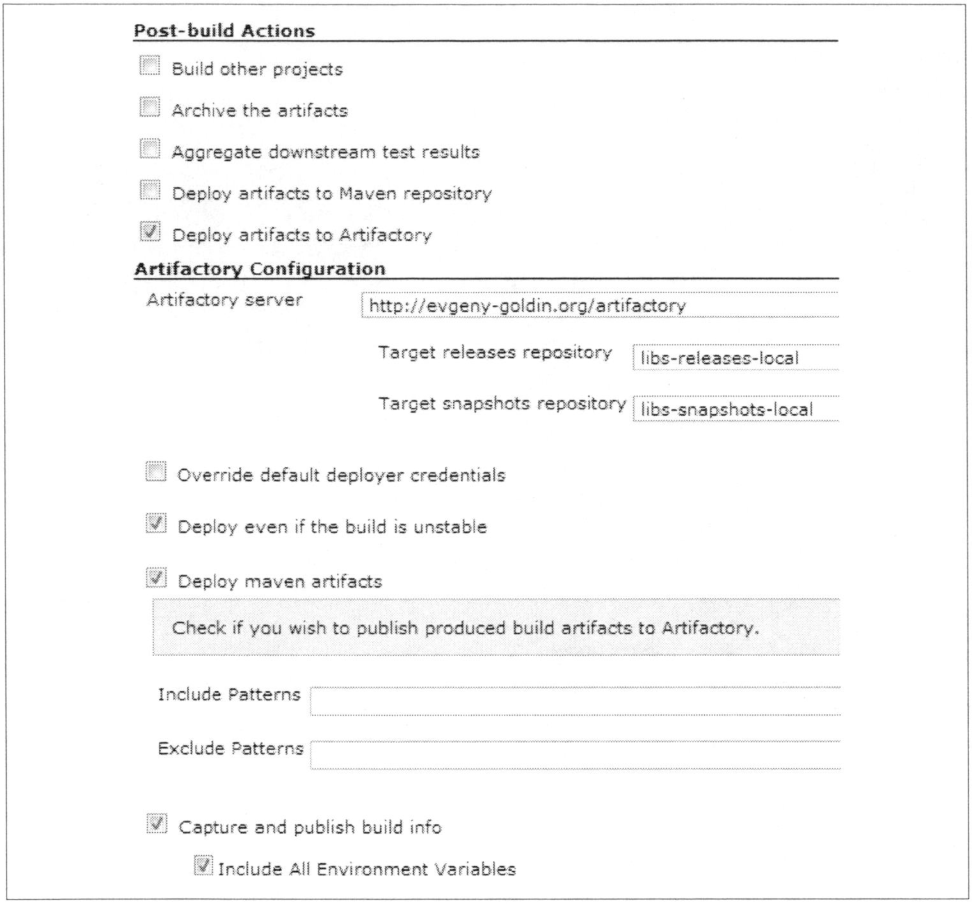

Figure 10-29. Artifactory Jenkins plugin configuration

to an Enterprise Repository Manager" on page 119, including an ability to deploy artifacts upon job completion or to send builds environment info together with artifacts for their better traceability.

You can also use the Artifactory Jenkins plugin in conjunction with the Maven Jenkins Plugin to deploy artifacts to Artifactory, as shown in the following example:

```
<job>
    ...
    <artifactory>
        <name>http://artifactory-server/</name>
        <deployArtifacts>true</deployArtifacts>
        <includeEnvVars>true</includeEnvVars>
        <evenIfUnstable>true</evenIfUnstable>
    </artifactory>
</job>
```

Default deployment credentials are specified when Jenkins is configured in the Manage Jenkins→Configure System screen. They can be also specified for each Jenkins job. The default Maven repositories are *libs-releases-local* and *libs-snapshots-local*. You can find more details in the plugin's documentation at *http://wiki.jenkins-ci.org/display/JEN KINS/Artifactory+Plugin*.

Freestyle Jobs

In addition to Maven jobs, the Maven Jenkins Plugin allows you to configure Jenkins freestyle jobs. An example is shown here:

```
<job>
    <id>free-style</id>
    <jobType>free</jobType>
    <scmType>git</scmType>
    <repository>
        <remote>git://github.com/evgeny-goldin/maven-plugins-test.git</remote>
    </repository>
    <tasks>
        <maven>
            <mavenName>apache-maven-3</mavenName>
            <jvmOptions>-Xmx128m -XX:MaxPermSize=128m -ea</jvmOptions>
            <properties>plugins-version = 0.2.2</properties>
        </maven>
        <shell><command>pwd; ls -al; du -hs .</command></shell>
    </tasks>
</job>
```

Freestyle jobs let you execute a shell or batch command, run Maven or Ant, and invoke other jobs. They provide a convenient run-time environment for system scripts or any other kind of activity not readily available with Jenkins or one of its plugins. Using this approach, you can generate Freestyle build job configuration files in a similar way to the approach we have seen for Maven build jobs, which can help make your build environment more consistent and maintainable.

Coordinating Your Builds

Triggering downstream build jobs is easy enough. However, when setting up larger and more complicated build job setups, you sometimes would like builds to be able to run concurrently, or possibly wait for certain build jobs to finish before proceeding. In this section, we will look at techniques and plugins that can help you do this.

Parallel Builds in Jenkins

Jenkins has built-in support for parallel builds—when a build job starts, Jenkins will assign it to the first available build node, so you can potentially have as many parallel builds running as you have build nodes available.

If you need to run slight variations of the same build job in parallel, multiconfiguration build jobs (see "Multiconfiguration Build Jobs" on page 263) are an excellent option. This can come in handy as a way of accelerating your build process. A typical application of multiconfiguration build jobs in this context is to run integration tests in parallel. One strategy is to set up an integration test build job that can be run in different ways to execute different subsets of the integration tests. You could define separate Maven profiles, for example, or configure your build to use a command-line parameter to decide which tests to run. Once you have set up your build script in this way, it is easy to configure a multiconfiguration build job to run the subsets of your integration tests in parallel.

You can also get Jenkins to trigger several downstream builds in parallel, simply by listing them all in the "Build other projects" field (see Figure 10-30). The subsequent build jobs will be executed in parallel as much as possible. However, as we will see further on, this may not always be exactly what you need.

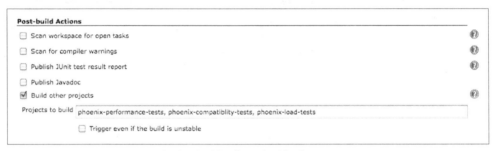

Figure 10-30. Triggering several other builds after a build job

Dependency Graphs

Before we investigate the finer points of parallel builds, it is useful to be able to visualize the relationships between your build jobs. The Dependency Graph View plugin analyzes your build jobs and displays a graph describing the upstream and downstream connections between your jobs. This plugin uses graphviz (*http://www.graphviz.org*), which you will need to install on your server if you don't already have it.

This plugin adds a Dependency Graph icon in the main menu, which displays a graph showing the relationships between all the build jobs in your project (at the dashboard level), or all of the build jobs related to the current build job (when you are inside a particular project [see Figure 10-31]). What's more, if you click on a build job in the graph, Jenkins will take you directly to the project page of that build job.

Joins

When setting up more complicated build pipelines, you frequently come across situations where a build job cannot proceed until a number of other build jobs have been

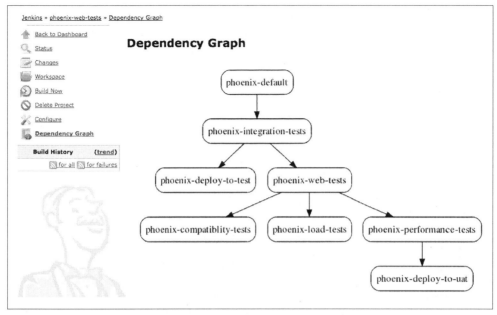

Figure 10-31. A build job dependency graph

completed, but that these upstream build jobs do not need to be executed sequentially. For example, in Figure 10-31, imagine that the *phoenix-deploy-to-uat* build job actually requires three jobs to succeed before it can be executed: *phoenix-compatibility-tests*, *phoenix-load-tests*, and *phoenix-performance-tests*.

We can set this up by using the Joins plugin, which you will need to install in the usual way via the Update center. Once installed, you configure a join in the build job that initiates the join process (in our example, this would be *phoenix-web-tests*). In our example, we need to modify the *phoenix-web-tests* build job so that it triggers the *phoenix-compatibility-tests*, *phoenix-load-tests*, and *phoenix-performance-tests* first, and then, if these three succeed, the *phoenix-deploy-to-uat* build job.

We do this by simply configuring the Join Trigger field with the name of the *phoenix-deploy-to-uat* build job (see Figure 10-32). The "Build other projects" field is not modified, and still lists the build jobs to be triggered immediately after the current one. The Join Trigger field contains the build jobs to be built once all of the immediate downstream build jobs have finished.

As a result, you no longer need the original build trigger for the final build job, as it is now redundant.

This new flow shows up nicely in the dependency graphs as illustrated in Figure 10-33.

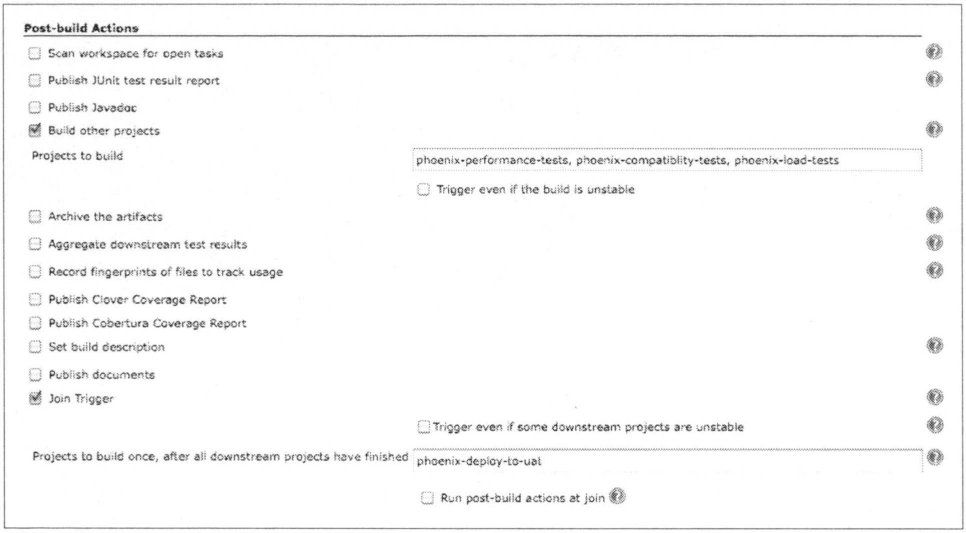

Figure 10-32. Configuring a join in the phoenix-web-tests build job

Locks and Latches

In other situations, you might be able to run a series of builds in parallel to some degree, but certain build jobs cannot be run in parallel because they access concurrent resources. Of course, well-designed build jobs should strive to be as independent as possible, but sometimes this can be difficult. For example, different build jobs may need to access the same test database or files on the hard disk, and doing so simultaneously could potentially compromise the results of the tests. Or a performance build job may need exclusive access to the test server, in order to have consistent results each time.

The Locks and Latches plugin lets you get around this problem to some extent. This plugin lets you set up "locks" for certain resources, in a similar way to locks in multi-threaded programming. Suppose, for example, in the build jobs depicted in Figure 10-33, that the load tests and the performance tests run against a dedicated server, but only one build job can run against this server at any one time. Imagine furthermore that the performance tests for other projects also run against this server.

To avoid contention over the performance server, you could use the Locks and Latches plugin to set up a "lock" reserving access to this server to a single build job at a time. First, in the System Configuration page, you need to add a new lock in the Locks section (see Figure 10-34). This lock will then be available to all build jobs on the server.

Next, you need to set up each build job that will be using the contended resource. In the Build Environment section, you will find a Locks field. Tick the checkbox and select the lock you just created (see Figure 10-35). Once you do this for each of the build jobs that need to access the resource in question, only one of these build jobs will ever be able to run at a given time.

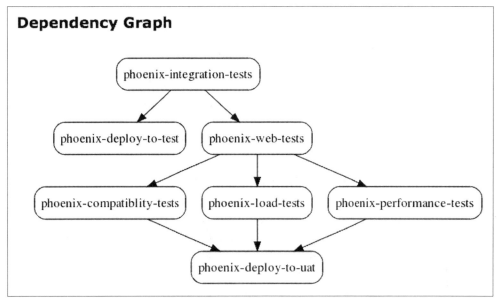

Dependency Graph

Figure 10-33. A more complicated build job dependency graph

Figure 10-34. Adding a new lock

Build Pipelines and Promotions

Continuous Integration is not just about automatically building and testing software, but can also help in the broader context of the software product development and release life cycle. In many organizations, the life of a particular version of an application or product starts out in development. When it is deemed ready, it is passed on to a QA team for testing. If they consider the version acceptable, they pass it on to selected users for more testing in a User Acceptance Testing (UAT) environment. And if the users are happy, it is shipped out into production. Of course, there are almost as many variations on this as there are software development teams, but one common principle is that specific versions of your software are selected, according to certain quality-related criteria, to be "promoted" to the next stage of the life cycle. This is known as build promotion, and the broader process is known as a build pipeline. In this section, we will look at how you can implement build pipelines using Jenkins.

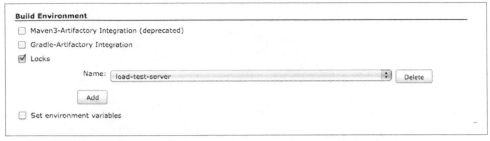

Figure 10-35. Configuring a build job to use a lock

Managing Maven Releases with the M2Release Plugin

An important part of any build pipeline is a well-defined release strategy. This involves, among other things, deciding how and when to cut a new release, and how to identify it with a unique label or version number. If you are working with Maven projects, using the Maven Release plugin to handle version numbers comes as a highly recommended practice.

Maven projects use well-defined and well-structured version numbers. A typical version number is made up of three digits (e.g., "1.0.1"). Developers work on SNAPSHOT versions (e.g.,"1.0.1-SNAPSHOT"), which, as the name would indicate, are not designed to be definitive. The definitive releases (e.g., "1.0.1") are built once and deployed to the local enterprise repository (or the central Maven repository for open source libraries), where they can be used in turn by other projects. The version numbers used in Maven artifacts are a critical part of Maven's dependency management system, and it is strongly advised to stick to the Maven conventions.

The Maven Release plugin helps automates the process of updating Maven version numbers in your projects. In a nutshell, it verifies, builds and tests your application, bumps up the version numbers, updates your version control system with the appropriate tags, and deploys the released versions of your artifacts to your Maven repository. This is a tedious task to do by hand, so the Maven Release plugin is an excellent way to automate things.

However the Maven Release plugin can be fickle, too. Uncommitted or modified local files can cause the process to fail, for example. The process is also time-consuming and CPU intensive, especially for large projects: it builds the application and runs the entire set of unit and integration tests several times, checks out a fresh copy of the source code from the repository, and uploads many artifacts to the Enterprise repository. Indeed, this is not the sort of thing you want running on a developer machine.

So it makes good sense to run this process on your build server.

One way to do this is to set up a special manual build job to invoke the Maven Release plugin. However, the M2Release plugin proposes a simpler approach. Using this plugin, you can add the ability to build a Maven release version in an existing build job.

This way you can avoid duplicating build jobs unnecessarily, making build job maintenance easier.

Once you have installed this plugin, you can define any build job to also propose a manual Maven Release step. You do this by ticking the "Maven release build" checkbox in the Build Environment section (see Figure 10-36). Here, you define the goals you want to execute to trigger the build (typically `release:prepare release:perform`).

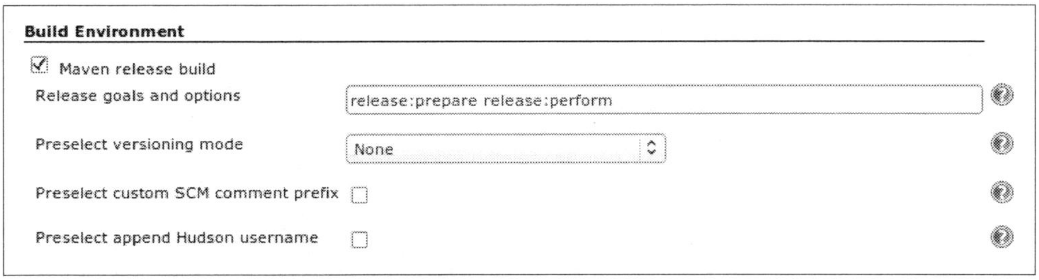

Figure 10-36. Configuring a Maven release using the M2Release plugin

Once you have set this up, you can trigger a Maven release manually using a new menu option called "Perform Maven Release" (see Figure 10-37).

Figure 10-37. The Perform Maven Release menu option

This will kick off a special build job using the goals you provided in the plugin configuration (see Figure 10-38). Jenkins gives you the option to either use the default version numbers provided by Maven (for example, version 1.0.1-SNAPSHOT will be released as version 1.0.1, and the development version number bumped up to 1.0.2-SNAPSHOT), or to provide your own custom numbers. If you want to release a major version, for example, you might choose to manually specify 1.1.0 as the release version number and 1.1.1-SNAPSHOT as the next development version number.

If you have a multimodule Maven project, you can choose to provide a single version number configuration for all modules, or provide a different version number update for each module. Note that it is generally not recommended practice to provide different version numbers for different modules in a multimodule project.

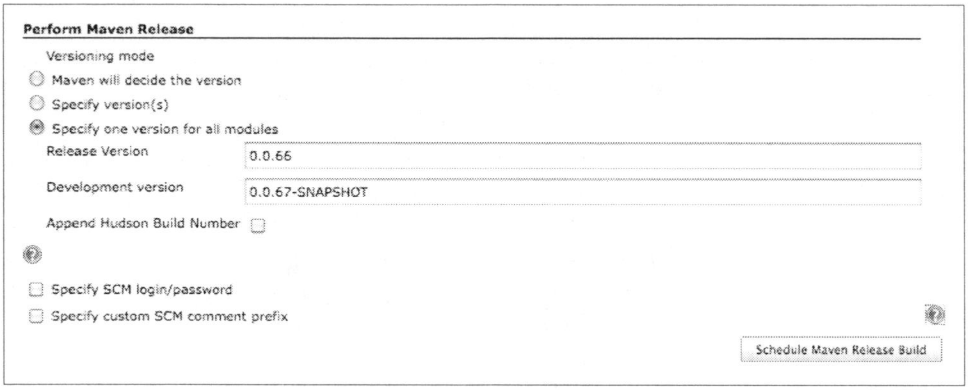

Figure 10-38. Performing a Maven release in Jenkins

Depending on your SCM configuration, you may also need to provide a valid SCM username and password to allow Maven to create tags in your source code repository.

The professional edition of the Nexus Enterprise Repository provides a feature called Staging Repositories, which is a way of deploying artifacts to a special staging area for further tests before releasing them officially. If you are using this feature, you need to fine-tune your build server configuration for best results.

Nexus Professional works by creating a new staging area for each unique IP Address, deploy users and HTTP User agent. A given Jenkins build machine will always have the same IP address and user. However, you will typically want to have a separate staging area for each build. The trick, then, is to configure Maven to use a unique HTTP User-Agent for the deployment process. You can do this by configuring the *settings.xml* file on your build server to contain something along the following lines (the ID must match the ID for the release repository in the deployment section of your project):

```
<server>
    <id>nexus</id>
    <username>my_login</username>
    <password>my_password</password>
    <configuration>
      <httpHeaders>
        <property>
          <name>User-Agent</name>
          <value>Maven m2Release (java:${java.vm.version} ${env.BUILD_TAG }</value>
        </property>
      </httpHeaders>
    </configuration>
</server>
```

Copying Artifacts

During a build process involving several build jobs, such as the one illustrated in Figure 10-33, it can sometimes be useful to reuse artifacts produced by one build job in a subsequent build job. For example, you may want to run a series of web tests in parallel on separate machines, using local application servers for improved performance. In this case, it makes sense to retrieve the exact binary artifact that was produced in the previous build, rather than rebuilding it each time or, if you are using Maven, relying on a SNAPSHOT build deployed to your enterprise repository. Indeed, both these approaches may run the risk of inconsistent build results: if you use a SNAPSHOT from the enterprise repository, for example, you will be using the latest SNAPSHOT build, which may not necessarily be the one built in the upstream build job.

The Copy Artifact plugin lets you copy artifacts from an upstream build and reuse them in your current build. Once you have installed this plugin and restarted Jenkins, you will be able to add a new type of build step called "Copy artifacts from another project" to your freestyle build jobs (see Figure 10-39).

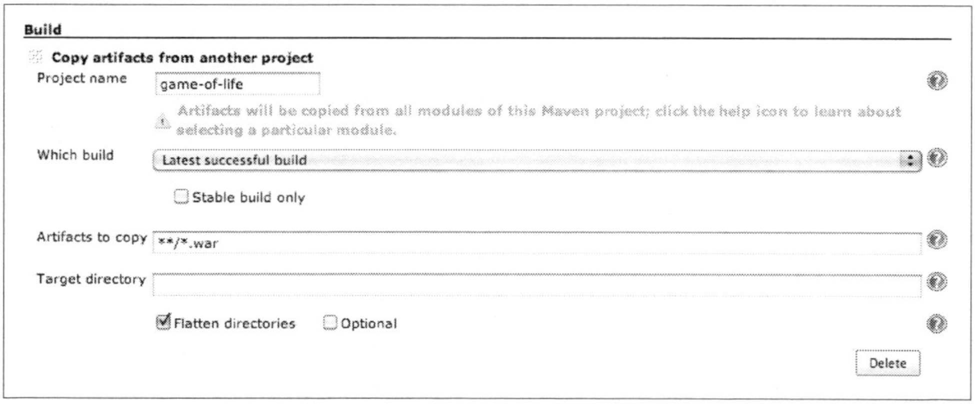

Figure 10-39. Adding a "Copy artifacts from another project" build step

This new build step lets you copy artifacts from another project into the workspace of the current project. You can specify any other project, though most typically it will be one of the upstream build jobs. And of course you can specify, with a great deal of flexibility and precision, the exact artifacts that you want to copy.

You need to specify where to find the files you want in the other build job's workspace, and where Jenkins should put them in your current project's workspace. This can be a flexible regular expression (such as **/*.war, for any WAR file produced by the build job), or it can be much more precise (such as gameoflife-web/target/gameoflife.war). Note that by default, Jenkins will copy the directory structure along with the file you retrieve, so if the WAR file you are after is nested inside the *target* directory of the gameoflife-web module, Jenkins will place it inside the *gameoflife-web/target* directory in your current workspace. If this is not to your tastes, you can tick the "Flatten directories" option to tell Jenkins to put all of the artifacts at the root of the directory you specify (or, by default, in your project workspace).

In many cases, you will simply want to retrieve artifacts from the most recent successful build. However, sometimes you may want more precision. The "Which builds" field lets you specify where to look for artifacts in a number of other ways, including the latest saved build (builds which have been marked to "keep forever"), the latest successful build, or even a specific build number.

If you have installed the Build Promotion plugin (see "Build Promotions" on page 288), you can also select the latest promoted artifact in a particular promotion process. To do this, choose "Specify by permalink", then choose the appropriate build promotion process. This is an excellent way of ensuring a consistent and reliable build pipeline. For example, you can configure a build promotion process to trigger a build that copies a generated WAR file from the latest promoted build and deploys it to a particular server. This ensures that you deploy precisely the right binary file, even if other builds have occurred since.

If you are copying artifacts from a multimodule Maven build job, Jenkins will, by default, copy all of the artifacts from that build. However often times you are only interested in one specific artifact (such as the WAR artifact in a web application, for example.

This plugin is particularly useful when you need to run functional or performance tests on your web application. It is often a useful strategy to place these tests in a separate project, and not as part of your main build process. This makes it easier to run these tests against different servers or run the subsets of the tests in parallel, all the while using the same binary artifact to deploy and test.

For example, imagine that you have a default build job called *gameoflife* that generates a WAR file, and you would like to deploy this WAR file to a local application server and run a series of functional tests. Furthermore, you want to be able to do this in parallel on several distributed machines.

One way to do this would be to create a dedicated Maven project designed to run the functional tests against an arbitrary server. Then, you would set up a build job to run these functional tests. This build job would use the Copy Artifact plugin to retrieve the latest WAR file (or even the latest promoted WAR file, for more precision), and deploy it to a local Tomcat instance using Cargo. This build job could then be set up as a configurable ("matrix") build job, and run in parallel on several machines, possibly with extra configuration parameters to filter the tests run by each build. Each build run would then be using its own copy of the original WAR file. An example of a configuration like this is illustrated in Figure 10-40.

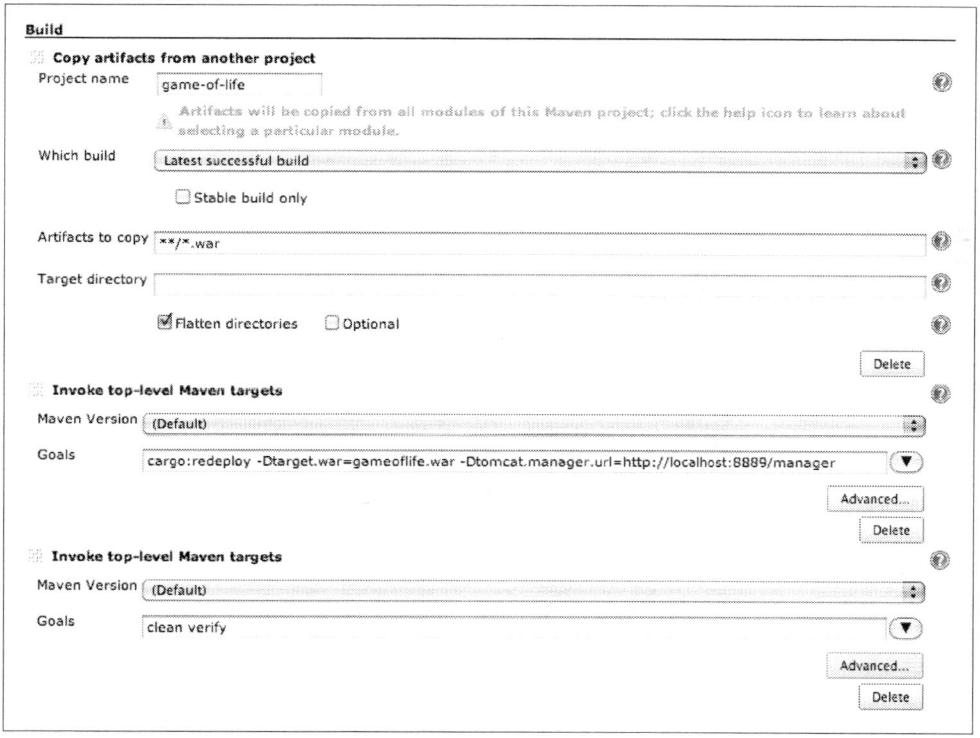

Figure 10-40. Running web tests against a copied WAR file

The Copy Artifact plugin is not limited to fetching files from conventional build jobs. You can also copy artifacts from multiconfiguration build jobs (see "Multiconfiguration Build Jobs" on page 263). Artifacts from each executed configuration will be copied into the current workspace, each in its own directory. Jenkins will build a directory structure using the axes that were used in the multiconfiguration build. For example, imagine we need to produce a highly-optimized version of our product for a number of different targeted databases and application servers. We could do this with a multiconfiguration build job like the one illustrated in Figure 10-41.

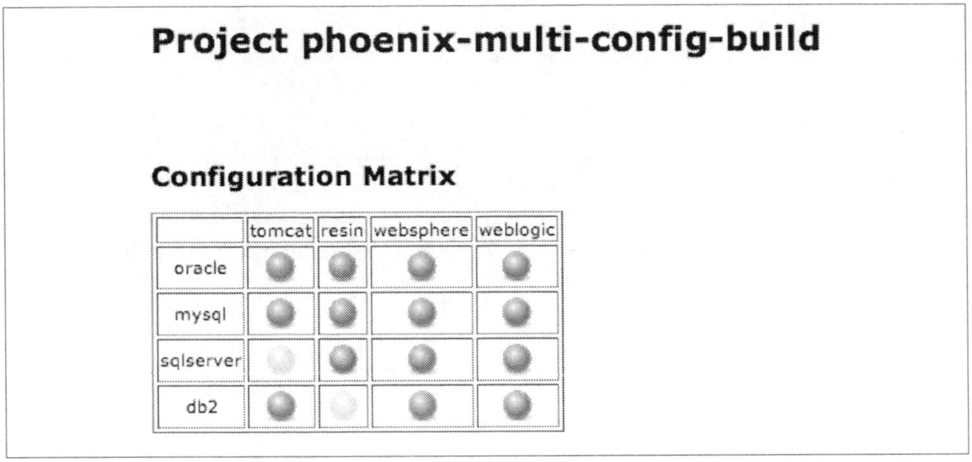

Project phoenix-multi-config-build

Configuration Matrix

	tomcat	resin	websphere	weblogic
oracle	●	●	●	●
mysql	●	●	●	●
sqlserver		●	●	●
db2	●		●	●

Figure 10-41. Copying from a multiconfiguration build

The Copy Artifacts plugin can duplicate any and all of the artifacts produced by this build job. If you specify a multiconfiguration build as the source of your artifacts, the plugin will copy artifacts from all of the configurations into the workspace of the target build job, using a nested directory structure based on the multiconfiguration build axes. For example, if you define the target directory as *multi-config-artifacts*, Jenkins will copy artifacts into a number of subdirectories in the target directory, each with a name corresponding to the particular set of configuration parameters. So, using the build job illustrated in Figure 10-41, the JAR file customized for Tomcat and MySql would be copied to the *$WORKSPACE/multi-config-artifacts/APP_SERVER/tomcat/DATA-BASE/mysql* directory.

Build Promotions

In the world of Continuous Integration, not all builds are created equal. For example, you may want to deploy the latest version of your web application to a test server, but only after it has passed a number of automated functional and load tests. Or you may want testers to be able to flag certain builds as being ready for UAT deployment, once they have completed their own testing.

The Promoted Builds plugin lets you identify specific builds that have met additional quality criteria, and to trigger actions on these builds. For example, you may build a web application in on build job, run a series of automated web tests in a subsequent build, and then deploy the WAR file generated to the UAT server for further manual testing.

Let's see how this works in practice. In the project illustrated above, a default build job (*phoenix-default*) runs unit and some integration tests, and produces a WAR file. This WAR file is then reused for more extensive integration tests (in the *phoenix-integration-tests* build job) and then for a series of automated web tests (in the *phoenix-web-test* build job). If the build passes the automated web tests, we would like to deploy the application to a functional testing environment where it can be tested by human testers. The deployment to this environment is implemented in the *phoenix-test-deploy* build job. Once the testers have validated a version, it can be promoted into UAT, and then into production. The full promotion strategy is illustrated in Figure 10-42.

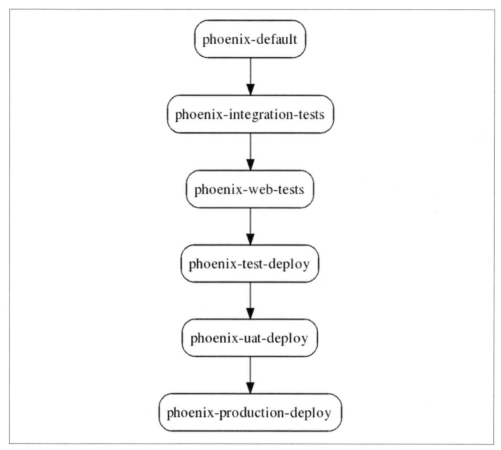

Figure 10-42. Build jobs in the promotion process

This strategy is easy to implement using the Promoted Builds plugin. Once you have installed this in the usual way, you will find a new "Promote builds when" checkbox on the job configuration page. You use this option to set up build promotion processes. You define one or more build promotion processes in the initial build job of process (*phoenix-default* in this example), as illustrated in Figure 10-43. A build job may be the starting point of several build promotion processes, some automated, and some manual. In Figure 10-43, for example, there is an automated build promotion process called *promote-to-test* and a manual one called *promote-to-uat*. Automated build promotion processes are triggered by the results of downstream build jobs. Manual promotion processes (indicated by ticking the 'Only when manually approved' checkbox) can only be triggered by user intervention.

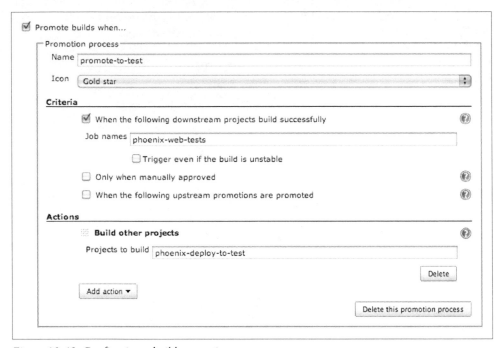

Figure 10-43. Configuring a build promotion process

Let's look at configuring the automated *promote-to-test* build process.

The first thing you need to define is how this build promotion process will be triggered. Build promotion can be either automatic, based on the result of a downstream build job, or manually activated by a user. In Figure 10-43, the build promotion for this build job will be automatically triggered when the automated web tests (executed by the *phoenix-web-tests* build job) are successful.

You can also have certain build jobs that can only be promoted manually, as illustrated in Figure 10-44. Manual build promotion is used for cases where human intervention is needed to approve a build promotion. Deployment to UAT or production are common examples of this. Another example is where you want to temporarily suspend automatic build promotions for a short period, such as nearing a release.

Manual builds, as the name suggests, need to be manually approved to be executed. If the promotion process is to trigger a parameterized build job, you can also provide parameters that the approver will need to enter when approving. In some cases, it can also be useful to designate certain users who are allowed to activate the manual promotion. You can do this by specifying a list of users or groups in the Approvers list.

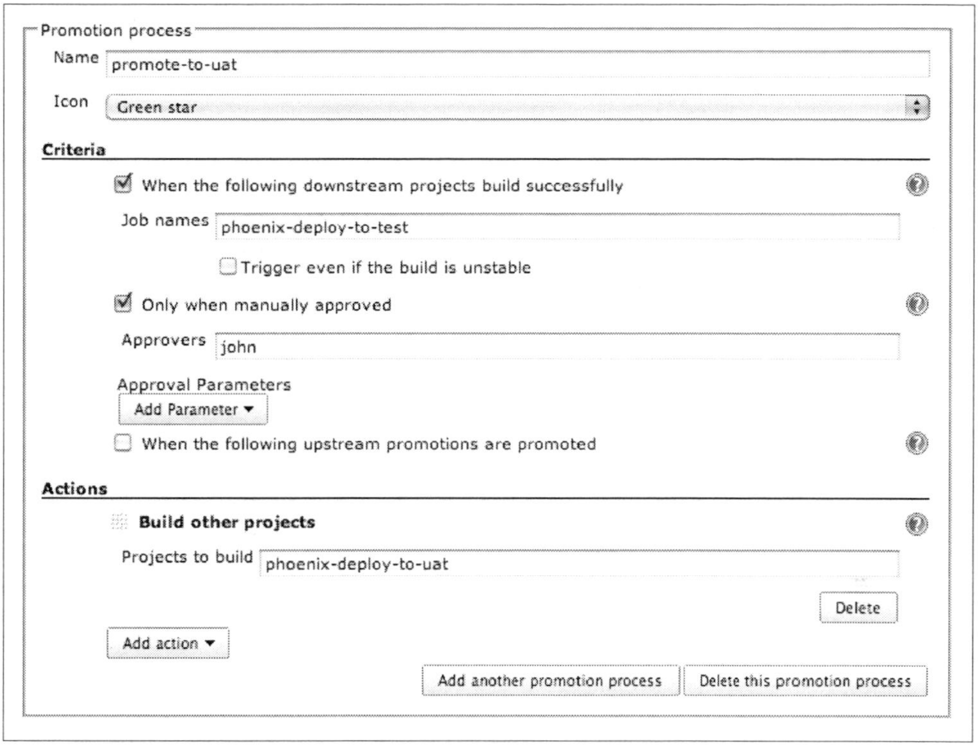

Figure 10-44. Configuring a manual build promotion process

Sometimes, it is useful to give some context to the person approving a promotion. When you set up a manual promotion process, you can also specify other conditions which must be met, in particular downstream (or upstream) build jobs which must have been built successfully (see Figure 10-45). These will appear in the "Met Qualifications" (for the successful build jobs) and in "Unmet Qualifications" (for the build jobs that failed or have not been executed yet).

Next you need to tell Jenkins what to do when the build is promoted. You do this by adding actions, just like in a freestyle build job. This makes build promotions extremely flexible, as you can add virtually any action available to a normal freestyle build job, including any additional steps made available by the plugins installed on your Jenkins instance. Common actions include invoking Maven or Ant scripts, deploying artifacts to a Maven repository, or triggering another build job.

One important thing to remember here is that you cannot rely on files in the workspace when promoting your build. Indeed, by the time you promote the build, either automatically or manually, other build jobs may have deleted or rewritten the files you need to use. For this reason, it is unwise, for example, to deploy a WAR file directly from the workspace to an application server from within a build promotion process. A more robust solution is to trigger a separate build job and to use the Copy Artifacts plugin

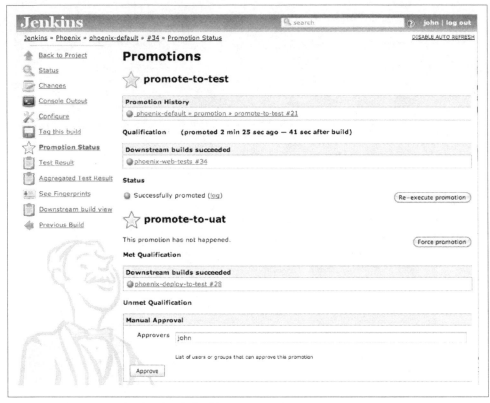

Figure 10-45. Viewing the details of a build promotion

(see "Copying Artifacts" on page 285) to retrieve precisely the right file. In this case, you will be copying artifacts that you have configured Jenkins to conserve, rather than copying the files directly from the workspace.

For build promotion to work correctly, Jenkins needs to be able to precisely link downstream build jobs to upstream ones. The more accurate way to do this is by using fingerprints. In Jenkins, a fingerprint is the MD5 checksum a file produced by or used in a build job. By matching fingerprints, Jenkins is able to identify all of the builds which use a particular file.

In the context of build promotion, a common strategy is to build your application once, and then to run tests against the generated binary files in a series of downstream build jobs. This approach works well with build promotion, but you need to ensure that Jenkins fingerprints the files that are shared or copied between build jobs. In the example shown in Figure 10-43, for instance, we need to do two things (Figure 10-46). First, we need to archive the generated WAR file so that it can be reused in the downstream project. Secondly, we need to record a fingerprint of the archived artifacts. You do this by ticking the "Record fingerprints of files to track usage" option, and specifying

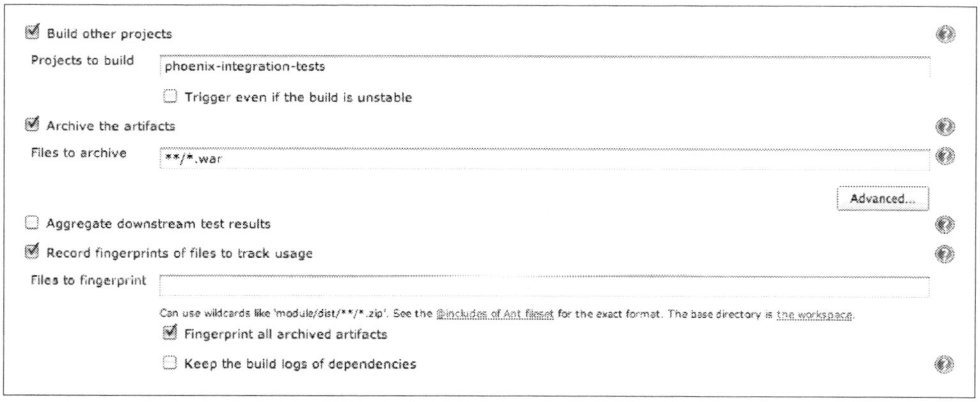

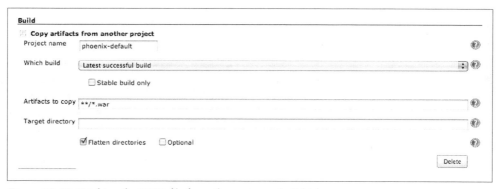

Figure 10-46. Using fingerprints in the build promotion process

the files you want to fingerprint. A useful shortcut is simply to fingerprint all archived files, since these are the files that will typically be retrieved and reused by the down-stream build jobs.

This is all you need to do to configure the initial build process. The next step is to configure the integration tests executed in the *phoenix-integration* build job. Here, we use the Copy Artifact plugin to retrieve the WAR file generated by the *phoenix-default* build job (see Figure 10-47). Since this build job is triggered immediately after the *phoenix-default* build job, we can simply fetch the WAR file from the latest successful build.

Figure 10-47. Fetching the WAR file from the upstream build job

This is not quite all we need to do for the integration tests, however. The *phoenix-integration* build job is followed by the *phoenix-web* build job, which executes the automated web tests. To ensure that the same WAR file is used at each stage of the build process, we need to retrieve it from the upstream *phoenix-integration* build job, and not from the original *phoenix-default* build job (which may have been executed again in the meantime). So we also need to archive the WAR file in the *phoenix-integration* build job (see Figure 10-48).

Figure 10-48. Archiving the WAR file for use in the downstream job

In the *phoenix-web* build job, we then fetch the WAR file from the *phoenix-integration* build job, using a configuration very similar to the one shown above (see Figure 10-49).

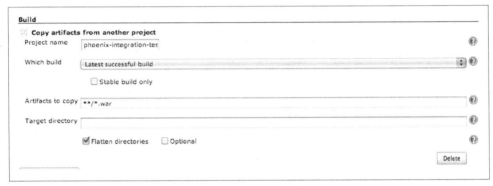

Figure 10-49. Fetching the WAR file from the integration job

For the build promotion process to work properly, there is one more important thing we need to configure in the *phoenix-web* build job. As we discussed earlier, Jenkins needs to be able to be sure that the WAR file used in these tests is the same one generated by the original build. We do this by activating fingerprinting on the WAR file we fetched from the *phoenix-integration* build job (which, remember, was originally built by the *phoenix-default* build job). Since we have copied this WAR file into the workspace, a configuration like the one in Figure 10-50 will work just fine.

Figure 10-50. We need to determine the fingerprint of the WAR file we use

The final step is to configure the *phoenix-deploy-to-test* build job to retrieve the last promoted WAR file (rather than just the last successful one). To do this, we use the

Copy Artifact plugin again, but this time we choose the "Specified by permalink" option. Here Jenkins will propose, among other things, the build promotion processes configured for the build job you are copying from. So, in Figure 10-51, we are fetching the last promoted WAR file build by the *phoenix-default* job, which is precisely what we want.

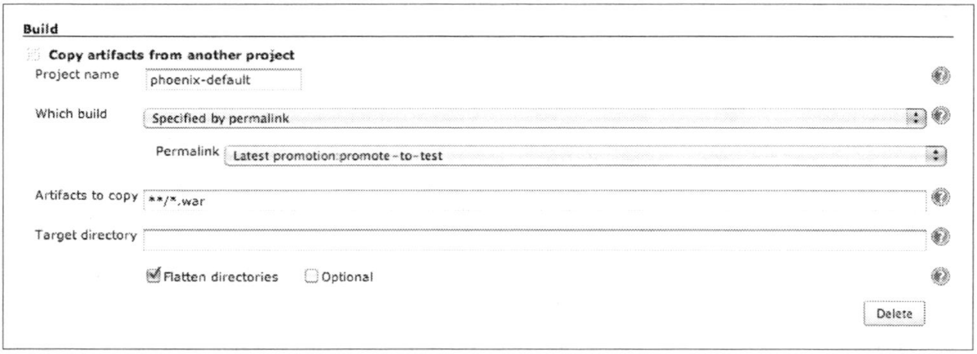

Figure 10-51. Fetching the latest promoted WAR file

Our promotion process is now ready for action. When the automated web tests succeed for a particular build, the original build job will be promoted and the corresponding WAR file deployed to the test environment. Promoted builds are indicated by a star in the build history (see Figure 10-52). By default, the stars are yellow, but you can configure the color of the star in the build promotion setup.

You can also use the "Promotion Status" menu entry (or click on the colored star in the build history) to view the details of a particular build promotion, and even to rerun a promotion manually (see Figure 10-45). Any build promotion can be triggered manually, by clicking on "Force promotion" (if this build job has never been promoted) or "Re-execute promotion" (if it has).

Aggregating Test Results

When distributing different types of tests across different build jobs, it is easy to loose a global vision about the overall test results. Test results are scattered among the various build jobs, without a central place to see the total number of executed and failing tests.

A good way to avoid this problem is to use the Aggregated Test Results feature of Jenkins. This will retrieve any test results recorded in the downstream jobs, and aggregate them in the upstream build job. You can configure this in the initial (upstream) build job by ticking the "Aggregate downstream test results" option (see Figure 10-53).

The aggregate test results can be seen in the build details page (see Figure 10-54). Unfortunately, these aggregate test results do not appear in the overall test results, but you can display the full list of tests executed by clicking on the Aggregate Test Result link on the individual build page.

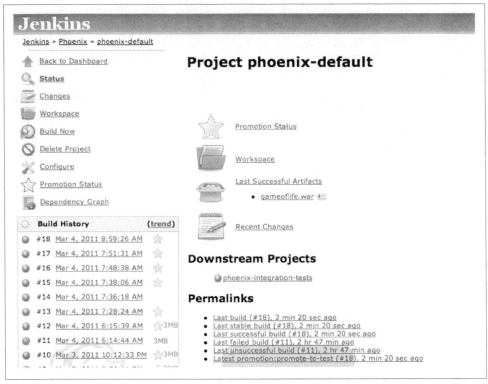

Figure 10-52. Promoted builds are indicated by a star in the build history

Figure 10-53. Reporting on aggregate test results

For this to work correctly, you need to ensure that you have configured fingerprinting for the binary files you use at each stage. Jenkins will only aggregate downstream test results from builds containing an artifact with the same fingerprint.

Build Pipelines

The final plugin we will be looking at in this section is the Build Pipeline plugin. The Build Pipelines plugin takes the idea of build promotion further, and helps you design and monitor deployment pipelines. A deployment pipeline is a way of orchestrating your build through a series of quality gates, with automated or manual approval processes at each stage, culminating with deployment into production.

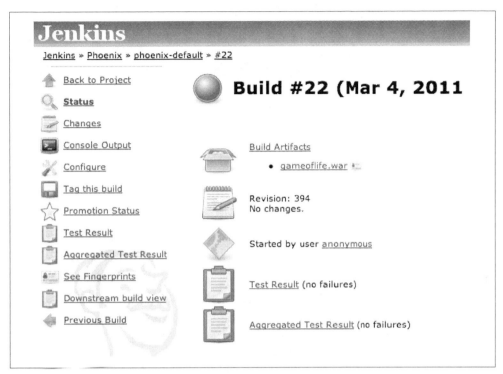

Figure 10-54. Viewing aggregate test results

The Build Pipeline plugin provides an alternative way to define downstream build jobs. A build pipeline, unlike conventional downstream dependencies, is considered to be a linear process, a series of build jobs executed in sequence.

To use this plugin, start by configuring the downstream build jobs for each build job in the pipeline, using the "Build other projects" field just as you would normally do. The Build Pipelines plugin uses the standard upstream and downstream build configurations, and for automatic steps this is all you need to do. However the Build Pipeline plugin also supports manual build steps, where a user has to manually approve the next step. For manual steps, you also need to configure In the *Post-build Actions* of your upstream build job: just tick the "Build Pipeline Plugin -> Specify Downstream Project" box, select the next step in your project, and tick the "Require manual build executor" option (see Figure 10-55).

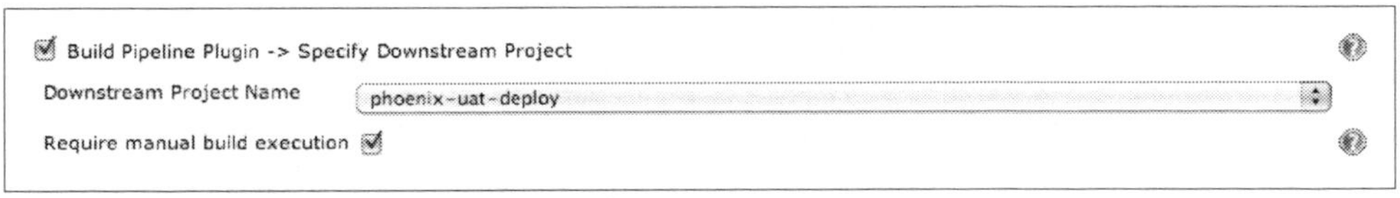

☑ Build Pipeline Plugin -> Specify Downstream Project	⑦
Downstream Project Name phoenix-uat-deploy	
Require manual build execution ☑	⑦

Figure 10-55. Configuring a manual step in the build pipeline

Once you have set up your build process to your satisfaction, you can configure the build pipeline view. You can create this view just like any other view (see Figure 10-56).

Figure 10-56. Creating a Build Pipeline view

There is a trick when it comes to configuring the view, however. At the time of writing, there is no menu option or button that lets you configure the view directly. In fact, you need to enter the URL manually. Fortunately, this is not difficult: just add */configure* to the end of the URL shown when you are displaying this view. For example, if you have named your view "phoenix-build-pipeline", as shown here, the URL to configure this view would be *http://my_jenkins_server/view/phoenix-build-pipeline*. (see Figure 10-57).

The most important thing to configure in this screen is the initial job. This marks the starting point of your build pipeline. You can define multiple build pipeline views, each with a different starting job. You can also configure the maximum number of build sequences to appear on the screen at once.

Once you have configured the starting point, you can return to the view to see the current state of your build pipeline. Jenkins displays the successive related build jobs horizontally, using a color to indicate the outcome of each build (Figure 10-58). There is a column for each build job in the pipeline. Whenever the initial build job kicks off, a new row appears on this page. As the build progresses through the successive build jobs in the pipeline, Jenkins will add a colored box in the successive columns, indicating the outcome of each stage. You can click on the box to drill down into a particular build result for more details. Finally, if a manual execution is required, a button will be displayed where the user can trigger the job.

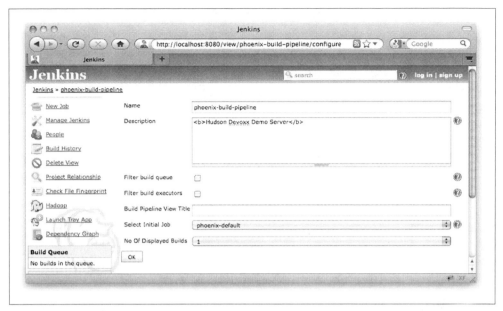

Figure 10-57. Configuring a Build Pipeline view

This plugin is still relatively new, and does not integrate with all of the other plugins we have seen here. In particular, it is really designed for a linear build pipeline, and does not cope well with branches or parallel build jobs. Nevertheless, it does give an excellent global vision of a build pipeline.

Conclusion

Continuous Integration build jobs are much more than simply the scheduled execution of build scripts. In this chapter we have reviewed a number of tools and techniques enabling you to go beyond your typical build jobs, combining them so that they can work together as part of a larger process. We have seen how parameterized and multiconfiguration build jobs add an element of flexibility to ordinary build jobs by allowing you to run the same build job with different sets of parameters. Other tools help coordinate and orchestrate groups of related build jobs. The Joins and Locks and Latches plugins helps you coordinate build jobs running in parallel. And the Build Promotions and Build Pipelines plugins, with the help of the Copy Artifacts plugin, make it relatively easy to design and configure complex build promotion strategies for your projects.

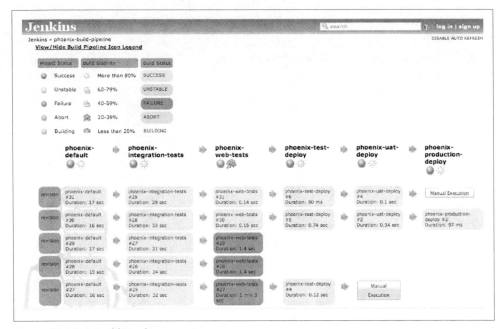

Figure 10-58. A Build Pipeline in action

CHAPTER 11

Distributed Builds

Introduction

Arguably one of the more powerful features of Jenkins is its ability to dispatch build jobs across a large number of machines. It is quite easy to set up a farm of build servers, either to share the load across multiple machines, or to run build jobs in different environments. This is a very effective strategy which can potentially increase the capacity of your CI infrastructure dramatically.

Distributed builds are generally used either to absorb extra load, for example absorbing spikes in build activity by dynamically adding extra machines as required, or to run specialized build jobs in specific operating systems or environments. For example, you may need to run particular build jobs on a particular machine or operating system. For example, if you need to run web tests using Internet Explorer, you will need to be use a Windows machine. Or one of your build jobs may be particularly resource-heavy, and need to be run on its own dedicated machine so as not to penalize your other build jobs.

Demand for build servers can also fluctuate over time. If you are working with product release cycles, you may need to run a much higher number of builds jobs towards the end of the cycle, for example, when more comprehensive functional and regression test suites may be more frequent.

In this chapter, we will discuss how to set up and manage a farm of build servers using Jenkins.

The Jenkins Distributed Build Architecture

Jenkins uses a master/slave architecture to manage distributed builds. Your main Jenkins server (the one we have been using up until present) is the master. In a nutshell, the master's job is to handle scheduling build jobs, dispatching builds to the slaves for the actual execution, monitor the slaves (possibly taking them online and offline as required) and recording and presenting the build results. Even in a distributed architecture, a master instance of Jenkins can also execute build jobs directly.

The job of the slaves is to do as they are told, which involves executing build jobs dispatched by the master. You can configure a project to always run on a particular slave machine, or a particular type of slave machine, or simply let Jenkins pick the next available slave.

A slave is a small Java executable that runs on a remote machine and listens for requests from the Jenkins master instance. Slaves can (and usually do) run on a variety of operating systems. The slave instance can be started in a number of different ways, depending on the operating system and network architecture. Once the slave instance is running, it communicates with the master instance over a TCP/IP connection. We will look at different setups in the rest of this chapter.

Master/Slave Strategies in Jenkins

There are a number of different ways that you can configure set up a distributed build farm using Jenkins, depending on your operating systems and network architecture. In all cases, the fact that a build job is being run on a slave, and how that slave is managed, is transparent for the end-user: the build results and artifacts will always end up on the master server.

Creating a new Jenkins slave node is a straightforward process. First, go to the Manage Jenkins screen and click on Manage Nodes. This screen displays the list of slave agents (also known as "Nodes" in more politically correct terms), shown in Figure 11-1. From here, you can set up new nodes by clicking on the New Node button. You can also configure some of the parameters related to your distributed build setup (see "Node Monitoring" on page 314).

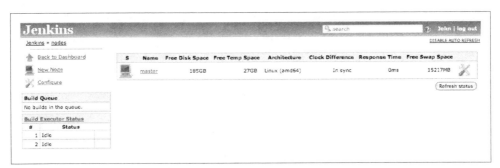

Figure 11-1. Managing slave nodes

There are several different strategies when it comes to managing Jenkins slave nodes, depending on your target operating systems and other architectural considerations. These strategies affect the way you configure your slave nodes, so we need to consider them separately. In the following sections, we will look at the most frequently used ways to install and configure Jenkins slaves:

- The master starts the slave agents via ssh
- Starting the slave agent manually using Java Web Start
- Installing the slave agent as a Window service
- Starting the slave agent directly from the command line on the slave machine from the command line

Each of these strategies has its uses, advantages, and inconveniences. Let's look at each in turn.

The Master Starts the Slave Agent Using SSH

If you are working in a Unix environment, the most convenient way to start a Jenkins slave is undoubtedly to use SSH. Jenkins has its own build-in SSH client, and almost all Unix environments support SSH (usually sshd) out of the box.

To create a Unix-based slave, click on the New Node button as we mentioned above. This will prompt you to enter the name of your slave, and its type (see Figure 11-2). At the time of writing, only "dumb slaves" are supported out of the box; "dumb" slaves are passive beasts, that simply respond to build job requests from the master node. This is the most common way to set up a distributed build architecture, and the only option available in a default installation.

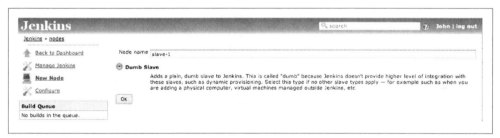

Figure 11-2. Creating a new slave node

In this screen, you simply need to provide a name for your slave. When you click on OK, Jenkins will let you provide more specific details about your slave machine (see Figure 11-3).

The name is simply a unique way of identifying your slave machine. It can be anything, but it may help if the name reminds you of the physical machine it is running on. It also helps if the name is file-system and URL-friendly. It will work with spaces, but you will make life easier for yourself if you avoid them. So "Slave-1" is better than "Slave 1".

The description is also purely for human consumption, and can be used to indicate why you would use this slave rather than another.

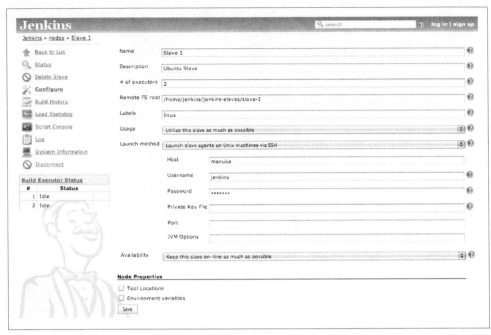

Figure 11-3. Creating a Unix slave node

Like on the main Jenkins configuration screen, the number of executors lets you define how many concurrent build job this node can execute.

Every Jenkins slave node also needs a place that it can call home, or, more precisely, a dedicated directory on the slave machine that the slave agent can use to run build jobs. You define this directory in the Remote FS root field. You need to provide a local, OS-specific path, such as */var/jenkins* for a Unix machine, or *C:\jenkins* on Windows. Nothing mission-critical is stored in this directory—everything important is transferred back to the master machine once the build is done. So you usually don't need to be so concerned with backing up these directories as you should be with the master.

Labels are a particularly useful concept when your distributed build architecture begins to grow in size. You can define labels, or tags, to each build node, and then configure a build job to run only on a slave node with a particular label. Labels might relate to operating systems (unix, windows, macosx, etc.), environments (staging, UAT, development, etc.) or any criteria that you find useful. For example, you could configure your automated WebDriver/Selenium tests to run using Internet Explorer, but only on slave nodes with the "windows" label.

The Usage field lets you configure how intensively Jenkins will use this slave. You have the choice of three options: use it as much as possible, reserve it for dedicated build jobs, or bring it online as required.

The first option, "Utilize this slave as much as possible", tells Jenkins to use this slave freely as soon as it becomes available, for any build job that it can run. This is by far the most commonly used one, and is generally what you want.

There are times, however, when this second option comes in handy. In the project configuration, you can tie a build job to a specific node—this is useful when a particular task, such as automated deployment or a performance test suite, needs to be executed on a specific machine. In this case, the "Leave this machine for tied jobs only" option makes good sense. You can take this further by setting the maximum number of Executors to 1. In this case, not only will this slave be reserved for a particular type of job, but it will only ever be able to run one of these build jobs at any one time. This is a very useful configuration for performance and load tests, where you need to reserve the machine so that it can execute its tests without interference.

The third option is "Take this slave on-line when in demand and off-line when idle" (see Figure 11-4). As the name indicates, this option tells Jenkins to bring this slave online when demand is high, and to take it offline when demand subsides. This lets you keep some build slaves in reserve for periods of heavy use, without having to maintain a slave agent running on them permanently. When you choose this option, you also need to provide some extra details. The "In demand delay" indicates how many minutes jobs must have been waiting in the queue before this slave will be brought online. The Idle delay indicates how long the slave needs to be idle before Jenkins will take it off-line.

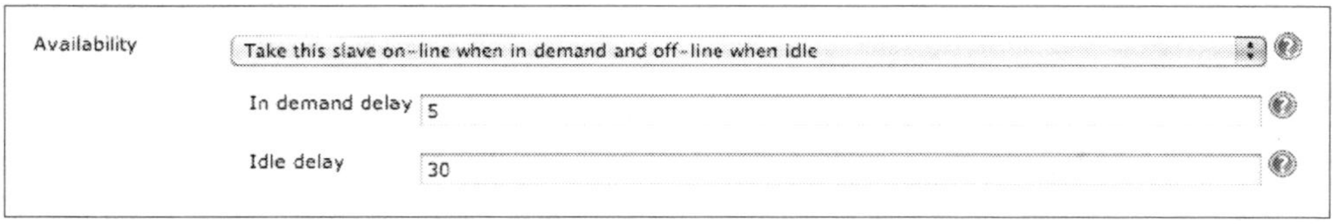

Figure 11-4. Taking a slave off-line when idle

The launch method is where you decide how Jenkins will start the node, as we mentioned earlier. For the configuration we are discussing here, you would choose "Launch slave agents on Unix machines via SSH". The Advanced button lets you enter the additional details that Jenkins needs to connect to the Unix slave machine: a host name, a login and password, and a port number. You can also provide a path to the SSH private key file on the master machine (e.g., id_dsa or id_rsa) to use for "password-less" Public/Private Key authentication.

You can also configure when Jenkins starts and stops the slave. By default, Jenkins will simply keep the slave running and use it whenever required (the "Keep this slave on-line as much as possible" option). If Jenkins notices that the slave has gone offline (for example due to a server reboot), it will attempt to restart it if it can. Alternatively, Jenkins can be more conservative with your system resources, and take the slave offline when it doesn't need it. To do this, simply choose the "Take this slave on-line when in demand and off-line when idle" option. This is useful if you have regular spikes and lulls of build activity, as an unused slave can be taken offline to conserve system resources for other tasks, and brought back online when required.

Jenkins also needs to know where it can find the build tools it needs for your build jobs on the slave machines. This includes JDKs as well as build tools such as Maven, Ant, and Gradle. If you have configured your build tools to be automatically installed, you will usually have no extra configuration to do for your slave machines; Jenkins will download and install the tools as required. On the other hand, if your build tools are installed locally on the slave machine, you will need to tell Jenkins where it can find them. You do this by ticking the Tool Locations checkbox, and providing the local paths for each of the tools you will need for your build jobs (see Figure 11-5).

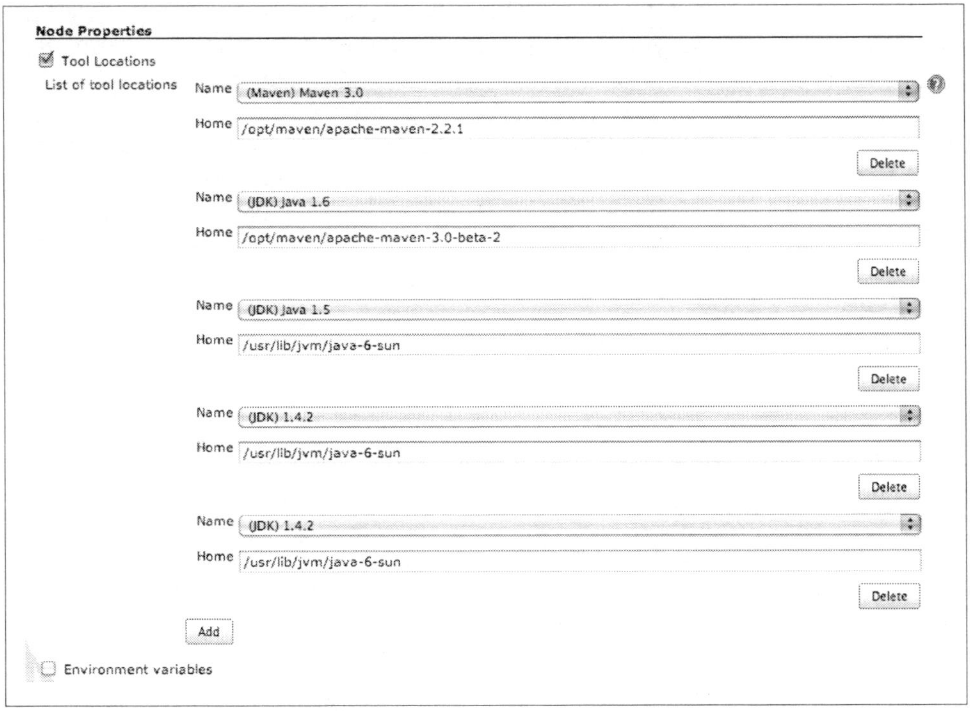

Figure 11-5. Configuring tool locations

You can also specify environment variables. These will be passed into your build jobs, and can be a good way to allow your build jobs to behave differently depending on where they are being executed.

Once you have done this, your new slave node will appear in the list of computers on the Jenkins Nodes page (see Figure 11-6).

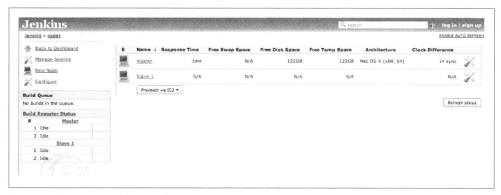

Figure 11-6. Your new slave node in action

Starting the Slave Agent Manually Using Java Web Start

Another option is to start a slave agent from the slave machine itself using Java Web Start (JNLP). This approach is useful if the server cannot connect to the slave, for example if the slave machine is running on the other side of a firewall. It works no matter what operating system your slave is running on, however it is more commonly used for Windows slaves. It does suffer from a few major drawbacks: the slave node cannot be started, or restarted, automatically by Jenkins. So, if the slave goes down, the master instance cannot restart it.

When you do this on a Windows machine, you need to start the Jenkins slave manually at least once. This involves opening a browser on the machine, opening the slave node page on the Jenkins master, and launching the slave using a very visible JNLP icon. However, once you have launched the slave, you can install it as a Windows service.

There are also times when you need to do this from the command line, in a Unix environment. You may need to do this because of firewalls or other networking issues, or because SSH is not available in your environment.

Lets step through both these processes.

The first thing you need to do in all cases is create a new slave. As for any other slave node, you do this by clicking on the New Node menu entry in the Nodes screen. When entering the details concerning your slave node, make sure you choose "Launch slave agents via JNLP" in the Launch Method field (see Figure 11-7). Also remember that if this is to be a Windows slave node, the Remote FS root needs to be a Windows path (such as *C:\jenkins-slave*). This directory does not have to exist: Jenkins will create it automatically if it is missing.

Once you have saved this configuration, Next, log on to the slave machine and open the Slave node screen in a browser, as shown in Figure 11-8. You will see a large orange Launch button—if you click on this button, you should be able to start a slave agent directly from within your browser.

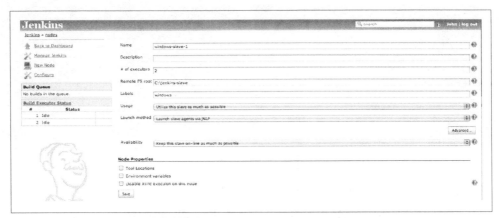

Figure 11-7. Creating a slave node for JNLP

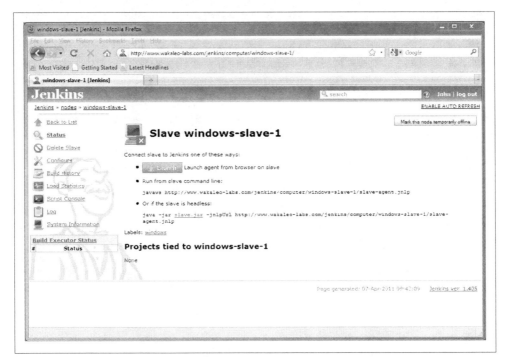

Figure 11-8. Launching a slave via Java Web Start

If all goes well, this will open up a small window indicating that your slave agent is now running (see Figure 11-9).

Browsers are fickle, however, and Java Web Start is not always easy to use. This approach usually works best with Firefox, although you must have the Java JRE installed beforehand to make Firefox Java-aware. Using JNLP with Internet Explorer requires

Figure 11-9. The Jenkins slave agent in action

some (considerable) fiddling to associate *.jnlp files with the Java Web Start executable, a file called *javaws*, which you will find in the Java *bin* directory. In fact it is probably easier just to start it from the command line as discussed below.

A more reliable, albeit low-level, approach is to start the slave from the command line. To do this, simply invoke the *javaws* executable from a command window as shown here:

```
C:> javaws http://build.myorg.com/jenkins/computer/windows-slave-1/slave-agent.jnlp
```

The exact command that you need to execute, including the correct URL, is conveniently displayed on the Jenkins slave node window just below the JNLP launch button (see Figure 11-8).

If security is activated on your Jenkins server, Jenkins will communicate with the slave on a specific nonstandard port. If for some reason this port is inaccessible, the slave node will fail to start and will display an error message similar to the one shown in Figure 11-10.

Figure 11-10. The Jenkins slave failing to connect to the master

This is usually a sign that a firewall is blocking a port. By default, Jenkins picks a random port to use for TCP communication with its slaves. However if you need to have a specific port that your firewall will authorize, you can force Jenkins to use a fixed port in the System configuration screen by selecting Fixed in the "TCP port for JNLP slave agents" option, as shown in Figure 11-11.

Figure 11-11. Configuring the Jenkins slave port

Installing a Jenkins Slave as a Windows Service

Once you have the slave up and running on your Windows machine, you can save yourself the bother of having to restart it manually each time your machine reboots by installing it as a Windows service. To do this, select the "Install as Windows Service" menu option in the File menu of the slave agent window (see Figure 11-12).

Figure 11-12. Installing the Jenkins slave as a Windows service

Once this is done, your Jenkins slave node will start automatically whenever the machine starts up, and can be administered just like any other Windows service (see Figure 11-13).

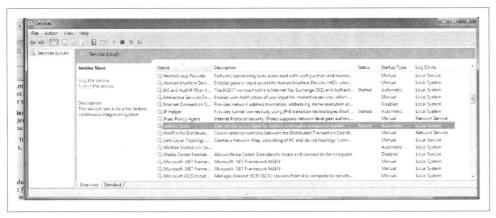

Figure 11-13. Managing the Jenkins Windows service

Starting the Slave Node in Headless Mode

You can also start a slave agent in headless mode, directly from the command line. This is useful if you don't have a user interface available, for example if you are starting a JNLP slave node on a Unix machine. If you are working with Unix machines, it is generally easier and more flexible just to use an SSH connection, but there are sometimes network or architecture constraints that prevent you from using SSH. In cases like this, it is still possible to run a slave node from the command line.

To start the slave node this way, you need to use Jenkins' *slave.jar* file. You can find this in *JENKINS_HOME/war/WEB-INF/slave.jar*. Once you have located this file and copied it onto the Windows slave machine, you can run it as follows:

```
java -jar slave.jar \
    -jnlpUrl http://build.myorg.com/jenkins/computer/windows-slave-1/slave-agent.jnlp
```

And if your Jenkins server requires authentication, just pass in the `-auth username:pass word` option:

```
java -jar slave.jar \
    -jnlpUrl http://build.myorg.com/jenkins/computer/windows-slave-1/slave-agent.jnlp
    -auth scott:tiger
```

Once you have started the slave agent, be sure to install it as a Windows service, as discussed in the previous section.

Starting a Windows Slave as a Remote Service

Jenkins can also manage a remote Windows slave as a Windows service, using the Windows Management Instrumentation (WMI) service which is installed out of the box on Windows 2000 or later (see Figure 11-14). When you choose this option, you just need to provide a Windows username and password. The name of the node must be the hostname of the slave machine.

This is certainly convenient, as it does not require you to physically connect to the Windows machine to set it up. However, it does have limitations—in particular, you cannot run any applications requiring a graphical interface, so you can't use a slave set up this way for web testing, for example. In practice this can be a little tricky to set up, as you may need to configure the Windows firewall to open the appropriate services and ports. If you run into trouble, make sure that your network configuration allows TCP connections to ports 135, 139, and 445, and UDP connections to ports 137 and 138 (see *https://wiki.jenkins-ci.org/display/JENKINS/Windows+slaves+fail+to+start +via+DCOM* for more details).

Figure 11-14. Letting Jenkins control a Windows slave as a Windows service

Associating a Build Job with a Slave or Group of Slaves

In the previous section, we saw how you can assign labels to your slave nodes. This is a convenient way to group your slave nodes according to characteristics such as operating system, target environment, database type, or any other criteria that is relevant to your build process. A common application of this practice is to run OS-specific functional tests on dedicated slave nodes, or to reserve a particular machine exclusively to performance tests.

Once you have assigned labels to your slave nodes, you also need to tell Jenkins where it can run the build jobs. By default, Jenkins will simply use the first available slave node, which usually results in the best overall turn-around time. If you need to tie a build job to a particular machine or group of machines, you need to tick the "Restrict where this project can be run" checkbox in the build configuration page (see Figure 11-15). Next, enter the name of the machine, or a label identifying a group of machines, into the Label Expression field. Jenkins will provide a dynamic dropdown showing the available machine names and labels as you type.

This field also accepts boolean expressions, allowing you to define more complicated constraints about where your build job should run. How to use these expressions is best illustrated by an example. Suppose you have a build farm with Windows and Linux slave nodes (identified by the labels "windows" and "linux"), distributed over three sites ("sydney", "sanfrancisco", and "london"). Your application also needs to be tested against several different databases ("oracle", "db2", "mysql", and "postgres"). You also use labels to distinguish slave nodes used to deploy to different environments (test, uat, production).

The simplest use of label expressions is to determine where a build job can or cannot be executed. If your web tests require Internet Explorer, for example, you will need

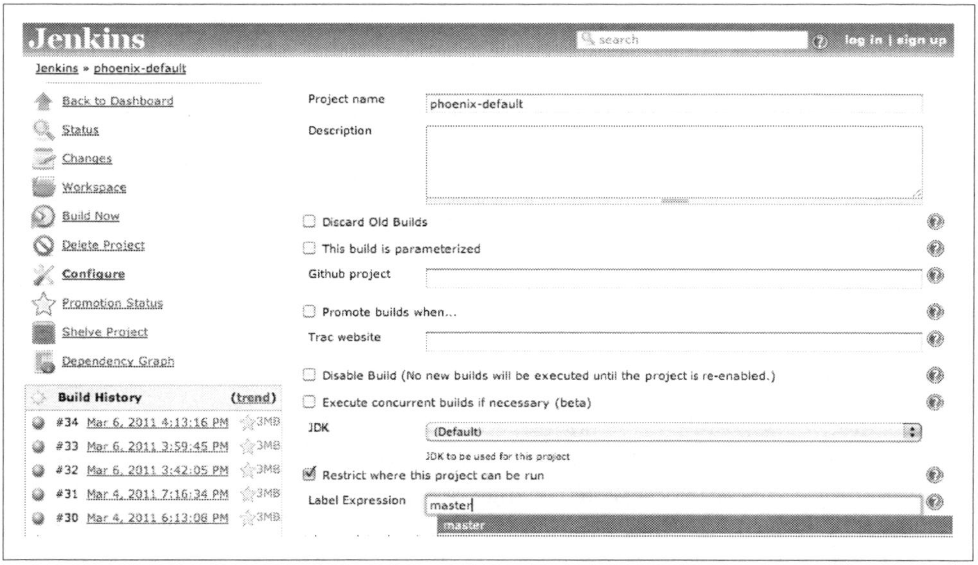

Figure 11-15. Running a build job on a particular slave node

them to run on a Windows machine. You could express this by simply quoting the corresponding label:

```
windows
```

Alternatively, you might want to run tests against Firefox, but only on Linux machines. You could exclude Windows machines from the range of candidate build nodes by using the ! negation operator:

```
!windows
```

You can also use the *and* (&&) and *or* (!!) operators to combine expressions. For example, suppose the Postgres database is only tested for Linux. You could tell Jenkins to run a particular build job only on Linux machines installed with postgres using the following expression:

```
linux && postgres
```

Or you could specify that a particular build job is only to be run on a UAT environment in Sydney or London:

```
uat && (sydney || london)
```

If your machine names contain spaces, you will need to enclose them in double quotes:

```
"Windows 7" || "Windows XP"
```

There are also two more advanced logical operators that you may find useful. The *implies* operator (=>) lets you define a logical constraint of the form "if A is true, then B must also be true." For example, suppose you have a build job that can run on any

Linux distribution, but if it is executed on a Windows box, it must be Windows 7. You could express this constraint as follows:

```
windows -> "Windows 7"
```

The other logical operator is the *if-and-only-if* (<=>) operator. This operation lets you define stronger constraints of the form "If A is true, then B must be true, but if A is false, then B must be false." For example, suppose that Windows 7 tests are only to be run in a UAT environment, and that only Windows 7 tests are to be run in the UAT environment. You could express this as shown here:

```
"Windows 7" <-> uat
```

Node Monitoring

Jenkins doesn't just dispatch build jobs to slave agents and hope for the best: it proactively monitors your slave machines, and will take a node offline if it considers that the node is incapable of safely performing a build. You can fine-tune exactly what Jenkins monitors int the Manage Nodes screen (see Figure 11-16). Jenkins monitors the slave agents in several different ways. It monitors the response time: an overly slow response time can indicate either a network problem or that the slave machine is down. It also monitors the amount of disk space, temporary directory space and swap space available to the Jenkins user on the slave machine, since build jobs can be notoriously disk-hungry. It also keeps tabs on the system clocks, as if the clocks are not correctly synchronized, odd errors can sometimes happen. If any of these criteria is not up to scratch, Jenkins will automatically take the server offline.

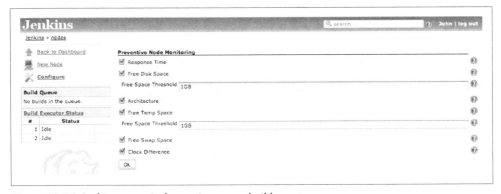

Figure 11-16. Jenkins proactively monitors your build agents

Cloud Computing

Cloud computing involves using hardware resources on the Internet as an extension and/or replacement of your local computing architecture. Cloud computing is expanding into many areas of the enterprise, including email and document sharing (Gmail and Google Apps are particularly well-known examples, but there are many others), off-site data storage (such as Amazon S3), as well as more technical services such as source code repositories (such as GitHub, Bitbucket, etc.) and many others.

Of course externalized hardware architecture solutions have been around for a long time. The main thing that distinguishes the cloud computing with more traditional services is the speed and flexibility with which a service can be brought up, and brought down when it is no longer needed. In a cloud computing environment, a new machine can be running and available within seconds.

However, cloud computing in the context of Continuous Integration is not always as simple as it might seem. For any cloud-based approach to work, some of your internal resources may need to be available to the outside world. This can include opening access to your version control system, your test databases, and to any other resources that your builds and tests require. All these aspects need to be considered carefully when choosing a cloud-based CI architecture, and may limit your options if certain resources simply cannot be accessed from the Internet. Nevertheless, cloud-based CI has the potential of providing huge benefits when it comes to scalability.

In the following sections, we will look at how to use the Amazon EC2 cloud computing services to set up a cloud-based build farm.

Using Amazon EC2

In addition to selling books, Amazon is one of the more well-known providers of cloud computing services. If you are willing to pay for the service, Amazon can provide you build machines that can be either used permanently as part of your build farm, or brought online as required when your existing build machines become overloaded. This is an excellent and reasonably cost-efficient way to absorb extra build load on an as-needed basis, and without the headache of extra physical machines to maintain.

If you want the flexibility of a cloud-based CI architecture, but don't want to externalize your hardware, another option is to set up a Eucalyptus cloud. Eucalyptus is an open source tool that enables you to create a local private cloud on existing hardware. Eucalyptus uses an API that is compatible with Amazon EC2 and S3, and works well with Jenkins.

Setting up your Amazon EC2 build farm

Amazon EC2 is probably the most popular and well-known commercial cloud computing service. To use this service, you will need to create an EC2 account with Amazon if you do not already have one. The process required to do this is well documented on the Amazon website, so we will not dwell on this here. Once you have created your account, you will be able to create the virtual machines and machine images that will make up your EC2-based build farm.

When using Amazon EC2, you create virtual machines, called instances, using the Amazon Web Services (AWS) Management Console (see Figure 11-17). This website is where you manage your running instances and create new ones. You create these instances from predefined images, called Amazon Machine Images (AMIs). There are many AMI images, both from Amazon and in the public domain, that you can use as a starting point, covering most of the popular operating systems. Once you have created a new instance, you can connect to it using either SSH (for unix machines) or Windows Remote Desktop Connection, to configure it for your purposes.

Figure 11-17. You manage your EC2 instances using the Amazon AWS Management Console

To set up a build farm, you will also need to configure your have one, just go to the Key Pairs menu in the Security build server to be able to access your EC2 instances. In particular, you will need to install the Amazon EC2 API tools, set up the appropriate private/public keys, and allow SSH connections from your server or network to your Amazon instances. Again, the details of how to do this are well documented for all the major operating systems on the EC2 website.

You can use Amazon EC2 instances in two ways—either create slave machines on Amazon EC2 and use them as remote machines, or have Jenkins create them for you dynamically on demand. Or you can have a combination of the two. Both approaches have their uses, and we will discuss each of them in the following sections.

Using EC2 instances as part of your build farm

Creating a new EC2 instance is as simple as choosing the base image you want to use. You will just need to provide some details about the instance, such as its size and capacity, and the private key you want to use to access the machine. Amazon will then create a new running virtual machine based on this image. Once you have set it up, an EC2 instance is essentially a machine like any other, and it is easy and convenient to set up permanent or semipermanent EC2 machines as part of your build infrastructure. You may even opt to use an EC2 image as your master server.

Setting up an existing EC2 instance as a Jenkins slave is little different to setting up any other remote slave. If you are setting up a Unix or Linux EC2 slave, you will need to refer to the private key file (see Figure 11-18) that you used to create the EC2 instance on the AWS Management console. Depending on the flavor of Linux you are using, you may also need to provide a username. Most distributions connect as root, but some, such as Ubuntu, need a different user name.

Figure 11-18. Configuring an Amazon EC2 slave

Using dynamic instances

The second approach involves creating new Amazon EC2 machines dynamically, as they are required. Setting up dedicated instances is not difficult, but it does not scale well. A better approach is to let Jenkins create new instances as require. To do this, you will need to install the Jenkins Amazon EC2 plugin. This plugin lets your Jenkins instance start slaves on the EC2 cloud on demand, and then kill them off when they are no longer needed. The plugin works both with Amazon EC2, and the Ubuntu Enterprise Cloud. We will be focusing on Amazon EC2 here. Note that at the time of writing the Amazon EC2 Plugin only supported managing Unix EC2 images.

Once you have installed the plugin and restarted Jenkins, go to the main Jenkins configuration screen and click on Add a New Cloud (see Figure 11-19). Choose Amazon EC2. You will need to provide your Amazon Access Key ID and Secret Access Key so that Jenkins can communicate with your Amazon EC2 account. You can access these in the Key Pairs screen of your EC2 dashboard.

You will also need to provide your RSA private key. If you don't have one, just go to the Key Pairs menu in the Security Credentials screen and create one. This will create a new key pair for you and download the private key. Keep the private key in a safe place (you will need it if you want to connect to your EC2 instances via SSH).

In the advanced options, you can use the Instance Cap field to limit the number of EC2 instances that Jenkins will launch. This limit refers to the total number of active EC2 instances, not just the ones that Jenkins is currently running. This is useful as a safety measure, as you pay for the time your EC2 instances spend active.

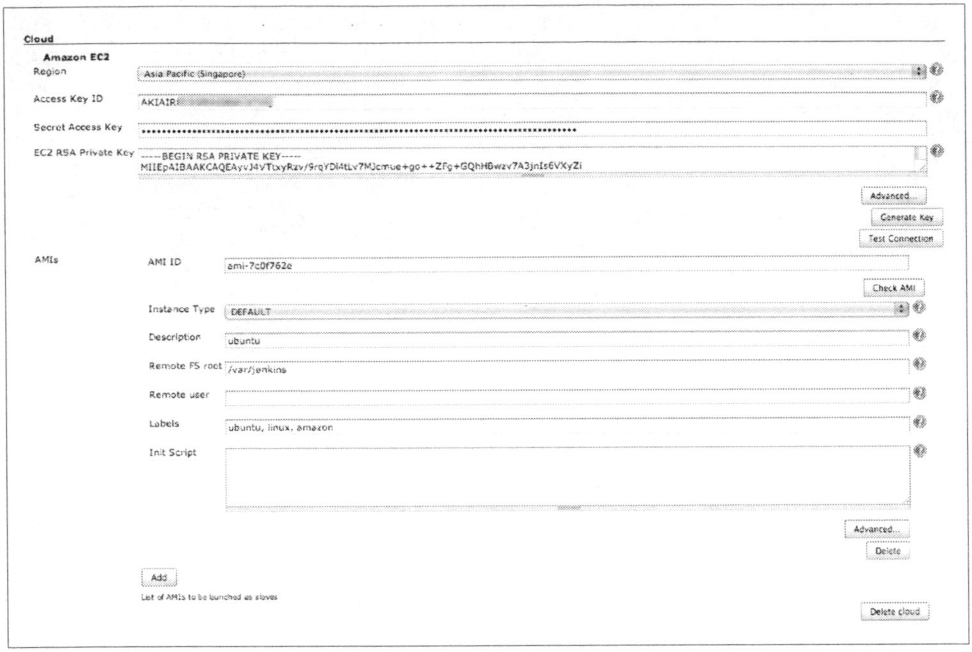

Figure 11-19. Configuring an Amazon EC2 slave

Once you have configured your overall EC2 connection, you need to define the machines you will work with. You do this by specifying the Amazon Mirror Image (AMI) identifier of the server image you would like to start. Amazon provides some starter images, and many more are available from the community, however not all images will work with EC2. At the time of writing, only certain images based on 32-bit Linux distributions work correctly.

The predefined Amazon and public AMI images are useful starting points for your permanent virtual machines, but for the purposes of implementing a dynamic EC2-based cloud, you need to define your own AMI with the essential tools (Java, build tools, SCM configuration and so forth) preinstalled. Fortunately, this is a simple process: just start off with a generic AMI (preferably one compatible with the Jenkins EC2 plugin), and install everything your builds need. Make sure you use an EBS image. This way, changes you make to your server instance are persisted on an EBS volume so that you don't lose them when the server shuts down. Then create a new image by selecting the Create Image option in the Instances screen on the EC2 management console (see Figure 11-20). Make sure SSH is open from your build server's IP address in the default security group on Amazon EC2. If you don't do this, Jenkins will time out when it tries to start up a new slave node.

Once you have prepared your image, you will be able to use it for your EC2 configuration.

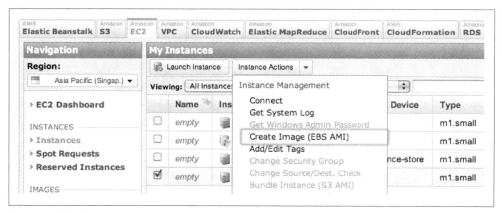

Figure 11-20. Creating a new Amazon EC2 image

Now Jenkins will automatically create a new EC2 instance using this image when it needs to, and delete (or "terminate," in Amazon terms) the instance once it is no longer needed. Alternatively, you can bring a new EC2 slave online manually from the Nodes screen using the Provision via EC2 button (see Figure 11-21). This is a useful way to test your configuration.

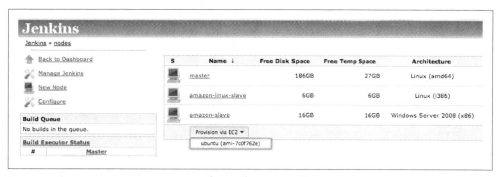

Figure 11-21. Bringing an Amazon EC2 slave online manually

Using the CloudBees DEV@cloud Service

Another option you might consider is running your Jenkins instance using a dedicated cloud-based Jenkins architecture, such as the DEV@cloud service offered by Cloud-Bees. CloudBees provides Jenkins as a service as well as various development services (like Sonar) around Jenkins. Using a dedicated Jenkins-specific service, there is no need to install (or manage) Jenkins masters or slaves on your machines. A master instance is automatically configured for you, and when you give a job to be built, CloudBees provisions a slave for you and takes it back when the job is done.

How does this approach compare with the Amazon EC2-based architecture we discussed in the previous section? The main advantage of this approach is that there is much less work involved in managing your CI architecture hardware. Using the Amazon EC2 infrastructure means you don't need to worry about hardware, but you still need to configure and manage your server images yourself. The CloudBees DEV@cloud architecture is more of a high-level, CI-centric service, which provides not only a Jenkins server but also other related tools such as SVN or Git repositories, user management, and Sonar. In addition, the pricing model (pay by the minute) is arguably better suited to a cloud-based CI architecture than the pay-by-the-hour approach used by Amazon.

Amazon EC2-based services are often, though not always, used in a "hybrid cloud" environment where you are offloading your jobs to the cloud, but a bulk of your builds remain in-house. The CloudBees DEV@cloud service is a public cloud solution where the whole build is happening on the cloud (though CloudBees does also offer a similar solution running on a private cloud).

Creating a CloudBees DEV@cloud account is straightforward, and you can use a free one to experiment with the service (note that the free CloudBees service only has a limited set of plugins available; you will need to sign up for the professional version to use the full plugin range). To signup for CloudBees, go to the signup page (*https:// grandcentral.cloudbees.com/account/signup*). You will need to enter some relevant information such as a user name, email information, and an account name. Once signed up, you will have access to both DEV@cloud and RUN@cloud (essentially the entire CloudBees platform) services.

At this point, you will have to subscribe to the DEV@cloud service. For our purposes, you can get away with simply choosing the "free" option. You will have to wait for a few minutes as CloudBees provisions a Jenkins master for you. The next step is to validate your account (this helps CloudBees prevent dummy accounts from running spurious jobs on the service). Click on the validation link, and enter your phone number. An automated incoming phone call will give your pin; enter the pin on the form. Once this is done, you can start running builds.

Your first port of call when you connect will be the management console (called GrandCentral). Click on the "Take me to Jenkins" button to go to your brand new Jenkins master instance.

From here, your interaction with DEV@cloud platform is exactly like in a standalone Jenkins. When you can create a new build job, just point to your existing source code repository and hit build. DEV@cloud will provision a slave for you and kick off a build (it may take a minute or two for the slave to be provisioned).

Conclusion

In Continuous Integration, distributed builds are the key to a truly scalable architecture. Whether you need to be able to add extra build capacity at the drop of a hat, or your build patterns are subject to periodic spikes in demand, a distributed build architecture is an excellent way to absorb extra load. Distributed builds are also a great way to delegate specialized tasks, such as OS-specific web testing, to certain dedicated machines.

Once you start down the path of distributed builds, cloud-based distributed build farms are a very logical extension. Putting your build servers on the cloud makes it easier and more convenient to scale your build infrastructure when required, as much as is required.

CHAPTER 12

Automated Deployment and Continuous Delivery

Introduction

Continuous Integration should not stop once your application compiles correctly. Nor should it stop once you can run a set of automated tests or automatically check and audit the code for potential quality issues. The next logical step, once you have achieved all of these, is to extend your build automation process to the deployment phase. This practice is globally known as Automated Deployment or Continuous Deployment.

In its most advanced form, Continuous Deployment is the process whereby any code change, subject to automated tests and other appropriate verifications, is immediately deployed into production. The aim is to reduce cycle time and reduce the time and effort involved in the deployment process. This in turn helps development teams reduce the time taken to deliver individual features or bug fixes, and as a consequence significantly increase their throughput. Reducing or eliminating the periods of intense activity leading up to a traditional release and deployment also frees up time and resources for process improvement and innovation. This approach is comparable to the philosophy of continual improvement promoted by lean processes such as Kanban.

Systematically deploying the latest code into production is not always suitable, however, no matter how good your automated tests are. Many organizations are not well prepared for new versions appearing unannounced every week; users might need to be trained, products may need to be marketed, and so forth. A more conservative variation on this theme, often seen in larger organizations, is to have the entire deployment process automated but to trigger the actual deployment manually in a one-click process. This is known as Continuous Delivery, and it has all the advantages of Continuous Deployment without the disadvantages. Variations on Continuous Delivery may also involve automatically deploying code to certain environments (such as test and QA) while using a manual one-click deployment for the other environments (such as UAT and Production). The most important distinguishing characteristic of Continuous De-livery is that any and every successful build that has passed all the relevant automated tests and quality gates can potentially be deployed into production via a fully automated one-click process and be in the hands of the end-user within minutes. However, the process is not automatic: it is the business, rather than IT, that decides the best time to deliver the latest changes.

Both Continuous Deployment and Continuous Delivery are rightly considered to rep-resent a very high level of maturity in terms of build automation and SDLC practices. These techniques cannot exist without an extremely solid set of automated tests. Nor can they exist without a CI environment and a robust built pipeline—indeed it typically represents the final stage and goal of the build pipeline. However, considering the sig-nificant advantages that Continuous Deployment/Delivery can bring to an organiza-tion, it is a worthy goal. During the remainder of this chapter, we will use the general term of "Continuous Deployment" to refer to both Continuous Deployment and Con-tinuous Delivery. Indeed, Continuous Delivery can be viewed as Continuous Deploy-ment with the final step (deployment into production) being a manual one dictated by the business rather than the development team.

Implementing Automated and Continuous Deployment

In its most elementary form, Automated Deployment can be as simple as writing your own scripts to deploy your application to a particular server. The main advantage of a scripted solution is simplicity and ease of configuration. However, a simple scripted approach may run into limits if you need to perform more advanced deployment ac-tivities, such as installing software on a machine or rebooting the server. For more advanced scenarios, you may need to use a more sophisticated deployment/configu-ration management solution such as Puppet or Chef.

The Deployment Script

An essential part of any Automated Deployment initiative is a scriptable deployment process. While this may seem obvious, there are still many organizations where de-ployment remains a cumbersome, complicated and labor-intensive process, including manual file copying, manual script execution, hand-written deployment notes, and so forth. The good news is that, in general, it does not have to be this way, and, with a little work, it is usually possible to write a script of some sort to automate most, if not all, of the process.

The complexity of a deployment script varies enormously from application to appli-cation. For a simple website, a deployment script may be as simple as resyncing a directory on the target server. Many Java application servers have Ant or Maven plugins that can be used to deploy applications. For a more complicated infrastructure, de-ployment may involve deploying several applications and services across multiple clustered servers in a precisely coordinated manner. Most deployment processes tend to fall somewhere between these extremes.

Database Updates

Deploying your app to the application server is often only one part of the puzzle. Databases, relational or otherwise, almost always play a central role in any application architecture. Of course, ideally, your database would be perfect from the start, but this is rarely the case in the real world. Indeed, when you update your application, you will generally also need to update one or more databases as well.

Database updates are usually more difficult to manage smoothly than application updates, as both the structure and the contents of the database may be impacted. However, managing database updates is a critical part of both the development and the deployment process, and deserves some reflection and planning.

Some application frameworks, such as Ruby on Rails and Hibernate, can manage structural database changes automatically to some extent. Using these frameworks, you can typically specify if you want to create a new database schema from scratch at each update, or whether you which to update the database schema while conserving the existing data. While this sounds useful in theory, in fact it is very limited for anything other than noncritical development environments. In particular, these tools do not handle data migration well. For example, if you rename a column in your database, the update process will simply create a new column: it will not copy the data from the old column into the new column, nor will it remove the old column from the updated table.

Fortunately, this is not the only approach you can use. Another tool that attempts to tackle the thorny problem of database updates is Liquibase (*http://www.liquibase .org/*). Liquibase is an open source tool that can help manage and organize upgrade paths between versions of a database using a high-level approach.

Liquibase works by keeping a record of database updates applied in a table in the database, so that it is easy to bring any target database to the correct state for a given version of the application. As a result, you don't need to worry about running the same update script twice—Liquibase will only apply the update scripts that have not already been applied to your database. Liquibase is also capable of rolling back changes, at least for certain types of changes. However, since this will not work for every change (for example, data in a deleted table cannot be restored), it is best not to place too much faith in this particular feature.

In Liquibase, you keep track of database changes as a set of "change sets," each of which represents the database update in a database-neutral XML format. Change sets can represent any changes you would make in a database, from adding and deleting tables, to creating or updating columns, indexes and foreign keys:

```
<databaseChangeLog
xmlns="http://www.liquibase.org/xml/ns/dbchangelog/1.6"
xmlns:xsi="http://www.w3.org/2001/XMLSchema-instance"
```

```
    xsi:schemaLocation="http://www.liquibase.org/xml/ns/dbchangelog/1.6
    http://www.liquibase.org/xml/ns/dbchangelog/dbchangelog-1.6.xsd">
      <changeSet id="1" author="john">
        <createTable tableName="department">
          <column name="id" type="int">
            <constraints primaryKey="true" nullable="false"/>
          </column>
          <column name="name" type="varchar(50)">
            <constraints nullable="false"/>
          </column>
          <column name="active" type="boolean" defaultValue="1"/>
        </createTable>
      </changeSet>
    </databaseChangeLog>
```

Change sets can also reflect modifications to existing tables. For example, the following
change set represents the renaming of a column:

```
    <changeSet id="1" author="bob">
      <renameColumn tableName="person" oldColumnName="fname" newColumnName="firstName"/>
    </changeSet>
```

Since this representation records the semantic nature of the change, Liquibase is capable of handling both the schema updates and data migration associated with this change
correctly.

Liquibase can also handle updates to the contents of your database, as well as to its
structure. For example, the following change set inserts a new row of data into a table:

```
    <changeSet id="326" author="simon">
      <insert tableName="country">
        <column name="id" valueNumeric="1"/>
        <column name="code" value="AL"/>
        <column name="name" value="Albania"/>
      </addColumn>
    </changeSet>
```

Each changeset has an ID and an author, which makes it easier to keep track of who
made a particular change and reduces the risk of conflict. Developers can test their
change sets on their own database schema, and then commit them to version control
once they are ready. The next obvious step is to configure a Jenkins build to run the
Liquibase updates against the appropriate database automatically before any integration tests or application deployment is done, usually as part of the ordinary project
build script.

Liquibase integrates well into the build process—it can be executed from the command
line, or integrated into an Ant or Maven build script. Using Maven, for example, you
can configure the Maven Liquibase Plugin as shown here:

```
    <project>
      <build>
        <plugins>
          <plugin>
            <groupId>org.liquibase</groupId>
```

```
            <artifactId>liquibase-plugin</artifactId>
            <version>1.9.3.0</version>
            <configuration>
            <propertyFileWillOverride>true</propertyFileWillOverride>
            <propertyFile>src/main/resources/liquibase.properties</propertyFile>
        </configuration>
    </plugin>
  </plugins>
</build>
...
</project>
```

Using Liquibase with Maven this way, you could update a given target database to the current schema using this plugin:

```
$ mvn liquibase:update
```

The default database connection details are specified in the *src/main/resources/liquibase.properties* file, and might look something like this:

```
changeLogFile = changelog.xml
driver = com.mysql.jdbc.Driver
url = jdbc:mysql://localhost/ebank
username = scott
password = tiger
verbose = true
dropFirst = false
```

However you can override any of these properties from the command line, which makes it easy to set up a Jenkins build to update different databases.

Other similar commands let you generate an SQL script (if you need to submit it to your local DBA for approval, for example), or rollback to a previous version of the schema.

This is of course just one example of a possible approach. Other teams prefer to manually maintain a series of SQL update scripts, or write their own in-house solutions. The important thing is to have a solution that you can use reliably and reproducibly to update different databases to the correct state when deploying your applications.

Smoke Tests

Any serious automated deployment needs to be followed up by a series of automated smoke tests. A subset of the automated acceptance tests can be a good candidate for smoke tests. Smoke tests should be unobtrusive and relatively fast. They should be safe to run in a production environment, which may restrict the number of modifications the test cases can do in the system.

Rolling Back Changes

Another important aspect to consider when setting up Automated Deployment is how to back out if something goes wrong, particularly if you are thinking of implementing Continuous Deployment. Indeed, it is critical to be able to roll back to the previous version if required.

How you will do this depends a lot on your application. While it is relatively straightforward to redeploy a previous version of an application using Jenkins (we will look at a technique to do this further on in this chapter), the application is often not the only player in the game. In particular, you will need to consider how to restore your database to a previous state.

We saw how it is possible to use Liquibase to manage database updates, and of course many other strategies are also possible. However rolling back a database version presents its own challenges. Liquibase, for example, lets you revert some, but not all changes to the database structure. However data lost (in dropped tables, for example) cannot be recovered using Liquibase alone.

The most reliable way to revert your database to a previous state is probably to take a snapshot of the database just before the upgrade, and use this snapshot to restore the database to its previous state. One effective strategy is to automate this process in Jenkins in the deployment build job, and then to save both the database snapshot and the deployable binary file as artifacts. This way, you can easily restore the database using the saved snapshot and then redeploy the application using the saved binary. We will look at an example of this strategy in action further on in this chapter.

Deploying to an Application Server

Jenkins provides plugins to help you deploy your application to a number of commonly-used application servers. The Deploy plugin lets you deploy to Tomcat, JBoss, and GlassFish. And the Deploy Websphere plugin tries to cater for the particularities of IBM WebSphere Application Server.

For other application servers, you will typically have to integrate the deployment process into your build scripts, or resort to custom scripts to deploy your application. For other languages, too, your deployment process will vary, but it will often involve some use of shell scripting. For example, for a Ruby on Rails application, you may use a tool like Capistrano or Chef, or simply a shell script. For a PHP application, an FTP or SCP file transfer may suffice.

Let's first look at some strategies for deploying your Java applications to an application server.

This is known as a hot-deploy, where the application is deployed onto a running server. This is generally a fast and efficient way of getting your application online. However, depending on your application and on your application server, this approach has been known to result in memory leaks or resource locking issues—older versions of Tomcat, for example, were particularly well-known for this. If you run into this sort of issue, you may have to force the application to restart after each deployment, or possibly schedule a nightly restart of the application server on your test machine.

Deploying a Java Application

In this section we will look at an example of how to deploy your Java web or JEE application to an application server such as Tomcat, JBoss, or GlassFish.

One of the fundamental principles of automated deployment is to reuse your binaries. It is inefficient, and potentially unreliable, to rebuild your application during the deployment process. Indeed, imagine that you run a series of unit and integration tests against a particular version of your application, before deploying it to a test environment for further testing. If you rebuild the binary before deploying it to the test environment, the source code may have changed since the original revision, which means you may not know exactly what you are deploying.

A more efficient process is to reuse the binaries generated by a previous build. For example, you may configure a build job to run unit and integration tests before generating a deployable binary file (typically a WAR or EAR file). You can do this very effectively using the Copy Artifact plugin (see "Copying Artifacts" on page 285). This plugin lets you copy an artifact from another build job workspace into the current build job workspace. This, when combined with a normal build trigger or with the Build Promotion plugin, lets you deploy precisely the binary file that you built and tested in the previous phase.

This approach does put some constraints on the way you build your application. In particular, any environment-specific configuration must be externalized to the application; JDBC connections or other such configuration details should not be defined in configuration files embedded in your WAR file, for example, but rather be defined using JDNI or in an externalized properties file. If this is not the case, you may need to build from a given SCM revision, as discussed for Subversion in "Building from a Subversion Tag" on page 259.

Using the Deploy plugin

If you are deploying to a Tomcat, JBoss, or GlassFish server, the most useful tool at your disposition will probably be the Deploy plugin. This plugin makes it relatively straightforward to integrate deployment to these platforms into your Jenkins build process. If you are deploying to IBM Websphere, you can use the Websphere Deploy plugin to similar ends.

Let's see how this plugin works in action, using the simple automated build and deployment pipeline illustrated in Figure 12-1.

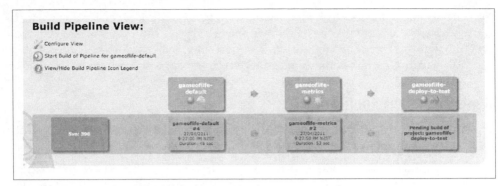

Figure 12 1. A simple automated deployment pipeline

Here, the default build (*gameoflife-default*) runs the unit and integration tests, and builds a deployable binary in the form of a WAR file. The metrics build (*gameoflife-metrics*) runs additional checks regarding coding standards and code coverage. If both these builds are successful, the application will be automatically deployed to the test environment by the *gameoflife-deploy-to-test* build job.

In the *gameoflife-deploy-to-test* build job, we use the Copy Artifact plugin to retrieve the WAR file generated in the *gameoflife-default* build job and copies it into the current build job's workspace (see Figure 12-2).

Figure 12-2. Copying the binary artifact to be deployed

Next, we use the Deploy plugin to deploy the WAR file to the test server. Of course it is generally possible, and not too difficult, to write a hand-rolled deployment script to get your application on to your application server. In some cases, this may be your only option. However, if a Jenkins plugin exists for your application server, it can simplify things considerably to use it. If you are deploying to Tomcat, JBoss, or GlassFish, the Deploy plugin may work for you. This plugin uses Cargo to connect to your application server and deploy (or redeploy) your application. Just select the target server type, and specify the server's URL along with the username and password of a user with deployment rights (see Figure 12-3).

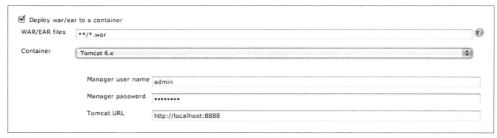

Figure 12-3. Deploying to Tomcat using the Deploy Plugin

This is known as a hot-deploy, where the application is deployed onto a running server. This is generally a fast and efficient way of getting your application online, and should be the preferred solution because of its speed convenience. However, depending on your application and on your application server, this approach has been known to result in memory leaks or resource locking issues—older versions of Tomcat, for example, were particularly well-known for this. If you run into this sort of issue, you may have to force the application to restart after each deployment, or possibly schedule a nightly restart of the application server on your test machine.

Redeploying a specific version

When you deploy your application automatically or continually, it becomes of critical importance to precisely identify the version of the application currently deployed. There are a several ways you can do this, which vary essentially in the role Jenkins plays in the build/deployment architecture.

Some teams use Jenkins as the central place of truth, where artifacts are both built and stored for future reference. If you store your deployable artifacts on Jenkins, then it may make perfect sense to deploy your artifacts directly from your Jenkins instance. This is not hard to do: in the next section we will look at how to do this using a combination of the Copy Artifacts, Deploy, and Parameterized Trigger plugins.

Alternatively, if you are using an Enterprise repository such as Nexus or Artifactory to store your artifacts, then this repository should act as the central point of reference: Jenkins should build and deploy artifacts to your central repository, and then deploy them from there. This is typically the case if you are using Maven as your build tool, but teams using tools like Gradle or Ivy may also use this approach. Repository managers such as Nexus and Artifactory, particularly in their commercial editions, make this strategy easier to implement by providing features such as build promotion and staging repositories that help you manage the release state of your artifacts.

Let's look at how you might implement each of these strategies using Jenkins.

Deploying a version from a previous Jenkins build

Redeploying a previously-deployed artifact in Jenkins is relatively straightforward. In "Using the Deploy plugin" on page 329, we saw how to use the Copy Artifacts and Deploy plugins to deploy a WAR file built by a previous build job to an application server. What we need to do now is to let the user specify the version to be deployed, rather than just deploying the latest build.

We can do this using the Parameterized Trigger plugin (see "Parameterized Build Jobs" on page 253). First, we add a parameter to the build job, using the special "Build selector for Copy Artifact" parameter type (see Figure 12-4).

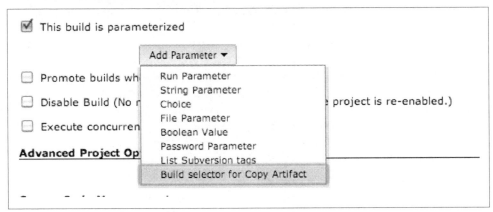

Figure 12-4. Adding a "Build selector for Copy Artifact" parameter

This adds a new parameter to your build job (see Figure 12-5). Here you need to enter a name and a short description. The name you provide will be used as an environment variable passed to the subsequent build steps.

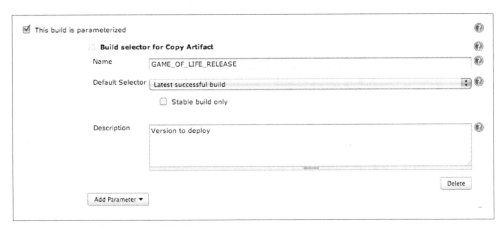

Figure 12-5. Configuring a build selector parameter

The build selector parameter type lets you pick a previous build in a number of ways, including the latest successful build, the upstream build that triggered this build job, or a specific build. All of these options will be available to the user when he or she triggers a build. The Default Selector lets you specify which of these options will be proposed by default.

When the user selects a particular build job, the build number will also be stored in the environment variables for use in the build steps. The environment variable is called COPYARTIFACT_BUILD_NUMBER_*MY_BUILD_JOB*, where *MY_BUILD_JOB* is the name of the original build job (in upper case and with characters other than A–Z converted to underscores). For example, if we copy an artifact from build number 4 of the *gameoflife-default* project, the COPYARTIFACT_BUILD_NUMBER_GAMEOFLIFE_DEFAULT environment variable would be set to 4.

The second part of the configuration is to tell Jenkins what to fetch, and from which build job. In the Build section of our project configuration, we add a "Copy artifacts from another project" step. Here you specify the project where the artifact was built and archived (*gameoflife-default* in our example). You also need to make Jenkins use the build specified in the parameter we defined earlier. You do this by choosing "Specified by a build parameter" in the "Which build" option, and providing the variable name we specified earlier in the build selector name field (see Figure 12-6). Then, just configure the artifacts to copy as we did in the previous example.

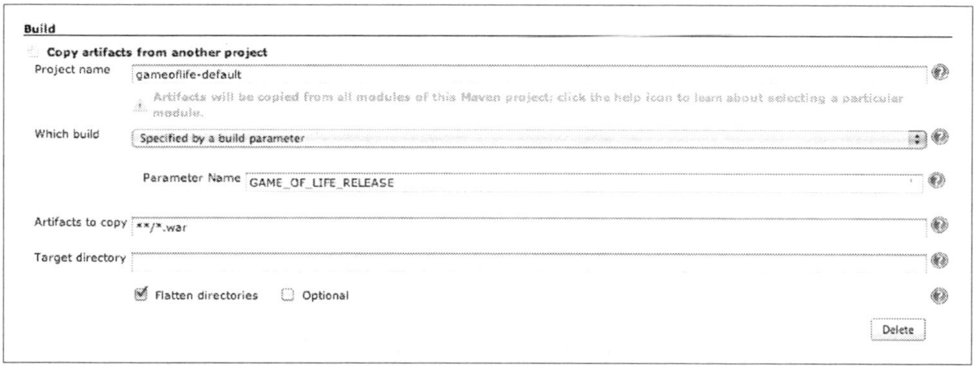

Figure 12-6. Specify where to find the artifacts to be deployed

Finally, we deploy the copied artifact using the Deploy plugin, as illustrated in Figure 12-3.

So let's see how this build works in practice. When we kick off a build manually, Jenkins will propose a list of options letting you select the build to redeploy (see Figure 12-7).

Most of these options are fairly self-explanatory.

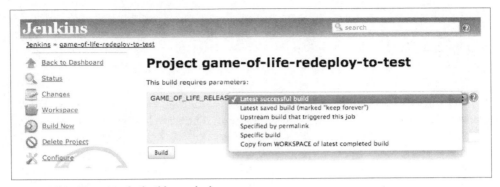

Figure 12-7. Choosing the build to redeploy

The "latest successful build" is the most recent build excluding any failing builds. So this option will typically just redeploy the latest version again. If you use this option, you will probably want to select the "Stable builds only" checkbox, which will exclude any unstable builds as well.

If you have opted to discard old builds, you will be able to flag certain build jobs to be kept forever (see "General Options" on page 81). In this case, you can choose to deploy the "Latest saved build".

A sensible option for an automated build job at the end of a build pipeline is "Upstream build that triggered this job". This way, you can be sure that you are deploying the artifact that was generated by (or promoted through) the previous build job, even if other builds have happened since. It is worth noting that, although this sort of parameterized build job is often used to manual deploy a specific artifact, it can also be effectively used as part of an automated build process. If it is not triggered manually, it will simply use whatever value you define in the "default selector" field.

You can also choose the "Specified by permalink" option (see Figure 12-8). This lets you choose from a number of shortcut values, such as the last build, the last stable build, the last successful build, and so on.

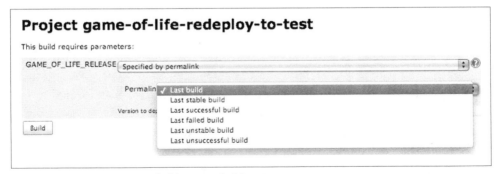

Figure 12-8. Using the "Specified by permalink" option

However if you want to redeploy a particular version of your application, a more useful option is "Specific build" (see Figure 12-9). This option lets you provide a specific build number to be deployed. This is the most flexible way to redeploy an application—you will just need to know the number of the build you need to redeploy, but this usually isn't too hard to find by looking at the build history of the original build job.

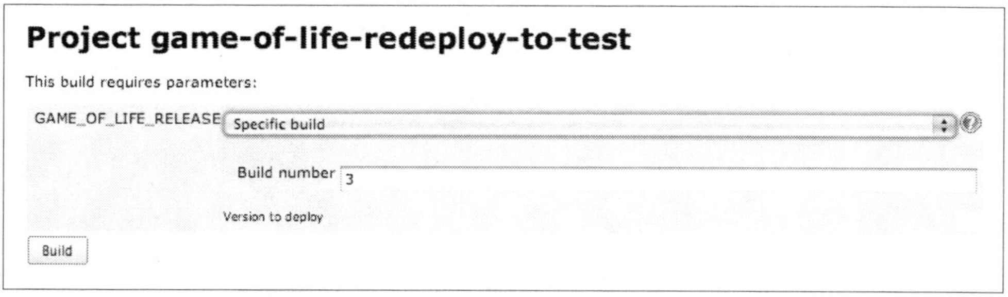

Project game-of-life-redeploy-to-test

This build requires parameters:

GAME_OF_LIFE_RELEASE | Specific build

Build number 3

Version to deploy

Build

Figure 12-9. Using a specific build

This is a convenient way to deploy or to redeploy artifacts from previous Jenkins build jobs. However, in some cases you may prefer to use an artifact stored in an enterprise repository like Nexus or Artifactory. We will look at an example of how to do this in the next section.

Deploying a version from a Maven repository

Many organizations use an Enterprise repository manager such as Nexus and Artifactory to store and share binary artifacts such as JAR files. This strategy is commonly used with Maven, but also with other build tools such as Ant (with Ivy or the Maven Ant Tasks) and Gradle. Using this approach in a CI environment, both snapshot and release dependencies are built on your Jenkins server, and then deployed to your repository manager (see Figure 12-10). Whenever a developer commits source code changes to the version control system, Jenkins will pick up the changes and build new snapshot versions of the corresponding artifacts. Jenkins then deploys these snapshot artifacts to the local Enterprise Repository Manager, where they can be made available to other developers on the team or on other teams within the organization. We discussed how to get Jenkins to automatically deploy Maven artifacts to an enterprise repository in Figure 12-10. A similar approach can also be done using Gradle or Ivy.

Maven conventions use a well-defined system of version numbers, distinguishing between SNAPSHOT and RELEASE versions. SNAPSHOT versions are considered to be potentially unstable builds of the latest code base, whereas RELEASE versions are official releases having undergone a more formal release process. Typically, SNAPSHOT artifacts are reserved for use within a development team, whereas RELEASE versions are considered ready for further testing.

A similar approach can be used for deployable artifacts such as WAR or EAR files— they are built and tested on the CI server, then automatically deployed to the Enterprise

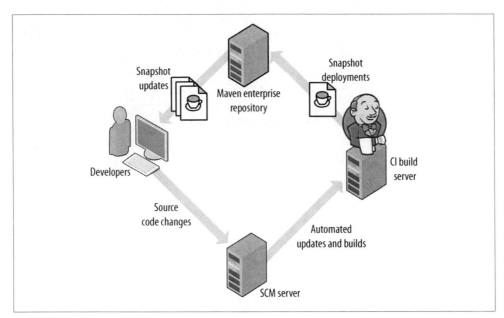

Figure 12-10. Using a Maven Enterprise Repository

Repository, often as part of a build pipeline involving automated tests and quality checks (see "Build Pipelines and Promotions" on page 281). SNAPSHOT versions are typically deployed to a test server for automated and/or manual testing, in order to decide whether a version is ready to be officially released.

The exact strategy used to decide when a release version is to be created, and how it is deployed, varies greatly from one organization. For example, some teams prefer a formal release at the end of each iteration or sprint, with a well-defined version number and corresponding set of release notes that is distributed to QA teams for further testing. When a particular version gets the go-ahead from QA, it can then be deployed into production. Others, using a more lean approach, prefer to cut a new release whenever a new feature or bug fix is ready to be deployed. If a team is particularly confident in their automated tests and code quality checks, it may even be possible to automate this process completely, generating and releasing a new version either periodically (say every night) or whenever new changes are committed.

There are many ways to implement this sort of strategy. In the rest of this section, we will see how to do it using a conventional multimodule Maven project. Our sample project is a web application called *gameoflife*, consisting of three modules: *gameoflife-core*, *gameoflife-services* and *gameoflife-web*. The *gameoflife-web* module produces a WAR file that includes JAR files from the other two modules. It is this WAR file that we want to deploy:

```
tuatara:gameoflife johnsmart$ ls -l
total 32
drwxr-xr-x  16 johnsmart  staff    544 16 May 09:58 gameoflife-core
```

```
drwxr-xr-x    8 johnsmart  staff     272  4 May 18:12 gameoflife-deploy
drwxr-xr-x    8 johnsmart  staff     272 16 May 09:58 gameoflife-services
drwxr-xr-x   15 johnsmart  staff     510 16 May 09:58 gameoflife-web
-rw-r--r--@   1 johnsmart  staff   12182  4 May 18:07 pom.xml
```

Earlier on in this chapter we saw how to use the Deploy plugin to deploy a WAR file generated by the current build job to an application server. What we want to do now is to deploy an arbitrary version of the WAR file to an application server.

In "Managing Maven Releases with the M2Release Plugin" on page 282, we discussed how to configure Jenkins to invoke the Maven Release Plugin to generate a formal release version of an application. The first step of the deployment process starts here, so we will assume that this has been configured and that a few releases have already been deployed to our Enterprise Repository Manager.

The next step involves creating a dedicated project to manage the deployment process. This project will be a standard Maven project.

The first thing you need to do is to set up a dedicated deployment project. In its simplest form, this project will simply fetch the requested version of your WAR file from your enterprise repository to be deployed by Jenkins. In the following *pom.xml* file, we use the *maven-war-plugin* to fetch a specified version of the *gameoflife-web* WAR file from our enterprise repository. The version we want is specified in the `target.version` property:

```xml
<project xmlns="http://maven.apache.org/POM/4.0.0" xmlns:xsi="http://www.w3.org/2001/
        XMLSchema-instance"
  xsi:schemaLocation="http://maven.apache.org/POM/4.0.0 http://
  maven.apache.org/maven-v4_0_0.xsd">
  <modelVersion>4.0.0</modelVersion>
  <groupId>com.wakaleo.gameoflife</groupId>
  <artifactId>gameoflife-deploy-with-jenkins</artifactId>
  <version>0.0.1-SNAPSHOT</version>
  <packaging>war</packaging>
  <dependencies>
    <dependency>
      <groupId>com.wakaleo.gameoflife</groupId>
      <artifactId>gameoflife-web</artifactId>
      <type>war</type>d
      <version>${target.version}</version>
    </dependency>
  </dependencies>
  <build>
    <plugins>
      <plugin>
        <artifactId>maven-war-plugin</artifactId>
        <configuration>
          <warName>gameoflife</warName>
          <overlays>
            <overlay>
              <groupId>com.wakaleo.gameoflife</groupId>
              <artifactId>gameoflife-web</artifactId>
            </overlay>
```

```
                </overlays>
            </configuration>
        </plugin>
    </plugins>
</build>
<properties>
    <target.version>RELEASE</target.version>
</properties>
</project>
```

Next, we configure a Jenkins build job to invoke this *pom.xml* file using a property value provided by the user (see Figure 12-11). Note that we have set the default value to RELEASE so that, by default, the most recent release version will be deployed. Otherwise, the user can provide the version number of the version to be deployed or redeployed.

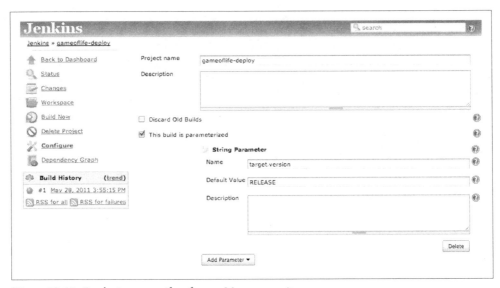

Figure 12-11. Deploying an artifact from a Maven repository

The rest of this build job simply checks out the deployment project and invokes the `mvn package` goal, and then deploys the WAR file using the Deploy plugin (see Figure 12-12). The `target.version` property will be automatically passed into the build job and used to deploy the correct version.

Similar techniques can be used for other project types. If you are deploying to an application server that is not supported by the Deploy plugin, you also have the option of writing a custom script in whatever language is most convenient, and getting Jenkins to pass the requested version number as a parameter as described above.

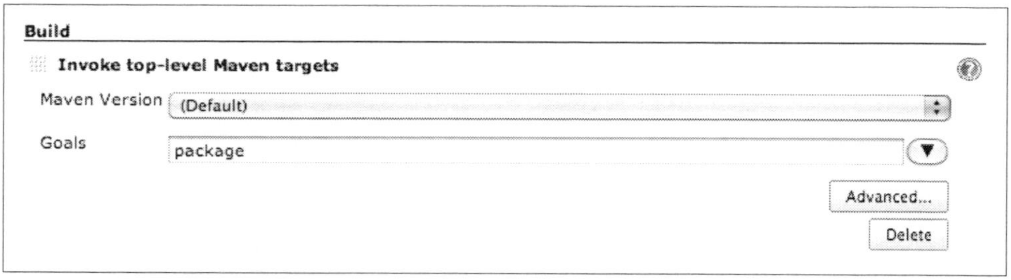

Build

Invoke top-level Maven targets

Maven Version (Default)

Goals package

Advanced...

Delete

Figure 12-12. Preparing the WAR to be deployed

Deploying Scripting-based Applications Like Ruby and PHP

Deploying projects using scripting languages such as PHP and Ruby is generally simpler than deploying Java applications, though the issues related to database updates are similar. Indeed, very often these deployments essentially involve copying files onto a remote server. To obtain the files in the first place, you have the choice of either copying them from another build job's workspace using the Copy Artifacts option, or checking the source code out directly from the source code repository, if necessary using a specific revision or tag as described for Subversion in "Building from a Subversion Tag" on page 259 and for Git in "Building from a Git Tag" on page 260. Then, once you have the source code in your Jenkins workspace, you simply need to deploy it onto the target server.

A useful tool for this sort of deployment is the Publish Over series of plugins for Jenkins (Publish Over FTP, Publish Over SSH, and Publish Over CIFS). These plugins provide a consistent and flexible way to deploy your application artifacts to other servers over a number of protocols, including CIFS (for Windows shared drives), FTP, and SSH/ SFTP.

The configuration for each of these plugins is similar. Once you have installed the plugins, you need to set up the host configurations, which are managed centrally in the main configuration screen. You can create as many host configurations as you like— they will appear in a drop-down list in the job configuration page.

Configuration of the hosts is fairly self-explanatory (see Figure 12-13). The name is the name that will appear in the drop-down list in the build job configurations. You can configure authentication using a username and password for FTP, or either an SSH key or a username and password for SSH. You also need to provide an existing directory on the remote server that will act at the root directory for this configuration. In the Advanced options, you can also configure the SSH port and timeout options.

Once you have configured your hosts, you can set up your build jobs to deploy artifacts to these hosts. You can do this either as a build step (see Figure 12-14) or as a post-build action (see Figure 12-15). In both cases, the options are similar.

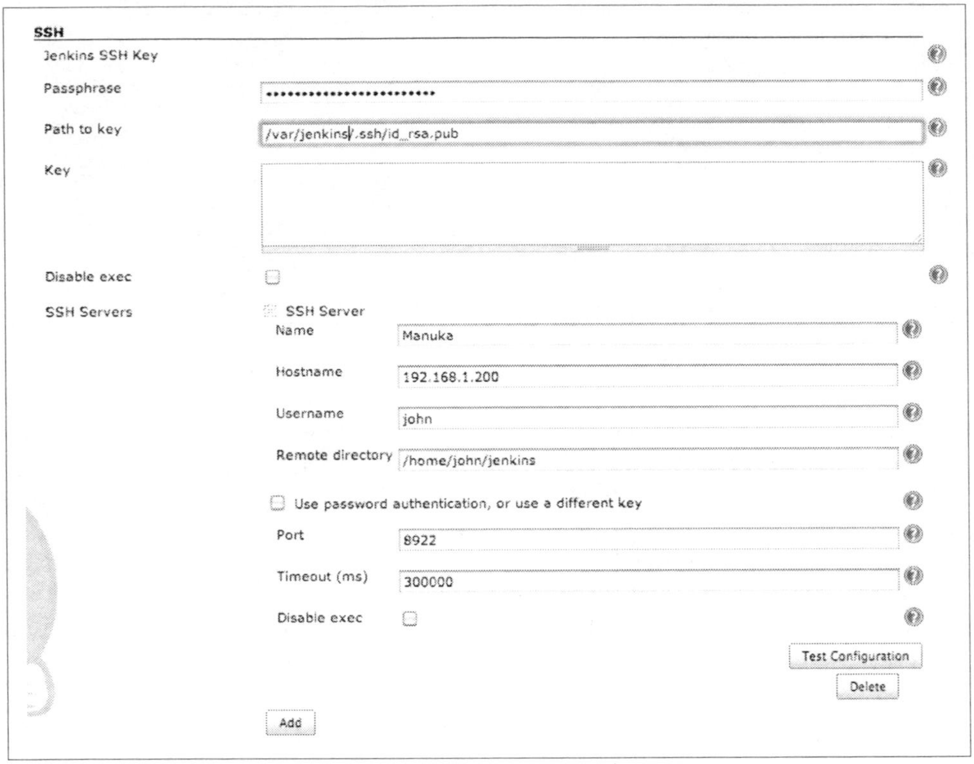

Figure 12-13. Configuring a remote host

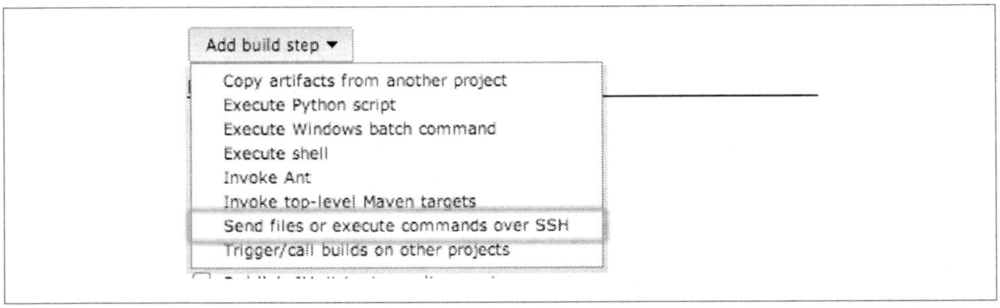

Figure 12-14. Deploying files to a remote host in the build section

First of all, you select the target host from the list of hosts you configured in the previous section. Next, you configure the files you want to transfer. You do this by defining one or more "Transfer sets." A Transfer set is a set of files (defined by an Ant fileset expression) that you deploy to a specified directory on the remote server. You can also provide a prefix to be removed—this lets you strip off unnecessary directories that you do not want to appear on the server (such as the *target/site* directory path in the

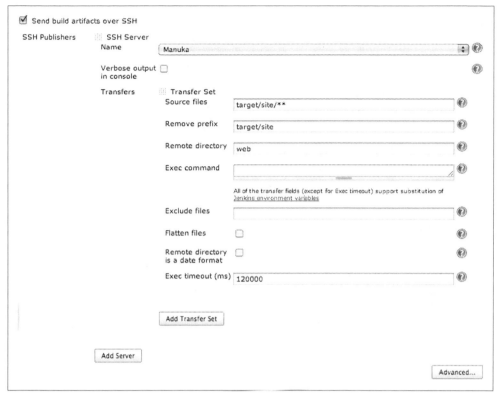

Figure 12-15. Deploying files to a remote host in the post-build actions

example). You can add as many transfer sets as you need to get the files you want onto the remote server. The plugin also provides options to execute commands on the remote server once the transfer is complete ("Exec command") or to exclude certain files or flatten the directories.

Conclusion

Automated Deployment, and in its most advanced form, Continuous Deployment or Continuous Delivery, can be considered the culminating point of a modern Continuous Integration infrastructure.

In this chapter we have reviewed several Automated Deployment techniques, mostly centered around Java-based deployments. However, the general principles discussed here apply for any technology. Indeed, the actual deployment process in many other technologies, in particular scripting languages such as Ruby and PHP, are considerably simpler than when using Java, and essentially involve copying files onto the production server. Ruby also benefits from tools such as Heroku and Capistrano to facilitate the task.

There are several important aspects you need to consider when setting up an Automated Deployment. First of all, Automated Deployment is the end-point of your CI architecture: you need to define a build pipeline to take your build from the initial compilation and unit tests, though more comprehensive functional and automated acceptance tests and code quality checks, culminating in deployment to one or more platforms. The degree of confidence you can have in your build pipeline depends largely on the degree of confidence you have in your tests. Or, in other terms, the less reliable and comprehensive your tests, the earlier in the build process you will have to fall back to manual testing and human intervention.

Finally, if at all possible, it is important to build your deployable artifact once and once only, and then reuse it in subsequent steps for functional tests and deployment to different platforms.

CHAPTER 13

Maintaining Jenkins

Introduction

In this chapter, we will be discussing a few tips and tricks that you might find useful when maintaining a large Jenkins instance. We will look at things like how to limit, and keep tabs on, disk usage, how to give Jenkins enough memory and how to archive build jobs or migrate them from one server to another. Some of these topics are discussed elsewhere in the book, but here we will be looking at things from the point of view of the system administrator.

Monitoring Disk Space

Build History takes disk space. In addition, Jenkins analyzes the build records when it loads a project configuration, so a build job with a thousand archived builds is going to take a lot longer to load than one with only fifty. If you have a large Jenkins server with tens or hundreds of build jobs, multiply this accordingly.

Probably the simplest way to keep a cap on disk usage is to limit the number of builds a project maintains in its history. You can configure this by ticking the Discard Old Builds checkbox at the top of the project configuration page (see Figure 13-1). If you tell Jenkins to only keep the last 20 builds, it will start discarding (and deleting) older build jobs once it reaches this number. You can limit them by number (i.e., no more than 20 builds) or by date (i.e., builds no older than 30 days). It does this intelligently, though: if there has ever been a successful build, Jenkins will always keep at least the latest successful build as part of its build history, so you will never loose your last successful build.

The problem with discarding old builds is that you loose the build history at the same time. Jenkins uses the build records to produce graphs of test results and build metrics. If you limit the number of builds to be kept to twenty, for example, Jenkins will only display graphs containing the last twenty data points, which can be a bit limited. This sort of information can be very useful to the developers, but it is often good to be able

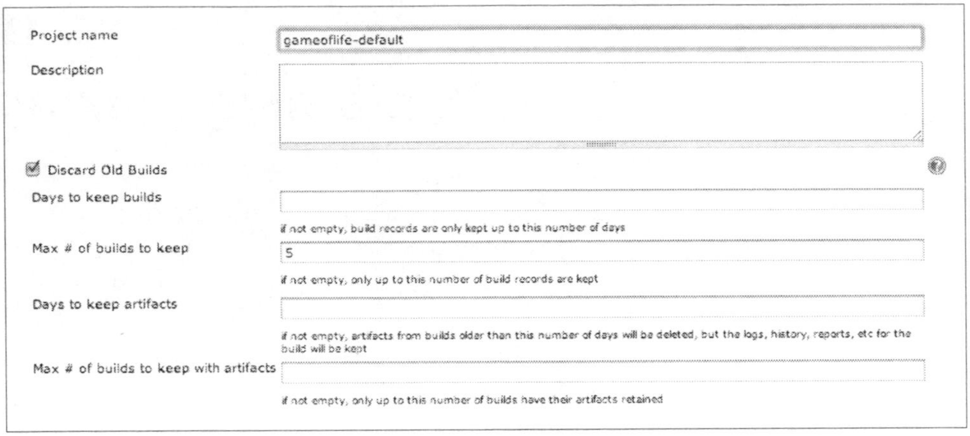

Figure 13-1. Discarding old builds

to see how the project metrics are doing throughout the whole life of the project, not just over the last week or two.

Fortunately, Jenkins has a work-around that can keep both developers and system administrators happy. In general, the items that take up the most disk space are the build artifacts: JAR files, WAR files, and so on. The build history itself is mostly XML log files, which don't take up too much space. If you click on the "Advanced..." button, Jenkins will let you discard the artifacts, but not the build data. In Figure 13-2, for example, we have configured Jenkins to keep artifacts for a maximum of 7 days. This is a great option if you need to put a cap on disk usage, but still want to provide a full scope of build metrics for the development teams.

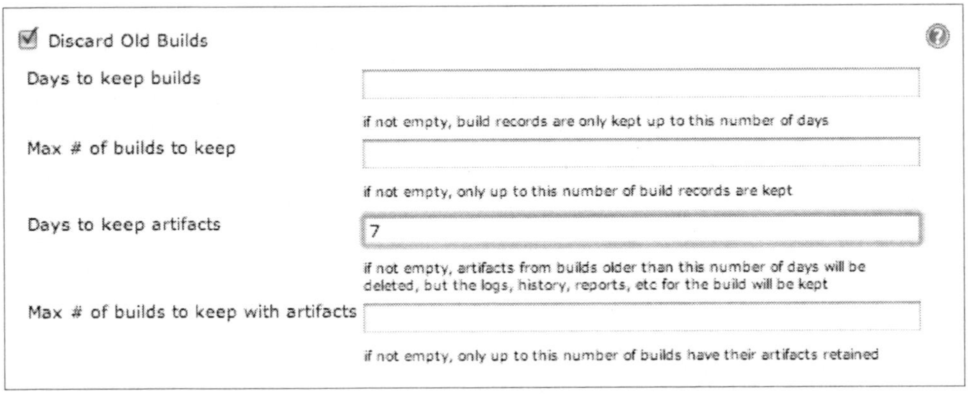

Figure 13-2. Discarding old builds—advanced options

Don't hesitate to be ruthless, keeping the maximum number of builds with artifacts quite low. Remember, Jenkins will always keep the last stable and the last successful builds, no matter what you tell it, so you will always have at least one working artifact (unless of course the project has yet to successfully build). Jenkins also lets you mark an individual build as "Keep this log forever", to exclude certain important builds from being discarded automatically.

Using the Disk Usage Plugin

One of the most useful tools in the Jenkins administrator's tool box is the Disk Usage plugin. This plugin records and reports on the amount of disk space used by your projects. It lets you isolate and fix projects that are using too much disk space.

You can install the Disk Usage plugin in the usual way, from the Plugin Manager screen. Once you have installed the plugin and restarted Jenkins, the Disk Usage plugin will record the amount of disk space used by each project. It will also add a Disk Usage link on the Manage Jenkins screen, which you can use to display the overall disk usage for your projects (see Figure 13-3).

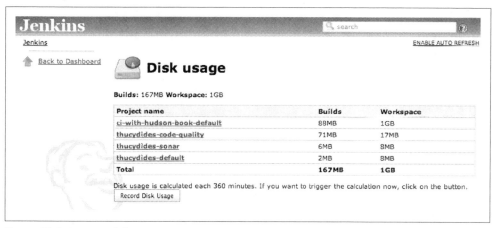

Figure 13-3. Viewing disk usage

This list is sorted by overall disk usage, so the projects using the most disk space are at the top. The list provides two values for each project—the Builds column indicates the total amount of space used by all of the project's build history, whereas the Workspace column is the amount of space used to build the project. For ongoing projects, the Workspace value tends to be relatively stable (a project needs what it needs to build correctly), whereas the Builds column will increase over time, sometimes at a dramatic rate, unless you do something about it. You can keep the space needed by a project's history under control by limiting the number of builds being kept for a project, and by being careful about what artifacts are being stored.

To get an idea of how fast the disk space is being used up, you can also display the amount of disk space used in each project over time. To do this, you need to activate the plugin in the System Configuration screen (see Figure 13-4).

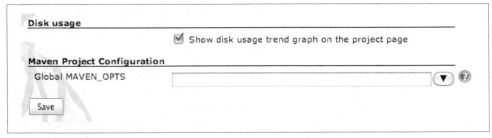

Figure 13-4. Displaying disk usage for a project

This will record and display how much space your projects are using over time. The Disk Usage plugin displays a graph of disk usage over time (see Figure 13-5), which can give you a great view of how fast your project is filling up the disk, or, on the contrary, if the disk usage is stable over time.

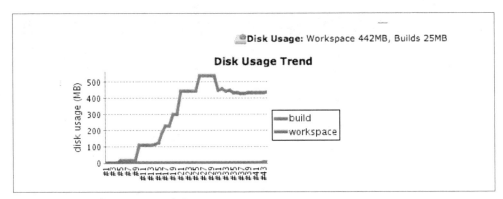

Figure 13-5. Displaying project disk usage over time

Disk Usage and the Jenkins Maven Project Type

If you are using the Jenkins Maven build jobs, there are some additional details you should know about. In Jenkins, Maven build jobs will automatically archive your build artifacts by default. This may not be what you intend.

The problem is that these SNAPSHOT artifacts take up space—a lot of it. On an active project, Jenkins might be running several builds per hour, so permanently storing the generated JAR files for each build can be very costly. The problem is accentuated if you have multimodule projects, as Jenkins will archive the artifacts generated for each module.

In fact, if you need to archive your Maven SNAPSHOT artifacts, it is probably a better idea to deploy them directly to your local Maven repository manager. Nexus Pro, for example, can be configured to do this and Artifactory can be configured to delete old snapshot artifacts.

Fortunately, you can configure Jenkins to this, go to the "Build" section of your build job configuration screen and click on the Advanced button. This will display some extra fields, as shown in Figure 13-6.

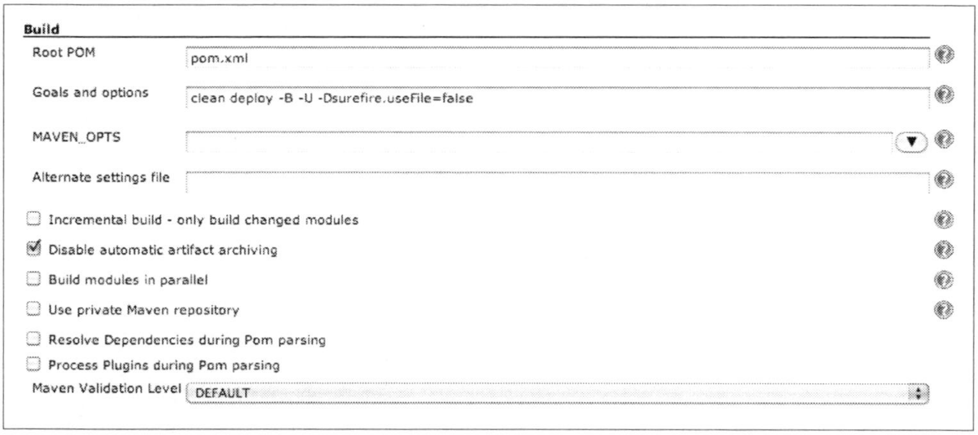

Figure 13-6. Maven build jobs—advanced options

If you tick the "Disable automatic artifact archiving" checkbox here, Jenkins will refrain from storing the jar files your project build generates. This is a good way of making your friendly system administrator happy.

Note that sometimes you *do* need to store the Maven artifacts. For example, they often come in handy when implementing a build pipeline (see "Build Pipelines and Promotions" on page 281). In this case, you can always choose to archive the artifacts you need manually, and then use the "Discard old builds" option to refine how long you keep them for.

Monitoring the Server Load

Jenkins provides build-in monitoring of server activity. On the Manage Jenkins screen, click on the Load Statistics icon. This will display a graph of the server load over time for the master node (see Figure 13-7). This graph keeps track of three metrics: the total number of executors, the number of busy executors, and queue length.

The *total number of executors* (the blue line) includes the executors on the master and on the slave nodes. This can vary when slaves are brought on and offline, and can be a useful indicator of how well your dynamic provisioning of slave nodes is working.

The *number of busy executors* (the red line) indicates how many of your executors are occupied executing builds. You should make sure you have enough spare capacity here to absorb spikes in build jobs. If all of your executors are permanently occupied running build jobs, you should add more executors and/or slave nodes.

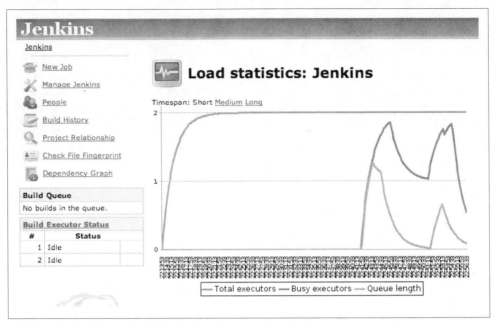

Figure 13-7. Jenkins Load Statistics

The *queue length* (the gray line) is the number of build jobs awaiting executing. Build jobs are queued when all of the executors are occupied. This metric does not include jobs that are waiting for an upstream build job to finish, so it gives a reasonable idea of when your server could benefit from extra capacity.

You can get a similar graph for slave nodes, using the Load Statistics icon in the slave node details page.

Another option is to install the Monitoring plugin. This plugin uses JavaMelody to produce comprehensive HTML reports about the state of your build server, including CPU and system load, average response time, and memory usage (see Figure 13-8). Once you have installed this plugin, you can access the JavaMelody graphs from the Manage Jenkins screen, using the "Monitoring of Jenkins/Jenkins master" or "Jenkins/ Jenkins nodes" menu entries.

Backing Up Your Configuration

Backing up your data is a universally recommended practice, and your Jenkins server should be no exception. Fortunately, backing up Jenkins is relatively easy. In this section, we will look at a few ways to do this.

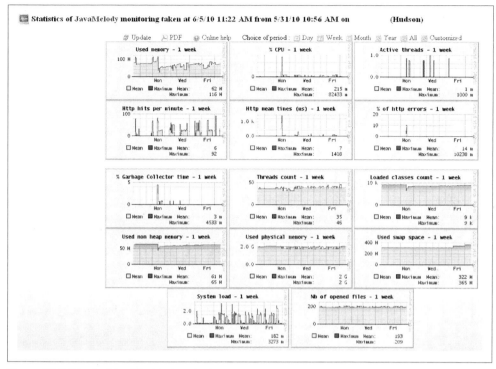

Figure 13-8. The Jenkins Monitoring plugin

Fundamentals of Jenkins Backups

In the simplest of configurations, all you need to do is to periodically back up your *JENKINS_HOME* directory. This contains all of your build jobs configurations, your slave node configurations, and your build history. This will also work fine while Jenkins is running—there is no need to shut down your server while doing your backup.

The downside of this approach is that the *JENKINS_HOME* directory can contain a very large amount of data (see "What's in the Jenkins Home Directory" on page 58). If this becomes an issue, you can save a little by not backing up the following directories, which contain data that can be easily recreated on-the-fly by Jenkins:

$JENKINS_HOME/war
    The exploded WAR file
$JENKINS_HOME/cache
    Downloaded tools
$JENKINS_HOME/tools
    Extracted tools

You can also be selective about what you back up in your build jobs data. The *$JEN-KINS_HOME/jobs* directory contains job configuration, build history and archived files for each of your build jobs. The structure of a build job directory is illustrated in Figure 13-9.

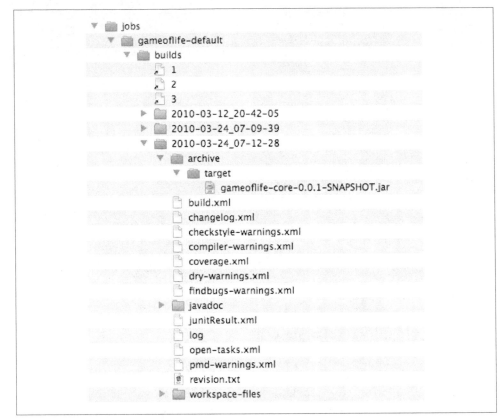

Figure 13-9. The builds directory

To understand how to optimize your Jenkins backups, you need to understand how the build job directories are organized. Within the *jobs* directory there is a subdirectory for each build job. This subdirectory contains two subdirectories of its own: *builds* and *workspace*. There is no need to backup the *workspace* directory, as it will simply be restored with a clean checkout if Jenkins finds it missing.

The *builds* directory, on the other hand, needs more attention. This directory contains the history of your build results and previously-generated artifacts, with a time-stamped directory for each previous build. If you are not interested in restoring build history or past artifacts, you don't need to store this directory. If you are, read on! In each of these directories, you will find the build history (stored in the form of XML files such as JUnit test results) and archived artifacts. Jenkins uses the XML and text files to produce the graphs it displays on the build job dashboard, so if these are important to you, you should store these files. The *archive* directory contains binary files that were generated and stored by previous builds. These binaries may or may not be important to you, but they can take up a lot of space, so if you exclude them from your backups, you may be able to save a considerable amount of space.

Just as it is wise to make frequent backups, it is also wise to test your backup procedure. With Jenkins, this is easy to do. Jenkins home directories are totally portable, so all you need to do to test your backup is to extract your backup into a temporary directory and run an instance of Jenkins against it. For example, imagine we have extracted our backup into a temporary directory called */tmp/jenkins-backup*. To test this backup, first set the *JENKINS_HOME* directory to this temporary directory:

```
$ export JENKINS_HOME=/tmp/jenkins-backup
```

Then simply start Jenkins on a different port and see if it works:

```
$ java -jar jenkins.war --httpPort=8888
```

You can now view Jenkins running on this port and make sure that your backup worked correctly.

Using the Backup Plugin

The approach described in the previous section is simple enough to integrate into your normal backup procedures, but you may prefer something more Jenkins-specific. The Backup plugin (see Figure 13-10) provides a simple user interface that you can use to back up and restore your Jenkins configurations and data.

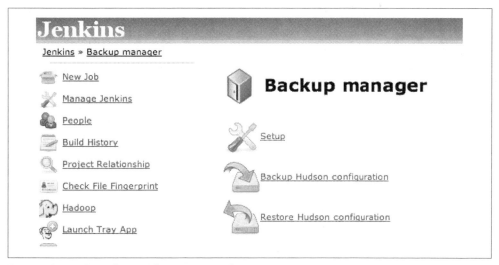

Figure 13-10. The Jenkins Backup Manager Plugin

This plugin lets you configure and run backups of both your build job configurations and your build history. The Setup screen gives you a large degree of control over exactly what you want backed up (see Figure 13-11). You can opt to only back up the XML configuration files, or back up both the configuration files and the build history. You can also choose to backup (or not to backup) the automatically-generated Maven artifacts (in many build processes, these will be available on your local Enterprise Repository Manager). You can also back up the job workspaces (typically unnecessary, as we discussed above) and any generated fingerprints.

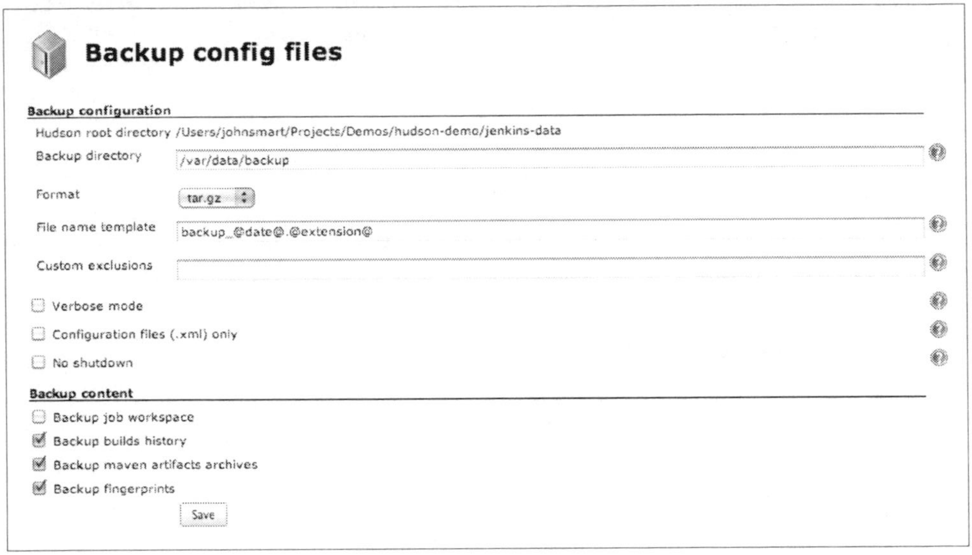

Figure 13-11. Configuring the Jenkins Backup Manager

You can trigger a backup manually from the Backup Manager screen (which you can access from the Manage Jenkins screen). The backup takes some time, and will shut down Jenkins during the process (unless you deactivate this option in the backup configuration).

At the time of writing, there is no way to schedule this operation from within Jenkins, but you can start the backup operation externally by invoking the corresponding URL (e.g., *http://localhost:8080/backup/backup* if your Jenkins instance is running locally on port 8080). In a unix environment, for example, this would typically be scheduled as a cron job using a tool like `wget` or `curl` to start the backup.

More Lightweight Automated Backups

If all you want to back up is your build job configuration, the Backup Manager plugin might be considered overkill. Another option is to use the Thin Backup plugin, which lets you schedule full and incremental backups of your configuration files. Because they don't save your build history or artifacts, these backups are very fast, and there is no need to shut down the server to do them.

Like the Backup plugin, this plugin adds an icon to the Jenkins System Configuration page. From here, you can configure and schedule your configuration backups, force an immediate backup, or restore your configuration files to a previous state. Configuration is straightforward (see Figure 13-12), and simply involves scheduling full and incremental backups using a cron job syntax, and providing a directory in which to store the backups.

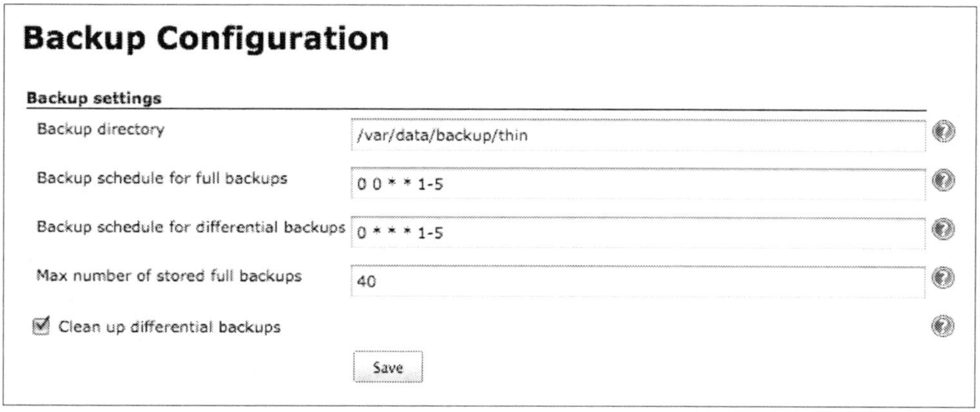

Figure 13-12. Configuring the Thin Backup plugin

To restore a previous configuration, just go to the Restore page and choose the date of the configuration you wish to reinstate (see Figure 13-13). Once the configuration has been restored to the previous state, you need to reload the Jenkins configuration from disk or restart Jenkins.

Restore Configuration

Restore options

restore backup from 2011-03-20 21:00

Restore

Figure 13-13. Restoring a previous configuration

Archiving Build Jobs

Another way to address disk space issues is to delete or archive projects that are no longer active. Archiving a project allows you to easily restore it later if you need to consult the project data or artifacts. Archiving a project is simple: just move the build project directory out of the job directory. Of course, typically, you would compress it into a ZIP file or a tarball first.

In the following example, we want to archive the *tweeter-default* project. So first we go to the Jenkins *jobs* directory and create a tarball (compressed archive) of the *tweeter-default* build job directory:

```
$ cd $JENKINS_HOME/jobs
$ ls
gameoflife-default    tweeter-default
$ tar czf tweeter-default.tgz tweeter-default
$ ls
gameoflife-default    tweeter-default         tweeter-default.tgz
```

As long as the project you want to archive is not running, you can now safely delete the project directory and move the archive into storage:

```
$ rm -Rf tweeter-default
$ mv tweeter-default.tgz /data/archives/jenkins
```

Once you have done this, you can simply reload the configuration from the disk in the Manage Jenkins screen (see Figure 13-14). The archived project will promptly disappear from your dashboard.

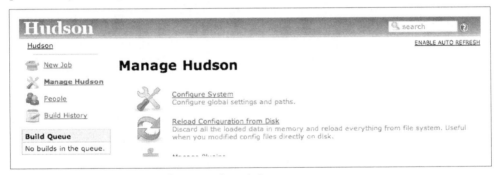

Figure 13-14. Reloading the configuration from disk

On a Windows machine, you can do exactly the same thing by creating a ZIP file of the project directory.

Migrating Build Jobs

There are times when you need to move or copy Jenkins build jobs from one Jenkins instance to another, without copying the entire Jenkins configuration. For example, you might be migrating your build jobs to a Jenkins instance on a brand new box, with system configuration details that vary from the original machine. Or you might be restoring an old build job that you have archived.

As we have seen, Jenkins stores all of the data it needs for a project in a subdirectory of the *jobs* directory in your Jenkins home directory. This subdirectory is easy to identify—it has the same name as your project. Incidentally, this is one reason why your project names really shouldn't contain spaces, particularly if Jenkins is running under Unix or Linux—it makes maintenance and admin tasks a lot easier if the project names are also well-behaved Unix filenames.

You can copy or move build jobs between instances of projects simply enough by copying or moving the build job directories to the new Jenkins instance. The project job directory is self-contained—it contains both the full project configuration and all the build history. It is even safe enough to copy build job directories to a running Jenkins instance, though if you are also deleting them from the original server, you should shut this one down first. You don't even need to restart the new Jenkins instance to see the results of your import—just go to the Manage Jenkins screen and click on Reload Configuration From Disk. This will load the new jobs and make them immediately visible on the Jenkins dashboard.

There are a few gotchas, however. If you are migrating your jobs to a brand new Jenkins configuration, remember to install, or migrate, the plugins from your original server. The plugins can be found in the *plugins* directory, so you can simply copy everything from this directory to the corresponding directory in your new instance.

Of course, you might be migrating the build jobs to a new instance precisely *because* the plugin configuration on the original box is a mess. Some Jenkins plugins can be a bit buggy sometimes, and you may want to move to a clean installation with a well-known, well-defined set of vetted plugins. In this case, you may need to rework some of your project configurations once they have been imported.

The reason for this is straightforward. When you use a plugin in a project, the project's *config.xml* will be updated with plugin-specific configuration fields. If for some reason you need to migrate projects selectively to a Jenkins installation *without* these plugins installed, Jenkins will no longer understand these parts of the project configuration. The same thing can also sometimes happen if the plugin versions are very different on the machines, and the data format used by the plugin has changed.

If you are migrating jobs to a Jenkins instance with a different configuration, it also pays to keep an eye on the system logs. Invalid plugin configurations will usually let you know through warnings or exceptions. While not always fatal, these error messages often mean that the plugin will not work as expected, or at all.

Jenkins provides some useful features to help you migrate your project configurations. If Jenkins finds data that it thinks is out of date or invalid, it will tell you so. On the Manage Jenkins screen, you will get a message like the one in Figure 13-15.

From here, you can choose to either leave the configuration as it is (just in case you roll back to a previous version of your Jenkins instance, for example), or let Jenkins discard the fields it cannot read. If you choose this option, Jenkins will bring up a screen containing more details about the error, and can even help tidy up your project configuration files if you wish (see Figure 13-16).

Figure 13-15. Jenkins will inform you if your data is not compatible with the current version

Manage Old Data

When there are changes in how data is stored on disk, Hudson uses the following strategy: data is migrated to the new structure when it is loaded, but the file is not resaved in the new format. This allows for downgrading Hudson if needed. However, it can also leave data on disk in the old format indefinitely. The table below lists files containing such data, and the Hudson version(s) where the data structure was changed.

Sometimes errors occur while reading data (if a plugin adds some data and that plugin is later disabled, if migration code is not written for structure changes, or if Hudson is downgraded after it has already written data not readable by the older version). These errors are logged, but the unreadable data is then skipped over, allowing Hudson to startup and function properly.

Type	Name	Version

The form below may be used to resave these files in the current format. Doing so means a downgrade to a Hudson release older than the selected version will not be able to read the data stored in the new format. Note that simply using Hudson to create and configure jobs and run builds can save data that may not be readable by older Hudson releases, even when this form is not used. Also if any unreadable data errors are reported in the right side of the table above, note that this data will be lost when the file is resaved.

Eventually, the code supporting these data migrations may be removed. Compatibility will be retained for at least 150 releases since the structure change. Versions older than this are in bold above, and it is recommended to resave these files.

No old data was found.

Unreadable Data

It is acceptable to leave unreadable data in these files, as Hudson will safely ignore it. To avoid the log messages at Hudson startup you can permanently delete the unreadable data by resaving these files using the button below.

Type	Name	Error
hudson.matrix.MatrixConfiguration	phoenix-multi-config-build/APP_SERVER=resin,DATABASE=mysql	NonExistentFieldException: No such field hudson.matrix.MatrixConfiguration.blockBuildWhenDownstreamBuilding
hudson.plugins.promoted_builds.PromotionProcess	phoenix-default/promotion/promote-to-test	NonExistentFieldException: No such field hudson.plugins.promoted_builds.PromotionProcess.blockBuildWhenDownstreamBuilding
hudson.matrix.MatrixConfiguration	phoenix-multi-config-build/APP_SERVER=tomcat,DATABASE=db2	NonExistentFieldException: No such field hudson.matrix.MatrixConfiguration.blockBuildWhenDownstreamBuilding
hudson.matrix.MatrixConfiguration	acceptance-test-suite/browser=chrome,os=OSX	NonExistentFieldException: No such field hudson.matrix.MatrixConfiguration.blockBuildWhenDownstreamBuilding
hudson.plugins.promoted_builds.PromotionProcess	gameoflife-deploy-to-uat/promotion/Deploy to Production	NonExistentFieldException: No such field hudson.plugins.promoted_builds.PromotionProcess.blockBuildWhenDownstreamBuilding
hudson.model.FreeStyleProject	game-of-life-freestyle-metrics	NonExistentFieldException: No such field hudson.model.FreeStyleProject.blockBuildWhenDownstreamBuilding
hudson.matrix.MatrixConfiguration	phoenix-multi-config-build/APP_SERVER=resin,D=mysql	NonExistentFieldException: No such field hudson.matrix.MatrixConfiguration.blockBuildWhenDownstreamBuilding

Figure 13-16. Managing out-of-date build jobs data

This screen gives you more details about the project containing the dodgy data, as well as the exact error message. This gives you several options. If you are sure that you no longer need the plugin that originally created the data, you can safely remove the redundant fields by clicking on the Discard Unreadable Data button. Alternatively, you may decide that the fields belong to a useful plugin that hasn't yet been installed on the new Jenkins instance. In this case, install the plugin and all should be well. Finally, you can always choose to leave the redundant data and live with the error message, at least until you are sure that you won't need to migrate the job back to the old server some day.

However, Jenkins doesn't always detect all of the errors or inconsistencies—it still pays to keep one eye on the system logs when you migrate your build jobs. For example, the following is a real example from a Jenkins log file showing what can happen during the migration process:

```
Mar 16, 2010 2:05:06 PM hudson.util.CopyOnWriteList$ConverterImpl unmarshal
WARNING: Failed to resolve class
com.thoughtworks.xstream.mapper.CannotResolveClassException: hudson.plugins.ciga
me.GamePublisher : hudson.plugins.cigame.GamePublisher
        at com.thoughtworks.xstream.mapper.DefaultMapper.realClass(DefaultMapper
```

```
.java:68)
        at com.thoughtworks.xstream.mapper.MapperWrapper.realClass(MapperWrapper
.java:38)
        at com.thoughtworks.xstream.mapper.DynamicProxyMapper.realClass(DynamicP
roxyMapper.java:71)
        at com.thoughtworks.xstream.mapper.MapperWrapper.realClass(MapperWrapper
.java:38)
```

The error is essentially telling us that it can't find a class called `hudson.plu`
`gins.cigame.GamePublisher`. In fact, the target installation is missing the CI Game plugin. And in this case (as sometimes happens), no warning messages where appearing on the Manage Jenkins page, so Jenkins was unable to correct the configuration files itself.

The simplest solution in this case would be to install the CI Game plugin on the target server. But what if we don't want to install this plugin? We could leave the configuration files alone, but this might mask more significant errors later on—it would be better to tidy them up.

In that case, we need to inspect and update the project configuration files by hand. On this Unix box, I just used `grep` to find all the configuration files containing a reference to "cigame":

```
$ cd $JENKINS_HOME/jobs
$ grep cigame */config.xml
project-a/config.xml:    <hudson.plugins.cigame.GamePublisher/>
project-b/config.xml:    <hudson.plugins.cigame.GamePublisher/>
project-c/config.xml:    <hudson.plugins.cigame.GamePublisher/>
```

In these *config.xml* files, I found the reference to the CI Game plugin in the `<publish`
`ers>` sect1 (which is where the configuration for the reporting plugins generally goes):

```
<maven2-moduleset>
  ...
  <publishers>
    <hudson.plugins.cigame.GamePublisher/>
    <hudson.plugins.claim.ClaimPublisher/>
  </publishers>
  ...
</maven2-moduleset>
```

To fix the issue, all I have to do is to remove the offending line:

```
<maven2-moduleset>
  ...
  <publishers>
    <hudson.plugins.claim.ClaimPublisher/>
  </publishers>

  ...
</maven2-moduleset>
```

The exact location of the plugin configuration data will vary depending on the plugin, but in general the *config.xml* files are quite readable, and updating them by hand isn't too hard.

So, all in all, migrating build jobs between Jenkins instances isn't all that hard—you just need to know a couple of tricks for the corner cases, and if you know where to look Jenkins provides some nice tools to make the process smoother.

Conclusion

In this chapter, we looked at a number of considerations that you should be aware of if your job is to maintain your Jenkins server, including how to monitor disk and server usage, how to back up your build jobs and Jenkins configuration files, and also how to migrate build jobs and upgrade build data safely.

Automating Your Unit and Integration Tests

Automating Your Tests with Maven

Maven is a popular open source build tool of the Java world, that makes use of practices such as declarative dependencies, standard directories and build life cycles, and convention over configuration to encourage clean, maintainable, high level build scripts. Test automation is strongly supported in Maven. Maven projects use a standard directory structure: it will automatically look for unit tests in a directory called (by default) *src/test/java*. There is little else to configure: just add a dependency to the test framework (or frameworks) your tests are using, and Maven will automatically look for and execute the JUnit, TestNG, or even Plain Old Java Objects (POJO) tests contained in this directory structure.

In Maven, you run your unit tests by invoking the *test* life cycle phase, as shown here:

```
$ mvn test
[INFO] Scanning for projects...
[INFO] ------------------------------------------------------------------------
[INFO] Building Tweeter domain model
[INFO]    task-segment: [test]
[INFO] ------------------------------------------------------------------------
...
------------------------------------------------------
 T E S T S
------------------------------------------------------
Running com.wakaleo.training.tweeter.domain.TagTest
Tests run: 13, Failures: 0, Errors: 0, Skipped: 0, Time elapsed: 0.093 sec
Running com.wakaleo.training.tweeter.domain.TweeterTest
Tests run: 3, Failures: 0, Errors: 0, Skipped: 0, Time elapsed: 0.021 sec
Running com.wakaleo.training.tweeter.domain.TweeterUserTest
Tests run: 4, Failures: 0, Errors: 0, Skipped: 0, Time elapsed: 0.055 sec
Running com.wakaleo.training.tweeter.domain.TweetFeeRangeTest
Tests run: 10, Failures: 0, Errors: 0, Skipped: 0, Time elapsed: 0.051 sec
Running com.wakaleo.training.tweeter.domain.HamcrestTest
```

```
Tests run: 8, Failures: 0, Errors: 0, Skipped: 0, Time elapsed: 0.023 sec

Results :

Tests run: 38, Failures: 0, Errors: 0, Skipped: 0
```

In addition to executing your tests, and failing the build if any of the tests fail, Maven will produce a set of test reports (again, by default) in the *target/surefire-reports* directory, in both XML and text formats. For our CI purposes, it is the XML files that interest us, as Jenkins is able to understand and analyze these files for its CI reporting:

```
$ ls target/surefire-reports/*.xml
target/surefire-reports/TEST-com.wakaleo.training.tweeter.domain.HamcrestTest.xml
target/surefire-reports/TEST-com.wakaleo.training.tweeter.domain.TagTest.xml
target/surefire-reports/TEST-com.wakaleo.training.tweeter.domain.TweetFeeRangeTest.xm
target/surefire-reports/TEST-com.wakaleo.training.tweeter.domain.TweeterTest.xml
target/surefire-reports/TEST-com.wakaleo.training.tweeter.domain.TweeterUserTest.xml
```

Maven defines two distinct testing phases: unit tests and integration tests. Unit tests should be fast and lightweight, providing a large amount of test feedback in as little time as possible. Integration tests are slower and more cumbersome, and often require the application to be built and deployed to a server (even an embedded one) to carry out more complete tests. Both these sorts of tests are important, and for a well-designed Continuous Integration environment, it is important to be able to distinguish between them. The build should ensure that all of the unit tests are run initially—if a unit test fails, developers should be notified very quickly. Only if all of the unit tests pass is it worthwhile undertaking the slower and more heavyweight integration tests.

In Maven, integration tests are executed during the *integration-test* life cycle phase, which you can invoke by running `mvn integration-test` or (more simply) `mvn verify`. During this phase, it is easy to configure Maven to start up your web application on an embedded Jetty web server, or to package and deploy your application to a test server, for example. Your integration tests can then be executed against the running application. The tricky part however is telling Maven how to distinguish between your unit tests and your integration tests, so that they will only be executed when a running version of the application is available.

There are several ways to do this, but at the time of writing there is no official standard approach used across all Maven projects. One simple strategy is to use naming conventions: all integration tests might end in "IntegrationTest", or be placed in a particular package. The following class uses one such convention:

```
public class AccountIntegrationTest {

  @Test
  public void cashWithdrawalShouldDeductSumFromBalance() throws Exception {
    Account account = new Account();
    account.makeDeposit(100);
    account.makeCashWithdraw(60);
    assertThat(account.getBalance(), is(40));
```

```
    }
  }
```

In Maven, tests are configured via the *maven-surefire-plugin* plugin. To ensure that Maven only runs these tests during the *integration-test* phase, you can configure this plugin as shown here:

```
<project>
  ...
  <build>
    <plugins>
      <plugin>
        <artifactId>maven-surefire-plugin</artifactId>
        <configuration>
          <skip>true</skip>❶
        </configuration>
        <executions>
          <execution>❷
            <id>unit-tests</id>
            <phase>test</phase>
            <goals>
              <goal>test</goal>
            </goals>
            <configuration>
              <skip>false</skip>
              <excludes>
                <exclude>**/*IntegrationTest.java</exclude>
              </excludes>
            </configuration>
          </execution>
          <execution>❸
            <id>integration-tests</id>
            <phase>integration-test</phase>
            <goals>
              <goal>test</goal>
            </goals>
            <configuration>
              <skip>false</skip>
              <includes>
                <include>**/*IntegrationTest.java</include>
              </includes>
            </configuration>
          </execution>
        </executions>
      </plugin>
      ...
```

❶ Skip all tests by default—this deactivates the default Maven test configuration.

❷ During the unit test phase, run the tests but exclude the integration tests.

❸ During the integration test phase, run the tests but *only* include the integration tests.

This will ensure that the integration tests are skipped during the unit test phase, and only executed during the integration test phase.

If you don't want to put unwanted constraints on the names of your test classes, you can use package names instead. In the project illustrated in Figure A-1, all of the functional tests have been placed in a package called *webtests*. There is no constraint on the names of the tests, but we are using Page Objects to model our application user interface, so we also make sure that no classes in the *pages* package (underneath the *webtests* package) are treated as tests.

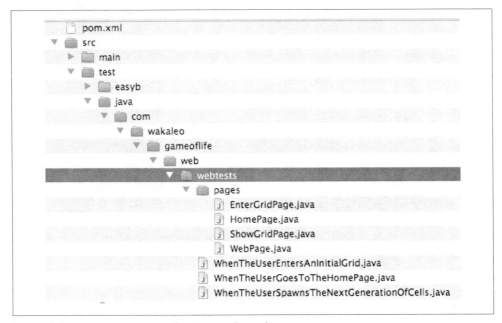

Figure A-1. A project containing freely-named test classes

In Maven, we could do this with the following configuration:

```
<plugin>
  <artifactId>maven-surefire-plugin</artifactId>
  <configuration>
    <skip>true</skip>
  </configuration>
  <executions>
    <execution>
      <id>unit-tests</id>
      <phase>test</phase>
      <goals>
        <goal>test</goal>
      </goals>
      <configuration>
        <skip>false</skip>
        <excludes>
          <exclude>**/webtests/*.java</exclude>
        </excludes>
      </configuration>
```

```
        </execution>
        <execution>
          <id>integration-tests</id>
          <phase>integration-test</phase>
          <goals>
            <goal>test</goal>
          </goals>
          <configuration>
            <skip>false</skip>
            <includes>
              <include>**/webtests/*.java</include>
            </includes>
            <excludes>
              <exclude>**/pages/*.java</exclude>
            </excludes>
          </configuration>
        </execution>
      </executions>
    </plugin>
```

TestNG currently has more flexible support for test groups than JUnit. If you are using TestNG, you can identify your integration tests using TestNG Groups. In TestNG, test classes or test methods can be tagged using the groups attribute of the @Test annotation, as shown here:

```
@Test(groups = { "integration-test" })
public void cashWithdrawalShouldDeductSumFromBalance() throws Exception {
    Account account = new Account();
    account.makeDeposit(100);
    account.makeCashWithdraw(60);
    assertThat(account.getBalance(), is(40));
}
```

Using Maven, you could ensure that these tests were only run during the integration test phase using the following configuration:

```
<project>
  ...
  <build>
    <plugins>
      <plugin>
        <artifactId>maven-surefire-plugin</artifactId>
        <configuration>
          <skip>true</skip>
        </configuration>
        <executions>
          <execution>
            <id>unit-tests</id>
            <phase>test</phase>
            <goals>
              <goal>test</goal>
            </goals>
            <configuration>
              <skip>false</skip>
              <excludedGroups>integration-tests</excludedGroups>❶
```

```
        </configuration>
      </execution>
      <execution>
        <id>integration-tests</id>
        <phase>integration-test</phase>
        <goals>
          <goal>test</goal>
        </goals>
        <configuration>
          <skip>false</skip>
          <groups>integration-tests</groups>❷
        </configuration>
      </execution>
    </executions>
  </plugin>
  ...
```

❶ Do not run the integration-tests group during the test phase.

❷ Run only the tests in the integration-tests group during the integration-test phase.

It often makes good sense to run your tests in parallel where possible, as it can speed up your tests significantly (see "Help! My Tests Are Too Slow!" on page 166). Parallel tests are particularly intensive with slow-running tests that use a lot of IO, disk or network access (such as web tests), which is convenient, as these are precisely the sort of tests we usually want to speed up.

TestNG provides good support for parallel tests. For instance, using TestNG, you could configure your test methods to run in parallel on ten concurrent threads like this:

```
<plugin>
  <groupId>org.apache.maven.plugins</groupId>
  <artifactId>maven-surefire-plugin</artifactId>
  <version>2.5</version>
  <configuration>
    <parallel>methods</parallel>
    <threadCount>10</threadCount>
  </configuration>
</plugin>
```

As of JUnit 4.7, you can also run your JUnit tests in parallel using a similar configuration. In fact, the configuration shown above will work for JUnit 4.7 onwards.

You can also set the `<parallel>` configuration item to `classes` instead of `methods`, which will try to run the test classes in parallel, rather than each method. This might be slower or faster, depending on the number of test classes you have, but might be safer for some test cases not designed with concurrency in mind.

Mileage will vary, so you should experiment with the numbers to get the best results.

Automating Your Tests with Ant

Setting up automated testing in Ant is also relatively easy, though it requires a bit more plumbing than with Maven. In particular, Ant does not come packaged with the JUnit libraries or Ant tasks out of the box, so you have to install them somewhere yourself. The most portable approach is to use a Dependency Management tool such as Ivy, or to place the corresponding JAR files in a directory within your project structure.

To run your tests in Ant, you call the `<junit>` task. A typical Jenkins-friendly configuration is shown in this example:

```xml
<property name="build.dir" value="target" />
<property name="java.classes" value="${build.dir}/classes" />
<property name="test.classes" value="${build.dir}/test-classes" />
<property name="test.reports" value="${build.dir}/test-reports" />
<property name="lib" value="${build.dir}/lib" />

<path id="test.classpath">❶
  <pathelement location="${basedir}/tools/junit/*.jar" />
  <pathelement location="${java.classes}" />
  <pathelement location="${lib}" />
</path>

<target name="test" depends="test-compile">
  <junit haltonfailure="no" failureproperty="failed">❷
    <classpath>❸
      <path refid="test.classpath" />
      <pathelement location="${test.classes}" />
    </classpath>
    <formatter type="xml" />❹
    <batchtest fork="yes" forkmode="perBatch"❺ todir="${test.reports}">
      <fileset dir="${test.src}">❻
        <include name="**/*Test*.java" />
      </fileset>
    </batchtest>
  </junit>
  <fail message="TEST FAILURE" if="failed" />❼
</target>
```

❶ We need to set up a classpath containing the *junit* and *junit-ant* JAR files, as well as the application classes and any other dependencies the application needs to compile and run.

❷ The tests themselves are run here. The `haltonfailure` option is used to make the build fail immediately if any tests fail. In a Continuous Integration environment, this is not exactly what we want, as we need to get the results for any subsequent tests as well. So we set this value to `no` and use the `failureproperty` option to force the build to fail once all of the tests have finished.

❸ The classpath needs to contain the JUnit libraries, your application classes and their dependencies, and your compiled test classes.

❹ The Junit Ant task can produce both text and XML reports, but for Jenkins, we only need the XML ones.

❺ The `fork` option runs your tests in a separate JVM. This is generally a good idea, as it can avoid classloader issues related to conflicts with Ant's own libraries. However, the default behaviour of the JUnit Ant task is to create a new JVM for each test, which slows down the tests significantly. The `perBatch` option is better, as it only creates one new JVM for each batch of tests.

❻ You define the tests you want to run in a fileset element. This provides a great deal of flexibility, and makes it easy to define other targets for different subsets of tests (integration, web, and so on).

❼ Force the build to fail *after* the tests have finished, if any of them failed.

If you prefer TestNG, Ant is of course well supported here as well. Using TestNG with the previous example, you could do something like this:

```
<property name="build.dir" value="target" />
<property name="java.classes" value="${build.dir}/classes" />
<property name="test.classes" value="${build.dir}/test-classes" />
<property name="test.reports" value="${build.dir}/test-reports" />
<property name="lib" value="${build.dir}/lib" />

<path id="test.classpath">
  <pathelement location="${java.classes}" />
  <pathelement location="${lib}" />
</path>

<taskdef resource="testngtasks" classpath="lib/testng.jar"/>

<target name="test" depends="test-compile">
  <testng classpathref="test.classpath"
          outputDir="${testng.report.dir}"
          haltonfailure="no"
          failureproperty="failed">
    <classfileset dir="${test.classes}">
      <include name="**/*Test*.class" />
    </classfileset>
  </testng>
  <fail message="TEST FAILURE" if="failed" />
</target>
```

TestNG is a very flexible testing library, and the TestNG task has many more options than this. For example, to only run tests defined as part of the "integration-test" group that we saw earlier, we could do this:

```
<target name="integration-test" depends="test-compile">
  <testng classpathref="test.classpath"
          groups="integration-test"
          outputDir="${testng.report.dir}"
          haltonfailure="no"
          failureproperty="failed">
    <classfileset dir="${test.classes}">
```

```
      <include name="**/*Test*.class" />
    </classfileset>
  </testng>
  <fail message="TEST FAILURE" if="failed" />
</target>
```

Or to run your tests in parallel, using four concurrent threads, you could do this:

```
<target name="integration-test" depends="test-compile">
  <testng classpathref="test.classpath"
          parallel="true"
          threadCount=4
          outputDir="${testng.report.dir}"
          haltonfailure="no"
          failureproperty="failed">
    <classfileset dir="${test.classes}">
      <include name="**/*Test*.class" />
    </classfileset>
  </testng>
  <fail message="TEST FAILURE" if="failed" />
</target>
```

Index

A

acceptance tests, automated, 7, 136, 155–158
Acceptance-Test Driven Development, 7
active (push) notifications, 195
Active Directory, Microsoft, as security realm, 176
administrator
    for Jenkins internal user database, 171
    for matrix-based security, 182
aggregate test results, 295–296
Amazon EC2 cloud computing service, 315–319
Amazon EC2 plugin, 317
Amazon Machine Image (AMI), 316
Amazon Web Services (AWS), 316
AMI (Amazon Machine Image), 316
analysis (see code coverage metrics; code quality metrics; tests)
Ant, 74–75
    automating tests, 365–367
    code coverage metrics with Cobertura, 148–150
    code quality metrics
        with Checkstyle, 228
        with CodeNarc, 236
        with FindBugs, 235
        with PMD and CPD, 231
    configuring, 74–75
    environment variables, accessing from, 107
    in freestyle build steps, 104
    installing, 75
ANT_OPTS environment variable, 54
application server
    automated deployment to, 328–341

Java applications, 329–338
    scripting-based applications, 339–341
    deploying Jenkins to, 16, 53–54
    upgrading Jenkins on, 63
archives of binary artifacts, 26
    deploying to Enterprise Repository Manager, 119–123
    disabling, 118
    in freestyle build jobs, 111–114
archiving build jobs, 353–354
Artifactory
    Enterprise Repository Manager, 121, 123
    Jenkins support for, 5
Artifactory plugin, 275
artifacts (see binary artifacts)
Atlassian Crowd, as security realm, 178
Audit Trail plugin, 190–191
auditing user actions, 189–193
authorization, 169
    (see also security)
    matrix-based security, 181–185
    no restrictions on, 170–171
    project-based security, 185–187
    role-based security, 188–189
automated deployment, 323–328
    to application server, 328–341
    database updates with, 325–327
    deployment script for, 324
    rolling back changes in, 328
    smoke tests for, 327
automated nightly builds, 6
automated tests (see tests)
AWS (Amazon Web Services), 316

Grails
    builds in, running with Jenkins, 125–126
    code quality metrics with CodeNarc, 237
Groeschke, Rene (contributor), xviii
Groovy scripts
    authentication script, 180–181
    code quality metrics with CodeNarc, 236–
        237
    environment variables in, 108
    running in build jobs, 108–110
    running on Script Console, 67
groups
    Active Directory, 176, 177
    Atlassian Crowd, 178
    LDAP, 176
    Unix, 177

H

headless mode, starting slave nodes in, 311
Hibernate, database updates with, 325
home directory for Jenkins, 46–47, 58–61, 68
home page, 16, 69
hot-deploy, 328, 331
HTML Publisher plugin, 156–158
HTTP proxy server, 77
Hudson, xvi, 3, 4, 5
    (see also Jenkins)
HUDSON_HOME environment variable, 46
HUDSON_URL environment variable, 107

I

IDE, code quality metrics with, 226
IM (see instant messaging)
information radiators, 202–203
installation
    Ant, 75
    Git, 10
    JDK, 71
    Jenkins, 41–44
        from binary distribution, 43
        on build server, 44–45
        on CentOS, 48
        on Debian, 47
        on Fedora, 48
        with Java Web start, 13–15
        on Linux, 43
        on OpenSUSE, 48–49
        on Redhat, 48

on SUSE, 48–49
    on Ubuntu, 47
    on Unix, 43
    from WAR file, 16, 42
    on Windows, 42, 43
    as Windows service, 54–58
    JRE, 10
    Maven, 18–19, 73
    plugins, 34
        (see also specific plugins)
    upgrading, 62–63
instant messaging (IM), 203–209
    IRC for, 208–211
    Jabber protocol for, 204–208
Instant Messaging plugin, 204
integration tests, 135, 137
    number of, 167
    performance of, 167
IRC (Internet Relay Chat), 208–211
IRC plugin, 209

J

Jabber Notifier plugin, 204
Jabber protocol, 204–208
Java applications
    deploying from Maven repository, 335–
        338
    deploying to application server, 329–338
    redeploying a specific version, 331
    redeploying from previous build, 332–335
    test reports from, 138
Java Development Kit (see JDK)
Java Runtime Environment (JRE), installing,
    10
Java version installed, checking, 41
Java Web Start
    installing and starting Jenkins using, 13–15
    starting slave nodes using, 307–309
Javadocs, 33–34
JAVA_ARGS parameter, 47
JAVA_HOME environment variable, 71, 107
JAVA_OPTS environment variable, 54
JBoss application server, deploying Java
        applications to, 329–338
JDK (Java Development Kit), 10
    configuring, 19
    configuring multiple versions of, 70–72
    installing, 71
    requirements for, 41

WebSphere Application Server, 328, 329
Windows
    installation package for Jenkins, 42
Windows services
    installing Jenkins as, 54–58
    installing slave node as, 310
    starting slave nodes as, 311
WMI (Windows Management
        Instrumentation), 311
workspace directory, 59
WORKSPACE environment variable, 107

X
XML format for test reports (see JUnit reports)
Xu, Juven (contributor), xviii
xUnit, 136, 138
xUnit plugin, 138

About the Author

John Ferguson Smart is a well-known international consultant, trainer, author, and speaker in open source and agile Java development and testing practices. He specializes in helping development teams improve their game with techniques such as Test-Driven Development (including BDD and ATDD), Automated Acceptance Tests, Continuous Integration, Build Automation, and Clean Coding practices. He provides training and mentoring in open source technologies, SDLC tools, and agile development processes.

John is the director of Wakaleo Consulting (*http://www.wakaleo.com*), a company that provides consulting, training, and mentoring services in open source and agile Java development practices.

Colophon

The animal on the cover of *Jenkins: The Definitive Guide* is an ornate chorus frog (*Pseudacris ornata*). These small amphibians, only 1–1.5 inches long, can be found on the coastal plains of North America from North Carolina to central Florida and eastern Louisiana. They prefer areas of shallow water without dense vegetation, such as ponds, roadside ditches, and flooded meadows.

The coloration of ornate chorus frogs varies depending on locale, and individuals can be predominantly black, white, brown, red, green, or some variation thereof. All specimens, though, display a dark stripe or collection of spots running from the nostril to the shoulder through the eye, and most have various other spots or stripes as well. The species breeds from November to March, and the calls of males can be heard from in or near areas of shallow water.

Ornate chorus frogs also owe their name to the sound of their mating call: *Pseudacris* comes from the ancient Greek for "false locust." The name was assigned in 1836 by American naturalist John Edwards Holbrook after he observed that the rapid shrill sound resembled that made by the infamous insect.

The cover image is from *Cassell's Natural History*. The cover font is Adobe ITC Garamond. The text font is Linotype Birka; the heading font is Adobe Myriad Condensed; and the code font is LucasFont's TheSansMonoCondensed.

Get even more for your money.

Join the O'Reilly Community, and register the O'Reilly books you own. It's free, and you'll get:

- $4.99 ebook upgrade offer
- 40% upgrade offer on O'Reilly print books
- Membership discounts on books and events
- Free lifetime updates to ebooks and videos
- Multiple ebook formats, DRM FREE
- Participation in the O'Reilly community
- Newsletters
- Account management
- 100% Satisfaction Guarantee

Signing up is easy:

1. Go to: oreilly.com/go/register
2. Create an O'Reilly login.
3. Provide your address.
4. Register your books.

Note: English-language books only

To order books online:
oreilly.com/store

For questions about products or an order:
orders@oreilly.com

To sign up to get topic-specific email announcements and/or news about upcoming books, conferences, special offers, and new technologies:
elists@oreilly.com

For technical questions about book content:
booktech@oreilly.com

To submit new book proposals to our editors:
proposals@oreilly.com

O'Reilly books are available in multiple DRM-free ebook formats. For more information:
oreilly.com/ebooks

O'REILLY®

Spreading the knowledge of innovators   oreilly.com

Have it your way.

O'Reilly eBooks

- Lifetime access to the book when you buy through oreilly.com

- Provided in up to four DRM-free file formats, for use on the devices of your choice: PDF, .epub, Kindle-compatible .mobi, and Android .apk

- Fully searchable, with copy-and-paste and print functionality

- Alerts when files are updated with corrections and additions

oreilly.com/ebooks/

Safari Books Online

- Access the contents and quickly search over 7000 books on technology, business, and certification guides

- Learn from expert video tutorials, and explore thousands of hours of video on technology and design topics

- Download whole books or chapters in PDF format, at no extra cost, to print or read on the go

- Get early access to books as they're being written

- Interact directly with authors of upcoming books

- Save up to 35% on O'Reilly print books

See the complete Safari Library at safari.oreilly.com

O'REILLY®

CPSIA information can be obtained at www.ICGtesting.com
Printed in the USA
266512BV00002B/1-72/P